AME
REAL

HISTORICAL
EPISODES

10652432

AMERICAN REALITIES

HISTORICAL EPISODES

Volume II

*From Reconstruction
to the Present*

Third Edition

J. WILLIAM T. YOUNGS

Eastern Washington University

Cover and text illustrations by Cecily Moon

■ HarperCollins *CollegePublishers*

Senior Editor: Bruce Borland
Development Editor: Carol Einhorn
Project Editor: David Nickol
Design Supervisor: Paul Agresti
Production Manager/Assistant: Willie Lane/Sunaina Sehwani
Compositor: K P Company
Printer and Binder: Courier Companies Inc.
Cover Printer: The Lehigh Press, Inc.

American Realities: Historical Episodes
Volume II From Reconstruction to the Present, Third Edition
Copyright © 1993 by J. William T. Youngs

All rights reserved. Printed in the United States of America. No part of this book may be used or reproduced in any manner whatsoever without written permission, except in the case of brief quotations embodied in critical articles and reviews. For information address HarperCollins College Publishers, 10 East 53rd Street, New York, NY 10022.

Library of Congress Cataloging-in-Publication Data

Youngs, J. William T. (John William Theodore), 1941—
    American realities : historical episodes / J. William T. Youngs. –
– 3rd ed.
        p.   cm.
    Includes bibliographical references and index.
    Contents: v. 1. From the first settlements to the Civil War —
v. 2. From Reconstruction to the present.
        ISBN 0-673-52239-3 (v. 1). — ISBN 0-673-52240-7 (v. 2)
        1. United States—History.   I. Title.
E178.6.Y68   1993   92-32282
973—dc20   CIP

93 94 95 9 8 7 6 5 4 3

Credits

MARY ANTIN. Quotations in Chapter 5 from *The Promised Land* by Mary Antin. Copyright 1912 by Houghton Mifflin Company. Copyright renewed 1940 by Mary Antin.

MARTIN LUTHER KING, JR. Quotations in Chapter 11 from "Letter from Birmingham Jail, April 16, 1963" in *Why We Can't Wait* by Martin Luther King, Jr. Reprinted by permission of Harper & Row, Publishers, Inc.

*To my mother
and the memory of my father*

Contents

Preface

American history is an epic composed of many events: colonists made their homes in a new world; soldiers fought for independence; capitalists built giant industries; civil rights activists struggled for equality. In such episodes we encounter the emotions, thoughts, and experiences that made up the distinct worlds of the past. In the two volumes of *American Realities* my goal has been to re-create some of those worlds, to capture the immediacy — the reality — of life as lived in other eras. I have not tried to reduce all these events to a single pattern, but in the aggregate the chapters trace the course of American history from the distant past to the present.

Each chapter is designed to lead the reader to a better understanding of major themes in United States history. Each volume can be read by itself or in tandem with a conventional American history textbook. The standard surveys present the general patterns of the past; this book reveals in greater depth the life beneath those patterns.

Like ourselves the people of the past were immersed in the issues of their times. But even while living fully in their own worlds, they bequeathed us ours. Their stories reveal the broad contours of the saga as well as the illustrative particulars. The death of Thomasine Winthrop leads us to know Puritanism better, and the flight of the *Enola Gay* to Hiroshima exhibits the harsh outlines of total war. The Lewis and Clark expedition reveals the marvelous land upon which the nation developed, and Charles Coughlin's career illuminates the personal turmoil of the depression years.

While writing *American Realities* I have often wished I had the novelist's poetic license to fill gaps not covered by the sources. But fortunately, facts can be as engaging as fiction. Documents are often colorful and evocative, allowing us to listen to the deathbed conversation of John and Thomasine Winthrop, to see the light of the South Pacific from a B-29, to enter imaginatively into the realities of other men and women.

We can find historical kinship in the ordinary circumstances of daily life. George Washington is comprehensible because he was stunned when his army in Manhattan collapsed. John Muir is like most of us because he was troubled once about choosing a career. If you have never faced a similar moment, when all your plans went awry, you are indeed lucky.

My touchstone in choosing topics for *American Realities* was that each should suggest our common humanity even while revealing worlds distinct from our own. More simply, I had to care about the subjects and believe others could care about them as well. Through such sympathy we come actually to live in history and feel our involvement with the past: his story and her story become our story.

The third edition of *American Realities* includes two new chapters and substantial revisions to three other chapters. In Volume I there is new material on the "Columbian exchange" through which Europeans and Native Americans influenced each other; the story of John Winthrop is carried from England to America; and new information is provided about Civil War soldier William Wheeler. In Volume II, "The New Computer Age: Bill Gates and Microsoft" explores the modern American software industry and its leading entrepreneur. A second new essay, "The Worlds of Osborne Jones," explores African-American life through an oral history.

The effort here to re-create history in words is supplemented by the imaginative drawings of Cecily Moon. Ms. Moon based her illustrations on careful reading of each chapter and on personal research in historical paintings and photographs. Each drawing highlights a major theme in the chapters.

For the instructor I have prepared a manual with chapter summaries, identification topics, multiple choice and discussion questions, and suggested research projects.

American Realities arrived at its present form with the help of many other scholars and writers. I am particularly grateful to Marian Ferguson, Dave Lynch, and Katie Carlone for their help on the first edition and to Brad Gray, Barbara Breese, and Dave Lynch for their work on the second edition. A writer could not ask for more congenial and intelligent assistance in nurturing his ideas than these editors provided. The book also owes a great deal to the assistance of Clair Seng-Niemoeller and Frank Kirk; to Lois Banner, Ron Benson, Peter Carroll, Joseph H. Cartwright, David Coon, Doris Daniels, Emmett M. Essin, Don Glenn, James Hunt, Donald M. Jacobs, Maury Klein, Ralph Shaffer, and Julius Weinberg; and to Charles Baumann, Joseph Corn, James Gale, Richard Johnson, William Kidd, Nancy Millard, Sue Murphy, Robert Toll, Albert Tully, and my students in American History. For their help on the previous revisions I am particularly grateful to Linda Stowe, Jay Hart, Russ Tremayne, Madeleine Freidel, August W. Giebelhaus, Emmett M. Essin, Paul W. Wehr, and James L. Gormly. For their help on the third edition, I would like to thank four helpful research assistants: Guy R. Breshears, Larry Cebula, Matthew A. Redinger, and Jason Steele. This edition benefited from astute comments by four reviewers: Brenda Cooper of Lee College, David Danbom of North Dakota State University, Paul Mertz of the University of Wisconsin at Stevens Point, and Carole Shelton of Middle Tennessee State University. I have been fortunate in working with several able and supportive editors at HarperCollins: Bruce Borland, Michele DiBenedetto, Carol Einhorn, and David Nickol. My wife, Linda Youngs, who is both the sternest and most sensitive critic of my work, gave me many valuable suggestions while pursuing her own busy schedule as a mother and an attorney. Finally, in dedicating *American Realities* to my mother, Marguerite Youngs, and to the memory of my father, J. W. T. Youngs, I wish to recognize their part in helping me find my own place in history.

J. WILLIAM T. YOUNGS

VOLUME II

FROM RECONSTRUCTION
TO THE PRESENT

1

BEYOND EMANCIPATION

Booker T. Washington and the Atlanta Compromise

In 1865 the long ordeal of slavery came to an end for four million blacks. Suddenly the freedom they had longed for during two centuries of bondage was theirs. The world opened before them: they could freely visit loved ones, attend schools, or run for public office. Blacks soon realized, however, that chains other than slavery still held them. Penniless, they could not afford to buy farms; untrained, they could not move into better jobs. In the 1870s and 1880s they lost many of the privileges they had gained when freed, including the right to vote. Booker T. Washington grew to maturity in years when blacks experienced both the exhilaration of freedom and the humiliation of segregation. He proved in his early life that an ex-slave could prosper by hard work. When in his later years he saw the cords of prejudice tightening around his people, he responded in the best way he knew, advocating self-help in the face of prejudice and segregation. Insisting on personal initiative, he was stubbornly loyal to individualistic ideals at a time when many Americans had apparently abandoned those ideals.

As the parade moved through the streets of Atlanta on its way to the opening of the Cotton States Exposition, Booker T. Washington, riding in a carriage near the end of the procession, was deeply troubled. He was a black man who would soon address a white audience, and in the South of 1895 he could not be certain of a friendly reception. Washington's fears contrasted strangely with the jubilation around him. Here in a city that Sherman had laid in ruins only thirty years before, the buildings were decorated with American flags and the citizens stood cheering a parade that symbolized the birth of a "new South." The procession ahead of Washington moved proudly along: white dignitaries in fine carriages; military officers glittering with gold trim and white helmets; rows of soldiers marching with bayonets gleaming in the sun; and cannon rumbling jauntily over rough cobblestones.

Sitting in the hot sun at the back of this long parade with a cluster of black soldiers and dignitaries, Washington felt the courage drain from his body. Thousands of blacks lining the road cheered when they saw him. But while their hands reached out to encourage him, they seemed to burden him with a heavy responsibility. How could he speak in a manner that would please the whites while doing justice to his own race?

The Atlanta Exposition had been designed to celebrate the achievements of both races. But blacks had been accepted grudgingly. The committee that had invited Washington to speak had done so reluctantly, anticipating at first that he would take part only in the opening of a separate Negro building. Although Washington was belatedly included in the opening day ceremonies, his people would be segregated into a "jim crow" section of the auditorium, just as their exhibits were segregated in a separate hall. Booker T. Washington knew that he could easily alienate the whites and damage his people if he spoke carelessly. If he simply flattered the whites, however, he would let down his black supporters.

Washington's carriage entered the fairgrounds, a magical place with 189 acres of grounds set off by a white fence three miles long. Hillsides at its edge sloped down to a flat green plain dotted with pine trees. He saw a broad lake, speckled with gondolas, rowboats, and steam launches; buildings covered with domes, minarets, and angels; and a midway crowded with Germans, Mexicans, plantation blacks, and native Americans dressed in traditional costumes.

The parade wound through this festive scene to the auditorium, a large building packed with noisy spectators, who had waited an hour or more for the speakers to arrive. They yelled as the dignitaries entered and took their seats on a broad platform, cheering boisterously for Rufus Brown Bullock, a popular former governor of the state, and for Charles A. Collier, who had inspired the exhibition. When Booker T. Washington entered the hall, the jim crow section of the audience applauded wildly, but there was only scattered applause among the whites: "What's that nigger doing on the stage?" several asked.

Washington felt faint as he took his seat and glanced over the large audience. A bishop in a colorful robe gave an invocation. A man read a poem celebrating the opening of the fair. These rather conventional performances made Washington feel all the more uneasy about the unusual speech he would soon present. When Charles Collier spoke, he must have given Washington heart. He discussed the genesis of the fair and praised various groups of people who had helped. Women had proved by their part in the exposition that they deserved wider horizons for their work. Blacks had given proof "of the progress they have made as freemen." The audience listened politely.

Washington continued to wait for his turn to speak. The setting sun filled the windows of the auditorium, casting its beams on the speaker's platform. Another speaker, Mrs. Joseph Thompson, talked about the women's part in the fair. Her hands trembled as she spoke in a low, timid voice. Washington knew how she felt.

When she finished there was a musical interlude. A band played "The Star-Spangled Banner," and the audience cheered happily. Then the band played "Dixie," and the auditorium was filled with rebel yells. As his time to speak neared, Washington reflected: in a moment he would seek to compress a lifetime of experience into a ten-minute oration. Perhaps he thought about his own journey — his odyssey of hardship and triumph — to this place.

Booker T. Washington was born the property of James Borroughs on a plantation near Hale's Ford, Virginia, on April 5, 1856. His mother, Jane Ferguson, had "high ambitions for her children." Washington did not know who his father was, assuming merely that he lived on a neighboring plantation. He knew even less about his ancestors but remembered "whispered conversations among the colored people" about the hardships endured by their forebears on slaveships in the Middle Passage to America.

His world was the daily life on a small plantation in Virginia. His mother was cook for the estate, preparing meals for the big house in the fireplace in her own small cabin. From childhood Washington was put to work, cleaning the yard, carrying water to the men in the fields, and taking corn to the mill. In later years he could not recall any period of his life that had been devoted to play.

His home was a log cabin with a dirt floor. The wind blew freely through cracks in the walls and doorway, making it bitterly cold in the winter. At night the children lay on the dirt floor with only a pile of rags

Booker T. Washington's childhood home. This drafty one-room slave cabin had a dirt floor and cracks large enough for a cat to pass through.

as bedding. They ate no regular meals as a family — snatching a bite here and there, eating from the skillet or from a pan balanced on their knees. Even the young slave's clothes were a burden: his wood-soled shoes hurt his feet, and his rough flax shirts pricked his skin like "a hundred small pin-points."

Despite such hardships, Washington recalled that the slaves felt affection toward their owners. Slaves guarded the big house when the whites went off to fight in the Civil War, and Washington believed that they would have died to protect their masters. Slaves mourned almost as much as the whites when young "Mars Billy," eldest son of the owner, was killed in the war, and they competed with each other for the opportunity to watch over two other wounded sons. With the end of the conflict in sight, the slaves could be trusted to help their masters hide their valuables from marauding soldiers.

Memories of plantation hardships blended in Washington's mind with memories of a sentimental kinship between slave and owner. But such mutual affection did not dispel the blacks' desire for freedom — a desire that had grown year by year over the previous decades. Even before the war the slaves had heard about abolitionist activities in the

North through a grapevine that reached even the most isolated blacks. They had learned about the election of Abraham Lincoln and followed the progress of the Civil War.

Out of deference to their southern masters, and perhaps from fear of punishment, they did not openly express their northern sympathies. But their excitement grew with each year of the war. Washington remembered awakening one night in his bed of rags and seeing his mother kneeling over her three children praying for the success of Lincoln's armies. The yearning for freedom pulsed through the slave quarters. Night after night the blacks stayed up late to sing their plantation songs, which contained words about freedom. The slaves had once associated these words — for their master's benefit — with the next world, but now the songs took on a new, bolder tone; the slaves "were not afraid to let it be known that the 'freedom' in these songs meant freedom of the body in this world."

At the end of the war the blacks were told to assemble outside the great house for an announcement. The master's family stood on the veranda while a visitor representing the U.S. government read the Emancipation Proclamation and told the slaves they were free. The blacks were ecstatic. Jane Ferguson kissed Booker and his brother and sister as tears ran down her face. All the newly freed blacks shouted and hugged one another, wild with joy.

Then a strange thing happened. Within a few hours the people became serious, even gloomy. Previously they had always thought of freedom merely as the removing of shackles. Without chains, it had seemed, life would be glorious. But now that the fetters had been removed, the people began to wonder what they would do with their lives. They realized that new trials would follow the blessing of freedom. Now they must plan for themselves. "It was very much like suddenly turning a youth of ten or twelve years out into the world to provide for himself," recalled Washington. "In a few hours the great questions with which the Anglo-Saxon race had been grappling for centuries had been thrown upon these people to be solved. These were the questions of a home, a living, the rearing of children, education, citizenship, and the establishment and support of churches."

Not all of these questions, of course, had to be settled at once. But the slaves did have to consider what they would do with their freedom. For the older people it was especially hard to contemplate moving. They had spent their lives on the plantation, and "deep down in their hearts," said Washington, "there was a strange and peculiar attachment to 'Old Marster' and 'Old Missus.'" Moreover, when the proclamation was read the owners themselves had seemed sad at the approaching loss of their people, at the departure of friends as well as workers. One by one the older slaves went up to the big house and carried on "whispered conversations" with their former masters. On the James Borroughs plantation and on other estates throughout the South some slaves chose to stay in their old homes, contracting with the owners to work on the lands with which they were so familiar.

But most ex-slaves wanted to do something to celebrate and observe their new freedom. Washington remarked that some blacks were content to leave the plantation for only a few days or weeks, simply "that they might really feel sure that they were free." Others reminded themselves of their new estate by changing their names. Throughout the South thousands of blacks took on names of their Civil War heroes, including Sherman and Lincoln. Washington had been named Booker Taliaferro by his mother but chose the additional surname by which he became famous.

Many slaves tested their new independence by going west as pioneers in Oregon, Washington, and other distant places, or riding the range as cowboys. Others went north to join relatives in the old free states; still others simply migrated within the South looking for free land or city jobs.

Booker T. Washington and his family left the Borroughs's lands. His mother had married a man on a neighboring plantation who had already fled from slavery on the heels of the Union army. Now this man, named Washington Ferguson, sent word from the Kanawah Valley in West Virginia that the family should join him. They set out across the mountains, traveling on foot and carrying their few possessions in a cart.

The family settled in Malden, West Virginia, in circumstances that showed little improvement over the years in slavery. They lived in a small cabin in an impoverished neighborhood where sanitary facilities were primitive and drunkenness was common. The boys worked long hours in the local salt furnaces and coal mines with their stepfather. Washington might easily have been overcome by poverty and hard work, but for the vision of a better life that drove him to improve himself.

Ever since he was a child on the plantation he had yearned for an education. When carrying books for the master's children, he had sometimes looked into the school and felt that "to get into a schoolhouse and study in this way would be about the same as getting into paradise." In his new home he used every opportunity to learn to read, first memorizing the number 18 marked on his stepfather's salt barrels, then pestering his mother until she bought him a copy of Webster's "blue-black" spelling book. When a young black man from Ohio opened a new school, he was one of its most enthusiastic students.

There was no uniform pattern of free education for blacks in the

South, but the federal government's Freedman's Bureau supported many educational programs for the ex-slaves, and in time the bureau would contribute to the support of the Malden school. The school's funding came mostly from black families, who pledged cash support and took turns boarding the teacher. Washington felt that the desire to learn was not unusual among the newly freed blacks. Most had been denied an education under slavery, and now that they were free, literacy seemed one of the precious opportunities of their new condition. Not only did the children attend the new schools, but many older people went, hoping to read the Bible before they died. "It was," said Washington, "a whole race trying to go to school."

Booker T. Washington learned to read and write in the simple, crowded school that his people set up in Malden, West Virginia. In these years he worked as houseboy for Mrs. Viola Ruffner, a Vermont Yankee and the wife of Gen. Lewis Ruffner, one of the mining aristocracy of the Kanawah Valley. She demanded that everything around her be clean and orderly, and she would not tolerate slovenly behavior. Her insistence on hard, systematic labor and her partiality for cleanliness impressed Washington. It became part of the poor ex-slave's vision of civilized life.

In 1872, when Booker Washington was sixteen years old, his horizons widened once more, and he set off on the most daring enterprise of his young life. He had heard that a college for blacks, called the Hampton Institute, had been set up in Virginia. He was not even clear where it was, but he was determined to attend. His parents were skeptical, even his normally supportive mother fearing his departure from home would be "a wild goose chase." But he saved a small amount of money and set out one fall day to find the school. Most of his black neighbors could not go to college, but the old people sought to help him along: some gave him a quarter, others a nickel or a handkerchief. Booker Washington carried with him the hopes of all the blacks in the Kanawah Valley.

His journey to the Hampton Institute has an epic quality, like Benjamin Franklin's flight from Boston to Philadelphia a century and a half before. Both men left home with little money in their pockets and endured hardships along the way; both arrived impoverished in a new home but triumphed over their circumstances.

When Washington left home, he was not certain exactly where he was going; he simply headed east across the mountains and learned quickly how difficult it was for a black man to travel in the white South. He was allowed to ride on a stagecoach across the Allegheny Mountains, but when the coach stopped at a small inn for the night and he sought to follow the white passengers in obtaining a room, he was told that the inn did not serve blacks. He spent the night huddled outside in the cold. He arrived penniless some days later in Richmond, Virginia, about eighty miles from Hampton. After walking around the city — the biggest he had ever seen — until midnight, he chose a place to sleep beneath a board sidewalk. The next day he found a job on the docks and earned enough money for a breakfast, which he long remembered as one of the best meals of his life.

Washington stayed in Richmond for a few days unloading ships and sleeping under the sidewalk. After saving a little money, he set out again for Hampton. As the school appeared before him, he was struck with wonder. The academic building was an imposing three-story edifice. Undoubtedly he had seen larger buildings in Richmond, but none dedicated to the education of his people. "It seemed to me," he later recalled, "to be the largest and most beautiful building I had ever seen."

Although the fall term was under way at Hampton, Washington was admitted to the institute and assigned a room in the boys' dorm in the schoolhouse attic. The school was coeducational, and the girls lived in nearby buildings that had once served as Union army barracks. Most of the students were older than Washington. Some had grown to adulthood as slaves and were in their late thirties. Even among these humble peers Washington stood out as a peculiarly rural and unsophisticated youth.

The students generally paid half of their room and board fee with labor and the other half with cash, but because of his acute poverty —he had arrived with only 50 cents in his pocket — Booker Washington was allowed to earn all his living expenses by working as a janitor. Like other students, he received his tuition from a northern benefactor, a man in New Bedford, Massachusetts. Even his clothes came from northern donors, who shipped barrels of discards to Hampton.

Washington's three years at the Hampton Institute were spent in rigorous physical and intellectual labor. The students arose at 5 :00 A.M. and were inspected for dress and grooming forty-five minutes later. At 6:00 A.M. they had breakfast, then prayers and room inspection. Classes and study hall occupied most of the remainder of the day. The curriculum included reading, geography, history, algebra, government, natural science, and moral philosophy. Hampton was a trade school as well as an academy, and the students worked as waiters, farmers, janitors, carpenters, painters, printers, and shoemakers. Education at Hampton did not proceed beyond secondary school level, largely because even the philanthropic northern educators who ran the school harbored racial stereotypes of the black intellect. One of the instructors was asked why the school did not teach more advanced courses and replied, "Oh, the colored people are not prepared for those studies yet. They are too ignorant. It will be time enough to talk about that, years from this time."

In later years black leaders would object to such condescension. But to ex-slaves like Washington who attended Hampton in the 1870s, the school was remarkable for the wonderful opportunities it did afford rather than for its limitations. Booker Washington seems to have spent his years at Hampton in a state of perpetual euphoria. Much as he enjoyed his classes and even his janitorial work, he was especially impressed by the opportunity to come into contact with "great men and women." There was, for example, Miss Mary F. Mackie, the female principal of the institute, a northern woman who was not above working side by side with Washington in cleaning the school before a new term. Above all, there was the head of the school, Gen. Samuel Chapman Armstrong, of whom Washington said, "I never saw a man who so completely lost sight of himself." Armstrong was a slender, soldierly man who had risen to command as a youth in his twenties during the Civil War. A northern idealist, he had resigned from the army after the war in order to devote his life to the education of the former slaves. As the school's head he seemed to embody its emphasis on hard work, liberal intelligence, and moral rectitude. The students were so devoted to him that one winter when the men's dormitory became overcrowded, almost everyone in one class volunteered to sleep outside in tents. Each morning during that cold season the general came by the tents to see how the boys were doing, and out of loyalty to him they never admitted their acute discomfort in the canvas dwellings. Armstrong became like a father to Washington, helping the young man with his career and providing a role model for his work as educator.

The promise and achievement of Hampton Institute was symbolized by the commencement exercises in June 1875, an impressive event attended by both black and white observers, including journalists from several northern newspapers and magazines. Several students recited poetry, and a chorus sang "Farewell My Own True Love" and "Nobody Knows the Trouble I've Seen." Seniors read their essays on "Beauty," "Compulsory Education," and "The Black Man as a Voter and Citizen." Washington and another student debated "The Annexation of Cuba," Washington taking the negative side and impressing several reporters with his forceful oratory and keen logic.

The most engaging performance of all was a lecture on slave music by a student, Joseph B. Towe. A reporter from the *Springfield Daily Republican* was spellbound by the presentation. "The writer," he said, "himself brimful of song, a powerful soloist, with a voice of wonderful sweetness, took us back into the past of slavery, and even further back, into Africa itself, for the original sources of this strange music." Towe described the work songs of his own plantation days "when the fields were full of music." Slave soloists were especially important, leading the field hands in song. They drew a large price from plantation owners, "for it paid well in the increased amount of work when the air was alive with work songs." Towe remembered one soloist, John Jones, who could speak an African language.

He recalled the cadences and variations of the work songs. "I will give you an instance," he said, and a chorus of students began to sing. The music, born in Africa, nourished through generations of slavery, uttered now by a chorus of young emancipated black students, swelled through the auditorium. Towe continued his lecture, pausing again and again while the students illustrated his points with song. The audience was entranced, and even former secessionists congratulated the school for its fine program.

Booker T. Washington's career at Hampton ended in a celebration of his people's past achievements, current attainments, and future hopes. But dark clouds hung over that promising future. Already many of the opportunities that had opened ten years before with emancipation were threatened by racial animosity. Many whites did not want to see the ex-slaves advance politically, economically, or intellectually. Among Washington's classmates was a man who had lost two friends and nearly been killed himself when bigots attacked the school where he taught. Through violence and legislation southern whites had begun to take away the basic rights the freedmen had seemingly won through emancipation.

During the years of Reconstruction following the Civil War southern blacks had made advances by their own initiative and with the help of governmental and private agencies. The very fact of freedom radically altered many lives. It allowed Washington and his family to move to West Virginia, enabling Booker T. Washington to attend Tuskegee and become a teacher — options that could be taken for granted in 1875 but had been unthinkable fifteen years before.

Many northerners believed that ending slavery should be only the first step in an extensive program to assist blacks in achieving equality with whites. One could not simply remove the chains of bondage and expect that blacks would immediately and automatically acquire the intellectual and material resources of their former masters. Washington had been assisted by the Freedman's Bureau, when it helped establish the Malden school, and by northern philanthropists who helped him pay his way at Hampton Institute. In addition to founding black schools, federal authorities supervised the operation of new state governments, encouraging blacks to vote and to seek public office. Because many whites were disfranchised for participating in the rebellion, ex-slaves temporarily controlled several southern governments. The United States also considered measures to assist blacks economically. In the early years of Reconstruction, experiments had been conducted on the Sea Islands of South Carolina; at Davis Bend, Louisiana, and elsewhere in the South, proving that if blacks were given land they could prosper.

For a time it had seemed that Reconstruction might revolutionize the political, economic, and intellectual lives of blacks as surely as emancipation had altered their legal status. But the reforms often proved fragile and incomplete. On the morning of emancipation a rumor had circulated widely among the freedmen that they would receive "40 acres and a mule," but the hope for economic assistance proved illusory. In an age that emphasized self-help, the government was unwilling to confiscate plantations or provide other lands for ex-slaves. Political reform, too, had its limits. In the 1870s the North became disenchanted with Reconstruction. The issue of black freedom and progress had agitated the nation for many decades, and many northerners now thought that other issues were more important. Perhaps it would be best, they reasoned, if the ex-slaves were now required to make their own way. The federal government ended its supervision of state politics and ex-Confederates were allowed to vote again.

Once local control returned to southern whites, blacks quickly lost one of Reconstruction's greatest benefits, the opportunity to vote and hold office. In the last quarter of the nineteenth century blacks who sought to vote were often beaten and sometimes killed. State laws formalized their political exile by requiring that voters be descendants of grandfathers who had voted or that they pass literacy tests that were crookedly administered, accepting even the most backward whites while excluding the best-educated blacks.

The freedmen were further disadvantaged by the growth of jim crow laws creating two spheres of life in the South: one the privileged existence of the white, the other the inferior place of the black. A third burden — poverty — combined with disfranchisement and segregation to limit black growth. Without property of their own, many blacks had been forced to enter contracts with white landlords whereby they farmed the land and paid a share of their crops as rent. They often fell into virtual serfdom by borrowing from owners against future profits.

At age twenty Booker T. Washington left Hampton to enter a world where prejudice and poverty threatened to take away the promise of freedom. He faced this world with a program for black advancement modeled on his own experience. Having transcended the squalor of his youth by working hard, he would teach others how to succeed. Quite simply, he believed that good character could overcome any hardship. He would build men and women of good character.

Booker T. Washington's teaching career began at home in Malden, West Virginia. He had contemplated entering politics but decided he could do more for his people as an educator than as a statesman. And surely the residents of the Kanawah Valley needed help as much as any people in the South. Work in the salt furnaces and the coal mines broke men's bodies and spirits, and tensions seethed between poor whites and poor blacks throughout the region. Interracial animosities often erupted into violence and lynchings. Washington brought to Malden his commitment to "assisting in laying the foundation of the race through a generous education of hand, head and heart." He established a day school, a night school, a reading room, and a debating society. He took a personal interest in his students and prepared the best of them for admission to the Hampton Institute.

In 1879 he received an invitation to teach at Hampton. General Armstrong had probably identified him as a prospective faculty member while Washington was at the school but wanted him to experience at first hand the hardships of primary school teaching before enabling him to prepare others to teach. At Hampton, Washington taught classes, directed a program for Indians, and headed the new night school. He particularly enjoyed the latter role. The men and women in this program were impoverished and had to work during the day. Washington grew fond of these students, who worked late into the night on their studies; he issued them honorary certificates over his signature designating them members of "The Plucky Class." The name stuck and the class grew. Washington's doctrine of hard work and self-help apparently touched many responsive souls.

After two years at Hampton, Washington received an invitation to assume a still greater responsibility. A group of citizens in Tuskegee, Alabama, had decided to establish a school for black students and needed a president; they wrote to General Armstrong asking him to recommend a candidate. They had expected him to name a white man, but Armstrong suggested Washington. The committee in Tuskegee agreed after a brief delay.

When he arrived in Tuskegee in 1881, Booker T. Washington was pleased with his new surroundings. The town's two thousand residents were half white and half black, and relations between the races appeared good. The letter asking for a school president had been signed by a black and a white. The only hardware store in town was owned by members of each race.

Before beginning the school year, Washington decided to spend a month traveling by mule through the region in order to gauge his clientele. He visited dozens of impoverished farms, sleeping often on the floor in one-room shacks and sharing simple meals of corn bread, black-eyed peas, and pork. He believed the people were poor mainly because they did not have the energy and the knowledge to improve themselves. They did not make the best use of their land, spent too much time loitering in town, and used their money unwisely — one family, so poor that they shared a single fork, possessed a $60 organ bought on time.

When Washington reflected on the troubles of his race, he usually thought of exactly this type of people — men and women who, in his estimation, did not know how to make the most of life. He felt that many blacks had taken the wrong road during Reconstruction, seeking a life of ease and luxury instead of building a firm foundation by useful labor. In Washington, D.C., for example, men would earn $4 in a week and spend $2 on a buggy ride down Pennsylvania Avenue. Or they lived in idleness, waiting for the federal government to provide jobs. Here and elsewhere too many blacks had devoted their energies to learning Latin and Greek when they should have studied agriculture or mechanics. They had snobbishly assumed that education meant freedom from manual labor. But their education, in many cases, was of no practical value. Or so Washington believed.

He assumed that his people needed to concentrate on the fundamentals: they should become better farmers, blacksmiths, carpenters, and teachers rather than lust after such gewgaws as $60 organs, $2 buggy rides, or superfluous learning. The person who could do some useful work would advance himself, even in the face of racial prejudice. He wrote: "My experience is that there is something in human nature which always makes an individual recognize and reward merit, no matter under what color of skin merit is found."

Washington hoped to mold the Tuskegee Institute into a school that would fill Alabama and the whole South with young men and women who followed his creed of self-help and who could, in turn, inspire other blacks to uplift themselves. But in 1881 his dream required its own foundation-building. There was not even a campus for the new university. At first Tuskegee occupied an old shanty and a black Methodist church, both of which leaked profusely. Then with borrowed money Washington purchased a run-down plantation and began to build Tuskegee by "a slow and natural process of growth."

His first students were shocked when they learned that he intended them to construct and maintain the school. Most had expected that the golden road of education would take them far away from such labor. But Washington intended "to teach them to study actual things instead of mere books alone." Besides, there was almost no money for the new school, and if the students didn't build it, no one else would. Washington carried the students along by precept and example, and in time they erected buildings, dug cellars, baked bricks, and crafted bedsteads and mattresses.

Washington gained the funds for these enterprises by seeking donations from every conceivable source. He traveled to the North where, with the help of General Armstrong, he learned how to open the purses of wealthy philanthropists. He appealed to the region's poor blacks, who sensed that their lives were caught up in some way in the growth of the school and gave generously of their own possessions — a pig, a quilt, sugar cane, or other farm products. Local whites helped the school, too, with loans, donations, or materials. With the aid of these donors, large and small, and the labor of Tuskegee's students, Washington was able to bring "order out of chaos" and establish the school.

Tuskegee offered a regular schedule of traditional courses as well as inculcating in students a "love of work for its own sake." Tuskegee's achievements even appeared to cement relations between blacks and whites in the region. Tuskegee's brickyard was a good example. After several unsuccessful efforts Washington finally built a kiln that could make good bricks. Since there was no other local brickyard, the white people soon came to Tuskegee to shop. "As the people of the neighborhood came to us to buy bricks," says Washington, "we got acquainted with them. Our business interests became intermingled. We had something which they wanted; they had something which we wanted. This, in a large measure, helped to lay the foundation for the pleasant relations that have continued to exist between us and the white people."

In 1881, when Tuskegee opened, only sixteen years had passed since it had been illegal to educate a black in Alabama. Within a decade Washington built Tuskegee into one of the best-known black colleges in the nation. By speaking at philanthropic gatherings and educational association meetings he acquired a modest national reputation as an effective orator with an interesting background. Thus, it was natural when in 1895 he was selected as a "responsible" representative of the black South at the opening of the Atlanta Exposition.

When Washington received the invitation to speak, he immediately recognized the importance of the occasion. The Atlanta Exposition was the first major trade fair held in the South since the Civil War, and so symbolized the resources and growth of the region. Washington had been called upon to address the largest white audience ever to hear a black speaker in the South, and he would never have a better chance to present his program for black progress and interracial cooperation.

In preparing his Atlanta address Washington combed through former lectures, selecting an image here, an idea there. After completing a draft of the talk, he read it to the Tuskegee faculty and won their

Tuskegee Institute, 1881–1895. Booker T. Washington began his school with a few crude buildings. With the help of local supporters, northern philanthropists, and cooperative students he built Tuskegee into a substantial academy.

approval. Despite this encouragement, however, he became increasingly apprehensive as the day for the speech drew near. Many southern newspapers had already published articles criticizing the fair committee for inviting a black man to speak. Washington recalled that when he left Tuskegee by train for Atlanta on September 17 he felt like a man "on his way to the gallows."

Everyone seemed to know he was going to deliver a major address. At stops along the way people pointed him out and discussed his forthcoming speech. In the station at Atlanta he heard an old black man say, "Dat's de man of my race what's gwine to make a speech at de Exposition to-morrow. I'se sho' gwine to hear him."

He was exceedingly uncomfortable in the spotlight. That night he hardly slept. In the morning he prayed for God's assistance. Then he took the long ride to the convention. Now, in a moment, he would speak.

When the band completed its musical interlude, Governor Bullock announced: "We have with us to-day a representative of Negro enterprise and Negro civilization." Washington rose to his feet and approached the platform. The sun's rays were flooding through the west windows, bathing the platform in light. Washington moved about, awkwardly trying to escape the brightness, but could not. He looked out at the silent crowd and the thousands of eyes upon him. He paused and then, his face aglow with the light of the setting sun, began his address.

The speech was fashioned around one essential point — that southern whites and blacks needed one another. "One-third of the population of the South," he began, "is of the Negro race. No enterprise seeking the material, civil, or moral welfare of this section can disregard this element of our population and reach the highest success." Washington advised each race to assist the other. He counseled whites to look to the black rather than to foreign immigrants to cultivate the surplus land and to labor in the factories. He urged them to recognize the ability of the ex-slaves who after only thirty years of freedom were engaged in the "production of agricultural implements, buggies, steam-engines, newspapers, books, statuary, carving, paintings, the management of drug-stores and banks." They had made this progress with the help of both southern and northern philanthropists, and with continued encouragement in the "education of head, hand, and heart" they would contribute further to southern prosperity. He reminded the whites that blacks had proved themselves constructive members of southern society. They had "tilled your fields, cleared your forests, builded your railroads and cities and brought forth treasures from the bowels of the earth." They had even been faithful to their slave masters, rearing their children, watching at their sickbeds, and following their dead "with tear-dimmed eyes to their graves." Over the years blacks had proved "the most patient, faithful, law-abiding, and unresentful people that the world has seen."

While reminding the whites of the importance of the blacks, Washington warned against abusing them. Injustice to the blacks, he said, would damage the whole society: "The laws of changeless justice bind oppressor and oppressed." If the blacks were treated fairly, their "sixteen million hands" would help in southern progress. If not, they would retard the growth of the whole South. "We shall constitute one third and more of the ignorance and crime of the South," he said, "or one-third of its intelligence and progress; we shall contribute one-third to the business and industrial prosperity of the South, or we shall prove a veritable body of death, stagnating, depressing, retarding every effort to advance the body politic."

Booker T. Washington's advice to his own people was equally frank. They must work hard to win the friendship and respect of their southern neighbors, engaging "in agriculture, mechanics, in commerce, in domestic service, and in the professions." In particular, they should recognize that "when it comes to business, pure and simple, it is in the South that the Negro is given a man's chance in the commercial world."

Washington said blacks must not expect to achieve social equality with whites immediately. They should begin at the bottom and work their way up, as Washington had done in his youth and in the foundation of the Tuskegee Institute. "No race can prosper," he asserted, "till it learns that there is as much dignity in tilling a field as in writing a poem." They must learn to distinguish between "the superficial and the substantial, the ornamental gewgaws of life and the useful."

The ideal relationship between the races could be summarized in one image. The black people, he told his white listeners, will work hard, "interlacing our industrial, commercial, civil, and religious life with yours in a way that shall make the interests of both races one. In all things that are purely social we can be as separate as the fingers, yet one as the hand in all things essential to mutual progress."

Both races should recognize that each had much to offer the other. Whites should seek the new industrial labor force among native blacks. Blacks should build their enterprises on southern soil rather than seeking refuge in the North. Both races were like a ship at sea that called to another for water and was told, "Cast down your bucket where you are." The thirsty crew reluctantly dropped a bucket expecting to find only salt water, but the water was fresh, for without their knowledge they had drifted into the broad mouth of the Amazon River. "Cast down your bucket where you are," Washington told both races, and you will find great opportunities lie before you.

Washington spun out these ideas in the best oratorical fashion of the times. He knew how to "sense' his audience, to recognize whether people were caught up in his ideas. Soon after he began the Atlanta address, his eyes shining in the sunlight, his feet planted firmly, his husky voice uttering the words in measured cadences, he knew that he had captured the crowd. People looked at him with admiration, some with tears in their eyes. When he came to the central metaphor in the speech, he held up his hand with fingers outstretched, then closed it into a fist as he said they would be "one as the hand in all things essential to mutual progress." Applause resounded through the auditorium. White gentry and black laborers alike jumped cheering to their feet.

When he had finished, applause again thundered through the hall. Governor Bullock rushed across the platform and clasped Washington's hand. Others followed. Clark Howell, editor of the *Atlanta Constitution,* wrote: "The address was a revelation. The whole speech is a platform upon which blacks and whites can stand with full justice to each other."

The Atlanta Exposition address catapulted Washington into local and national prominence, and after the address crowds gathered around him wherever he went in Atlanta. Washington was somewhat overwhelmed by the response and was glad to escape to Tuskegee on the following day. There congratulations also poured in. President Cleveland commended his speech, and the press, both North and South, was laudatory. The ten-minute oration had made Washington the foremost spokesman for his race, a position he would retain for the remaining twenty years of his life.

There were some, however, who criticized Washington's formula for interracial harmony. Some blacks felt he had conceded too much, put too much emphasis on the need for hard work and not enough on ending segregation and securing political rights. Even as Washington spoke, lawmakers in South Carolina were debating a measure that would disfranchise blacks in that state. In fact, within a few years every southern state passed such laws.

Washington was, of course, aware of injustice. He had been segregated in hundreds of jim crow hotels, restaurants, and railroad cars during his lifetime. Even on the day of the Atlanta Exposition address he was staying in a segregated hotel. His students had a taste of the racial animosity underlying such policies in 1896 when Alabama Governor William C. Oates addressed Tuskegee's graduating class. Annoyed by the liberality of a previous speaker, the governor threw away his prepared address and, glaring at his audience, told them: "I want to give you niggers a few words of plain talk and advice. . . . You might as well understand that this is a white man's country, as far as the South is concerned, and we are going to make you keep your place. Understand that. I have nothing more to say to you." Such astonishingly arrogant words might have provoked Washington to rage, but he was well acquainted with such men and ideas. His eyes twinkled as he heard the governor; then he dismissed the assembly on the grounds that everyone was "fagged out" from so much speaking. One of the guests later wrote, "Mr. Washington's imperturbably good nature alone saved the day."

Booker T. Washington's "good nature" struck many observers as acquiescence to white racism. In 1905 one of his chief critics, W. E. B. Du Bois, helped organize the Niagara movement, a forerunner to the National Association for the Advancement of Colored People, to foster resistance to disfranchisement and segregation. Such men believed that Washington was more remarkable for the limitations he accepted than for the opportunities he announced. Although Washington condemned racial oppression in the Atlanta Exposition address, he conceded that it mattered little if blacks were barred from opera houses, and at Tuskegee he emphasized manual labor rather than the professions. He gave two reasons for such policies. Sometimes he claimed that these limitations were appropriate, even beneficial to an emerging people who needed to begin with the fundamentals. At other times he claimed they were forced upon him by necessity. If he had become an agitator for equal rights, he would have lost support for Tuskegee. "When your head is in the lion's mouth," he liked to say, "you have to stroke that lion."

It was not Booker T. Washington's fashion to rail against injustice, to demand that the outside world conform to his ideals. Not that he quietly accepted disfranchisement and segregation as some writers have mistakenly claimed: he fought the movement to take away the black vote, remarked on the absurdity of segregation in public facilities, and condemned racial prejudice as a force that injured both blacks and whites. But the main thrust of his policy was to draw out the capabilities of his own people. Political and cultural disadvantages could, he believed, strengthen blacks. "With few exceptions," he said, "the Negro youth must work harder and must perform his task better than a white youth in order to secure recognition. But out of the hard and unusual struggle through which he is compelled to pass, he gets a strength, a confidence, that one misses whose pathway is comparatively smooth by reason of birth and race."

In 1895 in the midst of an age of industrial progress and self-made men his emphasis on individual initiative won admiration from both races. There were times of deeper insight when Booker T. Washington realized the terrible burden imposed on his people by racial prejudice. While he reigned at Tuskegee, hundreds of blacks throughout the South were burned to death or hanged by lynch mobs, and thousands were denied what he called "a man's chance" in business because of their color.

Despite these injustices, however, he continued to urge blacks to find strength in themselves and to make friends with their white neighbors. When those white neighbors did not merit his trust, Washington could still take consolation in the course of history. He had begun life, after all, as another man's property and had come a long way in material prosperity, public stature, and self-esteem. If he was not the white man's equal at least he was not his slave. In 1895 a man who vividly recalled sleeping in rags on a dirt floor in a slave cabin could be more impressed with what his people had achieved than by what they had been denied.

Washington's greatest strength — and his most serious limitation — lay in his ability to work within the historical situation. History freed him from slavery and allowed him to be a teacher: he worked hard and became a leading educator. History imposed barriers on him and his people: he encouraged them to live the fullest lives possible within those barriers. He would leave the removal of those barriers to other men and other generations.

QUESTIONS

1. Booker T. Washington had a strong, almost naive, faith in the real and potential harmony of whites and blacks. What instances of interracial cooperation did he recall in his own life? How did his Atlanta Exposition address evoke the ideal of cooperation?

2. How was Washington's life touched by racial injustice? What results does he predict if southerners don't treat his people fairly?

3. Washington believed that the black's best route to progress was through self-help. How did his life reflect this principle? In what ways did he believe that some blacks were responsible for their own poverty?

4. The author argues that Washington is wrongly accused of uncritically accepting segregation and placing the full burden of self-help upon his own people. In what phrases does Washington's Atlanta speech call on blacks to help themselves? In what words does he demand that whites treat them fairly? In what respects did Washington accept limitations on black initiative and freedom?

5. Washington justified the emphasis on manual labor at Tuskegee on the grounds that blacks needed to build from the ground up. In distinguishing between the "gewgaws" and the "useful" was he making a valid point about black needs, or was he rationalizing his acceptance of segregationist limitations on his race?

6. Washington was an optimist in 1895 because he had progressed so far from his slave rags of thirty years before. What would he have thought of contemporary black history if he had been born in 1875? What disadvantages did blacks as a race suffer at the time of the Atlanta address?

BIBLIOGRAPHY

COBEN, WILLIAM. *At Freedom's Edge* (1991). On black mobility and the southern white quest for racial control, 1861–1915.

DU BOIS, W.E.B. *Souls of Black Folk* (1903 and later editions). Poetic history of Reconstruction era by Washington's chief critic.

FREDERICKSON, GEORGE M. *The Black Image in the White Mind* (1971). Nineteenth-century attitudes about blacks and their future.

HARLAN, LOUIS R. *Booker T. Washington: The Making of a Black leader. 1856-1901* (1972). Fine biography revealing complexity of Washington and his times.

HARLAN, LOUIS R. *The Booker T. Washington Papers* (1972–). Includes many informative letters by Washington.

LITWACK, LEON F. *Been So Long in the Storm: The Aftermath of Slavery* (1979). Sensitive re-creation of the experience of southern blacks and whites in the first years of freedom.

ROSE, WILLIE LEE. *Rehearsal for Reconstruction* (1964). Describes northern efforts to provide a model at Port Royal for the economic and educational progress of ex-slaves.

STAMP, KENNETH M. *Era of Reconstruction. 1865–1877* (1965). Survey of the period emphasizing loss of voting rights and lack of property as the chief black weaknesses.

TRELEAJE, ALLEN W. *White Terror* (1971). Account of Southern vigilante groups, especially the Ku Klux Klan.

WASHINGTON, BOOKER T. *Up from Slavery* (1901 and later editions). Autobiographical account of Washington's life to the time of the Atlanta Exposition address.

WAYNE, MICHAEL. *The Reshaping of Plantation Society: From Slavery to Sharecropping in the Natchez District. 1860–1890* (1982). How emancipation changed plantation life.

2

THE NEW
INDUSTRIAL ERA

The Rise of
Andrew Carnegie

In three centuries the character of American life has undergone several dramatic changes. In the colonial period Euro-Americans replaced Indians as the dominant population on the eastern seaboard. During the Revolution thirteen British colonies formed an independent nation. Early in the nineteenth century a coastal people spread westward to the Mississippi. And after the Civil War 4 million slaves were freed from bondage. Each of these epochal events affected the American environment, but no change was more influential than industrialization in the late nineteenth century. The growth of big business affected where Americans lived, what they consumed, how they worked, and what they thought. If Rip Van Winkle had slept from 1870 to 1910, he would have seen changes far greater than those wrought by the American Revolution. The men who had led the industrial movement, entrepreneurs like Andrew Carnegie, were the most influential people of their time. Their histories reveal the massiveness of the new enterprises and suggest that even the captains of industry had trouble in adjusting to their own unprecedented power.

For two centuries America was a nation of wood. People came to the country in wood ships and moved about in carts, wagons, and coaches of wood. They used wood for their tables, chairs, plates, and bowls. They plowed their fields with wood plows pulled by oxen joined with wood yokes.

The economy built on wood was local, near to home. More than 90 percent of early Americans lived on farms. Most of what they ate, wore, and worked with they made themselves, lighting their dwellings with homemade candles and cutting their clothes from homespun cloth. Most of their products were just one step removed from nature. They wove the fleece from their sheep's backs into woolen cloth and ground the grain from their fields into bread. The fuel that warmed their houses came from nearby woods, as did materials for the houses themselves.

Wood may be said to symbolize something vital in early America: the comparative self-sufficiency of the family and the simple, close relationship to nature. By the same token, iron and steel were the basic ingredients of a new America that took form in the late nineteenth century. In the industrial age men traveled across the country behind an "iron horse" following iron rails. They crossed the oceans in steamships driven by iron machinery, fought their battles in ships protected by iron and steel armor, and constructed tall buildings with frameworks of steel. The dependence on these materials influenced new patterns in labor and business. Large concentrations of power began to replace individual enterprises; men worked in factories, not for themselves; they worked upon and with materials made from minerals, not living plants.

Iron was only one of many growing enterprises that revolutionized American life, but its history illustrates industrialization as a whole; and one business, the Carnegie Steel Company, illuminates trends throughout the industry. The company was created by Andrew Carnegie, a remarkable man in an age of incomparable entrepreneurs. He became interested in iron after the Civil War and concentrated his energy on steel in the 1870s. Buying and leasing other businesses, he pushed his company to dominance over the industry, producing almost as much steel as the whole of the British Isles. In 1901 Carnegie sold his company, retired from business, and became the nation's leading philanthropist.

Entrepreneurs like Carnegie have been both lauded and vilified, some critics regarding them as the indispensable leaders of an age of industrial wonders, other seeing them as narrow and greedy "robber barons" who exploited people and resources for their private benefit. Certainly they changed America, but at what cost to themselves and their society? By studying Carnegie's career we can explore the kinds of personal qualities that went into creating giant industries and consider the effects of their businesses on those they employed and served.

Andrew Carnegie's life began in Dunfermline, Scotland, a town on high ground above the Firth of Forth, looking out on Edinburgh, fourteen miles to the southeast, and the North Sea beyond. A center for the damask cloth trade, the town housed hundreds of looms on which half the population wove linen cloth, decorated with intricate designs of thistles, roses, and portraits. For centuries a tradition of fine craftsmanship had been passed from father to son.

Andrew Carnegie's family was typical of the town. The father, William, was a weaver. Shortly after his wife, Margaret, gave birth to Andy in their small cottage on November 25, 1835, he moved to a larger house and purchased three additional looms, worked by apprentices. As the eldest son, Andrew might expect to follow his father's trade.

But this future was not to be. Ironically, Andrew Carnegie, one day the greatest industrialist in the world, first experienced the industrial revolution as one of its victims. Shortly after his birth a power loom was established in Dunfermline, heralding an end to the old way of life. A group of protestors disguised in costumes attacked and burned the new mill, but they could not hold out for long against the lower cost of machine-produced linens. In winter 1847–48, six hundred of Dunfermline's weavers were out of work. William Carnegie had to sell his extra looms. His Scottish fortune ruined, he decided to take his family to America.

Years later Andrew would reflect on his Scottish legacy. He remembered relatives and friends who taught him a love for history and poetry and recalled simple childish pleasures such as raising rabbits. But along with these pleasant memories he had learned a painful lesson: how those unable to control their fortunes can be set adrift in the world.

The Carnegies left Dunfermline on May 17, 1848, setting sail from Glasgow for New York. Andrew was a bright and outgoing child. On shipboard he soon got to know the sailors and became so popular that he was invited to share their Sunday dessert. The family disembarked in New York City after fifty days at sea and continued on to Pittsburgh, whose history became thoroughly intertwined with Andrew Carnegie's.

Pittsburgh is located at the confluence of the Monongahela and Allegheny rivers in western Pennsylvania. Early visitors frequently commented on the great beauty of the two rivers and the narrow valleys they had cut through steep bluffs and green rolling hills. An English visitor commented on the pristine view that its only failing was that it lacked the noise and smoke of a great city. A century later an Englishman, Herbert Spencer, came to Pittsburgh in the company of Andrew Carnegie. By then the place was known as "The Smoky City." Clouds of coal dust darkened the skies, and torrents of factory waste discolored the rivers. Six months in Pittsburgh, Spencer believed, would justify anyone in committing suicide.

The transformation of this idyllic landscape into a commercial center is one of the great "success stories" in American urban history. Pittsburgh's favored location among huge supplies of iron and coal made it one of the fastest-growing cities in the United States. Its population swelled from 1,565 to 49,221 between 1800 and 1860. As early as 1820 the city was known as the iron capital of America. In 1842 Charles Dickens included Pittsburgh in his tour of the United States. The city, he wrote, "certainly had a great quantity of smoke hanging over it, and is famous for its iron works."

Many resourceful businessmen had a hand in the early economic success of Pittsburgh. But none did more than the Scottish boy making his slow progress westward in summer 1848. The Carnegies' trip from New York took three weeks by river and canal. In Pittsburgh they were greeted by relatives and a friendly Scottish community. They settled in an area known as "Slabtown," an ugly assortment of factories, stores, saloons, and jerry-built hovels.

It is tempting to let Andrew Carnegie's first days in Pittsburgh be colored by his later success. But to do so is to ignore the true harshness of those years. In 1848 the Carnegies could not dream that one day they would be worth millions of dollars. Their reality was poverty. Worse still, William Carnegie was a broken man. He knew only one craft and attempted to pursue it, weaving linens and peddling them along the Ohio River, but in America, as in Scotland, one could not make a decent living from hand-woven linens.

Andrew's mother was a strong, energetic woman. Shortly after their arrival in the New World she began to make money working for a shoe manufacturer and taking in laundry. But the skimpy parental earnings could barely support the family. Carnegie later wrote, "The prospect of want had become to me a frightful nightmare." The family fears burst to the surface one day in "the most tragic of all scenes I have ever witnessed." Andrew's uncle, visiting the family, tried to suggest ways for Andrew to help. He innocently suggested that the boy might get a basket of knickknacks and peddle them on the wharves.

Margaret Carnegie, outraged at the idea of her son doing such a thing, sprang toward the uncle. "What! My son a peddler and go among rough men upon the wharves! I would rather throw him into the Allegheny River. Leave me!" The shaken man retreated and Margaret broke down. Holding Andrew and his younger brother, Tom, her voice choked with emotion, she told them they must become honorable and respectable and not remain in a lowly, impoverished condition.

Yet the means of escape were by no means clear. Andrew's first jobs hardly seemed better than a peddler's. To help support the family he went to work in a factory, laboring from sunrise to sunset at $1.20 a week. A second job took him to a bobbin factory, where he worked in a "dark cellar" stoking a boiler. He must watch the gauges carefully — too little fuel and the machinery would not run properly, too much and the boiler could explode. At home "begrimed with coal dirt," he was unable to sleep soundly, wakening often to watch imaginary gauges. A promotion of sorts brought him out of the cellar but exposed him to an equally nasty task, dipping the bobbins in a foul-smelling oil that often caused him to vomit.

It is easy to understand why Carnegie saw his next task, with the O'Reilly Telegraph Company, as a wonderful opportunity. In the days before the telephone the rapidest form of communication was the telegraph. Business and personal letters were sent from city to city over telegraph lines by Morse code, then copied down and carried by delivery boys to the addressee. Unlike Carnegie's previous jobs, this one demanded initiative and mental effort and gave him an introduction, although a humble one, to members of Pittsburgh's business community. He soon memorized not only the location of every business establishment but also the faces of all the proprietors so that when he was bearing a telegram he could identify them on the street.

Between trips, waiting in the telegraph office, he taught himself to take messages by ear from the wire. Most operators had to copy out the code letter by letter and translate it; Carnegie was one of the few operators in the country then who could receive by ear. It was natural that soon, in 1851, he was given a position as operator. "I felt that my foot was upon the ladder," he later wrote, "and that I was bound to climb."

Even as a bobbinboy he had begun to plan his economic ascent. He heard that a new form of bookkeeping called double-entry was useful in business. Although he was working long hours, he went to school in the evening to learn the system, and in addition began an extensive reading program including works by Macaulay, Bancroft, Burns and Shakespeare. To develop his mind still more he joined the Webster Literary Club, which met to debate political questions and to study literature.

In these early years of his "career" (he was only sixteen in 1851) Carnegie might have been modeling his life on Benjamin Franklin's. He led a purposeful life, worked hard, advertised his abilities, and exploited every advantage that offered itself. But like most men on the make, Andrew Carnegie had little understanding of those who were unable to master their circumstances. Shortly after he became a telegraph operator, a sad event contrasted Carnegie's optimism with his father's tragic condition. Andrew had been sent out of town to help provide emergency telegraph service after a storm. By chance he met his father, who was traveling by ferryboat to Cincinnati to peddle his linens. Andrew was shocked to see that the old man was traveling not in a cabin, but on deck, exposed to the elements. William Carnegie admitted to his son that he could not afford a cabin. Andrew replied, "Never mind, Father, it won't be long before you and mother shall ride in your own carriage." His father paused for a long time, then, with difficulty, said, "Andra, I am proud of you." Andrew went back to work, and William went on to Cincinnati on the boat's open deck.

Without meaning to, without realizing that he had done so, the young man had humiliated his father as surely as if he had cursed him for a failure. William Carnegie died in 1855. He had known how to weave fine patterns in linen and to sing a good song. His son said of him, he was "one of the most lovable of men . . . not much of a man of the world, but a man all over for heaven." He hadn't known how to make his way in industrial America.

Andrew was very much a "man of the world," as he clearly proved in the decade before the Civil War. In the telegraph office he established a public reputation as a bright, industrious youth and met many of Pittsburgh's business leaders. One man he impressed was Thomas Scott, who in 1852 became superintendent of the Pennsylvania Railroad's western division. A year later Carnegie became his secretary and personal telegrapher.

The railroad was then an infant industry. By twentieth-century standards, the diminutive engines with their enormous polished lamps seem like carnival toys. The railroads at that time, however, were models of business efficiency — bigger and more carefully organized than any other enterprise. Formerly the largest economic units in the United States had been New England textile mills, some of them virtually occupying a whole town. The railroads were much larger, holding stations, warehouses, repair shops, offices, telegraph lines, and vast work forces. Even more impressive than their size was their organization. In order to operate efficiently — to move goods along the lines, collect payments, repair machinery, and regulate dozens of other activities — numerous functions had to be carefully planned and coordinated, requiring collection of impersonal statistical data on costs and labor.

The railroad became almost universally the standard for efficiency and order. Even the great nineteenth-century admirer of nature, Henry David Thoreau, paid tribute to railroads, recognizing their contribution to human development. Trains passed near his cabin at Walden Pond, and he contemplated their place in the American scene. "They go and come with such regularity and precision," he wrote, "and their whistle can be heard so far, that the farmers set their clocks by them, and thus one well-conducted institution regulates a whole country. Have not men improved somewhat in punctuality since the railroad was invented? Do they not talk and think faster in the depot than they did in the stage office? There is something electrifying in the atmosphere of the former place . . . To do things 'railroad fashion' is now the byword."

Between 1853 and 1865 Carnegie learned to do things "railroad fashion." The well-organized line from which he learned, the Pennsylvania Railroad, was known as "the standard railroad of the world." Its president, J. Edgar Thomson, and the superintendent of the western division, Thomas Scott, were two of the best managers of their day.

As Scott's right-hand man, Carnegie became familiar with all aspects of the railroad business. He observed the relationship between the railroad and its varied customers and learned about routing trains, maintaining equipment, and clearing wrecks. In 1859 Scott moved to Philadelphia as vice-president of the line, and Carnegie became superintendent of the western division. He was now twenty-four years old and earning $2,400 per year, a substantial sum in those days. As superintendent, Carnegie had new ideas for increasing the railroad's efficiency: clearing lines quickly after wrecks by burning the ruined cars and regularizing traffic flow by moving company goods only when customer traffic was light. These innovations show that Carnegie had mastered the *mental* art of business. Just as he had assembled a mental map of the business establishments of Pittsburgh, Carnegie now had a picture of the Pennsylvania Railroad system. He knew its equipment, workers, and customers; and he knew how changes in one area would affect conditions in another. Many businessmen were inclined to play hunches, taking risks with partial knowledge of a situation, but Carnegie possessed the mental acumen to evaluate all the intricate variables in a business decision. This ability made him an effective manager and helped him in another kind of business activity, that of financier.

While working for Thomas Scott, Carnegie had learned that it was possible to buy stocks in American companies, paper that would produce revenue for the holder without his working. With Scott's help he had made a number of good investments, including a one-eighth interest in the first sleeping car company in the United States. Thanks to such stocks, Carnegie had an income of almost $50,000 a year in 1863.

In 1865 Carnegie resigned his position with the Pennsylvania Railroad to devote full time to his financial interests. During the next seven years he was involved in a number of business enterprises, including telegraph lines, an oil company, grain elevators, Pullman cars, and railroads. Realizing a transcontinental railroad was imminent, he organized the Keystone Bridge Company in 1865 and built a crossing of the Mississippi at Saint Louis and another of the Missouri at Omaha.

His widely ranging activities in these years schooled his ability to evaluate business opportunities and showed him the many factors in capitalizing and running varied enterprises. He was now ready, as he later said, to "put all of his eggs into one basket and then watch that basket grow." There were many "baskets" from which to choose in post-Civil War America. Carnegie might easily have gone into Pullman cars, telegraph lines, or oil. But he was attracted to iron. It was a field that an entrepreneur might easily dominate. The oil business was too chaotic and speculative; in other fields, such as the telegraph, a single company, Western Union, already controlled the field. But the iron industry, though well established, was not monopolized by one large concern. In addition, iron seemed to be the essential material in a growing America.

When dealing with a person of Carnegie's stature, we run the danger of identifying the industry with the man, as if he had made a product where absolutely none had existed. But of course there was iron long before there was Carnegie. Man first began to work with iron some six thousand years before industrialists fashioned it into engines and ships and railroads. Early peoples made iron into tools and weapons that proved more effective — stronger and harder — than objects of copper, bronze, and stone. Over the centuries blacksmiths evolved better ways of working with their material and produced a widening group of products. By the mid-nineteenth century, new enterprises had placed heavy demands on iron products.

Several variables affected the character of iron, especially the carbon content and the time allowed for cooling. Wrought iron and steel had a low carbon content and were malleable. Cast iron had a higher carbon content and was firmer, but was also more brittle. In 1856 an Englishman, Henry Bessemer, invented a blast furnace that produced a new metal with the best qualities of both kinds of iron. It was malleable but strong, hard but not brittle. It was precisely the kind of metal the new industries required. Bessemer's invention was soon put to use in the United States.

Carnegie became involved in iron in 1872 when he and several partners formed Carnegie, McCandless and Company, the predecessor of Carnegie Steel. Carnegie had been interested in the Bessemer steel-making process for several years. At first it was not practical to build a Bessemer plant in Pittsburgh because it would require a kind of iron ore not generally available in the region. But the discovery of a suitable ore in Michigan solved the raw materials problem. Carnegie had a chance to observe the Bessemer process in England in 1872 and was impressed. An acquaintance later described Carnegie's reaction to the Bessemer converter: "Nothing that he had ever seen was so picturesque, so fascinating, so miraculous in its easily controlled force and fury. It was half a furnace and half a cyclone, yet it was obedient to the touch of a boy's hand. Give it thirty thousand pounds of common pig iron, and presto! the whole mass was blown into steel." It was a machine to match Carnegie's grand imagination.

Back in Pittsburgh, Carnegie began work on the plant that would become the J. Edgar Thomson Works. It was twelve miles from Pittsburgh on Braddock's Field, a pastoral area of farmland and virgin timber that had remained almost unchanged in the century and a quarter since General Braddock had met defeat there in the French and Indian War. The location took advantage of transportation facilities on two railroads and the Ohio River barges. At its completion in 1875 the plant was the largest and the best in America.

One would need only to observe the day-to-day activities of the Thomson Works to realize the remarkable difference between the old economy of home workshops and the new industry concentrated in giant plants. Every day tons of raw materials were shipped to Braddock. Ore was loaded into a furnace along with coke and limestone. The coke was ignited and blasts of air were forced through the mass; the iron became molten and was drained off into molds; later, with more refined technology, into giant ladles on freight cars. These were carried to a Jones mixer, a huge iron box capable of holding up to 250 tons of molten pig iron. In this vast cradle many loads of liquid iron were mixed to form a uniform composition. It was transferred from the mixer to the Bessemer converter, which one of Carnegie's associates called "the most beautiful and perfect piece of mechanism ever devised by the human mind." In the converter, jets of air were blown through the liquid iron, forcing out impurities and thereby transforming iron into steel. Then the molten steel was poured into molds and formed into ingots, which were, in turn, moved under heavy rollers and pressed into the necessary shape for later use. Carnegie produced some finished goods such as rails and iron plate. Other products were made in independent factories.

Building the plant was only the first step in the creation of a steel company. For the next twenty-five years Carnegie devoted his energies to matters of management, marketing, and expansion. He was fortunate from the start in securing a Civil War veteran and experienced steelmaster, Capt. William R. Jones, as plant supervisor, the man who would be at the plant every day ensuring that work progressed smoothly.

Jones refused Carnegie's offer of shares in the company, preferring to receive "one hell of a salary." As a measure of his assessment of Jones's responsibilities, Carnegie gave him the same salary as that of President Grant, $25,000 a year. Jones was bright and resourceful and could run and repair the machinery while identifying new equipment needs. The Jones mixer was his invention. Equally important, he was an incomparable leader. Known to the workers as "Captain Bill," he was an affable master who worked closely with his men. Pictures of him reveal a solid, handsome man with eyes of remarkable warmth. In his years as a steelmaster he occasionally knocked off work early to take his men to a

Steel plant and laborer. The raw human energy of industrialization was supplied by millions who worked long hours for low pay.

baseball game. When he heard of the Johnstown flood in 1889, he closed the mill, and he and his men went to help with rescue operations. He died soon afterward while inspecting a "hang" — a block in the flow of molten iron in one of his furnaces; the furnace exploded, killing him almost instantly. Carnegie was reduced to tears by the news. The plant was closed for the day of Jones's funeral, and nearly ten thousand men marched in his funeral procession. Jones was replaced by a close friend, Charles M. Schwab, who eventually became president of the United

States Steel Company and was, like his predecessor, a talented and affable steelmaster.

One of the reasons for Carnegie's success was his ability to identify and promote talented men like Jones and Schwab. He also devised management techniques to evaluate the effectiveness of each stage of steel manufacture. Traditionally, iron- and steelworks kept records of their overall profits and losses but had no way of accurately measuring results at each stage, to discover where improvements might be made. With detailed records Carnegie could replace ineffective parts, whether men or machines. He had learned the lessons of his early years well. Carnegie's was the first American manufacturing concern to do things "railroad fashion."

Careful management was an essential element in the growth of his steel interests. It enabled him to keep prices lower than those of his competitors and so to attract orders. Carnegie recognized, too, how valuable informal ties were in producing customers. Among his other talents, he was an accomplished salesman, telling amusing Scottish stories and cultivating his old friends from the railroad days. Businessmen would buy their steel from Carnegie for two good reasons: his prices were low and he was their friend. Carnegie was also able to anticipate new markets for steel. Late in the nineteenth century cities replaced railroads as the main buyers; Carnegie widened his contacts accordingly.

To careful management and imaginative marketing Carnegie added a third program, acquiring other companies. By this practice — known as horizontal integration — he increased his output and his domination of the industry. Among other businesses, he acquired the Homestead Works in 1889 and the Allegheny Bessemer Steel Company in 1890. In 1892 these interests were consolidated as the Carnegie Steel Company.

As he bought steel operations, Carnegie sought to control the businesses upon which steel depended. Producing steel required enormous supplies of coke, a hot-burning coal. In nearby Connollsville, a coal-rich region, Henry Clay Frick had gained control of 80 percent of the coke production. In 1889 Frick and Carnegie worked out an agreement whereby Frick became general manager of Carnegie's steel interests and Carnegie controlled Frick's coal. Carnegie gained a strong hold on another raw material, iron ore, by negotiating a long-term lease on ore lands in Minnesota's Mesabi Range, the richest in the world. To transport the ore he secured an interest in Great Lakes carriers and built a railroad from their Lake Erie terminus to his Monongahela furnaces.

By 1900 Carnegie accounted for one fourth of the nation's steel output. In that year the company's profits were $40 million, of which $25 million went to Carnegie himself. Carnegie steel could be found throughout the United States in railroads, battleships, bridges, and skyscrapers. It went into the Brooklyn Bridge and the Washington Monument.

Carnegie might have built his business even further. In 1900 he was considering the idea of constructing railroad lines and acquiring plants to produce such finished products as steel tubes, rods, and wire. But Andrew Carnegie had another ambition. Early in life he had written an article entitled "The Gospel of Wealth," in which he had argued that the man who dies rich "dies disgraced." A rich man, he had said, should use his money for the benefit of others. Over the years Carnegie had made a number of philanthropic bequests; now he wanted to devote himself entirely to this end. To do so he must convert his industrial wealth into liquid capital.

It was, of course, one thing to sell a ton of steel and quite another to sell a half-billion-dollar steel company. Fortunately at this moment the great financier J. P. Morgan was interested in expanding his steel interests. In 1898 Morgan had organized the Federal Steel Company with capital of $200 million. In December 1900 Morgan told Charles Schwab he was interested in buying Carnegie Steel. Schwab's boss was ready to sell and came up with the figure $492 million. Schwab communicated the price to Morgan, who took one look at the figure and accepted it without further negotiation. In January 1901 the bargain was formalized in a fifteen-minute meeting between Morgan and Carnegie. As Morgan left Carnegie's house, he shook his hand, saying, "Mr. Carnegie, I want to congratulate you on being the richest man in the world!"

Morgan formed his holdings into U.S. Steel, capitalized at $1.4 billion — the world's first billion-dollar corporation. The company controlled 60 percent of the steel industry. Charles Schwab became its first president, and Carnegie turned his energy to giving away his fortune.

In liquid assets — holdings that could easily be converted into cash — Carnegie may well have been the world's richest man. But in the late nineteenth century he was by no means unique. In Pittsburgh alone were a dozen men whose talents rivaled Carnegie's, including George Westinghouse, a pioneer in air brakes and electricity; Andrew Mellon, a leading financier; and Charles Schwab. Many of Pittsburgh's business leaders were self-made men. The telegraph office where Carnegie had worked as a boy also spawned David McCargo, a superintendent of the Allegheny Valley Railroad, and Henry W. Oliver, an oil millionaire. In the United States as a whole were many other brilliant entrepreneurs — men like John D. Rockefeller, J. P. Morgan, Thomas Edison, and Cornelius Vanderbilt, each exercising as much power as the presidents of the United States. Today, Carnegie, Edison, and Rockefeller are at least as well known as Presidents Hayes, Garfield, Arthur, Cleveland, and Harrison.

They lived in years of unprecedented opportunity. Just as the great changes brought about by the American Revolution made provincial lawyers, planters, and legislators into the founding fathers of the republic, the industrial revolution of a century later created an environment in which entrepreneurs who might otherwise have been local businessmen became industrialists with national and international interests. The outline of Carnegie's entrepreneurial role is relatively easy to trace. By managing his businesses efficiently, seeking out resources at the lowest possible price, and using new and effective machinery, he produced good, inexpensive steel. But when we attempt to evaluate Carnegie's career, we should know not only what he did but also how his work affected people. We need to consider the importance of the product he produced, the influence of his industrial management on others, and his role as a philanthropist.

In Andrew Carnegie's mind there was no question that he and other industrialists served America by building their enterprises. He was perhaps the most articulate of the entrepreneurs, and in some characteristics he was atypical — he was more literate than most (he memorized long segments of Shakespeare and Burns), and he devoted more of his resources and energy to philanthropy. But he typified the one characteristic most shared — the belief that the creation of wealth was a noble endeavor.

The nineteenth-century captain of industry was not merely a businessman; he was a miracle worker. No man believed more strongly than Carnegie in the "miracle" of modern civilization. His favorite motto was "all is well since all grows better." He wrote many essays reflecting his belief in human progress and frequently associated his confidence in mankind with his belief in America, as in his popular book, *Triumphant Democracy* (1886).

The philosophical basis of Carnegie's optimism was Social Darwinism. After Charles Darwin's *On the Origin of Species* was published in 1859, many businessmen applied a simplified version of Darwin's ideas to human society: the "survival of the fittest" would lead to higher and higher forms of civilization. Social Darwinism naturally appealed to successful businessmen who wanted to believe that their achievements were attributable to their own "fitness" and contributed to the elevation of all mankind. The man most associated with this idea was Herbert Spencer, an English philosopher, whose works Andrew Carnegie claimed to treasure above all others. Carnegie said that upon reading Spencer, "Light came in as a flood and all was clear." Spencer showed him that "Man was not created with an instinct for his own degradation, but from the lower he had risen to the higher forms. Nor is there any conceivable end to his march to perfection. His face is turned to the light, he stands in the sun and looks upward." In material achievement there can be no doubt that Carnegie contributed greatly to America's "march to perfection." America needed steel for buildings, ships, bridges, railroads — for the very sinews of the new industrial age, and Carnegie supplied it.

But at what cost? How did his career affect those it touched most closely, his business associates and laborers? Social Darwinism suggested that men succeed because they are virtuous, thus enabling businessmen to forget the brutal side of their success. Carnegie's unattractive side was his perpetual ruthlessness. He drove his managers and workers with all his energy, frequently playing off partners and plant managers against one another. Capt. Bill Jones parodied Carnegie's style: "Puppy dog number three, you have been beaten by puppy dog number two on fuel. Puppy dog number two, you are higher on labor than puppy dog number one." Those who could not stand the pace quit or were fired. Over the years Carnegie forced fifteen partners out of his steel business. Jones said of him, "Andy was born with two sets of teeth and holes bored for more."

If he was hard on his own colleagues, he was even harder on his competitors. When the Duquesne Steel Works began producing rails by a new, inexpensive process, Carnegie fostered a rumor throughout the railroad industry that the new rails lacked "homogeneity." It was a brilliant if unscrupulous propagandist's device. No one knew what "homogeneity" meant — in fact, it meant nothing at all — but the accusation inspired so much unwarranted suspicion that the market for the new product dried up. Soon afterward Carnegie bought the Duquesne Works at a bargain price.

Carnegie's opportunism was even more evident in his dealings with his work force. Many assume today that as soon as men were taken away from the loom and the blacksmith shop, where they made finished products, they lost the sense of pride in their work. Yet many of Carnegie's employees apparently shared their bosses' excitement in the achievement of the mills. Bill Jones, who worked closely with his men, preferred the noise and activity of a large mill to rural work, which he found dull. He believed "esprit de corps" among the workers was vital. The workers appear to have been proud of their productivity. There was a spirited competition among the Carnegie furnaces to see which would produce the most iron. At the end of each week a broom was placed atop the chimney of the most productive, announcing the week's victors to the whole area.

Under the direction of men like Jones, with his love of baseball, the esprit de corps among Carnegie workers may have been high. But baseball games and intraplant competition could not cloak the hardships of industrial labor. Carnegie's huge profits were made possible in part by low wages and long hours. The workers usually put in twelve hours a day, seven days a week in the hot mills. Author Hamlin Garland wrote his impressions of the mill life. First, there were the poor neighborhoods where the workers lived: "The streets were horrible; the buildings were poor; the sidewalks were sunken and full of holes. . . . Everywhere the yellow mud of the streets lay kneaded into sticky masses, through which groups of pale, lean men slouched in faded garments, grimy with soot and dirt of the mills." In the mills Garland learned the difficulty of steelwork. One man told him he had lost forty pounds in the first three months he worked. Others spoke of their exhaustion when they returned home. Then, too, gruesome accidents maimed or killed workers in explosions of molten iron. "The worst part of the whole business," said one man, "is, it brutalizes a man. You can't help it. You start to be a man, but you become more and more a machine, and pleasures are few and far between. It's like any severe labor; it drags you down mentally and morally just as it does physically."

One of America's first industrial unions, the Amalgamated Association of Iron, Steel and Tin Workers, sought to improve the worker's conditions. Carnegie had not allowed it to establish a foothold in his own plants, but the Homestead Works was highly unionized when he purchased it in 1889. Carnegie believed that the union contract that tied wages to production penalized the employers whenever they purchased improved equipment. In 1892 he authorized his tough manager, Henry Clay Frick, to break the union.

Frick began by lowering wages, which resulted in a strike. To secure the plant he hired three hundred men from Pinkerton's National Detective Agency as a private army. When the workers learned that these men were being moved to the plant in two barges, they lined the shore and opened fire on the Pinkerton men with rifles and a cannon; a battle continued through all of July 6, 1892. Finally the detectives, outnumbered by ten to one, agreed to withdraw. They were promised safe passage through the city by the union leaders, but the angry mob could not be restrained, and many of the Pinkerton men were badly beaten. The workers controlled Homestead for the next five days. Finally on July 12 state troops moved in and took over the plant. During the Homestead strike fourteen men were killed and 163 wounded. But Carnegie had won. The plant reopened with a nonunion crew. Historians generally agree that the union defeat at Homestead was instrumental in delaying industrial unionism in the United States for almost half a century.

Despite his victory, this episode was perhaps the most tragic event in Carnegie's career. He liked to think of himself as a friend of labor. Although he lacked close rapport with the workers and his wages were low in comparison with steel wages of sixty or seventy years later, his men were better housed and paid than many other nineteenth-century laborers.

Although Andrew Carnegie was in many ways a hard, even brutal man, he did not see himself this way. By his words and later by his deeds he drew a picture of another Andrew Carnegie — a loving, compassionate man who used his money to make the world a better place. His autobiography is full of tender memories: he makes a joyful, tearful return to Dunfermline; he tries to find a sailor who befriended him as a boy; he learns that a banker who knew him long ago remembers him with "deep affection." Carnegie even had a drawer in his desk reserved for appreciatory mail; it was marked, "Gratitude and sweet words."

There appear, then, to have been two Andrew Carnegies — one tender and caring, the other tough and greedy. The sensitive Carnegie was aware of his own ruthlessness and at age thirty-three, when his income was already more than $50,000 a year, he considered reforming his life. He chastened himself: "No idol [is] more debasing than the worship of money. . . . To continue much longer overwhelmed by business cares and with most of my thoughts wholly upon the way to make more money in the shortest time, must degrade me beyond the hope of permanent recovery." When he wrote these lines, he was considering retirement in two years, but instead he devoted three more decades to business.

During those years of pursuing wealth he did seek to avoid "debasing" himself. He chose steel over finance because he wanted to make money by producing something tangible and useful. He took pride in the quality of his steel. And he used some of his money for other people, beginning with an occasional gift of a church organ or a municipal swimming pool. During the rise of Carnegie Steel, his gifts were limited by his policy of plowing most of his profits back into the business. But after selling his company to J.P. Morgan, Andrew Carnegie could devote the remaining nineteen years of his life to philanthropy. He began with a $5 million donation to the benefits and pension fund of his employees. He built 2,811 public libraries around the world, 1,946 of them in the United States. He did not usually attend church but liked religious music, and he gave away almost eight thousand church organs. A few of his grants seem frivolous, like the $400,000 he gave Princeton for an artificial lake to encourage rowing and to "take the young men's minds off football." But most of his gifts were well conceived to educate and edify mankind. He built the Palace of Peace at the Hague; he contributed to Tuskegee Institute; and he helped to finance the movement to grant independence to the Philippines. To organize and perpetuate his philanthropic activities he established the Carnegie Corporation of New York with an endowment of $125 million. When he died on August 11, 1919, he had indeed given away most of his money; he had set aside about 10 percent of this wealth for his wife and daughter.

Through his charitable donations and accomplishments in business Carnegie sought to make real his belief that "all is well since all

Andrew Carnegie. Bill Jones said he was born with two sets of teeth and holes drilled for more.

grows better." He contributed to human progress by producing an important ingredient, steel, at a low price, as well as by building libraries and helping churches and universities. But his great resources came in part from the impoverishment of his laborers. A contemporary columnist, Finley Peter Dunne, questioned Carnegie's priorities by letting one of his characters, a workingman, say that it was all very well that Carnegie was giving away libraries, but that when his turn came to receive one, he would rather have food.

When we attempt to assess Andrew Carnegie, we are faced finally with contrasts. He was a ruthless businessman and a generous philanthropist; he built a great steel company but left his workers poorly clad and housed. He is so dynamic and complex that we seek underlying psychological explanations for his behavior. Historians have suggested that his father's failure and his mother's domination compelled him to seek continually to prove his manhood; or that his stature led him to compensate in business (he was four inches shorter than the average man of his time). It is possible that these factors helped form his personality, but other, more tangible qualities were there, too.

The poverty and helplessness of Carnegie's youth, the grim conditions of his early employment, made him desire a good income and engendered the sympathy for the underprivileged that was reflected in his philanthropy if not in his wages. He engaged in business because he enjoyed it and was good at it. He liked creating a large steel company that produced a good product. No doubt many other Americans wanted to do the same thing, but few had the skills of Carnegie: the memory that enabled him to survey every side of a business arrangement, the energy to manage dozens of enterprises, and the courage to take well-calculated risks. Such factors undoubtedly were much more important in Carnegie's triumph than his short stature or his father's failure.

The desire for wealth and native talent for business helped Carnegie and the other great industrialists of his age to prosper. The conditions of their age also facilitated their success: the exploding growth of new inventions, business techniques, and markets as well as the abundance of resources provided an enormous field of activity for the nineteenth-century capitalist. A half century later talented men would face a different world, dominated by large business, in which proportionately fewer poor youths would grow rich. The "organization man" became more common than the capitalist.

Men like Carnegie made possible this transition. One of his greatest achievements was applying careful management techniques to the production of material goods. The techniques of industry as well as its products, in turn, changed America.

Despite, or perhaps because of, the huge and impersonal character of his industry — the Bessemer converters with their gigantic cargoes of molten steel and the factories as populous as small cities — Carnegie tried to think of himself in human, even sentimental measures as the friend of humanity. The industrial world he made, however, was neither moral nor immoral in its own right. Great cities, industrial plants, transportation facilities, entertainment industries, and other features of twentieth-century prosperity grew out of the industrial revolution, radically altering the material conditions of American life. Later genera-tions would address the problems that industrialism created, seeking to improve the rewards of labor and to reduce industry's harm to the environment. But in doing so they would modify rather than remove the new world that men like Andrew Carnegie had built.

QUESTIONS

1. How did Andrew Carnegie's early life in Scotland influence his respect for industry and success?

2. What qualities enabled Carnegie to make the climb from laborer in a bobbin factory to Thomas Scott's personal secretary on the Pennsylvania railroad?

3. What were the most important contributions Carnegie made to the growth of his steel company? Notice especially his part in management, salesmanship, and expansion.

4. Many factors besides Andrew Carnegie's entrepreneurship made possible the creation of United States Steel. Explain the role of the following: the influence of railroad management, Henry Bessemer, the location of Pittsburgh, the expansion of the iron and steel markets, related industries such as coke manufacture, William R. Jones, the Mesabi Range, J.P. Morgan.

5. What evidence is there that Carnegie was insensitive or cruel to other human beings, especially his father, executive staff, business rivals, workers?

6. What was the attitude of Carnegie's workers toward their jobs? In what ways did they display their enthusiasm? their discontent?

7. How did Carnegie justify the sometimes harsh course of his business career? How did his belief in Social Darwinism and his philanthropy encourage his sense of self-worth?

8. What were Carnegie's main contributions to America as a businessman? as a philanthropist?

BIBLIOGRAPHY

CARNEGIE, ANDREW. *Autobiography* (1920). Carnegie's interesting and somewhat romanticized history of his life.

——. *Triumphant Democracy* (1886) and *The Gospel of Wealth* (1890). Carnegie's thoughts about industry and the stewardship of wealth.

GUTMAN, HERBERT. *Work, Culture, and Society in Industrializing America* (1976). Focuses on the traditional values and work ethic laborers brought to the factory.

HAYS, SAMUEL P. *The Response to Industrialism* (1957). Influence of industrialism on American society.

HOFSTADTER, RICHARD. *Social Darwinism in American Thought* (1959). Analyzes the social philosophy espoused by Carnegie and other business leaders.

JOSEPHSON, MATTHEW. *The Robber Barons* (1939). Lively narrative history of the new industrialists.

KIRKLAND, EDWARD C. *Industry Comes of Age* (1967). General history of the growth of big business.

LIVESAY, HAROLD C. *Andrew Carnegie and the Rise of Big Business* (1975). Fine brief biography of Carnegie.

WALL, JOSEPH FRAZIER. *Andrew Carnegie* (1970). Excellent, thorough biography.

WOLFF, LEON J. *Lockout: Story of the Homestead Strike* (1965). Describes the most tragic episode in Carnegie's relationship with labor.

WYLLIE, IRWIN G. *Self-Made Man in America* (1954). Description and analysis of the American belief in the self-made man.

3

THE BIRTH OF
ENVIRONMENTALISM

John Muir and the American Wilderness

The late nineteenth century was an era of business. Its heroes were men like Andrew Carnegie, who created giant industries, and its spirit was so strong that Booker T. Washington told his black students that in commerce they had "a man's chance" to prosper. In every age, however, some people oppose the prevailing values: Loyalists oppose a revolution; abolitionists reject an institution. In the age of enterprise some Americans challenged the business ideal of unfettered individualism. Labor unions sought the right to bargain; farmers attempted to regulate railroads and grain elevators. Those years also brought American conservationism to fruition. John Muir was the foremost spokesman for that movement, a pastoral voice in an age of steel. He was as bright and energetic as any business leader, but he chose to celebrate nature rather than transform it. His life illustrates the early conservation movement and illuminates the mysterious ways in which human beings make choices about who they will become.

One fine summer day in 1868 the young John Muir stood by a cliff edge hung over the Yosemite Valley. A half mile below, the land "seemed to be dressed like a garden — sunny meadows here and there, and groves of Pine and Oak." Nearby the Yosemite River cascaded through a channel in the rock, sped down a short incline, and sprang "out free in the air." Muir wanted a clear sight of the waterfall and began to work his way down the rock. Below he could see a narrow shelf that might support his heels over the sheer cliff. But he must slide down a steep incline to reach the ledge; if he missed, he would fall to his death. He wondered whether to go on.

The events of a lifetime, thirty years of growth in Scotland and America, had brought John Muir to this precarious position. As a child he had often taken chances for a better view of nature, and recently he had completed a solitary thousand-mile hike from Indiana to the Gulf of Mexico. He had risked his life before, but had never faced danger as overwhelming as this Yosemite cliff. Still he would go on. He filled his mouth with artemisia leaves, hoping the bitter taste would prevent giddiness. He then worked his way down to the ledge; it held him, and he was able to shuffle twenty or thirty feet to the side of the falls. There he found what he wanted — "a perfectly free view down into the heart of the snowy, chanting throng of comet-like streamers, into which the body of the fall soon separates." Muir could not later recall how long he had stood over the falls or even how he had gotten back to the rim. But in camp after dark that night he recorded in his journal that "the tremendous grandeur of the fall" had smothered all fear. He had had a "glorious time."

Muir survived and wrote about this and hundreds of his experiences in the wilderness, making the Yosemite Falls episode part of his legend, and Muir himself grew into the most popular and influential American conservation leader. Edwin Way Teale, another great figure in American wilderness history, said, "Of those who have written of nature surpassingly well . . . John Muir was the wildest. He was the most active, the most at home in the wilderness, the most daring, the most capable, the most self-reliant."

Despite such praise, Muir appears to have been out of step with his times. When he was born in 1838 the American population was barely 16 million. Half the territory that would become the fifty United States was controlled by native American tribal governments. In large sections of the country, buffalo, mountain lion, and grizzly bear roamed a wilderness hardly known to white men. The plow had barely crossed the Mississippi, and the great central valley of California was "one bed of golden and purple flowers" clothing millions of acres. When Muir died three quarters of a century later, the population had reached nearly 100 million. The land was intersected by 250,000 miles of railroad tracks. The forty-eight contiguous states were part of a federal union that stretched from ocean to ocean. The buffalo was nearly exterminated, and the mountain lion and grizzly bear had retreated to remote mountain refuges. The great American prairies and valleys had been broken by the plow.

Muir's career and personality ran against the grain of all this progress. In an age when a frontiersman named Tom Nixon became a hero for killing 140 buffalo in 40 minutes (and 7,000 in a month), John Muir argued that animals as well as human beings are God's creatures and have rights. Alive at the dawn of the automobile era, Muir complained that even the stagecoach moved too fast for passengers to see anything worthwhile. And in a nation that gloried in its ability to conquer nature — to convert redwoods into lumber and mountain meadows into grazing land — Muir held that wild nature must be preserved. Thus, while other men were inventing the light-bulb, building giant corporations, or laying railroad tracks, John Muir was exploring the American wilderness.

It is possible to see Muir as a cantankerous individualist, one of those men whom Henry David Thoreau described as marching to the beat of a "different drummer." Certainly he was exceptional. More perhaps than any other American, Muir sought continually to expose himself to the wilderness. He climbed a tree in a windstorm, rode down a mountainside on an avalanche, and stood in the open to watch the progress of a Yosemite earthquake. On his hiking expeditions he frequently carried only a metal cup, tea leaves, and some dry bread, preferring simple fare and a bed of pine needles to a cluttered campsite.

But John Muir was not a hermit or a misanthrope. In fact, he was to become one of the most influential men of his day. During these years when Americans were settling the last frontiers, respect for nature became part of the American credo. Muir helped make it happen. He wrote articles in national magazines, founded a wilderness preservation society, and fought for the protection of wilderness areas. Eventually his name would adorn campsites, lakes, mountains, and forests. It appears more often in California's nomenclature than that of any other man. The Muir Woods near San Francisco, the John Muir Trail along the Sierra Nevada crest, and the Muir Grove in Sequoia National Park are a few of the more famous sites bearing his name.

John Muir's life began in Dunbar, Scotland, in 1838. He was raised in a substantial house in the center of town, but most of his early memories were of expeditions into nearby fields and to the sea. In later years he wrote, "When I was a boy in Scotland I was fond of everything that was wild." He and other boys took long runs on country lanes and explored the rocks and pools along the shore of the North Sea. They grew hardy in scraps at school and in competitions to prove their bravery. As a boy John climbed down the sheer walls of a dungeon in the ruins of Dunbar Castle and scaled the steep roof outside his bedroom window. He later recalled sitting on the rooftop in the night and "looking at the scenery over the garden wall while the wind was howling and threatening to blow me off."

Muir remembered his youthful adventures as a wonderful beginning to a life lived close to nature. But unfortunately his complicated and overbearing father thought otherwise. Daniel Muir was a merchant and a farmer by trade, but he was above all obsessed with religion. He constantly read the Bible and other religious works such as Fox's *Book of Martyrs.* His view of the godly household was austere and foreboding. He allowed no pictures, considering them graven images forbidden by the Scriptures; he sprinkled his conversation with biblical allusions; and he frowned on gaiety. John's mother, Ann, a naturally cheerful person, was jovial only when her husband was absent. John said his father "devoutly believed that quenching every spark of pride and self-confidence was a sacred duty."

Daniel saw his son's wilderness forays as wasteful, devilish behavior. Every time John went exploring, he realized he might be severely beaten. But, as he later recalled, "no punishment, however sure and severe, was of any avail against the attraction of the fields and woods."

John spent his first eleven years in Dunbar. For education he received mainly lessons in French, English, and Latin, with some work also in spelling, arithmetic, history, and geography. He later compared his early learning with the "progressive" educational philosophies in vogue at the turn of the century. In Scotland, he said, "there was nothing said about making the seats easy or the lessons easy." If a student failed to learn a lesson, he was beaten, "for the grand, simple, all-sufficing Scotch discovery had been made that there was a close connection between the skin and the memory." His father added to John's assignments the memorizing of several biblical verses each day, and before he was eleven John had learned most of the Scriptures "by heart and by sore flesh." Even in the schoolyard, however, the wilderness was not far away. From the playground the boys could look out over the sea and watch sailing ships moving past. "In stormy weather," Muir recalled, "they were all smothered in clouds and spray, and showers of salt scud torn from the tops of the waves came flying over the playground wall."

While John was learning lessons from man and nature, his father was formulating a plan to move the family to America. It is not entirely clear why he decided to leave Scotland, for he was able to provide well for himself and his family in Dunbar. His spiritual restlessness may have moved him. In recent years he had changed from one religious denomination to another before becoming a Disciple of Christ. He may have hoped to find more people with similar religious views in America. And the New World appeared to offer more economic opportunities for his large family.

At any rate, one day he announced that they were going to the New World. He sold his business and booked passage on a ship from Glasgow. John was delighted. To him, America meant "no more grammar, but boundless woods full of mysterious good things." John enjoyed his first ocean voyage, climbing all over the ship and helping with the work when the crew would let him. But it was a hard voyage. For forty-five days they were on the ship, often in heavy seas making it too dangerous to light cook fires on deck or lanterns and candles below. They ate salt pork and potatoes and sometimes bits of candy their father had brought along. John's sister, Sarah, dreadfully seasick, stayed in her bunk for the whole trip.

They reached the United States in early spring 1849. Daniel carefully collected information on places to live and settled on Wisconsin after learning from a Buffalo, New York, grain dealer that most of his wheat was from that region. By packet boat, lake steamer, and horse-drawn wagon they traveled to Portage, a boom town on the path of a proposed canal that would unite the Fox and Wisconsin rivers, providing a water route between the Great Lakes and the Mississippi River. With the help of a friend they located some land by Fountain Lake, ten miles from Portage. There they built a small shack and began to clear the land.

Fountain Lake, surrounded by forest, meadow, and water, was a beautiful place. It was alive with wildlife, especially such birds as wood ducks, chickadees, nuthatches, prairie chickens, and bobwhites. The children played hide-and-seek in the fields and explored the countryside. Muir later recalled there nature streamed "into us, wooingly teaching her wonderful glowing lessons . . . every wild lesson a love lesson, not whipped but charmed into us. Oh, that glorious Wisconsin wilderness."

But John's father was no more sympathetic to play in Wisconsin than in Scotland. He turned increasingly to religious studies and became a lay preacher in the local Disciples church. He left John and the other children to do most of the farmwork. They turned the virgin soil with a "breaking plow," then grubbed out the roots and bushes. When they burned these on a great bonfire, Daniel characteristically used the occasion to lecture the children on the terrors of hell. At twelve John was put to work guiding the heavy plow behind an ox team. Even the girls had to work in the fields. The boys slept upstairs in an unheated room, three in a bed, where the quilt froze by their faces on the cold mornings and they rushed downstairs in bare feet to dress before the kitchen stove. Their food was scanty. For a time Daniel Muir put the whole family on an unbalanced vegetable diet that slowly drained their strength. He allowed more food only after a neighbor accused him of ruining the family's health.

One of John Muir's worst experiences came in digging a well for his father. Day after day he had to chisel his way through sandstone down a hole three feet wide. Eighty feet down he was nearly killed by poisonous gas in the shaft. Neighbors told the Muirs how to clear out the gas, and John had to cut through another ten feet to strike water. It is no wonder that he later wrote, "Farming was a grim, material, debasing pursuit under Father's generalship."

Never close to his father, John did come to respect other adults in the neighborhood. One man lent him books, such as Scott's Waverly novels. Others loved to recite poetry and encouraged John's interest in literature. In these early years, his greatest achievements were in mechanics. He found that with a simple penknife and pieces of wood he could build clocks, barometers, and a waterwheel. His father allowed him no time during the day for such exercises but said he could work on them before breakfast. Delighted to have some time he could call his own, John began rising at 1:00 A.M. In the basement he built all kinds of gadgets. From an old iron wagon-box rod he fashioned a huge thermometer that could be seen from far out in the fields, so sensitive that it could record the heat change caused by someone approaching within five feet. He also built a contraption to raise a sleeper out of bed at a designated hour and another to feed the horses automatically.

Some of the neighbors thought John was a crank. Others recognized his inventive genius, and one of these encouraged him to exhibit at the Wisconsin State Fair and to enter a mechanical trade. John was now twenty-one and could legally determine his own course of life, but the choice was difficult. His father wanted him to stay at home and work on the farm. His friends encouraged his inventiveness. John was still drawn to the wilderness. But in those days before the National Park and Forest services were created, there seemed to be no way to combine a love of wilderness with a career. John sometimes walked the roads around his house all night pondering his course. "I used to spend hours with my head up in the sky," he writes. "I soared among the planets and thought."

He finally decided to leave home, taking with him as many of his inventions as he could carry. His father refused to say good-bye, but his mother gave him a gold coin to help him on his way. At the station in

Portage the conductor was impressed by Muir's collection of inventions and introduced him to the engineer. With the engineer's approval John rode across Wisconsin on the cowcatcher platform at the front of the train.

In Madison John exhibited his inventions at the state fair. They attracted large crowds and were reported enthusiastically in the local press. One paper called Muir a "genuine genius." When word of his success reached home, it provoked joyful congratulations from his mother, brother, and sisters — and a solemn letter from his father on the danger of vanity.

John was offered several jobs. He worked for a time with a man who had invented a steam-powered iceboat. But he soon came back to the University of Wisconsin at Madison. Muir gained incalculably from his college education. His good mind and buoyant personality made him popular on campus. He was slender and almost six feet tall. He let his light red hair and beard grow long — he never shaved and he bothered little about grooming. His sisters said that he looked "wild as a loon," which he took as a compliment. Those who knew him often commented on his eyes, and one of his admirers said that he had "the twinklingest blue eyes" she had ever seen. He soon became known for his inventions, which he set up in his room along with several new gadgets, including a desk with a mechanism that put books in front of him at intervals to keep his work on schedule, a contraption to light a fire in the morning, and a "loafer's chair" that fired off a pistol when anyone sat in it. Muir's room became a college showplace and was visited even by members of the state legislature.

Muir's years at the university might easily have led the inventive student into a career in mechanics, engineering, or business. Instead, higher education reinforced his taste for wilderness. Previously his relationship to nature had been recreational and intuitive. He enjoyed being outdoors and observing plant and animal life, but these pleasures had no apparent relationship to an adult world of thought and action. At Wisconsin he learned that religion, science, and literature might all be involved in the study of the wilderness.

He studied geology under Ezra Slocum Carr, who had worked at Harvard under Louis Agassiz, one of the foremost scientists of the nineteenth century. Many geologists at that time relied on the biblical account of the Great Flood to explain characteristics of the earth. Agassiz and Carr argued that scientists should study the land itself with a "seeing eye." They believed such studies revealed that a "universal ice age" had helped shape the earth's contours. Taking to their studies a traditional faith in divine omnipotence, they relied more on God's handiwork than on Scripture. Agassiz wrote: "The glacier was God's great plow and when it vanished from the surface of the land, it left it prepared for the hand of the husbandman." To help his students read the land Professor Carr frequently took them into the country on field trips, and so he taught Muir that one could go into the wilderness for scientific and theological reasons as well as for recreation.

Muir took a similar lesson from his studies in botany. A fellow student, Milton Griswold, showed him how plants can be identified by their leaves and other organs. Muir remarked, "Why Griswold, that's perfectly wonderful!" He purchased a botany book and began to study the characteristics of, and relationships among, plants.

Another valuable lesson came from his literature professor, James Davie Butler, who introduced Muir to the works of Ralph Waldo Emerson and urged his students to keep "commonplace books" with accounts of the day-to-day events in their lives. Emerson's writings on nature revealed that the wilderness is a realm filled with literary and philosophic inspiration, and a journal gave Muir a way of recording the details of wilderness experience for later literary use.

Muir also encountered men who were beginning the battle to conserve natural resources. In the early years of European settlement, America had so much land and so few people that no thought had been given to preserving the wilderness; it was considered something that could be taken for granted. But by the time Muir entered the university, American forests were falling with fearful rapidity. Railroads and steamboats alone used 10 million cords of wood a year. Wood was the primary building material and fuel for 30 million Americans. A few farsighted individuals were warning against unchecked exploitation of the wilderness. Increase A. Lapham, Wisconsin's foremost conservationist, actively campaigned for restrictions on timber companies. Alexander von Humboldt, author and naturalist, claimed that destroying trees would eventually destroy the watershed. At the university Muir heard these ideas, and they helped develop his sensitivity to the wilderness as something to preserve as well as to cherish.

In retrospect, Muir's Wisconsin education was admirably suited to his later career. But in 1864 when he departed from the university, his course was by no means clear. Muir considered specializing in a branch of natural studies, such as astronomy: instead, for the next few years he combined short wilderness expeditions with work in factories.

In 1863 he explored sections of the Wisconsin and Mississippi rivers, and in the following summer he walked through Upper Michigan and Ontario, Canada, collecting plants and keeping a journal. But when it came to earning a living he turned to activities in which his mechanical ability and inventiveness were most useful. From 1864 to 1866 he worked in an Ontario sawmill and rake factory. He invented several machines that doubled production and was offered a partnership in the company. He refused, explaining frankly, "I love nature too well to spend my life in a work that involves the destruction of God's forests."

In 1866 he moved on to Indianapolis, Indiana, and went to work for Osgood, Smith, and Company, which manufactured hubs, spokes, and other carriage parts. Again he invented machinery and rose quickly in his employer's esteem. He was asked to write a report on the management of the factory, and he made a number of suggestions for more efficient operation. Once more he was offered a management position and a partnership.

John Muir clearly had the ability to become a successful business-man. His inventive and organizational abilities suggest that he might have become another Thomas Edison or Henry Ford. But the wilderness was always there. While working in Ontario and Indiana, Muir spent his weekends in the woods. His enthusiasm for the outdoors was so infectious that numerous friends in both places frequently accompanied him into the forests.

He later described these years as a time of great inner turmoil. The nation, recovering from the ravages of the Civil War, needed business leaders; his family might need financial help. His talents in manufactur-ing were apparent. Surely he could pursue a career in business and devote his spare moments to his wilderness avocation.

But then in March 1867 an event forced him to reevaluate once more what he wanted to do with his life. Late one day he was working with a sharp file on one of the machines. It slipped and pierced the cornea of his right eye. He recalled, "I would gladly have died where I stood." Both eyes were affected, and Muir's doctor declared that Muir would not see again. For weeks he lay in a darkened room. "My days," he wrote, "were terrible beyond what I can tell, and my nights were if possible more terrible. Frightful dreams exhausted and terrified me."

One of his friends brought another doctor, a specialist who told Muir that the injured eye would recover and in time he would be able to see again with both eyes. Muir felt like a man "arisen from the grave." He now decided to delay no longer before going to the wilderness and wrote, "God has to nearly kill us sometimes to teach us lessons."

It was still not clear to Muir how he might spend his whole adult life in the wilderness, but he was determined at least to pass the next three years "botanizing." Afterward he would settle down, but the long stay in nature, he said, would be "sufficient to lighten and brighten my afterlife in the gloom and hunger of civilization's defrauding duties."

Before setting out he made a final visit to his Wisconsin home. There he affirmed his relationship to nature. Daniel Muir still identified wilderness with evil and told John his study of geology and botany was blasphemous. The son replied, "I'll tell you this, Father, I've been spending my time a lot nearer the Almighty than you have." In the years ahead he would continue to believe that he was close to God in the wilderness.

In fall 1867 Muir set out on his thousand-mile walk from Indiana to the Gulf of Mexico. "I wandered afoot and alone," he wrote, "with a plant-press on my back, holding a generally southward course, like the birds when they are going from summer to winter." He carried a few supplies and little cash. His route over the hills and mountains of Kentucky and Tennessee took him through country that had been devastated by the Civil War. He encountered bands of outlaws more than once. Along the way he collected botanical specimens that he sent to his brother in Wisconsin for safekeeping. His description of the journey in *A Thousand-Mile Walk to the Gulf,* an account published many years later, displays his youthful enthusiasm. His ability to justify this wandering life was exhibited in an encounter with a blacksmith in the mountains of eastern Tennessee.

He stopped at the man's house to seek lodging. The blacksmith appeared, "Hammer in hand, bare-breasted, sweaty, begrimed, and covered with shaggy black hair." He invited Muir to spend the night but during dinner questioned him closely about what he was doing. When he learned that Muir was wandering through the South collecting plants, he told him that he should be doing something more useful. "These are hard times," he said, "and real work is required of every man that is able. Picking up blossoms doesn't seem to be a man's work at all in any kind of times." John Muir was undaunted; he reminded the blacksmith that the great King Solomon had studied plants and that Christ had told his disciples to "consider the lilies." He asked his host, "Whose advice am I to take, yours or Christ's?" The blacksmith was impressed by Muir's reply, calling him "a very strong-minded man," and admitted that he had "never thought of blossoms in that way before." It was one of Muir's strengths that he could do things that were unusual and also persuade others that what he was doing was worthwhile. He used the "consider the lilies" text again in his later writings when he wanted to encourage his readers to visit the national parks.

John Muir's walk finally took him to the southern tip of Florida; from there he went by boat to Cuba where he spent several weeks in botanical explorations. He had intended to go to South America and visit the Amazon, but his funds were low. It hardly mattered. "All the world was before me," he wrote, "and every day was a holiday, so it did not seem important to which of the world's wildernesses I first should wander." He had seen pictures of the Yosemite Valley in California and decided he would continue his travels in the Far West. He took steerage passage on a crowded ship to the Isthmus of Panama and then traveled to San Francisco. He arrived on March 28, 1868, but did not linger. On the streets he asked a carpenter how to get out of the city. The man asked him where he wanted to go, and Muir replied, "Anywhere that is wild."

Once out of San Francisco, Muir crossed the coastal range by Pacheco Pass and looked down on the Great Central Valley, "level and flowery, like a lake of pure sunshine." He called it "the floweriest piece of the world." He camped there for a time and then walked on toward the Sierra Nevada. When he saw the mountain range, it was "so gloriously colored and so radiant, it seemed not clothed with light, but wholly composed of it, like the wall of some celestial city." He hiked up the Merced River to Yosemite Valley. "No temple made with hands can compare with Yosemite," he later wrote. "Every rock in its walls seems to glow with life." His health, damaged by the malarial swamps of the South, recovered quickly in the clean mountain air.

In the months and years ahead John Muir became as much a feature of Yosemite Valley as the forests and rocks. He spent his winters in a small cabin in the valley, sharing its snowy isolation with a few other white men and Indians. He worked intermittently as a shepherd and sawmill hand to earn his keep, but he spent most of his time exploring. He was an adventurer, a philosopher, a botanist, and a geologist. It was in this period that he stood on the brink of Yosemite Falls. That episode and others like it reflect his constant effort to see the whole region from every possible angle of vision and in every possible condition.

When an earthquake rocked the valley on March 26, 1872, and other men huddled in their beds in deathly fear, Muir was delighted. Here is how he describes the scene: "One morning about two o'clock, I was aroused by an earthquake; and though I had never before enjoyed a storm of this sort, the strange, wild thrilling motion and rumbling could not be mistaken, and I ran out of my cabin, near the Sentinel Rock, both glad and frightened, shouting, 'A noble earthquake!' feeling sure I was going to learn something." As Muir stood outside, he watched a great rock split away from a cliff and shower down on the valley, "making a terribly sublime and beautiful spectacle." Muir had theorized that the valley's sharp sides were fashioned by earthquakes. Now he had seen evidence.

In a less dramatic way he discovered how glaciers had shaped Yosemite Valley. In months of hiking and climbing in the region he saw on the rocks many signs of ancient glacial activity. At that time the leading theory on the valley's origins was that of Josiah D. Whitney, a Harvard professor, who had been hired by the state of California to do a geological survey of the state. Whitney spent many years on his work, publishing authoritative volumes on California's geology. He held that

John Muir's wilderness worlds. From Florida to California he visited the American wilderness, helping to create a conservation ethic.

the Yosemite Valley had come into being when a section of the Sierra Nevada had sunk into a great hole beneath. Muir was unconvinced, remarking wryly, "the bottom never dropped out of anything that God made." While working at the sawmill in the valley, he had spent part of his time as a tourist guide. He used these encounters with visitors to state his views on the origins of the valley. In 1871, at the urging of friends, he published the first of several articles explaining his glacial theory. When Josiah Whitney heard of Muir's work, he vehemently dismissed his arguments as those of "a mere sheepherder" and "an ignoramus." It was several decades before scientists generally accepted Muir's views. But many important men were impressed with his work. The president of the Massachusetts Institute of Technology, one of the tourists he conducted around the valley, was so taken by Muir that he urged him to come east and teach at the institute. The great Louis Agassiz, among the first to propose the theory of universal glaciation, so admired Muir's work that he wrote, "Here is the first man who has any adequate conception of glacial action."

With all this recognition Muir once more had to reevaluate his choice of a career. He still had no vocation in the traditional sense, calling himself "an unknown nobody in the woods." He had planned to take up a conventional career after three years of wandering, but now those having passed, he saw no reason to leave the mountains, which so intrigued and inspired him. "I only went out for a walk," he wrote, "and finally concluded to stay out till sundown, for going out, I found, was really going in."

Fortunately, his new-found popularity as a writer was a way to earn a living from his wilderness travels. He did most of his writing while living with friends in Oakland and San Francisco. He complained about these periods of forced absence from the mountains but nonetheless developed a fine flowing style that conveyed his enthusiasm for nature. A century later his word pictures still lure readers out of their urban homes into the mountains and forests he so beautifully described. His writing is characterized by strong adjectives and metaphors. On the ability of the juniper and the rock pine to resist the wind he says: "Their stiff, crooked roots grip the stormbeaten ledges." Sunrise in the Yosemite brings "another reviving morning. Down the long mountain-slopes the sunbeams pour, guiding the awakening pines, cheering every needle, filling every living thing with joy." The Bridal Veil waterfall is "clad in gauzy, sun-sifted spray."

Describing the flora and fauna of the wilderness led Muir to a philosophy of nature. He believed that civilization makes men competitive, narrow, and dull. The wilderness calls forth their more generous impulses and inspires them with its vitality. Man is out of tune with the whole cosmos, with the primary force that creates and sustains the world. Although Muir rejected the biblical idea of an anthropomorphic god, he did believe that the universe, and man with it, was guided by a great spiritual force. To see the force, all one has to do is go into the wilderness and observe how nature operates. He wrote: "Heaven knows that John the Baptist was not more eager to get his fellow sinners into the Jordon than I to baptize mine in the beauty of God's mountains."

In the 1870s Muir preached a gospel of the wilderness while continuing his wanderings. After his early explorations of the Yosemite region he began to travel farther afield. In 1873 he hiked the whole length of the Sierra Nevada. In the years following he explored sections of the Rocky Mountains, the Pacific Northwest, and Alaska.

As he approached his fortieth birthday his enthusiasm for wild nature was unabated, but he began to envy his brothers and sisters who had married and were rearing families. In 1879 he began courting Louie Strentzen, daughter of a wealthy fruit rancher in the Alhambra Valley, a few miles east of San Francisco. On April 14, 1880, they were married, and the couple settled on her father's land, where John immediately became involved in running the orchards. Louie well understood John's need for nature and encouraged him to take the three months before the busy fall harvest to go on with his travels. In 1880 and 1881 he returned to Alaska, exploring several regions where no white man had been before. Muir loved these forays into the wilderness but was ambivalent about leaving his family. When he was on a ship off the coast of Alaska in the midst of beautiful sea and mountains, he wrote Louie: "I was just thinking . . . of our warm, sunny home, and Annie [their infant] in her soft blankets . . . and of the red cherries down the hill. . . . Oh, if I could touch my baby and thee." During the next seven years John Muir spent most of his time managing the orchards, raising Bartlett pears and Tokay grapes. He worked hard and managed the business efficiently, so that he quickly became one of the most successful ranchers in his area. In 1886 a second daughter was born.

Muir sought to teach his children a religious creed quite different from that of his father's, encouraging them to revere God, "not as a person, but as a loving, intelligent spirit creating, permeating, and controlling the universe." In many ways John Muir was an ideal father and husband — devoted, resourceful, open. But the years as a rancher wore at him. He complained of "the eternal grind, grind, grind" and compared himself to a wild animal in a cage. His friends and his wife urged him to spend more time exploring and writing about the wilderness. Louie regretted what the ranch was doing to him and even urged him to sell it. His health began to deteriorate.

Finally in 1888 Muir took his first extensive trip to the mountains in many years. The high point of the journey was a climb to the top of Mount Rainier. ("Did not mean to climb it," he wrote to Louie, "but got excited and soon was on top.") In the next year he went to Yosemite with Robert Underwood Johnson, an editor for *Century* magazine, one of the foremost periodicals in the nation. Muir was shocked at the deterioration caused by sheep and tourists. At Underwood's urging he agreed to write a series of articles in *Century* urging that Yosemite be made into a national park. At that time the valley belonged to California, and although it was a state park it was open to exploitation by timber and grazing interests.

By 1890 Muir's brother-in-law arrived in California to help manage the orchards. From then on he was able to devote more time to the wilderness. In that year, partly because of Muir's articles in *Century*, Yosemite became a national park. In the following years Muir enveloped himself more in conservation issues. In his youth he urged people to appreciate rather than to conserve the wilderness. In the 1870s, when many sections of the Sierra Nevada had not even been explored, men did not seem to pose a threat. But by the 1890s timber and livestock companies were tearing away at the mountains. By illegally claiming lands or by simply stealing trees from public lands, lumbermen destroyed some of the finest redwood groves in the mountains. Often they used dynamite to blast the big trees, wasting three quarters of the timber. Simultaneously hundreds of thousands of sheep — which Muir called "hoofed locusts" — were destroying the native flowers and grasses of the mountain meadows.

When John Muir returned to the wilderness in 1890 after almost a decade away, he was not only a writer but a propagandist for conservation. In 1892 with a few friends he founded the Sierra Club, which planned outings in the wilderness and lobbied for conservation issues. In 1897 Muir became associated with a National Forest Commission, appointed to survey the nation's wilderness areas. The most influential member was a young man named Gifford Pinchot. At first Muir and Pinchot got along well. Both loved the outdoors, and both opposed careless exploitation of the wilderness. But it soon was apparent that Pinchot's goal was planned use of the wilderness, not preservation. Muir told Pinchot he wanted nothing more to do with him after the younger man favored allowing sheep to graze in the forest reserves. The conflict between their ideals — planned use and preservation — would split the conservation movement for many years to come.

To promote his views Muir published a series of influential articles in the *Atlantic Monthly* in 1899. These were so popular that the editor, Walter Hines Page, declared that they improved the magazine's circulation enormously. The articles helped win support for the growing conservation movement and added to Muir's reputation as its foremost leader.

John Muir was at the height of his popularity and influence a few years later in 1901, when he made one of his most extraordinary visits to

Yosemite. Over the years he had escorted many important men and women into the mountains. Now he learned that President Theodore Roosevelt wanted to visit the park in Muir's company. Muir may have anticipated no more than a few private minutes with the president, but Roosevelt had other plans. After traveling to Yosemite in a large party, Muir and the president rode away alone on horseback to a remote section of the park. They set out their sleeping bags and cooked over a large fire. "Now this is bully!" said Roosevelt. That night the president sat by the crackling flames and listened to Muir talk about the wilderness. They awakened with four inches of snow on their sleeping bags, but the president, undaunted, insisted on spending two more nights in the wilderness. At the end of the trip he told Muir, "I've had the time of my life!"

The trip with Roosevelt reflected Muir's national prominence as a conservationist and outdoorsman. He was now in his sixties and could not make the long backcountry trips that he had taken as a younger man. But he still traveled extensively. In 1901–2 he made a trip around the world. He spent many hours in Europe's leading museums. ("A monstrous dose of civilization," he called it.) But he particularly enjoyed seeing new wildernesses — the Himalayas from Darjeeling, Australia from atop a stagecoach. Nine years later he made a long trip through South America and Africa. He also made many shorter trips to the Sierra Nevada and to the Petrified Forest in Arizona.

During these years he pulled together his notes from journals and articles written many years before and arranged them in a series of books. The *Atlantic* articles became *Our National Parks*. His other books in this period included *The Yosemite* and *The Story of My Boyhood and Youth*. These and other volumes helped spread Muir's philosophy of the wilderness.

He was also involved more and more in battles to preserve wilderness. The most important of these involved the effort to prevent a dam in the Sierra. To the south of Yosemite canyon lies another known as Hetch Hetchy. This valley consists of rock formations that rival Yosemite's, and in Muir's time its vegetation was even lovelier than that of its sister canyon. It was included in the boundaries of Yosemite Park, but influential San Franciscans fancied it as a place to build a reservoir. Hetch Hetchy aroused a classic struggle between those who believe the wilderness should be preserved and admired and those who would "conquer" and use it. Arguments initiated by each side in this encounter have been repeated again and again in subsequent conflicts over the wilderness.

The dam's proponents claimed it was essential to create a reservoir in Hetch Hetchy to give San Francisco a stable water supply. They painted sensational images of people suffering in a city without water, argued that the canyon was a practical site for an inexpensive dam, and contended that the new lake would actually enhance the beauty of the region. They even said that the site could be easily acquired because it was public land.

Muir met their arguments at every point. Yes, he said, men have practical needs, but they also have spiritual needs. Men should not attempt to make everything "immediately and selfishly commercial," for they need "beauty as well as bread." He argued that nature is essential to man's health; it heals and cheers body and soul. Moreover, he pointed out that there were several alternative damsites — surely San Francisco could serve its utilitarian needs in some other region. Finally, he criticized the idea that the reservoir would increase the area's beauty; it would bury the lovely valley floor. His essay, which appears in *The Yosemite,* concludes: "Dam Hetch Hetchy! As well dam for water-tanks the people's cathedrals and churches, for no holier temple has ever been consecrated by the heart of man."

Muir fought the Hetch Hetchy battle in every possible arena. He wrote articles, organized a massive public campaign, and persuaded such friends as railroad magnate Edward H. Harriman to lobby against the bill. In his seventy-fifth year he was still fighting the dam. He wrote to one friend that he hoped the struggle would end soon; it was killing him. That year the conflict did end. Muir and his supporters met defeat when the dam proposal bill passed Congress in December 1913.

The old mountaineer took the loss well; many other wilderness areas would survive. He could also take comfort because his belief in the worth of wilderness to man was now shared by millions of Americans. The life that had begun with a personal love of nature had matured into a useful career and encouraged a historic movement.

Muir continued to write in the following year. At Christmastime he went south to visit his daughter, Helen. While with her, he caught pneumonia. He died on December 24, 1914. He had often reflected on death and had faced it many times in the mountains. He spoke of it as "going home." After death the soul would be free to wander through the wilderness uninhibited by a physical body and earthly cares. He once described how he would begin that pilgrimage: "My first journeys would be into the inner substance of flowers, and among the folds and mazes of Yosemite's falls. How grand to move about in the very tissue of falling columns, and in the very birthplace of their heavenly harmonies, looking outward as from windows of ever-varying transparency and staining!"

QUESTIONS

1. What was John Muir's attitude toward formal religion? How did his father's religiosity affect him? In what sense did religion enter into his relationship with nature?

2. What is the evidence that John Muir could have been a successful inventor or industrialist? In what ways did he take his scientific interests and organizational skills into the wilderness?

3. How did Muir come to devote himself to the wilderness? Explain the role of the following: his boyhood, the university, business experience, a sharp file, the thousand-mile walk, writing, Louie, timber, and sheep interests.

4. In what ways did John Muir contribute to the preservation of American wilderness? Explain why he became a conservationist as well as a naturalist.

5. What is the difference between conservationism and planned use?

6. What arguments were voiced on each side in the Hetch Hetchy fight?

BIBLIOGRAPHY

BADE, WILLIAM F. *The Life and Letters of John Muir* (2 vols., 1923). Especially useful for its selection of Muir letters.

HAYS, SAMUEL. *Conservation and the Gospel of Efficiency* (1959). Conservation in the early twentieth century.

MCGEARY, M. NELSON. *Gifford Pinchot: Forester-Politician* (1960). Biography of leading advocate of planned use of the wilderness.

NASH, RODERICK. *Wilderness and the American Mind* (1967 and later editions). Excellent historical analysis of American attitudes toward the wilderness.

PETULLA, JOSEPH M. *American Environmental History* (1977). Survey of the exploitation and conservation of American natural resources.

RUNTE, ALFRED. *National Parks: The American Experience* (1979). How America's national parks came into being.

TEALE, EDWIN WAY, EDITOR. *The Wilderness World of John Muir* (1976). The best one-volume anthology of Muir's writings.

WOLFE, LINNIE MARSH. *Son of the Wilderness: John Muir* (1945). A well-researched and lively biography.

4

IMPERIAL
AMERICA

Dewey and Aguinaldo at Manila Bay

As former rebels against British imperial rule Americans have opposed colonialism, believing that all people have the right to govern themselves. In attempting to support democracy abroad, however, America has frequently intervened in other countries, leading to the impression that the United States is an imperial power. During the Spanish-American War in 1898 the paradox of anti-imperial intervention was acutely visible. The United States went to war with Spain ostensibly to end Spanish cruelty in Cuba but within a year was using brutal Spanish tactics to maintain control over the Philippines. Many forces then at work in America — the racism that segregated and disfranchised blacks, the industrialism that expanded the nation's wealth, and the settling of the West that removed the last internal frontier, among others — affected American policy in the Philippines. Two men whose paths crossed in Manila Bay, George Dewey and Emilio Aguinaldo, symbolized the power of a rapidly growing America and the rising hopes of the long-colonized Philippines.

When the Spanish-American War began in April 1898, few Americans were aware of the Philippines. The country had gone to war to drive Spain out of Cuba without giving thought to other Spanish possessions. Even President McKinley professed ignorance about Spain's Pacific islands. But within a few weeks the Philippines would be front-page news in the United States, and in less than a year the islands would be an American territory. Why would the United States want to acquire a distant and obscure country seven thousand miles beyond her western shores? And how would her action affect the Filipinos themselves? The careers of the American admiral George Dewey and the Philippine insurrectionist Emilio Aguinaldo suggest answers to these questions.

In 1898 the American vitality that had forged democratic institutions, conquered a continent, and given birth to giant industries seemed to flow naturally into overseas expansion. Adm. George Dewey, whose Philippine exploits would make him a national hero, embodied the self-confident spirit that America took into the country's first overseas adventure.

Dewey was born in Montpelier, Vermont, in 1837. He entered the navy in 1854 as a student in the newly founded Naval Academy at Annapolis and received much of his early training from veterans of the War of 1812. At the beginning of the Civil War, Dewey became executive officer of the steam frigate *Mississippi,* a distinguished vessel that had served as Perry's flagship in Japan. In 1862 his ship was part of the fleet that wrested control of the Mississippi River from the Confederate forces. The commander of the fleet was David G. Farragut, a resourceful officer who won immortality at Mobile Bay for his order, "Damn the torpedos! Full steam ahead!" Almost a half century after serving under him Dewey wrote, "Farragut has always been my ideal of the naval officer, urbane, decisive, indomitable."

After the exhilarating years of the Civil War the navy entered a long, frustrating period of inertia. "It was easy then," wrote Dewey, "for an officer to drift along in his grade, losing interest and remaining in the navy only because he was too old to change his occupation." Dewey's description of one of his ships, the *Juanita,* reflects his feeling about the navy of the 1870s and 1880s. A round-bottomed sloop built in 1861, she rolled heavily even in light seas. Sailing her into the Mediterranean, Dewey was mortified to find that she and other dated American ships were "the laughing stock of the nations." While Europe was building armored battleships and fast cruisers, the typical American vessel was "a relic of a past epoch."

By 1890, however, Dewey had begun to feel a new "pulse" in the country as Americans grew more interested in their position in the world. The Reverend Josiah Strong reported that his countrymen had spread across their own land and now needed to expand overseas as an outlet for their energies. Capt. Alfred Thayer Mahan wrote a widely read book, *The Influence of Sea Power upon History,* arguing that nations grew to greatness through control over the seas. Politicians Henry Cabot Lodge and Theodore Roosevelt claimed that strong nations were warrior nations. These ideas were translated into public policy in the building of a new "steel navy" in the 1890s.

George Dewey was stationed in Washington during the period of expansion, serving as president of the Board of Inspection and Survey, which examined new vessels for fitness. Although he was nearly sixty years old, he projected the optimistic, outgoing spirit of the era and thought of himself as "a man of action." While in Washington he won the respect of Theodore Roosevelt, then assistant secretary of the navy, who supported his promotion to commander of the Pacific squadron. At the time "not one man in ten" in Washington expected a war with Spain. But Dewey prepared for the possibility, knowing that the Philippines, a Spanish possession, would be an American target if war came. During his last month in Washington he studied charts and descriptions of the Philippines and, with Roosevelt's "vigorous support," arranged for more munitions for his fleet.

On January 3, 1898, Dewey, now a commodore, took command of the Asiatic squadron in Nagasaki, Japan. The squadron was "hardly a formidable force," consisting of only two cruisers, a gunboat, and a Civil War paddlewheel steamer. Apart from the steamer, however, they were fine, up-to-date ships, well supplied with modern rapid-fire guns accurate at distances of five miles and more.

Pictures of Dewey standing on the deck of the flagship *Olympia,* a bright, trim vessel, show him to be a solid man, with short white hair, a thick walrus mustache, and warm, piercing eyes. We can hear him saying, as he later wrote, that he would go to Manila whether or not he had sufficient ammunition, "for such were our orders and such was the only thing to do."

Although war had not yet begun, on February 11, 1898, he set sail from Japan for Hong Kong, which he regarded as the "most advantageous position from which to move to attack." He arrived on February 17 and learned about the sinking of the *Maine* in Havana. War now seemed inevitable. Eight days later Theodore Roosevelt sent Dewey a cable advising him to "keep full of coal." Dewey sought information on Manila's defense, drilled his men, put his machinery in top condition, repainted his ships to make them less conspicuous, and loaded coal and other supplies. Since international law prevented neutrals from supplying armed belligerents in wartime, he established a base at Shanghai, reasoning that "so loosely organized a national entity as the Chinese Empire could not enforce the neutrality laws."

On April 25, 1898, he received a cable from Secretary of the Navy John D. Long telling him to "Proceed at once to the Philippine Islands. Commence operations particularly against the Spanish fleet." Two days later, at two o'clock in the afternoon, the American fleet set out across the China Sea toward Manila Bay.

Commodore Dewey was confident that he could defeat the Spanish, but he was sailing toward a well-fortified position. The Hong Kong papers had frequently mentioned the presence of minefields at the entrance to the bay, and in the gambling clubs no one would bet on the Americans, even at heavy odds. The fleet proceeded toward Manila in two columns, fighting ships forward and auxiliaries twelve hundred yards behind, all lights extinguished in the night except a carefully screened lamp at the stern of each vessel, allowing others to follow. The only other illumination came from the phosphorescent wake at the bow and stern of each ship.

At daybreak on April 30 Luzon, the Philippines' main island, was in plain view. The fleet continued south along the coast, staying a safe three to four miles from shore. Dewey had received intelligence that the enemy was waiting in Subic Bay, a well-protected deep-water harbor thirty miles north of Manila Bay, but this information proved false. Pleased that the enemy had not elected to stand in this formidable position, he sailed toward the narrow channel leading into Manila. "Now we have them," said Dewey.

Waiting until dark, he approached the channel under a pale moon. Ahead several fortified islands were dimly visible. The passage reminded him of a night thirty-six years before when he had followed Farragut up the Mississippi toward New Orleans. As the ships passed El Fraile, the outermost island, the Americans braced themselves, expecting soon to encounter mines, torpedo launches, and cannon shot. The El Fraile battery opened fire but was quickly silenced by the American guns. The ships encountered no other resistance, and a little after midnight, marveling at their good fortune, they steamed unscathed into the wide expanse of Manila Bay.

Through the night they went on toward the city, planning to engage the Spanish fleet at dawn. Dewey allowed the men to sleep at their guns but awakened them for coffee at 4:00 A.M. The fleet approached Manila and discovered the Spaniards off Cavite Peninsula some five miles away.

Dewey was elated. "Before me now," he writes, "was the object for which we had made our arduous preparations, and which, indeed, must ever be the supreme test of a naval officer's career." He led his fleet of six vessels on an oblique course toward the Spanish position, keeping the guns on the enemy. The ships moved at eight knots, two hundred yards apart, "the dun, war-colored hulls of the squadron followed in column behind the flag-ship, keeping their distance excellently." The Americans were under fire from batteries in Manila, Cavite, and the Spanish fleet, but these shots were inaccurate. At 5:40 A.M. the distance to the Spanish fleet was five thousand yards. Dewey turned to the captain of his flagship, saying: "You may fire when you are ready, Gridley."

American shells rained down upon the Spanish ships; then Dewey circled and came past four more times, accurately raking the Spaniards. A single eight-inch shell struck the Spanish flagship, *Reina Cristina*, killing and wounding 20 men and destroying the steering gear. Another disabled the crews of four rapid-fire guns. Shells carried away the mizzenmast with the admiral's flag and exploded in the ammunition room and sick bay. The *Reina Cristina's* losses were 150 men killed and 90 wounded. Finding his ship almost completely disabled, Admiral Montojo ordered her abandoned and sunk. Five years later, when she was raised from the mud, she was found to have fifteen holes in her hull.

At 7:35 A.M. Dewey learned that he was low on ammunition and ordered his fleet to withdraw and evaluate the situation, but the information proved inaccurate. Taking advantage of the lull, Dewey ordered a meal prepared before returning to the battle.

Shortly after eleven o'clock the American ships approached the remnants of the Spanish fleet, quickly overwhelming the remaining ships. At about noon a Spanish flag on the government buildings in Cavite was lowered and a white flag raised. The Spanish had lost 8 ships and 381 men, and Admiral Montojo was wounded. Dewey did not lose one man, and he now commanded Manila Bay. The Spanish offered to surrender their chief city, but the commodore refused to accept a capitulation until American land forces arrived.

After a day of intense action the Americans settled down to the comparatively dull job of blockading Manila. They occupied the military base at Cavite and disabled the guns at Corregidor in the mouth of Manila Bay. On May 4 Dewey sent a ship to the Chinese mainland with his report on the remarkable victory. The short, fierce Battle of Manila Bay was America's most successful encounter with a foreign foe since Andrew Jackson's lopsided victory over the British at New Orleans in 1815. Like Jackson's victory, Dewey's was overwhelming, and he received congratulatory cables from all around the world. One of his favorites, from Theodore Roosevelt, read: "Every American is your debtor."

By defeating the Spanish fleet, Dewey had won a bay, a city, and an empire. Like an efficient businessman he had surveyed the situation in advance, built up his resources, discovered his adversary's weaknesses, and seized the victory. The most significant thing about Dewey's action was its decisiveness. It had been so simple that it seemed providential.

The victory at Manila Bay was deceptive, however. Dewey may have matched steel against steel, bested the enemy's ships, and cut off his capital, but the Philippines were not merely a navy and a city. The islands were crowded with people who looked on with aloof curiosity as the Western powers blasted away at one another. Dewey would form only a dim idea of the Philippine people, and most Americans would never begin to comprehend them. But the Filipinos had a history and ambitions of their own that would soon disrupt the course of the American empire.

The Philippines consist of a long chain of several thousand islands. Most of the population is clustered on the eleven largest islands, particularly Luzon and Mindanao, both about the size of Indiana. Ancient volcanoes rise from the islands, and thick forests shelter cockatoos, parrots, iguanas, monkeys, and water buffalo. The natives are mainly Malays who came to the islands from the south thousands of years ago. Some of the islands are so remote that in the 1970s anthropologists would discover Stone Age tribes living in the thick forests.

The Filipinos first encountered Western man in 1521 when Ferdinand Magellan, claiming Spanish sovereignty over the islands, landed a small army in the face of fifteen hundred warriors led by the native chief Lapu-Lapu. The natives fought fiercely, killing Magellan and driving the Spaniards back to their ships. Lapu-Lapu is regarded today as a hero — the first Filipino to successfully resist foreign domination.

The Spaniards returned forty-four years later and, after six years of warfare, subjugated the natives and established Manila as their capital. They imposed their government, religion, and society upon the Filipinos for the next three centuries, Christianizing the natives and forcing them to build roads, churches, and convents. The Spaniards monopolized the most lucrative positions in the church, state, and economy.

In the nineteenth century Filipino life centered on small dusty villages with large churches and on farms whose chief crops were hemp, sugar, tobacco, coconuts, and rice. Village bands, religious processions, and cockfights added color to native life. The Filipino houses were sometimes large and well built, but more often the people lived in "nipa" huts made of bamboo. The Americans, who burned many of these huts after liberating the Philippines from Spain, reckoned they took $5 worth of material and three days' work to rebuild.

Emilio Aguinaldo, hero of the Philippine independence movement and in many respects a typical Filipino, was born on March 22, 1869, in Kawit, a few miles south of Manila, in a large house with a steep thatch roof. His father was a well-to-do landowner, lawyer, and town official. The imprint of Spanish rule was evident throughout the region. The towns bore Spanish names: Rosario, Las Piñas, Santa Rosa, Manila. The higher officers in church, army, and government were Spaniards. And life was highly flavored by Catholicism. Religious training had an important part in Aguinaldo's education. His mother taught him to "pray to the mysteries of the rosary every night."

While young Aguinaldo learned that as a Filipino he belonged to an inferior caste in his own land. Capable leaders like his father were not allowed to occupy high office. The Spanish priest in Kawit was treated with all the deference accorded an Oriental potentate. After mass on Sundays a teacher took Aguinaldo and his classmates to Father Toribio Minguella to pay their respects. Aguinaldo recalls: "The priest was seated in a big armchair. One by one we would kneel down to kiss his hand which he would raise in a gesture of blessing us."

After attending school, Emilio went to work to help support his family. With his brother Críspulo he bought a *paraw,* a native sailing vessel. They carried cargoes between their home province and the adjoining islands of Mindoro, Panay, and Tamblas, carrying salt and bolos, large knives for which their region was famous, to exchange for forest products, tallow, cattle, and material for making fish traps. For several years they lived agreeably at sea, lying on the deck at night and watching "the twinkling stars," catching fish for their meals, looking at "beautiful maidens wading in the shallow seashore."

During his years as a trader Aguinaldo grew in stature in his home village of Kawit. When he was twenty he began holding local offices and at twenty-five he became municipal captain, thus occupying the highest office open to a Filipino. A year later he married Hilaria del Rosario, and in the fall of 1896 their first child was born, welcomed into the world with a celebration of fireworks, and baptized soon afterward in the local Catholic church.

Aguinaldo's life in the Spanish-ruled Philippines was pleasant but confining. He was a successful trader, a respected leader, a proud husband and parent. In a sense he was a free man; yet there were constant reminders that he and his people were regarded as inferiors by the Spanish. In May 1896 Aguinaldo and other town officials had just paid their respects to Father Fidél de Blas and were on their way to the council hall. A Spanish lieutenant saw Aguinaldo and called out to him, "Hey, you, Municipal Captain, come here. Prepare me a calesa right now, do you understand?" A calesa was a buggy, and the lieutenant was treating Aguinaldo like a lackey. Aguinaldo, humiliated and embarrassed, answered meekly, "Yes, sir." He asked his servant to fetch the vehicle and went on to the council chamber. After the meeting had begun, the

lieutenant entered the room and shouted at Aguinaldo, again demanding a buggy. Aguinaldo lost his temper and shouted back, "We are
holding a meeting. If you want anything, you may tell us about it after
giving our meeting due respect."

The lieutenant replied, "To whom shall I pay my respects? Why
should I salute any one of you?"

Aguinaldo lacked the confidence to tell the lieutenant he should
show deference to the town meeting but pointed to a painting of the
Spanish queen regent hanging behind the council, saying that the
lieutenant should salute it. A few minutes later the Spaniard got his
buggy. He then lodged a complaint with his superior against the Filipino
for discourtesy to military authority.

Aguinaldo was not punished for his part in the affair, but neither
was the lieutenant. The Spanish soldier had acted on the common
assumption that a colonized people are inferior, that even their most
constructive activities are foolish pretenses. Among his people Aguinaldo
might be a municipal captain, but to the Spanish officer he was a servant.

After the buggy incident Aguinaldo went to Manila to join the
Katipunan, a secret anti-Spanish fraternity. He recruited new members
in his own province, meeting clandestinely with recruits in the fields and
on his paraw. In summer 1896 Spanish authorities learned about the
Katipunan, and on August 19 they began to round up its members,
provoking scattered resistance.

Aguinaldo joined the insurrection on August 31. He and his
followers took over Kawit by disarming the town's three Filipino civil
guards and confiscated the parish funds after the priest fled. Aguinaldo
sent out a message declaring, "We have started to rebel against this
tyrannical race" and urging others to join him in rising against Spain and
breaking "the chains of slavery that have bound us with her all these
hundred years."

He embarked upon the Revolution in a spirit of determination
mixed with trepidation. After resigning his civic post and changing into
the rough clothes of a guerrilla, he found it difficult to eat. "As my heart
pounded furiously," he recalled, "I could not swallow any morsel of food
without gulping water." He fully expected to die within a few months.

Aguinaldo's fears were well founded. The Spanish forces used
ruthless tactics to suppress the rebellion. At the beginning of the
movement there were only some fifteen hundred Spanish troops in the
Philippines, but within a few months this number had swelled to more
than twenty thousand. At first the Filipinos were poorly armed, fighting
chiefly with bolos and spears. But late in 1896 they won several impressive victories and captured many Spanish guns. For ammunition they
collected unexploded Spanish shells and removed the powder, picked up

empty cartridges from the battlefields, and if necessary used nails and wire as projectiles. The Revolution quickly gained momentum, the people supporting the soldiers with food and lodging and welcoming them to town with bamboo arches, bells, bands, and the singing of the *Te Deum.*

On December 30, 1896, the Revolution gained its foremost martyr, José Rizal, the most respected Filipino of that time. Born in 1861, Rizal was a brilliant young man who had traveled in Spain, France, Italy, Germany, and England. A surgeon, philosopher, poet, and artist, his novel, *Do Not Touch Me,* became the *Uncle Tom's Cabin* of the movement for Philippine freedom. Rizal was not a revolutionary. A gentle, humane person, he favored gradual change. But when the Revolution began, he was arrested and charged with sedition. Confronted in court with false confessions gained by torture, he was found guilty and condemned to die. On the morning of December 30 he was taken from his cell to face a firing squad. The walls around were crowded with picnicking Spaniards who regarded the execution as a great social event. Amid their laughter and applause Rizal was killed.

The insurgents meanwhile had formed several independent governments. The people associated with Aguinaldo created an elective government, with Aguinaldo at the head of its military forces. This "little republic" controlled the province of Cavite. According to Aguinaldo, the government was patterned after that of the United States; the region was free from crime and disorder; and "everybody greeted each other as brothers and sisters."

Factionalism, however, damaged the Filipino position, and with the arrival of fresh Spanish troops in 1897 the regime was able to win back most of the insurgent territory in Cavite. Spain now clearly had the initiative against the rebels. Bur problems at home, disease among the troops, and the possibility of a war over Cuba all inclined her to seek a quick negotiated settlement. On the promise that Spain would adopt reforms, Aguinaldo agreed to leave the country, departing for Hong Kong in 1897.

Emilio Aguinaldo and his fellow revolutionaries had hardly settled on the mainland when the Spanish-American War began. Aguinaldo reasoned that because the United States had gone to war to end Spanish oppression in Cuba, surely America would help the Filipinos. Already in November 1897, and again in January 1898, he had written to Washington appealing for help. The declaration of war against Spain and the Teller amendment, promising that the United States would not annex Cuba, encouraged hopes that America would be equally generous to the Philippines.

At the outbreak of the war, the Spanish governor general of the

Philippines sought to dissuade Filipinos from relying on America, claiming that the United States would destroy their churches and enslave them. But the people scoffed at Spanish warnings, even helping Dewey find his way into Manila Bay: the Spaniards had turned off all coastal lighting, but Filipinos built a huge bonfire on shore as a signal.

E. Spenser Platt, the U.S. consul to Singapore, encouraged Aguinaldo to expect American support for Filipino independence and cited the Teller amendment as evidence of America's good intentions. On May 16 by Dewey's orders Aguinaldo and seventeen of his followers were taken aboard the *McCulloch* at Hong Kong and brought to Manila. On May 19 Aguinaldo met with Dewey and slept aboard the flagship *Olympia*.

We have no record of their conversations. Aguinaldo claimed that Dewey assured him the United States would grant independence to the Philippines and encouraged him to fight the Spanish. Dewey said he made no such promise, but he appears to have been sympathetic toward independence. He allowed Aguinaldo to occupy buildings the Spanish had abandoned and supplied him with arms. He avoided, however, any gesture that could be regarded as recognition of Philippine independence. On June 18, 1898, the insurgents proclaimed their independence; Dewey turned down an invitation to attend their ceremonies on the weak pretext that it was mail day. But when he sent news of the declaration home, he added, "In my opinion these people are superior in intelligence and more capable of self-government than the natives of Cuba, and I am familiar with both races."

The Filipinos gave credibility to their claim of independence by winning several victories over the Spaniards. By late June they had thirty thousand men under arms and were the de facto government of Luzon Island, except for Manila, which they had surrounded with trenches.

Dewey remained in the Philippines through the spring and summer of 1898, waiting for the arrival of the soldiers that would make possible the occupation of Manila. Most of his men stayed in the ships anchored off Cavite. The climate was hot and damp; periods of torrential rain were followed by steaming tropical heat and "lifeless air." The sailors subsisted on sea rations, supplemented occasionally with fresh fruit and eggs purchased from the natives and meat, vegetables, and other "Chinese delicacies" brought from Hong Kong.

Despite the fact that they were thousands of miles from home, there was something natural about the presence of the Americans in the Philippines. As Dewey looked over the hills of Luzon from his flagship, they reminded him of the Green Mountains of Vermont. The harbor was now effectively a part of America, to be administered efficiently.

"American supremacy and military discipline," wrote Dewey, "must take the place of chaos." Dewey did not address himself to the larger question of whether the Philippines should become permanently a part of America. This, he realized, "Was a question to decide at home." Now he was required simply to provide for its stable government under a blockade.

Great as Dewey's victory was, it was comparatively simple in contrast to the problems that lay ahead. The Spanish fleet had been defeated, but what should be done with the Philippines? There were four apparent possibilities: they could be returned to Spain, declared independent, turned over to another foreign government, or retained by the United States. These options were represented by the presence of four forces in Manila Bay at the time: Americans, Spaniards, other Europeans, and Filipinos.

The United States appeared to be in charge. In his efficient leadership, which John Hay, the Secretary of State, described as a mingling of "wisdom and daring," Dewey ably embodied America's claim to world power. He had been mortified by the knowledge in the 1870s and 1880s that the American navy could easily be demolished by a modern fleet. But the fight at Manila had won the admiration of foreigners and allowed Americans to respect themselves. The United States was now a power to be reckoned with.

What of the Spanish? They had occupied the Philippines for more than three centuries and had built Manila, and yet they had shown a curious lethargy in their defense. Heavy guns that should have been along the shore before Dewey's arrival were found unmounted. The gunners at the entrance to the bay had let Dewey's large fleet slip through with almost no resistance. No torpedo boats greeted him inside the bay, and the shore batteries at Manila and Cavite had been ineffective. Moreover, Admiral Montojo had chosen a curious position for his stand. Dewey believed he could have hurt the Americans had he confronted them in Subic Bay. Montojo had refused to fight in the deep water of Subic Bay because, as he put it, "Our vessels could not only be destroyed, but they could not save their crews." In other words, the timorous Spaniard was preparing for defeat.

If the story of the Battle of Manila Bay reflected the energy and ability of a new nation now a world power, it also displayed the indolence of an older country that had lost its confidence. The contrast was tragically dramatized by an incident the night after the battle. Crowds had gathered along the Manila waterfront to gaze at the conquering fleet lying offshore. Out of solicitude for the people, Dewey had the band play "La Paloma" and other Spanish tunes. Dewey writes, "While the sea-breeze wafted the strains to their ears the poor colonel of artillery who had commanded the battery, feeling himself dishonored by his disgraceful failure, shot himself through the head."

The Spanish were clearly demoralized and offered no more resistance. Dewey had to consider, however, another possible threat to his position from other nations whose navies were in the harbor. He was particularly worried about an increasingly formidable fleet of German vessels. He realized that it was common in wartime for neutrals to send naval vessels as observers, and some of the foreign ships in Manila seemed friendly enough. Along with the Germans there were small contingents from England, France, and Japan. But Germany's show of power was worrisome. Dewey recognized that the Philippines were "a rich prize for any ambitious power." Germany had more ships than needed for observation and, at one time, actually had a more formidable fleet in the bay than Dewey. Worse, the ships frequently disregarded common blockade rules. They steamed into the bay and dropped anchor without first reporting to Dewey, and they occupied small sections of territory around the bay, making surveys.

Dewey was frankly alarmed and sent urgent requests to the United States for more ammunition, later admitting that the German attitude was one reason for his worry about stores. When the time came to take the city of Manila, the English fleet, which had been much friendlier to Dewey, positioned itself between the Americans and the Germans, giving rise to rumors that if the Germans should attack the Americans the English and American fleets would "fire in the same language." It is more likely that the fleet wanted to observe the action from a favorable vantage point, but Dewey regarded their activity as an amicable gesture. Long after Dewey left Manila, German records were made public that proved Germany had not planned to attack the Americans but did intend to take the islands if the Americans decided not to. At the least, the presence of other foreign vessels in Manila Bay was a reminder of the international implications of the Philippine situation.

The fourth element at Manila Bay was the Filipinos, whose significance the United States was strangely reluctant to acknowledge. Aguinaldo's appeals to McKinley asking him to guarantee the independence of his country went unanswered. Newspapers in the United States carried little news of Filipino activities, and Americans were either apathetic or hostile toward the natives. On May 15 Gen. Wesley Merritt, commander of an American army bound for the islands, wrote McKinley suggesting he might have to fight the Filipinos. Merritt's soldiers knew nothing about the natives, and aboard the transports they joked about the Filipino "cannibals" and referred to them as "niggers." When the American troops reached Manila, they were landed without regard to the Philippine army or government. The first American general in the

Philippines, Thomas Anderson, sought to reassure Aguinaldo, telling him, "In 122 years we have established no colonies." Anderson wrote to Washington saying that the Filipinos "are not ignorant savage tribes, but have a civilization of their own." Yet nothing was done to establish formal relations with the insurgents.

One wonders how the history of America's involvement in the Philippines would have changed if Dewey had been able to work more closely with the people. At Subic Bay, Americans and insurgents had cooperated in taking a strategic Spanish gun emplacement. Surely Dewey and the rebels together could have taken Manila shortly after his arrival. He claimed he had no troops to occupy it, but why not let the Filipinos occupy their own capital? Apparently, America wanted to help the Filipinos on America's terms.

As more American troops arrived, they persuaded a reluctant Aguinaldo to turn over the Filipino trenches along the south side of Manila. By now his troops controlled most of Luzon. General Merritt, in charge of the army in the Philippines, was under orders to "avoid all sign of alliance with the insurgents." With sufficient support to hold Manila, Dewey began negotiations with the commander of the Spanish forces, General Jaudenes. The Spaniards, surrounded by American and Philippine troops, bereft of their navy, cut off from contact with Madrid, and vulnerable to bombardment by the American fleet, were quite willing to surrender.

But the commander did not want to lose face by quitting without firing a shot. The two sides finally agreed that the American army would attack; Dewey would move his fleet into position but not bombard the city. In exchange, the Spanish shore batteries would not shell his fleet. The Spanish would resist for a time; then Dewey would signal a request for surrender, and the Spanish would comply. It would proceed like a military drill, but real ammunition would be used — and real lives would be lost.

On August 13 this drama was enacted. The Americans stormed Fort San Antonio outside Manila and took it. The fleet moved into position and demanded a Spanish surrender. A white flag appeared, and the Americans then occupied the city. As part of the capitulation agreement America promised not to allow any insurgents to enter Manila. The Spanish feared reprisals from the Filipinos, and the Americans were glad enough to occupy the capital themselves. One great power had thus supplanted another in the Philippines.

In America the conquest of the Philippines seemed a magnificent triumph. Dewey was the most popular man in the United States, the country's first military hero since the Civil War. Across the land stores were flooded with Dewey buttons and hats. A popular song celebrated his victory, and he was awarded a new rank, Admiral of the Navy.

What did Dewey's victory mean? On the one hand, it was a military achievement, plain and simple. The destruction of Spain's Pacific fleet and American control of the Philippines had given the United States an initial advantage in the war with Spain. Subsequent victories in the Caribbean would persuade Spain to accept peace terms favorable to the United States.

The war was fought for two explicit reasons: to end Spanish oppression in Cuba and to achieve political stability in the Western Hemisphere. One goal was humanitarian, the other political. Neither suggested the need to acquire territory, a fact underscored by the Teller amendment. With victory in Manila, however, Americans began to think of new territory, justifying expansion on economic, humanitarian, and strategic grounds.

American business had not been enthusiastic about entry into the Spanish-American War, but with Dewey's victory a new attitude appeared, and the stock market rose sharply. Businessmen and politicians began to talk about the economic value of the Philippines. The islands were regarded as good sources of hemp, minerals, sugar, tobacco, and forest products; and they were a doorway to the great Chinese market. Henry Cabot Lodge claimed that their "value to this country is almost beyond imagination."

While American businessmen were thinking of coaling stations and hemp, another group of Americans thought about Philippine souls. Humanitarians saw the Filipinos as backward people who should be elevated by Christian missionaries and educators. There were flaws in this argument. The natives were neither ignorant nor heathen. Three and a half centuries of Spanish rule had won most to Catholicism, and an extensive educational system existed on the islands. Nor was the United States in a good position to claim solicitude for nonwhite peoples. Ironically, the American mission to uplift Filipinos would occur at the same time as jim crow laws were removing the benefits of citizenship from American blacks. Apparently it was easier to aid nonwhites abroad than to bring about equality at home.

But the idea of America as defender of human rights had tremendous appeal. The islanders were frequently referred to as our "Little Brown Brothers." A poem by Rudyard Kipling, which first appeared in February 1899, called upon Americans to "Take up the White Man's Burden" and civilize the Filipinos. The Filipinos might not be grateful for American help, but President McKinley remarked, "Do we need their consent to perform a great act for humanity?"

Coupled with humanitarian and economic reasons for keeping the Philippines was a third strain of thought, a delight in expansion for its own sake. Taking new land was quite simply something that great powers did. Their activity was usually justified by the word "destiny" — Americans had been destined to spread across the continent and were now destined to take the Philippines. Albert J. Beveridge had summarized the expansionist idea in a speech several days before Dewey's victory. "We are a conquering race," he said. "We must obey our blood and occupy new markets, and, if necessary, new lands."

Events during summer 1898 encouraged the movement to annex the Philippines. Victories in Cuba and Puerto Rico as well as the army's entry into Manila confirmed American strength. President McKinley, a strong Methodist, decided to support annexation after spending many a late night walking the floor in the White House and kneeling in prayer. Finally one night, in a kind of revelation, as he reported to a meeting of fellow Methodists, he considered the alternative ways of disposing of the Philippines: we could not give them back to Spain or to another European power, he decided, nor could we allow them to govern themselves without preparation. And so, he decided, "There was nothing left for us to do but to take them all, and to educate the Filipinos, and uplift and civilize and Christianize them."

When the peace commission had convened in Paris, McKinley's original instructions on the Philippines had been vague, but on October 25 he cabled the American negotiators telling them to demand that Spain concede the islands to the United States. Spain reluctantly agreed in return for a payment of $20 million. According to the treaty that was signed on December 10, Spain relinquished sovereignty to Cuba and ceded Guam, Puerto Rico, and the Philippines to the United States.

The Paris negotiations had gone smoothly, but the treaty still had to come before the Senate. And despite the popularity of imperialism, a strong coalition of anti-imperialists had begun to form. McKinley himself had encouraged anti-imperialistic sentiments in a December 6, 1897, message to Congress on Cuba. "I speak not of forcible annexation," he had said, "for that cannot be thought of. That by our code of morality would be criminal aggression." McKinley was later embarrassed by these words.

By late 1898 "imperialist" and "anti-imperialist" had come to designate those who supported or opposed expansion. In fall 1898 anti-imperialist leagues were formed around the country, devoted to defeating the treaty in the Senate. Some members were veterans of reform campaigns — men and women who had fought for Indian rights, abolition, Prohibition, and civil service reform. This group included Carl Schurz, Charles Francis Adams, and Jane Adams. Others were educators and literary figures, among them President David Starr Jordon of Stanford, philosopher William James, and writers William

Dean Howells and Mark Twain. Businessmen like Andrew Carnegie helped finance the anti-imperialists. Labor opposition was led by Samuel Gompers, president of the American Federation of Labor.

The anti-imperialists claimed that acquisition of colonies was contrary to the American ideal of government by the consent of the governed. Ever since the American Revolution, the United States had acquired territory with the usual expectation that the new land would become a part of the United States. The Philippines would be an exception, for even the supporters of annexation did not intend that the islands would join the Union.

The anti-imperialists reminded the American public of their cherished traditions. William Jennings Bryan, the Democratic presidential candidate of 1896, asked an audience in Omaha on June 14, 1898: "Our guns destroyed a Spanish fleet, but can they destroy that self-evident truth, that governments derive their just powers, not from superior force, but from the consent of the governed?" In another talk Bryan echoed Lincoln's "house divided" speech: "This nation cannot endure half republic and half colony — half free and half vassal."

Historians have questioned whether the apparently altruistic feeling for the Philippine people was the real reason for opposition to colonialism. Many Americans opposed annexation, not because of sympathy for, but out of prejudice against, the Filipinos. In the atmosphere of racial bigotry that prevailed in the late nineteenth century, it was assumed that Filipinos were unfit to become American citizens. Samuel Gompers called them a "semi-barbaric population, almost primitive in their habits and customs." A high proportion of the senators who opposed annexation were from southern states that had recently passed jim crow laws and disfranchised the blacks.

Practical considerations also led the anti-imperialist movement. Some businessmen feared competition from cheaper Philippine agricultural products, and labor leaders feared importation of cheap labor. Many anti-imperialists believed it would be too difficult to maintain and protect distant colonial possessions.

In the winter of 1898–99 the opponents of annexation were strong enough to threaten the treaty, but they faced a difficult tactical problem. Should they refuse to support the treaty, thereby continuing the technical state of war with Spain? Or should they accept the treaty and then fight imperialism in a separate Philippine vote or in the elections of 1900? Many anti-imperialists wanted to block the treaty, but others supported it, planning to consider annexation separately. The result was a 57 to 27 Senate vote on February 6, 1899, only 2 votes more than the necessary two-thirds majority required for treaty confirmation.

The Senate then considered a separate Philippine measure, the

Bacon resolution, which would have granted independence to the islands. Hostility to annexation was so strong that the vote on February 14, 1899, resulted in a tie. Vice-President Garret A. Hobart cast the deciding vote against the measure. In its place another bill, the McEnery resolution, was adopted, promising that in "due time" the United States would "make such disposition of said islands as will best promote the interests of the citizens of the United States and the inhabitants of said islands." This vague statement was hardly comforting to the anti-imperialists.

The opponents of annexation had made a grave tactical error. There were enough of them to have insisted on a self-denying measure, such as the Bacon resolution, before the treaty vote as a condition of their support for the treaty itself. By voting on the treaty first they failed to win any important concessions and badly divided their own movement.

In the presidential campaign of 1900 the Democrats nominated William Jennings Bryan and adopted a strong anti-imperialist platform. Bryan lost badly, but the election was not a mandate for imperialism, for the Democrat's domestic policies were at least as much of an issue as his foreign policy. Nonetheless, the election effectively ended the anti-imperialist movement. The American possession of the Philippines was now a matter of fact.

In the meantime, Philippine opposition to colonial rule had led to an insurrection against America. When it became apparent that the United States was not planning to grant the islands their independence, the Filipino troops that had helped defeat the Spaniards began to rebel against their new rulers. In 1899 guerrilla war quickly spread throughout the islands, with Emilio Aguinaldo as the nominal leader of the Filipinos.

The rebellion was so formidable that the United States had to send seventy thousand troops, four times as many as had fought in Cuba, to suppress it. It dragged on for three years and took more American lives than the war with Spain. The United States soon adopted many Spanish antiguerrilla tactics, using torture and establishing concentration camps. The most successful officers were men like "Hell Roaring Jake" Smith, who told his men to make the island of Samar into "a howling wilderness" and to "kill everything over ten." A congressional investigation of the conduct of the war revealed the seamy side of America's endeavors to "uplift" the Filipinos.

The Philippine insurrection came to an end in 1901 with the capture of Aguinaldo. Frederick Funstan, general in charge of a Kansas volunteer regiment, arranged to have himself and four other Americans taken to Aguinaldo's camp, deep in the Luzon mountains, in the guise of prisoners. Their "captors" were friendly Filipino scouts. Once the group reached Aguinaldo's camp they abandoned their pretense and took the rebel leader captive. In Manila the demoralized Aguinaldo signed a proclamation urging his people to end hostilities and enjoy their new lives under the "liberty promised by the generosity of the great American nation."

The United States had already begun to establish civil government in the islands. In 1900 William Howard Taft was inaugurated as governor. A few months later three Filipinos were added to the governing commission. The American record in the Philippines was considerably more liberal than the Spanish. American teachers were sent to the islands. Filipinos were allowed to fill important positions in the government. The United States attempted to "train" the Filipinos for independence. The islands became an American commonwealth in 1935 and were given full independence after World War II.

America's initial involvement in the Philippines had been a curious blend of humanitarianism and expansionism. Although United States rule was more liberal than Spain's and another power probably would have taken the islands if America had withdrawn, colonialism, even in its most benevolent form, brought economic opportunism and racial prejudice — and of course military conquest in the first place. Dewey's stunning victory made expansion seem simple but blinded America to Filipino aspirations.

Three days after United States forces captured Manila, Dewey visited the city and found the Americans well established. "The people had already resumed their peaceful avocations," he wrote, "and if it had not been for the colors over the citadel, the American sentries posted here and there, and the presence in the streets of the tall, stalwart, good-natured volunteers, who made the little Filipinos seem diminutive in contrast, one would never have imagined that a state of war had lately existed or that the sovereignty of the centuries had been changed."

QUESTIONS

1. How was the United States able to gain control of the Philippines? Evaluate the role of the following: American naval power, Spanish indolence, Dewey's preparation and skill.

2. Why did Emilio Aguinaldo and other Filipinos rebel against Spanish rule?

3. How did the United States treat the Filipinos at Manila Bay? In what ways did Americans encourage Filipino hopes for independence? In what ways were they insensitive in their treatment of the natives?

4. For what reasons did the United States decide to annex the Philippines? What evidence is there that some other power would have annexed the islands if America had not? What arguments were used to oppose annexation? Why did America annex the Philippines but not Cuba?

5. Why did the Filipinos rebel against the United States? How was the United States able to quell the uprising?

6. In what respect were the Filipinos in no better condition under American rule than under Spain? In what ways was the government more liberal?

BIBLIOGRAPHY

AGUINALDO, EMILIO. *My Memoirs* (1967). Aguinaldo's autobiography.

BEISNER, ROBERT. *Twelve Against Empire* (1968). Studies twelve anti-imperialists, including Andrew Carnegie.

DEWEY, GEORGE. *Autobiography* (1913). Interesting and well-written account of the admiral's career.

FREIDEL, FRANK. *The Splendid Little War* (1958). Focuses on the soldiers' experience in the Spanish-American War.

LAFEBER, WALTER. *The New Empire* (1963). History of American expansion between 1860 and 1898.

LEROY, JAMES A. *Americans in the Philippines* (2 vols., 1914). Exhaustive history of early American involvement.

PRATT, JULIUS W. *Expansionists of 1898* (1936). Explores American motives in annexing Hawaii and the Philippines.

TRASK, DAVID F. *The War with Spain in 1898* (1981). Lengthy, comprehensive account of the war.

WOLFF, LEON. *Little Brown Brother* (1961). History of American war against the Philippine insurrection.

5

NEW IMMIGRANTS

Russian Jews in the United States

America has long been a place of refuge for the outcasts of other lands. Puritans fleeing religious persecution and Irishmen escaping famine immigrated to the New World to begin their lives anew. Waves of immigrants from Northern Europe peopled the United States in the early years, but at no time did the country receive more immigrants than during the years 1880 to 1915 when millions of people from Eastern and Southern Europe came to America and created ethnic communities in the new land. Seeking to perpetuate their customs while adjusting to American life, they sought also, like earlier immigrants, to discover their identity in the new land. The Russian Jews and other immigrants faced many hardships in the United States, but none more difficult than maintaining their cultural identity in an America that both stimulated and under-mined their traditional ways.

When did America begin? The American national holiday cele-brates the events of 1776 in Philadelphia, Pennsylvania. But the United States is not exclusively the product of the Revolution. America had many births — after 1776 as well as before; her origins lay in the streets of Dublin, the villages of Russia, the fields of China, and the fjords of Norway as well as in farms and towns of the thirteen colonies. In 1900, 15 percent of the people living in the United States had been born elsewhere. Between 1840 and 1914 more than 30 million people came from foreign countries to settle in the United States. The Great Migration of Puritans to Massachusetts Bay from 1630 to 1640 brought about forty thousand people; late in the nineteenth and early in the twentieth centuries, as many immigrants frequently passed through Ellis Island in a week. In the years 1905, 1906, and 1907 more people came to America than the whole population of the United States at the time of the Revolution. Ireland, Great Britain, Scandinavia, Russia, Italy, and Germany each gave birth to more than a million future Americans between 1840 and 1915.

These immigrants were changed by the United States, but America was changed by them at the same time. The story does not lend itself to neat chronological boundaries or to the listing of key episodes; it is much more subtle and amorphous than the history of an individual or event. But the story of one group will help clarify this gradual, fundamental change. The Russian Jewish experience is remarkable in itself, but is the more important because it is not unique; a dozen or more immigrant sagas have similar scope. The Chinese in San Francisco, the Irish in Boston, the Scandinavians in Wisconsin and Minnesota, and scores of other groups combined immigrant backgrounds with an American future.

The Russian Jews who began arriving in the United States in large numbers after 1880 were far from the earliest members of the Jewish faith to arrive. The first Jews came to America in 1654 and settled in New Amsterdam. At the time of the American Revolution, some 2,000 Jews were in the United States, with congregations in Newport, New York, Philadelphia, Richmond, and Savannah. In the next thirty years the population climbed slowly to 2,000 in an American population of more than 9 million, but after 1820 Jewish immigration began to increase rapidly. By 1850 the Jewish population was 50,000; in 1860 it reached 150,000. Most of the new immigrants were refugees from political and social turmoil in Germany. They mainly engaged in trade and settled throughout the United States.

Just before 1900, immigration to the United States changed dra-matically. Hitherto most immigrants, non-Jewish as well as Jewish, had been from Central and Northern Europe: France, Germany, Scandinavia, Great Britain, and Ireland. But now "new immigrants" began to arrive from Southern and Eastern Europe: Austria-Hungary, Poland, Russia, Romania, Italy, and Greece. Most Jewish immigrants after 1880 were from Eastern Europe.

At first the German Jews were ambivalent about the arrival of their religious fellows from Eastern Europe. On the one hand, they sympathized with Jews escaping from oppression. On the other, they were embarrassed by the curious customs of the new immigrants: the men with long, curly beards; the women with wigs; the strange accents; the poverty; the reputation of some for radicalism. The old Jews commonly feared that the strange new immigrants would damage their own image of respectability. But despite these reservations, the German Jews became active in immigrant aid societies and lobbied to keep immigration policies liberal. Between 1881 and 1914, more than 2 million Jews immigrated to America. More than three-fourths of these came from Russia; most of the remainder from other regions of Eastern Europe, especially Austria-Hungary and Romania. Most new immigrants settled in, or at least passed through, New York's Lower East Side. Between 1880 and 1910 the Jewish population in New York City increased from 80,000 to 1,250,000.

The Jews who came to the United States had no nation of their own but lived scattered across Europe and through other quarters of the globe. Wherever they lived they depended on their host nation to allow them to worship in peace. In Germany, Italy, Austria-Hungary, Russia, and elsewhere, they provided services as artisans and businessmen and accordingly were tolerated. But their position was always precarious. They usually had no political power and often were oppressed by hostile citizens and rulers.

The Russian Jews were mainly the descendants of men and women who had settled in Poland in the thirteenth and fourteenth centuries. There they had become moneylenders, tax collectors, innkeepers, artisans, and grain merchants. For several centuries they lived in relative peace, but in the eighteenth century Poland was partitioned — divided among Russia, Prussia, and Austria — and many Polish Jews came under Russian domination.

Under the tsars the position of the Jews rapidly deteriorated. They were not allowed to live outside of a region known as the Pale of Settlement, which consisted of Poland, Lithuania, Byelorussia, and the Ukraine. Within the Pale itself, their political and economic activities were restricted. They were usually not allowed to own land, and they were barred from higher education by restrictive quotas and tests. Early in the nineteenth century, Jews were drafted into the Russian army for twenty-five-year periods of service and were expected to become Christians. Those who managed to preserve their faith through this long ordeal became heroes among their people.

For civilians as well as for soldiers, the challenge of maintaining Judaism in a hostile environment strengthened faith. Religion provided the Jewish people with a sense of community, integrity, and purpose. Being a Jew involved not only special forms of worship but also distinctive patterns of dress, behavior, and speech — most spoke Yiddish, a composite of Hebrew and other languages. They observed special holidays, prayers, and laws. Religious learning was the essential part of education: young men frequently spent many years studying Jewish law, and the scholar was highly esteemed.

Thus, the Russian Jews were effectively a nation within a nation, drawn together by a common faith and driven together by Russian prejudice. But despite their disadvantages they established strong, healthy communities within the Pale. Most lived in towns that dotted the predominantly agricultural landscape. Barred from landownership, they provided goods for the agrarian population by working as artisans, small manufacturers, and merchants. In the Russian population as a whole, a much larger proportion of Jews than Gentiles were involved in manufacturing, commerce, and the professions. These economic activities provided a livelihood but not great riches. Some 5 to 10 percent of Russian Jews were moderately wealthy; 20 percent were impoverished; the majority lived in modest comfort with simple food, clothing, shelter, and furnishings.

Still, by several measures of achievement the Russian Jews may be said to have prospered. They maintained close family ties, had high standards of hygiene, and experienced no problem with alcoholism. These indications of personal and communal health are reflected in Russian vital statistics: the Jewish death rate was much lower than that of other Russians. The caliber of Jewish life is reflected also in a relatively high literacy rate: twice as many Russian Jews as non-Jews could read at the end of the nineteenth century.

The life of the Russian Jew with its mixture of hardship and triumph is told in the story of a girl who migrated from the Pale to the United States. After a few years of life in the New World she decided to write an account of her youth, not, as she indicated in her preface, because it was unique, but because it was "typical of many. " Her American name was Mary Antin, and the title of her book was *The Promised Land.*

Mary was born in Polotzk, a village some three hundred miles west of Moscow. Her father was a prosperous merchant who provided well for his family: his daughter remembered embroidered linen, silver candlesticks, kitchen shelves "lined with copper and brass," and "feath-erbeds heaped halfway to the ceiling." It was a world in which match-makers arranged marriages, and people wore a ribbon around the neck to ward off disease. Above all, it was a world tinctured by the Jewish faith. Religion touched almost every corner of Mary's life. Whenever her mother discovered a peculiar mark on a chicken she was preparing to cook, she would send it to the rabbi, who would "look in his big books" and decide whether the chicken could be eaten. The Antins observed the Sabbath with a rigor that even the early American Puritans could not have matched. On the Sabbath, Mary was not allowed to work or even to touch any instrument of labor or commerce, as an axe or a coin. It was "forbidden to light a fire, or to touch anything that contained a fire, or had contained fire, were it only a cold candlestick or a burned match."

As a little girl Mary learned that "The world was divided between Jews and Gentiles." A girl named Vanka threw mud at her; her mother brushed off the dirt and explained that there was nothing to do because Vanka was a Gentile, and "The Gentiles do as they like with us Jews." Mary learned quickly, and later when Vanka spat at her she wiped her face and, she writes, "thought nothing at all. I accepted ill-usage from the Gentiles as one accepts the weather."

As she grew older, she saw other signs of prejudice. Jewish mer-chants had to pay special fees for the right to travel on business. A local capmaker went to a city to practice his trade, passed the proper tests, and paid his fees, but the authorities claimed he had not done so. He returned impoverished to Polotzk. The young men of Polotzk were drafted into an army that made no provision for their faith. Many sought to avoid the service by inflicting temporary injury on themselves. Mary Antin recalled that the deformities often proved incurable, so that "there were many men in Polotzk blind of one eye, or hard of hearing, or lame, as a result of these secret practices."

If such hardships were the daily bread of Jews in the Pale of Settlement, they lived always with the fear of much worse oppression. At any moment the Gentiles in a community might take it into their minds to massacre the Jews. These outbreaks of mass violence, known as pogroms, were frequently encouraged by priests, police, even by the tsar. They were rare under the benevolent rule of Alexander II (1855–81), but they occurred much more often after his assassination in 1881. In the following year the government instigated a massacre of Jews at Nizhny Novgorod. During the next few years Jews were slain or driven from their homes in scores of local pogroms throughout Russia.

Fear haunted the Jews in Polotzk, especially on Christian holidays; then they locked their doors and stayed inside, "knowing that the least disturbance might start a riot, and a riot lead to a pogrom." Mary Antin recalled seeing people who had been caught in pogroms. "Jews who escaped the pogroms," she writes, "came to Polotzk with wounds on them, and horrible, horrible stories, of little babies torn limb from limb before their mothers' eyes. Only to hear these things made one sob and sob and choke with pain. People who saw such things never smiled any more, no matter how long they lived; and sometimes their hair turned white in a day, and some people became insane on the spot."

To be a Jew in the Pale of Settlement was to be constantly humiliated and threatened by hostile neighbors and a hostile regime. Yet it was an economic crisis rather than fear of oppression that finally drove the Antins to migrate to America. During the nineteenth century large new industries had forced many East Europeans out of work. Simultaneously, rapidly growing population strained the resources of food and shelter. The Jews were especially injured by these changes. Between 1800 and 1900 the number of Russian Jews increased from 1 million to 4 million. Many Jewish artisans lost their jobs when factories began to produce goods more cheaply than they could. At the same time, government regulations prevented most Jews from becoming industrialists.

Mary Antin's father was ruined by these changes. At first Antin was a successful merchant, but then he became ill and was no longer able to support his family. To survive, the Antins had to sell many of their belongings, and Mary's mother had to go to work as a peddler. When the father finally recovered, economic conditions were so bad that he could not reestablish himself in business. Like millions of other Europeans, he began to think of America.

A Russian Jew could not go to Moscow, Kiev, or Saint Petersburg to improve his condition. But he could go to New York, Boston, or Chicago, to find more economic opportunities and fewer prejudicial restrictions. Prior to 1880 very few East Europeans had come to America, but in the next thirty-five years one Russian Jew in three would make the trip. Steamship companies encouraged them by offering rapid passage at a low fare. The first settlers helped others by sending back information and money and by establishing households and neighborhoods in America where the immigrant could settle among friends.

After 1880 the migration developed an astonishing momentum. Between 1881 and 1914, when World War I interrupted the flow of immigrants, more than 1.5 million Russian Jews came to the United States. Migration became an obsession in the Pale of Settlement. Mary Antin recounts:

> America was in everybody's mouth. Businessmen talked of it
> over their accounts; the market women made up their
> quarrels that they might discuss it from stall to stall; people

who had relatives in the famous land went around reading
their letters for the enlightenment of less fortunate folk . . .
children played at emigrating.

Mary's father listened carefully to such talk. If others could go,
then so too might he. Finally he gathered his courage and set out alone
for America. He could not afford to bring his family, but in America he
borrowed the necessary money and wrote for the family to join him.
Mary was ecstatic. "So at last," she writes, "I was going to America!
Really, really going at last! The boundaries burst. The arch of heaven
soared. A million suns shone out for every star. The winds rushed in
from outer space, roaring in my ears, 'America! America!'" Mary compared going to America with going to Jerusalem or crossing the Red Sea.
It was not merely a journey — it was the fulfillment of life's promise.

With such thoughts, Mary Antin and hundreds of thousands of
other East Europeans set out for America. The trip was filled with
hardships. First one must pack together the few belongings that could be
easily carried on a long journey by cart, rail, and ship. With these
possessions — pots and pans, a samovar, and perhaps goose-down
bedding — the emigrant departed from the native village into a world
whose language and customs were unfamiliar. At every step were
unscrupulous trainmen, innkeepers, and government officials who
might prey on the ignorant. At the borders many had to cross illegally,
because the tsar often denied passports to Jews. Many a refugee crossed
into Germany or Austria in the black of night and on foot, following a
guide through isolated fields or forests. Once outside Russia, the
immigrants boarded trains, usually riding in fourth-class accommodations that were little better than boxcars, and journeyed on to port cities
such as Hamburg or Bremen. Even then the ordeal was frequently
prolonged, as they lived in prisonlike quarantine enclosures while
waiting for their vessels. Finally, on the voyage to America the passengers
were exposed to acute discomfort. They commonly traveled in crowded
steerage quarters deep in the bowels of the ship, which were poorly
ventilated and shook with the engines' vibrations. Many travelers
recalled the poor food, filthy toilets, and the constant stench of vomit.
One man echoed the feelings of many when he described the journey as
"a kind of hell that cleanses a man of his sins before coming to the land
of Columbus."

The Antins experienced many hardships on their travels. After
journeying across Russia they learned that they could not enter Germany unless they purchased second-class rail tickets (instead of the
fourth-class tickets they held). They could not afford the extra cost and
had to remain in a border town until a friend helped them across. They
then passed through Germany, packed like cattle into a fourth-class car.

Once all the passengers were unceremoniously removed from the train
and forced to take showers, apparently as a precaution against disease,
though no explanation was given. At their destination they were herded
into a building where they had to wait for many days before boarding a
ship.

Finally they went to sea for a sixteen-day voyage. Crowded together
with other passengers as seasick as themselves, they encountered storms
that tossed passengers from their beds. "We frightened immigrants,"
writes Mary Antin, "turned our faces to the wall and awaited our watery
graves." Despite such difficulties, the voyage was not entirely painful.
When the weather cleared there were "happy hours on deck, with
fugitive sunshine, birds atop the crested waves, band music and dancing
and fun." And then there was the fine moment when the ship finally
neared the American shore.

At Ellis Island, where most of the immigrants entered America,
they came face to face with the first of the blunt realities that would
shape their new lives. This immigrant depot, a huge brick edifice lying
just off Manhattan in New York Bay, was opened in 1892, a year after the
United States government had taken over supervision of immigration
from the states. As immigrants disembarked, they were given numbers
and herded into a great central hall where they were formed into lines
and led past several doctors who scrutinized them for disease. The laws
of that time imposed no quotas on immigrants but did stipulate that
each entrant be in good health and be able to provide for himself. Those
who appeared to be sick with tuberculosis, venereal disease, ringworm,
or other serious ailments were marked with chalk and held for further
examination. The immigrants who passed the medical tests were then
asked a barrage of questions about their character, politics, skills, money,
and family status. Frequently their assimilation began here at the hands
of clerks who simplified East European names into shorter Anglo-Saxon
forms. Most were allowed to leave Ellis Island after a day. Others had to
remain for one or two weeks for further examination. The least fortunate — between 1 and 2 percent of the immigrants between 1880 and
1914 — had to return to Europe.

The ordeal at Ellis Island was softened for Jewish immigrants by
the Hebrew Immigrant Aid Society, founded in 1892. Its representatives,
identified by the letters HIAS on their blue caps, helped the immigrants
answer questions and served as advocates for those the government
sought to exclude. They also provided information on housing and jobs.

After completing their examinations on Ellis Island, the immigrants boarded one of the ferries that ran twenty-four hours a day
between the island and Manhattan. A short voyage past the Statue of

Liberty took the travelers to Battery Park. Behind them now were the loathsome railroad and steamship accommodations and intimidating customs and immigration officials. Disembarking amid the cries of seagulls and the throb of the ferry engine, the immigrants were finally set free in America.

But who were they now? Where would they go? How would they make a living? Because immigrants landed in New York with an average of only $8 in their pockets, the end of the long journey from Europe was only the beginning of a much longer struggle to make a living in America.

The Russian Jews who came to America were mostly young, and many came with their families. The majority were skilled laborers; 40 percent were clothing workers. After an abortive Russian revolution in 1905, a higher proportion of wealthy and educated Jews began to immigrate. Some artisans were able to use their European skills in America, but many found that the industrial forces that rendered their crafts obsolete in Europe were also at work in America.

Whatever their backgrounds, the immigrants had first to search for shelter and work. Some went to other cities — Boston, Cleveland, Detroit, even Los Angeles — but most stayed in New York. Of the Jews who landed at Ellis Island, three-fourths remained in the city. New York was vital in shaping the East European Jewish experience in America.

New York had grown rapidly during the nineteenth century. In 1800 its population was 60,000; by 1850 it had climbed to 515,000; and in 1900, after it absorbed Brooklyn and other outlying areas, the population was more than 3 million. The city owed its growth in part to the forces that were redistributing the American population from farm to city across the country. With new railroads, telegraphs, and steamships, urban centers acquired greater importance. Cities became centers of manufacturing, distribution, and finance in an economy where interdependence was rapidly replacing self-sufficiency.

Even without the immigrants New York would have grown in the nineteenth century, but newly arriving Americans greatly accelerated the expansion. Once a Russian Jew had arrived in Manhattan he had many reasons to stay. New York had jobs in manufacturing enterprises, department stores, and printshops. Opportunities for individual enterprise were there, too; one could easily become a street peddler or proprietor of a small store. Another attraction was one's fellow countrymen, a whole neighborhood with tens of thousands of men and women who had grown up in Russia, bringing with them Yiddish newspapers, plays, stores, doctors. They created a comfortable, familiar community in the midst of a strange land.

Most East Europeans lived on the Lower East Side of New York, an area that had become a Jewish ghetto during the past eighty years. Early in the nineteenth century a small colony of Jewish immigrants settled there. In the 1830s and 1840s, Dutch, German, and Polish Jews followed them. With the later arrival of East European Jews, the Lower East Side became a nation within a nation — or, more accurately, a cluster of nations within a nation. A map of the settlement patterns of Russian, Galician, Austro-Hungarian, Romanian, and Levantine Jews reveals boundaries among the groups as distinct as national frontiers. By 1900 the Lower East Side was one of the most crowded places in the world, with more than a half million Jews in concentrations of as many as seven hundred per acre. This was the most crowded section of the city, containing only about one-eightieth of the land, but one-sixth of the population. One observer wrote: "The architecture seemed to sweat humanity at every window and door."

Such crowding was made possible in part by new building techniques and in part by forbearance by the inhabitants. New York City lots were twenty-five feet wide and roughly a hundred feet deep. The first tenements consisted of private houses that were converted into apartments. But with increased crowding, a more efficient system was required. In 1879 a contest was held with the prize going to the best apartment design. The winning plan was the now infamous "dumbbell" tenement, so named because it was shaped like a weightlifter's bar and weights.

The typical dumbbell tenement had from six to seven stories, each floor with four apartments containing a kitchen, a sitting room, and one or two bedrooms. Only the rooms facing the street or the ten-foot deep backyard had fresh air. Other rooms faced a foul air shaft or had no windows. One toilet served all the inhabitants on each floor. Under the best of conditions these rooms would seem confining, even for a small family. But many were occupied by families with five or six children. Also there were boarders, individuals or whole families, who shared an apartment with the renters, sleeping in the kitchen or sharing the other rooms and helping to pay the rent of $10 to $20 a month. Through the summer men and women slept in the yards or on roofs or fire escapes to avoid the stifling closeness of the tenement apartments. In one week during August 1896 the temperature averaged 90 degrees and 420 New Yorkers died of the heat.

With all its limitations, the tenement apartment still offered shelter, both physical and psychological, from the abrasive world in which the immigrant must find work. The search for steady employment was frequently the most trying and disorienting feature of immigrant life. Many artisan immigrants had to find work in new areas. Some

went to work in sweatshops, small manufacturing establishments producing clothing, cigars, and other products. Others became small
merchants — with a pushcart and a bushel of apples one could easily
become a peddler on the busy ghetto streets. With a little more money,
one could rent a small street-front store with a tenement apartment in
the rear.

Mary Antin's father was one of many immigrants who drifted —or
rather was beaten — from one job to another. Her family settled in
Boston, but their experience coincided with that of Russian Jews in New
York, Cleveland, and elsewhere. At first, Mary's father and a partner ran
a refreshment stand on Crescent Beach, selling cold lemonade; hot
peanuts; pink popcorn; and their own potato chips, which were "thin as
tissue paper, crisp as dry snow, and salty as the sea." Mary writes: "I
admired greatly our shining soda fountain, the rows of sparkling glasses,
the pyramids of oranges, the sausage chains, the neat white counter and
the bright array of spoons. . . . I thought my father looked very well in
a long white apron and shirt sleeves. He dished out ice cream with
enthusiasm. So I supposed he was getting rich."

Then a problem arose with the law — something about the business license and selling on Sunday, the Christian Sabbath. At any rate,
the family had to abandon the beautiful refreshment stand. Mr. Antin
rented a basement store, purchased a stock of sugar, flour, crackers,
potatoes, kerosene, kindling wood, and penny candy, and again he was
in business. But trade was not brisk. Mary's older sister and mother had
to go to work. And even then they dreaded the landlady's weekly visits
and the humiliating need to ask for more time to pay the rent.

Experiences such as these awaited many immigrants. Russian Jews
frequently wrote boastful letters to their countrymen, saying that in
America all men were equal, that the peddler was as respected as the
capitalist. But the egalitarian dream could not hide the miserable
working conditions of many immigrants. Ephraim Lisitzky, a poet,
described a poignant scene in which he first encountered the reality of
immigrant labor on the sordid fringes of the American economy. As a
fifteen-year-old boy he traveled from Russia to the United States to join
his father, who had immigrated eight years before. After a confusing
search, he found the roominghouse in Boston where his father lived.
There he waited at the doorstep for his father's return. "Suddenly," he
writes, "a figure came towards me through a rosy mist. As it approached,
the mist lifted and I saw it, radiant and compassionate. I leaped up —it
was my father. In the dusk my father's face loomed up from the street.
He walked heavily, bent under a sack filled with rags and bottles. His
face was dark and hard with an expression of mingled humiliation and
forgiveness." Like many other immigrants, Lisitzky spent his days

picking through trash cans, selecting the few items that could be resold.

Soon the younger Lisitsky had to go to work himself. Unable to find other employment, he borrowed a peddler's basket and strove to make a living. He writes:

> I chose Tuesday, a lucky day in Jewish tradition, to embark on my peddling experience.
>
> It was a rainy autumn day. The wind shook my basket and whipped the shoelaces dangling from my hand into my face. I trudged down the street like a doomed man on his way to the gallows. Whenever anybody looked at me I lowered my eyes in shame. I approached a house whose number was the numerical equivalent of a verse of Scripture I had in mind, timidly mounted the stairs and couldn't bring my hand to knock at the door. At last I knocked diffidently. The door opened. I stood in the doorway with downcast face, and inquired clumsily in a low voice:
>
> "Maybe the lady wants matches?"
>
> "Matches?" The woman at the door responded sardonically. "Come in and I'll show you the piles of matches the peddler already supplied me with — enough to burn up all of the houses in Boston!"

Lisitzky moved on to other houses, but at the end of day he had not sold a thing. Not only was he forced to become a peddler, but he was not even good at it. At the synagogue he wept inwardly. Life was hard in the land of the free.

Most East European Jews on the Lower East Side made their livings in ways only slightly more rewarding than the Lisitzkys'. The majority eked out a humble existence as peddlers, small shopkeepers, or factory workers. In 1890 the garment trade alone employed thirteen thousand workers on the Lower East Side. In 1900, 50 percent of the city's industrial labor force worked in the area, laboring many hours for small wages.

With poor housing and employment, one would expect the Lower East Side to have been a depressing place. And yet, surprisingly, it was not. The area was crowded, and most of its people were poor, but it displayed an impressive vitality. Jacob Epstein, one of America's finest artists in this century, traced his creativity to his youth among the ghetto's "unique and crowded humanity." Bertha, a character in Henry Roth's classic novel, *Call It Sleep,* preferred the ghetto to her small European home because, she said, "There's always a stir here." Even William Dean Howells, a distinguished visitor well acquainted with the wealthiest and most cultivated homes in America, was impressed with the vigor of New York's Jews. "I found them," he wrote, "usually cheerful in the Hebrew quarter. . . . I was struck by men's heroic superiority to their fate, if their fate is hard."

Observations such as these — and there are scores of them — suggest that our account of poor housing and hard work only touches the surface of the immigrant experience. Despite these hardships an infectious vigor enlivened the Lower East Side. Its people were among the healthiest in the city; drunkenness, suicide, and crime rates were relatively low. Their families were strong. An energy affected the newcomer and startled the visitor who walked among the merchants on Hester Street who hawked trinkets, food, and clothes; through crowded streets with their signs in Yiddish and Hebrew where half-crazed Christian missionaries sometimes sought to win converts; past the tenement apartments, so closely packed that one could smell the neighbors' cooking and hear the neighbors' arguments; and among the shops and theaters of the Lower East Side.

What was the source of this energy? In part it was a sense of expectation: a better world was at hand. America meant freedom and opportunity. We may read that same anticipation in a letter written by John Winthrop in frontier Boston almost three centuries before. Settled among people who were ill fed, poorly housed, and wracked by disease, he had written home to his wife, "We are here in a Paradise." Like the Puritans before them, the East European Jews believed that they were on the brink of a better life.

Sometimes this confidence was broken by too many days spent picking rags from gutters and trash cans or by too many nights of hunger and crowding. But it could feed on many things: the sight of exotic new objects such as a rocking chair; the availability of inexpensive goods — peaches for a penny a quart, eyeglasses for 35 cents, fancy underwear for less than a dollar. And then, too, the chance to prosper was there. The man with the cart might own a store. The storekeeper could build a chain of stores. The tenement dweller might one day have a real tub, hot running water, an inside toilet, and — to vanquish winter's chill — "stimm hitt."

Around them were indications that such visions were not entirely fanciful. Already a few German Jewish merchants had become fabulously wealthy in merchandising. Isidor and Nathan Straus had built Macy's into the largest department store in the world. Julius Rosenwald increased sales at Sears, Roebuck to $50 million per annum. Other Jews entered the professions. By 1900 New York City had five hundred Jewish doctors. Jewish intellectuals included philosophers Felix Adler and Morris Cohen, social scientists E.R.A. Seligman and Franz Boas, and journalists Walter Lippmann and Joseph Pulitzer.

Signs of success appeared on the Lower East Side. Physicians and dentists occupied fancy brownstone houses along East Broadway, the grand boulevard of the new community. The avenue was also the Jewish newspaper row, commanded by the ten-story *Jewish Daily Forward* building on Seward Park. Nearby were the Educational Alliance and the Jewish Maternity Hospital. On Grand Street were several large department stores, and the Bowery had the world's largest savings bank. Few immigrants, of course, ever became department store owners, or newspaper editors, or doctors. But for them there were other rewards. After becoming a citizen, one could vote just like any other American. On the Lower East Side, as in the rest of New York City, celebration bonfires were lit on election day. One could move freely from one part of the country to another and send one's children to free public schools. If a man's own dreams seemed unattainable, he could at least provide his children a chance for advancement. One of the most eloquent passages in Mary Antin's *Promised Land* tells of her father's taking his three daughters to their first day in school. Business success, even the ability to learn English, had eluded Mr. Antin. But his daughters could aspire to a better life. She writes:

> So it was with a heart full of longing and hope that my father led us to school on that first day. He took long strides in his eagerness, the rest of us running and hopping to keep up.
>
> At last the four of us stood around the teacher's desk; and my father, in his impossible English, gave us over in her charge, with some broken word of his hopes for us that his swelling heart could no longer contain. . . .
>
> I think Miss Nixon [the teacher] guessed what my father's best English could not convey. I think she divined that by the simple act of delivering our school certificates to her he took possession of America.

By entering the public school, the Jewish child gained the opportunity to learn the American language and customs. At home, in the street, and in the Jewish cheder, which supplemented public education with Jewish training, he met the rich culture of his own ancestors. Like the Puritans and other early American immigrants, the Russian Jews hoped to keep alive their heritage while living a fuller life in a new country. This aspiration nourished the remarkable cultural activity of the Lower East Side, with its journals, clubs, and plays. One of the foremost agencies of Jewish culture at the turn of the century was the Yiddish theater, with the finest drama in New York for its time. The shows were inexpensive, exciting, and responsive to audience interests.

In 1900 New York had three Yiddish theaters — the Jewish Peoples, the Thalia, and the Windsor. The plays usually revolved around leading stars, such as Jacob P. Adler and Bertha Kalish, Sigmund Feinman, David Kessler, and Boris Tomashefsky, all idols of the Lower East Side, onstage and off. The plots dealt with stock situations, and one of the foremost writers, "Professor" Horowitz, could write a play a day. The plays often dealt with a topic of paramount interest to immigrants in a new land, the tension between Jewish traditions and a more secular America. Many plays pitted unfaithful children against parents who had sacrificed for them.

For many years a number of Yiddish theater performances were more compelling than anything on Broadway, which mainly featured light musicals and vaudeville. Musicals fared best with the Yiddish audience when songs inspired by Russian cantors' chants were added to programs. The Yiddish theater began its decline only when the American mass media began to draw the best Jewish theatrical talents: men such as the Warner brothers, Sam Goldwyn, Douglas Fairbanks, and Louis B. Mayer, who became pillars of the motion-picture industry.

Other agencies of Jewish culture came along: social clubs where people went for company, debate, and intellectual discussion; the Young Men's Hebrew Association; and various charitable associations. When Jews were denied access to Christian hospitals, they formed their own, including Mt. Sinai in New York and Beth Israel in Boston. Other cultural activities took place in cafes, centers for talk, of which there were three hundred in New York in 1905.

The most important Jewish cultural agency was, of course, the synagogue. As new immigrants came and new religious beliefs spread, the number of synagogues spread rapidly. In New York there were 14 in 1854, 150 in 1890, and 300 in 1900. Many were simply storefronts and other simple edifices and were administered from day to day by a *shamas,* a religious functionary with little status, because rabbis were in short supply. The work of shamas and rabbi was supplemented by that of other religious figures, notably the *shohet,* or ritual slaughterer; a *mohel,* who performed the traditional circumcision; and the *maschgiach,* who inspected dietary regulations.

Despite the proliferation of synagogues and religious functionaries, religious devotion tended to decline. Proportionately fewer rabbis than laymen migrated, and a tendency to reduce the number of the essential elements of the faith spread. And so, too, followed a trend toward religious apathy. Also many men and women became actively antireligious — secular in their outlook on life. Mainly socialists, anarchists, and freethinkers, they claimed that organized religion was reactionary and took the fervor of faith into advocacy for secular reform. At their most extreme, they scoffed at Jewish religious laws and customs, and even held Yom Kippur balls on the night of the recitation of the *Kol Nidre* when most Jews were in the synagogue praying and fasting.

Such events were exceptional and transitory. For the most part, immigrants sought to perpetuate their traditional culture. After all, for centuries they had preserved a distinctive Jewish culture in a hostile European environment. In New York they formed the largest concentration of Jews anywhere in the world and throughout America were comparatively free to worship, think, and behave as they pleased. In newspapers, cafes, clubs, and the theater they now had the freedom to fulfill their traditions as Jews.

But despite these influences for continuity, the American experience began subtly to undermine Jewish traditions. Even if the adults tried to maintain the old traditions, the children were frequently drawn away. The free public schools, which gave them opportunities undreamed of in Russia, taught them a new language and exposed them to a new religion — the Lord's Prayer and other Christian customs were observed in many schools. Children who used Yiddish rather than English were laughed at, and they quickly learned English, sometimes even refusing afterward to speak Yiddish at home. Immigrants established schools to provide supplementary Jewish training, but they were often poorly taught and ill attended. Many boys would attend special classes only for a few weeks before the Bar Mitzvah, the ceremonial observance of their passage to manhood. But in 1908 only 28 percent of New York's Jewish children were receiving any Jewish training. As the children grew up, most did not support the Yiddish journals and theater.

For some immigrants this casting off of the old ways was a matter for self-congratulation. Mary Antin considered that she had been reborn in America. She was pleased to have abandoned the "medieval" practices and beliefs of her native Russian village and to have adopted the seemingly wider vision of her new land. She did not even object to saying the Lord's Prayer in school, and she called herself by the Christian name, Mary, given her by the immigration officials.

As the twentieth century progressed, the Jewish standard of living improved until it matched that of other Americans. Many Jews moved out of the Lower East Side to other communities and to the suburbs. In 1892, 75 percent of New York's Jews lived on the Lower East Side; by 1916 the proportion was only 23 percent. These were signs of material success, but some of the best Jewish spokesmen feared that success might debase the immigrant, that American materialism might be more damaging than Russian tyranny, that a priceless heritage might be lost.

Ironically, these laments found their counterpart among white Anglo-Saxon Protestant Americans, who worried that their own heritage would be undermined by Jews and other nonwhite or non-Protestant Americans. The new immigration with its heavy concentration on East and South Europeans brought to America millions of people who seemed disturbingly different from the descendants of earlier, North European immigrants. In 1916 Madison Grant published the classic statement of these fears, *The Passing of the Great Race.* Grant claimed that ethnic minorities were undermining primitive American virtues.

Prejudice against the new immigrants found its way into public policies. Restaurants, hotels, clubs, jobs, even whole neighborhoods were closed to Jews. Organizations such as the Immigration Restriction League lobbied to curtail immigration to the United States.

During the 1920s hostility to Jews, as well as to other ethnic minorities, was formalized in prejudicial quotas in educational institutions and hospitals. It found the highest sanction in the adoption of the National Origins Act of 1924, a law restricting immigration to the United States to 150,000 annually and establishing quotas that favored the North European peoples over the new immigrants of the previous fifty years. It remained substantially unchanged until 1965 when a new system, based on America's need for skills, was adopted.

The enactment of the National Origins Act should remind us that American nativistic hostility toward East European Jews included other immigrant groups. Like the Jews, Italian, Irish, Greek, Chinese, and Japanese immigrants hoped to improve themselves by becoming Americans. Like the Jews, these other groups have retained ethnic characteristics in their religion, culture, food, and holidays. And all have had to overcome the prejudice spawned by that side of the American character which fears change or diversity. For years many employment ads included the warning, "No Irish Need Apply." Chinese and Japanese immigrants have faced even worse persecution: in Tacoma, Washington, all the Chinese were driven out of town in 1885, and throughout the West in the 1940s hundreds of thousands of Japanese Americans were interned in detention camps.

Despite the enormity of such events that isolated and wounded the immigrants, the constructive relationships between old and new Americans have been many. Historians and sociologists have argued about the correct way of describing this accommodation. One description, using the image of a melting pot, suggests that all Americans have merged into a common national character, composed of its many antecedents. Another thesis suggests that America is a "pluralistic" society or a "mosaic" consisting of many kinds of people. Surely there is truth in each of these propositions. Jewish Americans, Irish Americans, Chinese Americans, Anglo Americans, black Americans, and native Americans all have distinctive heritages. But at the same time, radio, television, and films, as well as American mobility, democracy, and business have formed an amalgamated society in which all Americans take some part.

We miss some of the richness of American history, however, if we move too quickly from the early to the late twentieth century. For history is not only what people become. It is also what they are and were. And not so long ago when Admiral Dewey conquered the Spanish fleet in Manila, and Theodore Roosevelt was elected president, and John Muir advocated a Yosemite National Park, America was the home of 10 million men, women, and children from other quarters of the globe. We might close with a picture of the sons and daughters of the Russian Jewish immigrants teaching public school or producing Hollywood films. Let us leave them, rather, in history — attending classes in the cheder, shopping in the open-air markets on Hester Street, hurrying to a Yiddish play at the Thalia — part Jewish, part Russian, part American: bemused, challenged, and intensely alive.

QUESTIONS

1. In what respects did Jews prosper in Russia? In what ways did they have a distinct culture? How were they discriminated against?

2. Why was Mary Antin so enthusiastic about going to the United States? What did America mean to her?

3. The author claims that despite their hardships the Russian Jews built strong, healthy communities in the United States. What hardships did they encounter? How were they discriminated against? What evidence do we have of their vitality?

4. In what respects were Jewish immigrants able to preserve their traditional cultures in the New World? In what ways did the new environment undermine their traditions?

5. Why was the National Origins Act passed in 1924?

6. The United States has been described as a melting pot and as a mosaic. Which analogy best summarizes the early experience of the East European Jews? Explain your answer.

BIBLIOGRAPHY

ANTIN, MARY. *The Promised Land* (1912). Autobiography by a young woman who adapted readily to American life.

DINNERSTEIN, LEONARD, AND DAVID REIMERS. *Ethnic Americans: A History of Immigration and Assimilation* (1982). Good overview of immigrant history.

HANDLIN, OSCAR. *The Uprooted* (1951 and later editions). Evocative recreation of immigrant experience.

HIGHAM, JOHN. *Strangers in the Land* (1955). Classic history of American nativism.

HOWE, IRVING. *World of Our Fathers* (1976). Thorough and beautifully written account of East European Jewish immigration.

RISCHIN, MOSES. *The Promised City* (1970). Focuses on Jews in New York City, 1870-1914

ROTH, HENRY. *Call It Sleep* (1934). Haunting novel about Jewish immigrant life in New York.

SCHULBERG, BUDD. *What Makes Sammy Run* (1941 and later editions). Lively account of an unscrupulous second-generation American who claws his way from New York poverty to Hollywood splendor.

Takaki, Ronald. *Strangers from a Different Shore* (1989). Describes the Asian-American immigrant experience.

6

EXPANDING
AMERICAN DEMOCRACY

The Woman Suffrage Victory

Critics of woman suffrage predicted dire consequences if men abandoned their monopoly on politics. Women's weak minds and delicate temperaments could not survive the hurly-burly of public life. The complexity of politics and the rough election-day crowds would either frighten women into simpering fools or transform them into unnatural amazons. Gone would be the charm and serenity of the tender sex, the woman's capacity to create havens of domestic tranquility in a tumultuous world. With such arguments many Americans sought to deny women the ballot. But woman suffragists said "Nonsense!" to the romantic fiction of the female incapacity for electoral politics. In a democracy, they argued, it was indecent to leave half the citizens unrepresented because of their sex. These reformers, men as well as women, fought seventy years for woman suffrage. Their campaigns won success at the height of the Progressive movement, and yet many progressives, while embracing other reforms, were reluctant to support woman suffrage. A woman's right to vote would soon seem as natural as her right to live, but the change came only after a long struggle.

On the bright cold afternoon of March 4, 1913, hundreds of thousands of spectators crowded the streets of Washington, D.C., hoping to catch a glimpse of a colorful parade. This was inauguration week for Woodrow Wilson, the country's first Democratic president in sixteen years, but the pageant was designed to impress rather than honor Wilson. Planned by women's-rights suffragists, it advertised women's accomplishments and dramatized the need for woman suffrage.

The affair began with an allegory presented by dancers and an orchestra on the steps of the Treasury Building. The air was chill, but the sky overhead was a perfect blue. Thousands stood watching as the performers, dressed in rainbow-colored robes representing Justice, Charity, Liberty, and Hope, moved across the steps. The dancers paused, and a woman in pure white depicting Peace appeared from behind one of the massive columns of the Treasury. While the orchestra played the "Lohengrin Overture," she held out her hands and released a dove into the bright sky. The cold wind blew ripples through the light airy costumes of the dancers, and detractors predicted that the whole cast would be confined to their beds the following day. But, according to a *New York Times* reporter, "The real suffragists said it was heroic."

When the pageant ended, the suffrage advocates, five thousand strong, took their places in the women's parade. This was one of the most elaborate processions ever assembled in the national capital. Floats depicted the worldwide struggle for woman suffrage, the history of the American struggle for equality, and the activities of women in households, farms, the professions, and government. Some of the women rode on the floats; others marched between them carrying their state flags or yellow banners with the slogan "VOTES FOR WOMEN."

The marchers had come from all over the United States. Illinois women reserved a whole train and employed women porters; their "manless special" attracted much attention, and at every stop along the route the women gave speeches and poured tea for visitors. Among the women in the parade were all the notable leaders of the suffrage movement, including Dr. Anna Howard Shaw, president of the National American Woman Suffrage Association. The most popular figure with the crowd was "General" Rosalie Jones, who had left New York several weeks before, leading her women on a long march to the Capitol. Now she walked along briskly with her followers, carrying a yellow pilgrim staff and a large bouquet of roses. Among the marchers were large contingents of black women, writers, artists, physicians, lawyers, businesswomen, and "just wives."

A group of women rode on horseback at the front of the parade, led by Inez Milholland, a striking figure in a white broadcloth cossack suit. As she turned on to Pennsylvania Avenue, she beheld an astonishing sight. Along the route hundreds of thousands of spectators filled the Capitol mall. The crowd surged on to the avenue, pressing upon the marchers. The police, not having anticipated so many people, were virtually helpless.

The proximity of marching women and audience elicited a range of responses to the suffrage cause. Everywhere there were signs of support. Houses were decorated with yellow bunting, representing the women's movement, intertwined with the patriotic red, white, and blue. Thousands of spectators wore yellow "VOTES FOR WOMEN" buttons. Men expressed their support by wearing badges or marching with the National Men's League for Woman Suffrage. Boy Scout troops and National Guard units helped control the crowd. Maj. J.M. Shindel of the Pennsylvania National Guard threw flowers in the path of Rosalie Jones and her pilgrims, shouting, "Nothing's too good for you!"

There were, however, other men and women who were less friendly to the suffragists. Some wore satirical badges proclaiming "VOTES FOR MEN" or depicting men's trousers with "VOTES FOR WOMEN" patches sewed over the bottoms. Others jeered or threw cigarette butts at the marchers. Drunken men tried to climb aboard the floats. A policeman shouted at Genevieve Stone, the wife of an Illinois congressman, "If my wife were where you are, I'd break her head."

The sun set before the last of the parade moved down Pennsylvania Avenue, marking the end of a day both exhilarating and exhausting. One of the featured speakers, the blind deaf-mute Helen Keller, was so tired that she was unable to take part in the concluding ceremonies. The parade and its audience had symbolized better than its planners might have wished both the excitement and the frustration of the woman suffrage movement.

Although the pageant and march had been successful productions, the opposition along the route had best represented the predominant mood of the American people. One hundred and forty years had passed since the beginning of the American Revolution, but in 1913 women still did not enjoy equal rights. The American democracy was primarily a male democracy. Representative government still meant representation for men only.

There were many reasons for the long postponement of woman suffrage. Political machines that ran many state and local governments were reluctant to introduce a new set of voters into the electoral system. Organizations like Tammany Hall in New York were accustomed to working with traditional male clientele and considered women voters an unknown force that might threaten their power. Businessmen feared the influence of women's votes on working conditions in their factories: nonvoting women and children could be employed in poor conditions at low wages, and their bosses feared that woman suffrage might damage this profitable arrangement. The liquor interests felt threatened by sexual equality at the polls because the Prohibition crusade drew much of its strength from women.

All these groups considered woman suffrage a direct challenge to their power. Other Americans opposed the movement on ideological grounds. Voting would overtax women's inferior intellects. Popular journals ran articles on such subjects as "Why the Vote Would Be Injurious to Women" and "Famed Biologist's Warning on the Peril in Votes for Women." A woman's proper place was in the home. Here she should create a comfortable atmosphere, a haven of decency sheltered from the abrasive struggles of the outside world. All these advantages could be lost if women began to vote. When women went to the polls, they would be exposed to the corrupt influence of dissolute men. Worse, by choosing their own political candidates they might become independent of their husbands and lose their traditional attitude of subservience. The pillars of civilization would come crashing down, and all would be chaos.

It was ironic that such attitudes toward woman suffrage should come out in a time generally known as the Progressive era. During the presidential administrations of Roosevelt, Taft, and Wilson, the government passed many laws designed to reform American society. Theodore Roosevelt's "trustbusting" along with his creation of the Department of Commerce and Labor curtailed some abusive actions of big business. The Pure Food and Drug Act and the Meat Inspection Act guaranteed a better diet for Americans. Other acts strengthened the Interstate Commerce Commission, regulated the railroads, and provided for equitable use of the national forests. Wilson would continue the earlier Republican reform momentum with new trust regulations, the Federal Reserve Act, and laws protecting labor.

The apparent interest of progressivism in the underdog makes the delay in woman suffrage seem inexplicable. But the continuing opposition to expanding the electorate was not entirely inconsistent with the Progressive impulse. Reforms early in the twentieth century were understood mostly from a conservative point of view. Political reform would return the government to the traditional middle- and upper-middle-class leaders. Business regulation would restore the traditional competitive marketplace. The ideal Progressive world was mostly white, male, and native. It mattered little to the reformers that in the early twentieth century most blacks lost the chance to vote and that restriction of immigration gained popularity. Blacks and immigrants were not part of the traditional ruling elite.

Some women's leaders even tried to capitalize on the prevailing mood of ethnic conservatism to strengthen their demands for woman suffrage, arguing that their votes would strengthen the white middle-class electorate, because proportionately fewer immigrants than natives had wives. Others took part in reform programs, advocating Prohibition and conducting social welfare programs, thereby gaining administrative experience and wider support for suffrage.

Despite such efforts, however, the suffrage movement had failed to register many gains in the early Progressive period. In fact, the history of woman suffrage in the sixty-five years since the demand for votes was first made at the Seneca Falls Convention in 1848 had been painfully slow. At that gathering Elizabeth Cady Stanton had introduced a resolution stating: "It is the duty of women of this country to secure to themselves their sacred right to the elective franchise." The meeting and its suffrage resolution had been ridiculed by the press, but once the issue was raised Stanton devoted much of her life to the suffrage cause. In 1850 she met Susan B. Anthony, the Quaker daughter of a local mill operator, and tried to win her over to the cause. Anthony was a temperance reformer who initially showed little interest in women's rights issues. But when she was barred from speaking at a major temperance convention because she was a woman, she recognized the significance of Stanton's interest. In 1852 the two women formed a partnership that would be the most important factor in the first half century of the suffrage movement.

They campaigned for a broad program of reform, organizing meetings, speaking, distributing pamphlets, and circulating petitions. In 1860 they won a major victory in persuading the New York Legislature to adopt a law giving married women the right to their wages — which had formerly belonged to their husbands — and allowing them for the first time to sue in court. With the beginning of the Civil War they turned to the cause of emancipation, identifying their own aspirations for liberation with that of the slaves.

When constitutional amendments were proposed guaranteeing rights to former slaves, they hoped they would be so worded as to encompass women's rights. But many male abolitionists refused to support their demands, holding that "This is the Negro's hour," and the amendments did nothing for women. Despite this setback, women pursued a variety of strategies to publicize their cause. In 1866 Elizabeth Cady Stanton ran for Congress as an independent, and Susan B. Anthony presented a suffrage petition to Congress with several thousand signatures. Stanton lost by 12,000 votes to 24, and Anthony's petition failed to persuade Congress to act. In 1867 the two women campaigned unsuccessfully for a state woman suffrage law in Kansas. In the following year they persuaded a supporter to introduce a woman

Susan B. Anthony. For almost sixty years she was one of the most dedicated and skillful leaders of the women's rights movement.

suffrage amendment in Congress, but the bill received no support. Defeat followed upon defeat, but the women continued their work.

In 1869, twenty-one years after the Seneca Falls Convention, the two women founded the National Woman Suffrage Association, with Stanton as president. Stanton's keynote address to that organization was one of her most forceful statements on behalf of women's rights. She compared women with peasants, serfs, and slaves. "Of all kinds of aristocracy," she declared, "that of sex is the most odious and unnatural; invading, as it does, our homes, desecrating our family altars, dividing those whom God has joined together, exalting the son above the mother who bore him, and subjugating, everywhere, moral power to brute force."

Stanton, Anthony, and other members of the new association traveled throughout the country speaking on women's rights and forming suffrage organizations. Stanton was the more eloquent speaker; Anthony was particularly adept at arranging meetings, hiring halls, and handling the other details of administration. But progress was slow. During the first two decades of their organization they won only a few, widely scattered victories. In 1869 the Territory of Wyoming, where men greatly outnumbered women, became the first region in the United

States to adopt woman suffrage. (In 1890 Wyoming was admitted to statehood and so became the first state to permit women to vote.) In 1876 Stanton won publicity for the cause by drafting the Woman's Declaration of Rights at the Philadelphia Centennial Exposition. Two years later she and Anthony persuaded California Senator Aaron A. Sargeant to introduce the federal woman suffrage amendment into Congress. The amendment would be reintroduced periodically until 1919.

In 1890 the National Woman Suffrage Association joined forces with a rival organization, the American Woman Suffrage Association, to form the National American Woman Suffrage Association with Stanton as president. She retired two years later, and Anthony followed in the office until 1900. During the last decade of the century many suffragists attempted to capitalize on the nativistic mood of the times and emphasized their deep roots in the nation's past. Many had felt cheated by the Civil War experience, where they had supported the underdog blacks, only to have the ex-slaves receive freedom before they did. They were less willing now to take up the cause of the immigrant.

By 1900 both Stanton and Anthony were in their eighties and had to curtail their suffrage activities. Stanton died in 1902, and Anthony died in 1906, a few weeks after delivering an address to a Baltimore suffrage convention in which she declared, "Failure is impossible." During the final years of the founders, new suffragists began to emerge on the national scene. The most important was Carrie Chapman Catt, who had grown up in Iowa, where she was a teacher, school principal, and journalist. In 1890 she attended the first convention of the National American Woman Suffrage Association and immediately became one of its foremost supporters. Her husband, a wealthy California civil engineer, supported her reform interests and even signed a personal contract with Carrie allowing her to spend two months in the spring and two more in the fall devoted entirely to the suffrage movement. In the 1890s Catt assumed many of Susan B. Anthony's administrative responsibilities, raising funds and organizing branch offices for the NAWSA. In 1900 when Anthony retired, Carrie Chapman Catt took over as president. She immediately worked to strengthen the nationwide organization and to build up the suffrage treasury. She remained president until 1904 when her husband's illness required her to retire temporarily.

Catt's successor, Anne Howard Shaw, was a licensed preacher and physician who had received a theological degree from Boston University in 1886. She is generally credited with being one of the ablest and sincerest suffrage orators of her day, and under her guidance the NAWSA grew from seventeen thousand to two hundred thousand members. But she was less adept at administration than Anthony and

Catt. During the eleven years of her presidency, the NAWSA lost much of its administrative control over local activities.

The fortunes of woman suffrage were not dependent, however, solely on the activities of the national president. The movement gained strength early in the twentieth century through the activities of hundreds of local suffragist organizers and thousands of workers. Pauline Agassiz Shaw, for example, became one of the movement's great financial supporters. Her husband, a New England mining magnate, encouraged her to use the family fortune for many benevolent activities, including experimental kindergartens and day-care centers. Through the child-care centers Shaw became acquainted with the problems of working mothers and began to think about the larger issues of women's rights. She regarded woman suffrage not only as a desirable goal but, even more important, as a means to greater ends. If women could vote, she believed, they would reform politics, improve working conditions, and increase chances for world peace. In 1901 she founded the Boston Equal Suffrage Association for Good Government.

Jane Addams, the best-known social worker of the Progressive era, also came to see woman suffrage as a way of achieving wider social reform. She believed that the greatest problem in city life was the dismal condition of urban households; because women were closest to the problems of home life, they would be most likely to rectify them if they had the power to vote.

Another suffragist, Harriot Stanton Blatch, was brought up with sensitivity to women's issues by her mother, Elizabeth Cady Stanton. Harriot Blatch lived in England for many years with her husband before returning to the United States in 1902. She brought with her appreciation for the more dramatic tactics of the British woman suffrage movement, and she organized such activities as parades, political campaigns against suffrage opponents, and the organization of working women.

The suffragists represented a wide gamut of political sensibilities. Some, like Bell Kearney of Mississippi, believed that woman suffrage would help maintain the superiority of America's traditional rulers. She argued that woman suffrage with a literacy requirement would greatly increase the ratio of white to black voters in the South. The South, she said, should "look to its Anglo-Saxon women as the medium through which to retain the supremacy of the white race over the African." Others, however, like Jane Addams and Pauline Shaw, believed that suffrage would help elevate the poorer classes.

In the early 1900s the movement gained increasing support from poorer women laborers. Caroline A. Lowe, a suffragist from Kansas City, Missouri, and a wage earner herself, presented an eloquent appeal on behalf of 7 million working women to the 1912 NAWSA Convention. "From the standpoint of wages received," she said, "we wage earners know it to be almost universal that the men in the industries receive twice the amount granted to us although we may be doing the same work. We work side by side with our brothers; we are children of the same parents, reared in the same homes, educated in the same schools, ride to and fro on the same early morning and late evening cars, work together the same number of hours in the same shop and we have equal need of food, clothing and shelter. But at 21 years of age our brothers are given a powerful weapon for self-defense, a larger means for growth and self-expression." Lowe argued that this weapon, the vote, being denied to women, left her a victim of the economic marketplace.

Relying on the activities of thousands of local organizers like Caroline Lowe, the suffragist movement pinned its hopes on local victories. Throughout the United States suffragists delivered speeches from automobiles and on street corners, lobbied in state legislatures, gave speeches, published tracts, and circulated petitions. In 1915 they nearly won one of the most important local contests, the fight for the vote in New York. In that campaign they held block parties and street dances; established special days for visiting firemen, policemen, railroad workers, and other groups of men; and campaigned from door to door in every section of the state. To dramatize the prejudice that gave new immigrants the vote before women, they sent delegates of university women to sit in the audience clad in cap and gown, unenfranchised, as new males were sworn as citizens. On the morning of election day when the suffrage issue went before the voters, they sent poll watchers to every voting place, armed with coffee and sandwiches for themselves and for male poll workers, and watched to see that the election was honest. But on election eve they learned that they had been defeated. In New York City when the news arrived, there was a moment's silence, then one of the women declared, "Who'll go with me now and start a new campaign with a street meeting." Manhattan soon had its first suffragist rally of the new campaign.

Elsewhere the local campaigns had already produced suffrage victories. At the time of the great 1913 Washington suffrage parade, nine states had adopted laws allowing women to vote. The suffrage states — Wyoming, Colorado, Utah, Idaho, Washington, California, Arizona, Kansas, and Oregon — were all western states with relatively small populations in which men generally outnumbered women. Altogether, the suffrage states commanded only fifty-four electoral votes.

It was a start, but some of the suffragists felt that the movement was going too slowly and that more should be done on the national level. The foremost leader of the militant suffragists was a young woman named Alice Paul. Like many other women's rights leaders, she was reared in a Quaker household. In 1908 she had gone to England to do research for a doctorate in social work from the University of Pennsylvania. She joined the British suffragist movement and became acquainted with its leader, Emmeline Pankhurst.

English suffragists employed tactics far more radical than those of their American counterparts. They planted bombs, destroyed mail, burned men's clubs and social pavilions, damaged golf courses, and even attempted to take the royal jewels from the Tower of London. Alice Paul did not engage in these more violent forms of protest, but she did become a suffragist speaker and attempted to interrupt public meetings with suffrage demands. She was arrested seven times, including once in Norwich when she attempted to deliver a suffrage speech outside a hall where a young politician, Winston Churchill, was delivering a speech. "You didn't have to be a very good speaker," she once reflected, "because the minute you began you were arrested."

Upon returning to America in 1910 she joined the National American Woman Suffrage Association. She was disappointed by the organization because of its lack of militancy and its failure to push for the federal suffrage amendment, but through the influence of Jane Addams in 1912 she was appointed head of the NAWSA congressional committee. At the time she was only twenty-seven years old.

Her appointment at such an early age indicated the relative unimportance of the committee. Although it was responsible for encouraging congressional suffrage action, it had received a budget of only $10 during the previous year, and the former chair had managed to return change from that! Alice Paul inherited a list of suffrage supporters with her new job and found that most were either dead or had left the capital. The suffrage amendment, introduced so many years before through the influence of Susan B. Anthony and Elizabeth Cady Stanton, had not been reported out of committee since 1896.

Alice Paul was challenged rather than discouraged by the situation. With the help of Lucy Burns, whom she had met in prison in England, she instigated a vigorous suffrage campaign in the capital. With the approval of the NAWSA she organized the great Washington parade of 1913, sending invitations across the country, lining up families in Washington to house the visiting suffragists, and handling the details of parade organization. When a group of southern suffragists refused to march in the parade with black representatives of the National Association for the Advancement of Colored People, she appeased their delicate racial sensibilities by placing a men's contingent between them and the NAACP marchers. Alice Paul marched in a university section among scores of voteless women dressed in caps and gowns. Sixty years later in an interview for *American Heritage* she remembered the parade with fondness. The crowd was boisterous but friendly, she said. "Of course, we did hear a lot of shouted insults, which we always expected. You know, the usual things about why aren't you home in the kitchen where you belong."

In the following year Alice Paul established the Congressional Union for Woman Suffrage to raise funds for her congressional committee. Because the NAWSA provided almost no money for the federal campaign, she believed that she needed a separate budget. She soon established a strong organization, and with the help of fellow lobbyists she was able to persuade Congress to bring the suffrage bill to the House floor. The Congressional Union popularized the measure by calling it "the Susan B. Anthony Amendment." The bill was defeated that year in both the House and the Senate.

The leaders of the NAWSA observed the Congressional Union's activity with some apprehension. The parent organization was committed to a state-by-state movement and emphasized the grass-roots education of the voters. Alice Paul preferred the national approach, reasoning that Congress provided a smaller and more manageable group of people to work with. In 1914 NAWSA required Paul to resign her leadership of either the congressional committee or the Congressional Union. She chose to remain in charge of her own organization. Soon afterward the Congressional Union was deprived of its affiliation with the NAWSA and went its separate way.

The Congressional Union thrived as an independent organization. After the suffrage bill's congressional defeat in 1914, the Union campaigned against Democrats seeking reelection, contending that the party in power should be blamed for the failure of the suffrage amendment. Many of the women's targets were defeated, and suddenly the suffrage movement acquired political clout. In 1916 historian Charles Beard wrote an admiring description of the organization — now called the National Woman's party — in *The New Republic*. "It has ideas," he said, "but it does not wear them on its sleeve. . . . It does not beg, it does not wheedle, it does not whine. It wages a trench warfare with exactly the kind of weapons that men use. It knows that no other kind is effective. It speaks a language which the most seasoned and cynical politician can understand. It has money and organization and will and votes."

In 1916 woman suffrage states elected one fifth of the Senate, one seventh of the House of Representatives, and one sixth of the presidential electors. In that year, under heavy pressure from women's groups, both major parties adopted woman suffrage planks in their national platforms. But they both hedged their support by advocating state-by-state decisions rather than supporting the national suffrage amendment.

Acting on the principle that the party in power should be blamed for suffrage failure, the Woman's party campaigned against Woodrow Wilson. In so doing they gained their first martyr to their cause. Inez Milholland, who had led the Washington parade, was considered by the suffragists to be the most striking of their supporters, and they customarily placed her at the head of their parades. Her suffrage activism had begun in her undergraduate days at Vassar, where she held an illegal women's rights meeting in a local cemetery after the college president refused to allow the meeting on campus.

Inez Milholland was not struck down by bullets or bayonets, but she died dramatically, nonetheless. She and her sister, Vita, were touring the western states in 1916, campaigning against Wilson, when she collapsed from exhaustion while delivering an address in Los Angeles. Her legendary last words were: "Mr. President, how long must women wait for liberty?"

Woodrow Wilson would see those words hundreds of times in the next two years, for the Woman's party had them embroidered on suffrage banners and displayed them before the White House along with their party's purple, white, and gold standards. On January 7, 1917, Wilson, who had ridden to victory on the slogan "He Kept Us Out of War," received a delegation from the Woman's party but told them that he continued to favor a state-by-state approach to the suffrage question. On the following day the women created a "perpetual delegation" to the White House. Wilson refused to meet with any more delegates, claiming that the impending war required all his time. And so the women sent pickets to the White House from 10:00 A.M. to 5:30 P.M. six days a week. President Wilson was gracious enough, removing his hat and bowing to the women when he left the White House grounds for his daily drive, but he still refused to support the Anthony amendment.

On April 6, 1917, the United States entered the war with Germany, and many suffragists believed that women should postpone their activities until the end of the war. But the Woman's party, recalling that the same logic had damaged the women's movement during the Civil War, insisted on maintaining their daily vigil at the White House. They now came to be regarded as disloyal and suffered abuse from opponents, some of whom tore up their banners. The police made periodic sweeps of the picket lines, arresting several hundred women before the year's end for allegedly obstructing traffic.

On October 20, 1917, Alice Paul was arrested. She spent five horrifying weeks in prison, first in stuffy overcrowded cells with other suffragists, and then alone in a psychopathic ward. She was already so weakened by poor prison food that she could hardly walk, but she decided to dramatize her cause by going on a hunger strike. The prison hospital responded by force-feeding her through hard tubes pushed into her nose, a tactic that had been used in British prisons to break suffragist hunger strikes. Alice Paul knew that women had received permanent damage to their nasal passages and eyes from this technique. But she persisted.

Her situation was all the more intimidating because the prison doctors implied to her that she would be committed to an insane asylum, a move they could make without intervention by judge, jury, or lawyers. In the mental wing of the hospital she was further intimidated by an "observation" procedure that involved awakening her with a bright light once every hour all night long. Her cell window was boarded up.

Alice Paul was cut off from all friends and attorneys for several weeks, but finally Dudley Field Malone, one of the country's foremost lawyers, had the opportunity to see her. As often happens when a government abuses a well-known person, the tide of public sentiment shifted strongly in favor of Paul and her fellow suffragists. Through President Wilson's influence they were released from prison on November 27 and 28, 1917. Less than two months later, on January 19, 1918, Wilson came out in favor of woman suffrage. The next day the House of Representatives passed the Anthony amendment. But there remained the problems of winning Senate support for the measure and of persuading the necessary three fourths of the states to ratify.

Alice Paul's contribution to the woman suffrage movement was more dramatic than that of the moderate suffragists. But while she was capturing national headlines with confrontation tactics, thousands of suffragists were at work winning support state by state, city by city, and precinct by precinct. In New York City, Lillian D. Wald, who ran the Henry Street Settlement House on the Lower East Side, was especially influential. She took her commitment to suffrage into meetings with immigrants, housewives, and politicians. Her settlement house ran a visiting nurse program that sent one hundred nurses on 250,000 house calls throughout New York City in 1917. By their activity the nurses showed immigrant wives that a woman could be as resourceful as a man, and they frequently encouraged them to support the suffrage movement. The wives, in turn, influenced their husbands. When New York adopted woman suffrage in 1917, the Lower East Side approved by better than two to one.

The National American Woman Suffrage Association also took a crucial part in the final suffrage battles. In 1915 Carrie Chapman Catt again became president of the organization. Under her direction the NAWSA adopted the "Winning Plan" in its national convention in 1916. This was a combination of local and national activity. In Washing-

Carrie Chapman Catt. In the 1890s she and her husband agreed that she could devote four months a year to women's rights.

ton, Catt was an effective lobbyist, winning even President Wilson's personal admiration. In the states her workers helped win an impressive series of victories between 1916 and 1918.

The war also helped the women's cause. It required hundreds of thousands of women to fill "men's jobs" when male workers joined the armed forces. The idealistic Wilsonian war rhetoric, stressing human rights, further aided the suffragists. Alice Paul, in particular, turned the Wilsonian demand for justice abroad into another reason for justice to women at home. Moreover, woman suffrage now appeared to be on the threshold of worldwide approval. Russia and England had already given women the vote by 1918, and most Canadian provinces had enfranchised women. (England, however, required a woman to be thirty before she could vote.)

In May 1919 President Wilson called a special session of Congress to consider the suffrage amendment. Six more states had passed suffrage bills. The Eighteenth Amendment, prohibiting the sale of alcoholic beverages, had already passed, removing the incentive for the liquor lobby's opposition to woman suffrage. The momentum was now clearly on the side of ratification. On May 20, 1919, the House again voted its approval. On June 4, after a sometimes bitter debate, the Senate finally added its consent.

The states soon began to ratify the Anthony amendment. Many had already approved state laws for woman suffrage and ratified almost immediately. But the Deep South was strongly opposed, and it would be necessary to sweep the rest of the country to win the necessary three-fourths majority required for ratification. The issue was in doubt until the bill came before the Tennessee house on August 26, 1920. With that body almost evenly divided, the youngest representative, twenty-four-year-old Harry Burns, cast a decisive vote in favor of the amendment. His mother, an ardent suffragist, had written him, "I've been watching to see how you stood but have noticed nothing yet. Don't forget to be a good boy and help Mrs. Catt."

With the passage of the Nineteenth Amendment, women throughout the United States were able to vote in the presidential election of 1920. For many, who had longed for enfranchisement all their lives, the first opportunity to vote seemed the verge of a new age. One of the suffragists, Charlotte Woodward, had been in the movement since a June day in 1848 when she had ventured forth from her farm to attend the Seneca Falls Convention. She alone of the members of that first women's rights convention lived to see the nationwide enfranchisement of her sex.

Victory was particularly sweet to those who had worked for it as active suffragists. But it was pleasing also to millions of other women who enjoyed the fruits of the suffrage victory. One was a woman named Sally Gold, who had been born in Austria sometime before 1818 when John Adams and Thomas Jefferson were still alive. She remembered that in Austria there had never been any talk of woman suffrage; in fact, she could remember seeing women "harnessed to carts like donkeys." When she was about sixty she immigrated to the United States and came to live in New York City. When woman suffrage was adopted in New York, she lived in an apartment behind a small store where she sold eggs, butter, and other groceries. On the first election day under the new law, her granddaughters urged her to go right out and vote. But Sally Gold was more than a hundred years old and knew how she wanted to observe this day. She carefully washed the dishes and swept the floor. Then she went out to cast her ballot.

The suffrage victory was a product of many factors. Although it took place in an era of broad social reform, it existed, ironically, in an uncomfortable relationship with the Progressive movement. Its members gained experience by working in progressive causes such as temperance unions and settlement houses. But the male leadership of the Progressive movement was generally slow in embracing woman suffrage.

The movement benefited, however, from the atmosphere of reform in the United States in the early twentieth century. Suffragists saw reform occur in other areas and were encouraged that they, too, might accomplish their goal.

The suffrage victory drew on women with many backgrounds and temperaments. The more liberal members of the movement had to work side by side with suffragists who welcomed the disfranchisement of blacks and restrictions of immigrants. The movement also divided between militant and moderate suffragists. The mix of characteristics was apparent in the personalities of the movement's two best-known leaders. Although they favored different tactics and headed different organizations, Alice Paul and Carrie Catt needed one another. The National Woman's party dramatized the cause and revealed the political power of women. The NAWSA was more active in organizing the local campaigns that were essential to ratification. Both recognized, moreover, that women could not achieve full social and political equality simply by the fact of having the ballot. After ratification Catt lent her energies to the newly created League of Women Voters, an organization designed to help women make the most intelligent possible use of their ballots. And Paul began to work for an equal rights amendment, guaranteeing women full equality with men. In 1919 women tended to feel that other feminist reforms would follow naturally on the suffrage victory. But discrimination in property laws, employment practices, and other areas continued unaltered and did not come under effective attack until the 1960s.

Looking back on the disparate forces that contributed to the suffrage movement, its long history, and its unfinished business, we find that Alice Paul's assessment a half century after the passage of the Anthony amendment is particularly apt: "I always feel . . . the movement is a sort of mosaic. Each of us puts in one little stone, and then you get a great mosaic at the end."

QUESTIONS

1. For what reasons did people oppose woman suffrage? Why did many Progressives, who supported other reforms, oppose it?

2. In what ways did Elizabeth Cady Stanton and Susan B. Anthony foster the suffrage movement?

3. Why was Alice Paul dissatisfied with the NAWSA program, and what was her contribution to the suffrage movement?

4. Describe the contribution of each of the following to the suffrage

movement and mention the factors you consider to have been most important: Alice Paul, Carrie Chapman Catt, local suffragist workers, World War I, the Progressive movement, Woodrow Wilson. Explain your answer.

5. Why did Alice Paul and Carrie Catt believe that the battle for women's rights could not end with the passage of the Susan B. Anthony amendment? What further measures did they advocate?

BIBLIOGRAPHY

BUHLE, MARI JO, and PAUL BUHLE, EDITORS. *The Concise History of the Woman Suffrage Movement* (1978). Documentary overview of suffrage movement.

CATT, CARRIE CHAPMAN and NETTIE ROGERS SHULER. *Woman Suffrage and Politics* (1923). Suffrage history by foremost NAWSA administrator.

DANIELS, DORIS. "Building a Winning Coalition: The Suffrage Fight in New York State." *New York History* (January 1979): 59–80. Emphasizes role of settlement house workers, especially that of Lillian Wald.

FLEXNER, ELEANOR. *Century of Struggle: The Women's Rights Movement in the United States* (1970). Standard survey on the feminist movement.

GALLAGHER, ROBERT S. "I was arrested, of course. . . ." *American Heritage* 25 (February 1974): 16–24 and 92–94. Illuminating interview with Alice Paul focusing on suffrage battle.

IRWIN, INEZ HAYES. *The Story of Alice Paul and the National Woman's Party* (1964). Popular account of Paul's suffrage activities, 1913–20.

KRADITOR, AILEEN S. *The Ideas of the Woman Suffrage Movement, 1890–1920* (1965). Analysis of arguments for and against woman suffrage.

LUNARDINI, CHRISTINE A. *From Equal Suffrage to Equal Rights* (1986). Alice Paul and women's rights.

SHAW, ANNA HOWARD. *The Story of a Pioneer* (1915). Autobiography of a NAWSA leader.

STANTON, ELIZABETH CADY, ET AL. *The History of Woman Suffrage* (6 vols., 1899–1922). Extensive account by participants.

7

MODERNITY VERSUS TRADITION

The Scopes Trial and the American Character

Americans have always admired both progress and tradition. Frequently while remodeling their lives and their society they have looked with nostalgia to earlier times. Puritans created a new commonwealth in America but claimed that their civil and religious innovations restored ancient Christian practices. American Revolutionaries built a new republic but believed that they were regaining traditional liberties they had enjoyed as colonists. Similarly, many Americans in the 1920s walked forward while looking backward, enjoying the marvels of industrial technology but longing for the simplicity of a preindustrial, prescientific age. Their anxieties came to the surface when a young man was brought to trial in Dayton, Tennessee, for teaching about evolution. Even as they disapproved of his conduct, the townspeople were curiously divided about the relative merits of tradition and the modern world.

In our imaginations the 1920s is a decade of fun and fads. It is the Jazz Age, the Roaring Twenties, or as columnist Westbrook Pegler styled it, "The Era of Wonderful Nonsense." Unlike the previous decade and the two that followed, no one event shaped life in the 1920s, no Great War or Great Depression. The people focused instead on a string of mini-events. It was an age in which thousands sought to outdo each other in sitting atop flagpoles or setting records in marathon dances. When we think of the 1920s, our minds turn immediately to such glamorous icons of popular culture as bootleg whiskey, Babe Ruth, and the Charleston.

Certainly beneath the surface glitter large forces were at work. But even these came to notice and were dramatized by colorful episodes, tawdry as the Leopold-Loeb murder case or triumphant as Charles Lindbergh's transatlantic flight. One of the decade's most talked of events was the trial in Dayton, Tennessee, of the young John Thomas Scopes, who had committed the crime of teaching evolution to his high school biology class. In the hot summer of 1925 more than a hundred reporters would converge on Dayton and send out a million words of news to a fascinated nation. Two of the most renowned public figures in America, Clarence Darrow and William Jennings Bryan, argued the case.

In part America was fascinated by the "Great Monkey Trial" because of its carnival atmosphere and its famed protagonists. But the nation also paid attention because the trial was one of those episodes in which America attempts to define itself. It dramatized several important conflicts: urban versus rural values, progress versus tradition, modernism versus fundamentalism.

To see what the Scopes trial meant, we must begin by examining these underlying tensions. Between 1900 and 1925 dozens of new products were standard fixtures in American life. Thousands of families had replaced their horse and buggy with an automobile. Electric power was available throughout the nation. People could hear music and news on radios in their own homes. New buildings called skyscrapers had changed the profiles of big cities. And airplanes carried men into the hitherto impregnable skies.

These abundant signs of material progress encouraged confidence in American technology. Individual productivity increased rapidly, and new selling devices such as time payments helped expand the American market. The American businessman was hero of the day. An author, Bruce Barton, even ventured to compare successful entrepreneurs with Christ: After all, wasn't the Lord the greatest salesman of all time? Barton's *The Man Nobody Knows* was enormously popular. The people's glib confidence in the inevitability and rightness of American business prosperity found an apt representative in laconic Calvin Coolidge, the last American president to enjoy a two-hour nap every afternoon.

Among the young, the materialism of the 1920s found expression in relaxed moral standards. In the past girls had been the guardians of social virtue. Now young ladies frequently went out on dates unchaperoned, wearing rouge, sleeveless dresses, and stockings rolled down to the knee. They danced cheek to cheek with boyfriends to passionate jazz rhythms and scoffed when their parents called the saxophone an instrument of the devil. They smoked, drank bootleg whiskey, and rode — or parked — in autos till sunrise, kissing and petting freely. Their sexual exploits may seem tame to a more jaded age, but compared with their parents they were scandalously unrestrained. In 1900 a kiss had implied a promise of marriage. In 1925 a girl in an F. Scott Fitzgerald novel could brag, "I've kissed a dozen men. I suppose I'll kiss dozens more." A college newspaper featured the rhyme: "She doesn't smoke / she doesn't pet / she hasn't been / to college yet." Everywhere the old standards seemed to be breaking down.

Some Americans happily embraced the freedom and materialism of the 1920s. Others were more cautious. Few objected to such conveniences as the radio and the telephone, but many rejected the new permissiveness; they emphasized traditional values and sought to combat change. Some supported legislation aimed at improving public behavior, including the proper length of skirts. Others demanded enforcement of Prohibition laws, restricted immigration, and subordination of minorities. They frequently identified virtue with small towns and vice with cities.

Some opponents of change joined the Ku Klux Klan, which claimed to protect white Anglo-Saxon Protestant America from threats to traditional morality. Klan members met in white robes and hoods, burned crosses, beat up gamblers and prostitutes, and lynched blacks — all in the name of morality. In 1925 the organization had about 3 million members throughout the United States and helped elect at least sixteen U.S. senators and eleven governors.

The fundamentalist movement was less inclined to racism and violence than the KKK but did share many of the Klan's aims. Both emphasized Scripture, the American heritage, rural life, and the common man, while fearing intellectuals and change. Fundamentalism was distinguished, however, by one elemental issue, the truth of Scripture, especially the Biblical view of Creation, the Virgin Birth, and the Resurrection. For fundamentalists these beliefs were the underpinning of personal morality. If men doubted the sacredness of their history, they would behave like beasts.

Fundamentalists generally accepted the First Amendment prescription about teaching religion in public schools, but they sought to influence school curriculum by preventing the teaching of anything contradictory to the Bible. They identified the Darwinian theory of evolution as their foremost enemy.

Since the publication a half century before of Charles Darwin's *On the Origin of Species,* scientists had come to accept his view that human life had evolved over millions of years from more primitive forms of life. Their theories did not necessarily undermine the belief in God, because evolution could be seen as God's way of peopling the earth. Christians who accepted evolutionary theory were called modernists and believed the Bible should be reconciled with modern science. These religious progressives saw God as the first cause or absolute energy. Their weakness lay in making God so abstract as to be unapproachable. One New England modernist clergyman confessed that when he thought of God he imagined a "sort of oblong blur."

The modernist creed proved less compelling than the fundamentalist views, and in the 1920s the latter group captured many Christian denominations and passed resolutions upholding a literal understanding of the Bible. To further "protect" their children from competing ideas, fundamentalists campaigned against evolution in the schools. In Oklahoma and Florida they passed laws banning Darwinism from public education, and they sponsored thirty-five other antievolution bills between 1921 and 1929. Tennessee was not the first state to pass such legislation, and the great test case heard there might easily have taken place in hundreds of other towns. Fundamentalism was as much a part of the American scene in the 1920s as the Charleston or the automobile.

Tennessee joined the antievolution crusade in 1925 when an obscure legislator, John Washington Butler, a Macon County farmer, introduced a bill in the state house of representatives making it illegal in a state-supported school to "teach any theory that denies the story of divine creation of man as taught in the Bible, and to teach instead that man has descended from a lower order of animals." No significant opposition confronted the measure, even from the University of Tennessee, and the bill passed in the house and senate by a wide margin.

With the passage of the Butler Act, the American Civil Liberties Union decided that the time had come to fight the antievolution movement in the courts. Holding that such laws threatened freedom of speech, the ACLU announced that it would provide legal and financial assistance to any teacher who wanted to test the act.

This was a tempting offer, for it promised not only support for the defendant but also publicity for his community. The test case might have come from anywhere in Tennessee, but the small rural community of Dayton provided the first case. One afternoon in April 1925 two local attorneys who supported the law and a mining engineer who opposed it discussed evolution while relaxing at the soda fountain in Robinson's drugstore. The evolutionist, George Rappelyea, suggested that Dayton stage a test case; he was seconded enthusiastically by F.E. Robinson, the drugstore proprietor, who exclaimed that the case would put Dayton on the map.

Anyone who taught biology in Tennessee might have served as defendant, for the state-required biology textbook, written in a more liberal era, included material on evolution. The men decided to ask John Thomas Scopes to challenge the law. Scopes was a twenty-four-year-old biology teacher at Dayton High School and, because he was an intelligent, modest, and popular young man, known to the townspeople as "Professor," he would represent the community well.

One of the men went out and fetched Scopes from a tennis court. Back at the drugstore, Scopes readily admitted that he could not teach biology without teaching evolution, whereupon Rappelyea urged him to help overturn an unjust law. Scopes was at first reluctant to expose himself to a court action but was soon persuaded to help. A few days later he was charged with breaking the law.

The trial rapidly took shape. Rappelyea contacted the ACLU, which promised its support, agreeing to take the case to the Supreme Court, if necessary, "to establish that a teacher may tell the truth without being thrown in jail." The prosecution sought to identify attorneys who could best argue — and publicize — the case. William Jennings Bryan was a logical choice.

Bryan was a leading spokesman for the fundamentalist movement. After passage of the Butler Act he had written to the governor of Tennessee, Austin Peay, telling him: "The Christian parents of the state owe you a debt of gratitude for saving their children from the poisonous influence of an unproved hypothesis." Sue K. Hicks, a Dayton attorney (whose unlikely first name came from his mother, who died giving him birth), invited Bryan to take part, anticipating that he would attract international attention to the case. In reply to Hicks's telegram, Bryan wired back his enthusiastic acceptance.

Although no longer an active politician, Bryan was still one of America's best-known public figures. Born in Salem, Illinois, in 1860, he practiced law in Illinois and Nebraska for eight years before being elected to Congress in 1890. He served for two terms, then tried unsuccessfully to win election to the U.S. Senate. Between 1894 and 1896 he was editor of the *Omaha World Herald*.

In 1896 Bryan was already known as a capable public speaker and a popular politician, but nothing in his career suggested the fame he would win overnight in the Democratic Convention in Chicago that year. The convention was controlled by "Silver Democrats," who identified themselves with that elusive figure, the common man, and claimed that a currency based on silver would save the people from oppression by an economic elite. Bryan, a prosilver delegate to the convention, gave a speech that electrified the delegates. He identified his party with the farms, the "plain people," and "the producing masses" of the nation. Blaming the gold standard for the country's ills, he thundered, "You shall not press down upon the brow of labor this crown of thorns, you shall not crucify mankind upon a cross of gold."

The speech joined the handful of American rhetorical masterpieces. High school students across the country soon presented the talk in speech contests. Bryan himself repeated it thousands of times to rapt audiences long after the campaign of 1896 was over. The convention was so moved by the "Cross of Gold" speech that the young and hitherto unknown Bryan was chosen on the third ballot as the Democratic presidential candidate.

Bryan appeared in Dayton almost three decades after his first presidential campaign; yet a continuity between the two episodes is evident. In each case a basic moral issue seemed to be at stake. In each Bryan proposed a simple, even a simplistic, solution to a complex problem. And both times he inspired a devoted following.

In the campaign of 1896 and in subsequent campaigns and activities Bryan won a reputation as defender of the plain people. After losing the 1896 election he returned to Lincoln, Nebraska, and established *The Commoner,* a journal that spread his political views for almost three decades. His personality so dominated Democratic politics that he was chosen as the party's presidential candidate in three elections: 1896, 1900, and 1908. He lost all to more popular Republican candidates, but he held a large following within the party. He might even have secured a fourth nomination in the badly deadlocked convention of 1912 had he not bent his energies to supporting the New Jersey Progressive, Woodrow Wilson.

Wilson became the first Democratic president in sixteen years and rewarded Bryan for his service by offering him any post in the administration. Bryan chose the most prestigious, secretary of state, and undertook to educate himself on foreign affairs. His uncompromising rectitude was soon apparent. A teetotaler, he substituted mineral water and grapefruit juice for wine at diplomatic functions. A man of peace, he negotiated thirty treaties providing for peaceful resolution of disputes. With the outbreak of World War I, Bryan threw all his influence behind neutrality and objected to any act that might draw the United States into war. When Woodrow Wilson insisted on sending two harsh notes to Germany after its submarine sank the British ocean liner *Lusitania,*

Bryan resigned rather than sign the second one. In retirement Bryan was free to campaign for peace, an enterprise he undertook with evangelical fervor.

But when he learned that Congress had declared war, he immediately wired Wilson offering to serve as a private in the armed forces. Although he did not find his way to the trenches — the army would have little need for a fifty-seven-year-old private — he did throw his support behind the war. Now that the majority had decided for war, he declared, dissent was no longer proper. In *The Commoner* he quoted Thomas Jefferson's maxim: "Acquiescence in the will of the majority is the first principle of republics." Such would be his position later in the Scopes case. During the war Bryan was most conspicuous as a campaigner for prohibition, which he called "the greatest moral reform" of the generation.

In his work for neutrality and Prohibition, Bryan implicitly associated religion and politics. In later years he turned increasingly to religious activities. He was encouraged to abandon his lifelong preoccupation with politics by his failure to lead the 1920 Democratic Convention as he had guided others. In politics his influence was waning, but in religion he might still play a role in leading America to righteousness. The new emphasis was hardly a radical shift from his earlier views. His religious roots were deep. As a child in Illinois he and his father had memorized sections of the Bible together. There was even something of the religious prophet in his appearance. His unflinching righteousness, his commanding presence, and his powerful voice invited comparison with religious leaders. He had been called a "Moses come to lead the people from the wilderness" and a second Saint Paul. Theodore Roosevelt said of him, "By George, he would make the greatest Baptist preacher on earth."

In his last years Bryan stridently advocated the Bible's literal truth and moral precepts. In Miami, Florida, where he spent the winter, he taught an adult Sunday school class in a city park. Thousands of men and women sat in the open air beneath the palm trees and listened as the earnest, gray-haired evangelist held forth each Sunday from a wood bandstand. After the meetings he distributed copies of his books to likely converts, even pursuing some to their own doorsteps. On one mission to deliver a book to a young man who had said he wanted to begin a Christian life, Bryan came upon a muddy street torn up for sewer construction. His wife urged him to return when the road was fixed, but he continued on foot. "The boy may need the book," he said. "We cannot tell." It was typical of Bryan to see a chance to improve the world in even a small gesture.

Bryan was ever alert to occasions to save a soul or cure a nation. By

1923, six years after he had begun delivering Sunday lectures, they were being reprinted in 110 newspapers with more than 20 million readers. Bryan had also become an important figure in the Presbyterian church and a leader of its conservative element against such modernists as Harry Emerson Fosdick. In 1924 he was elected vice-moderator of the national Presbyterian Convention.

At this time he came closer to the fundamentalist movement. He began to publish tracts with titles like *The Menace of Darwinism* and *The Bible and Its Enemies,* and he attacked both the scientific basis and the moral implications of Darwinism. The theory of evolution, he said, is simply a theory. Its scientific basis is questionable, and it is contrary to common sense as well as opposed to the Bible. In comparing men with monkeys, Darwin confused the superficial with the essential. Certainly there are superficial similarities between men and beasts, but in man the body was less important than the mind, and the mind inferior to the soul. The human intellect and the human spirit argue for a unique divine creation. "We are not the progeny of the brute," he wrote. "We are the handiwork of the Almighty."

Darwinism was thus inaccurate. It made bad science; worse still, it made bad morality. Bryan claimed that Darwinism replaced Christian love with elemental hate as "the law of development." When translated into Social Darwinism, it justified economic oppression and class pride and so undermined democracy itself. Bryan insisted that men's beliefs about the origins of life affect their actual behavior. Only "a sense of responsibility to God" could make men aspire to "that which is highest and best."

Darwinism was sapping traditional American values. "The greatest menace to the public school system today," he told the 1920 Nebraska Constitutional Convention, is "its Godlessness. We have allowed the moral influences to be crowded out." Because Darwinism had infected the public school curriculum, its influence must be fought in the legislature and on the school board as well as in the private conscience. He constructed an ingenious rationale for this restriction on intellectual freedom. The individual, he said, will remain free to study evolution, but only as a private citizen. In the schoolroom he must accept the limitations set by school board and legislature. Quite simply the people, who pay the taxes that support the schools, have a right to determine what is taught. It is a simple matter of majority rule. For once, after years of political defeat, Bryan was confident that the majority was on his side.

After each Sunday school lecture or public address, people crowded around Bryan, eager to tell him how his faith had encouraged them or their children.

"I have been slipping away from the church," a young man told him, "but you have brought me back."

"My daughter is a student at the University," a father told him, "and your lecture has steadied her."

Their comments assured the white-haired patriarch of fundamentalism that his cause was just. Each of Bryan's many causes had held the promise of a better world, with peace, democracy, and temperance, but this final crusade absorbed and transcended all the others. If men would follow God with simple faith in His Word and strong determination to do His will, all war, oppression, and injustice would end — so Bryan believed.

He began to see progress when the Florida legislature, at his urging, passed a law in 1924 forbidding instructors to "teach *as true* Darwinism or any other hypothesis that links men in blood relationship to any other form of life." When the Tennessee legislature met a year later to consider a similar law, Bryan was in touch with several legislators, one of whom distributed five hundred copies of his pamphlet, *Is the Bible True?* to his colleagues.

When the test case was prepared at Dayton, it was natural that Bryan should be identified as the man who could best publicize the fundamentalist cause as well as prosecute the case. Immediately after he agreed to participate, he was showered with letters from wellwishers. His senior in the Presbyterian hierarchy, the Reverend Mr. J. Frank Norris, wrote him: "You are now in the great work of your life and are rendering ten thousand times more service to the cause of righteousness than a dozen presidents."

While Bryan reaped encouragement from his fundamentalist supporters, the opponents of the Butler Act had identified an equally fitting representative of their cause. A brilliant trial lawyer, Clarence Darrow, had offered his services to the defense as soon as he learned that Bryan had agreed to assist the prosecution. The Scopes case appealed to Darrow because throughout his legal career he had defended the underdog. He thought of himself as a representative of the people against all forms of oppression.

Perhaps he inherited this trait from his father, Amirus Darrow, an Ohio furniture maker and undertaker who had rejected Christianity after testing it as a student at Meadville Theological Seminary. Clarence was born in 1857 and reared on his father's rationalistic principles. While Bryan was learning about the Bible, Darrow was learning about science. After attending Allegheny College and the University of Michigan, Darrow was admitted to the Ohio bar in 1878. Following nine years of practice in Ohio, he moved to Chicago, where he quickly established a reputation as an adept civil lawyer and involved himself in local politics.

In 1894 his career was given direction by two cases. First he handled

Clarence Darrow (left) and William Jennings Bryan. They represented not only opposite sides in the Scopes trial, but also different views of American character and purpose.

an appeal for young Robert Prendergast, who had shot and killed the mayor of Chicago. Darrow lost and Prendergast was executed. The experience appears to have solidified Darrow's opposition to capital punishment. Men should not be held entirely responsible for their acts, he believed, because they were shaped by their birth and upbringing. The state might imprison a bad person to prevent injury to others, but there is no justice in executions. After the Prendergast assassination case Darrow tried fifty more capital cases and never again lost a client to the death penalty.

In 1894 he also defended Eugene Debs, who had refused to honor a court order in the Pullman boycott. Darrow lost the case but defended Debs so ably that he was much sought after in other labor cases.

Darrow's reaction to World War I suggests several similarities to Bryan. He had considered himself a pacifist, but "when Germany invaded Belgium," he wrote, "I recovered from my pacifism in the twinkling of an eye." He favored support for England and France but believed that people could in good conscience oppose the war. Whereas Bryan believed that there were issues on which all reasonable people should agree, Darrow was suspicious of the tyranny of the majority. If

Bryan's contribution to the war had been saving soldiers from vice, Darrow's involved saving dissenters from jail.

After the war Darrow faced his most difficult case, which he called the "Loeb-Leopold Tragedy." Nathan Leopold was a brilliant eighteen-year-old in his second year at the University of Chicago Law School. In summer 1924 he persuaded a friend, Richard Loeb, to help him commit the "perfect crime." They abducted fourteen-year-old Robert Franks, killed him, dumped the body in a culvert, and sent a ransom note to his father. A few days later they were apprehended, traced by a pair of eyeglasses Leopold had dropped near the body. When the boys confessed the crime, there seemed little chance of saving them from the death penalty. The crime was reprehensible, and Leopold and Loeb were the sort of people many Americans disliked anyway — they were wealthy, intellectual, Jewish, and homosexual. But Darrow attempted to show that their minds "were not normal." After a long trial, which he said, "exhausted all the strength I could summon," he finally heard Chicago Judge John Caverly sentence the murderers to life in prison.

After the moral ambiguities of the Leopold-Loeb trial, the Scopes case must have strongly appealed to Darrow. Here the "crime" was teaching an important and widely accepted scientific theory, and the "culprit" was a personable young man. Moreover, Darrow was as partial to the principle of scientific inquiry as Bryan was to the Bible. Darrow had helped form an intellectual club in Chicago that regularly heard local professors lecture about life and the universe. He had already challenged Bryan on the Bible's reliability as a source of scientific truth in an article in a Chicago newspaper.

Darrow and Bryan held opposing views about dissent and science, but both thought themselves champions of the oppressed. Their difference lay in their perception of reality. Bryan believed that the plain, honest people of America were threatened by big-city intellectuals who scoffed at their traditional virtues and their traditional God. Darrow believed that intelligent, honest Americans were thwarted by bigots and ignoramuses who preferred make-believe truths to reality.

As the attorneys for both sides prepared to come to Dayton, the town busily prepared for its moment in the national spotlight. The people, fundamentalists and modernists alike, were jubilant at the publicity they would receive. Dayton was a small town that had flirted once with the chance to grow. Twenty years earlier it seemed destined to become a major industrial center. But the blast furnace on which expansionists had pinned their hopes had been forced to close. Dayton's dream had faded, and nearby Chattanooga had grown into the regional metropolis.

Dayton had remained a small town, hub of an agricultural county whose chief products were peaches, tomatoes, and strawberries. It was a stable, conservative community where, as in most small towns, blacks "knew their place" and women were excluded from public affairs. The town had no saloons, gambling, or whiskey. The Scopes trial would bring people, publicity, and business to the town — put it on the map. But even while growing Dayton could preserve its values. In fact, it would call attention to itself precisely because it was defending its values.

Late in spring 1925 the trial obsessed Dayton. When news arrived that Chattanooga might upstage Dayton with an earlier trial, the outraged people held a meeting where feelings ran high. Modernist George Rappelyea sought to strike a blow for Darwinism and Dayton by declaring, "there are as many evolutionists in Dayton as there are monkeys in Chattanooga." In response the owner of a local barbershop, outraged at Rappelyea's support of a doctrine that appeared to associate his family with the beasts, attacked — and bit — the evolutionist.

Rappelyea and Dayton survived the evening's excitement, and Dayton's leadership in the evolution test was soon fixed when Judge John T. Raulston convened a special grand jury to hasten the trial. Raulston was a native of the region, born in Gizzard's Cove in the nearby mountains. He dreamed of higher office and reckoned the trial would aid his promotion. In various ways scores of other Dayton residents calculated their personal stake in the trial. Businessmen repainted their stores; innkeepers prepared extra rooms. With typical opportunism, a businessman by the name of Darwin posted a large sign outside his shop reading "DARWIN IS RIGHT" and added, in small letters underneath, "inside."

Despite such preparations, the reporters who began to arrive early in July were more impressed with Dayton's pastoral qualities than its entrepreneurial ambition. Many had traveled by train and bus from the crowded streets of New York and other large cities; they were impressed by Dayton's trim houses, cool lawns, and stately trees. They commented on the beautiful hills and rich fields surrounding the town. They were intrigued by the soft-spoken farmers who strode about in felt Stetsons. The reporters stayed in places like the Aqua Hotel, named for the clear spring water bubbling from the surrounding hills, where all guests were awakened by a rap at the door at quarter to seven, calling them to a communal breakfast. The citizens, eager to create a good impression, shook hands and smiled affably; chairs lined the streets outside the stores, beckoning the visitors to settle into Dayton's leisurely pace.

Sooner or later the strangers found their way to Robinson's drugstore, now the most famous landmark in town. Inside, discussion of the trial, the attorneys, evolution, and the Bible never stopped. John

Scopes usually came to the store in the late afternoon after swimming in a local pond. His good nature and serious demeanor seemed to characterize the local citizenry's attitude toward the trial.

Two sides of the American temperament — religiosity and curiosity — existed comfortably in Dayton. A walk through the town revealed its dedication to Christianity. A dozen churches, including Southern Methodists, Southern Baptists, and Presbyterians, competed among themselves and with smaller denominations. Outside town the fields bore religious signs as naturally as they produced potatoes and strawberries. "Take care lest thy sins find you out," read one. Farther on in the hills strange sects practiced curious rites learned from a literal reading of the Bible. In Dayton the people told of a farmer who had *seen* God and a minister who had wrestled with Him.

Although most of the people did not claim to have seen, much less to have wrestled, with the Lord, nearly all were church members. Religion gave them recreation, communal spirit, topics of discourse. One reporter, seeming to be overwhelmed by the atmosphere, wrote in astonishment, "The whole region is saturated with religion."

Still, sentiment in Dayton was curiously tolerant of Scopes and evolution. Even H.L. Mencken, America's greatest contemporary critic of the "small town mentality," was impressed that no "poisonous spirit" surrounded the trial. The majority may have been fundamentalists and disapproved of teaching evolution in the schools, but most were also interested in learning more about the world. Several jurors admitted after the trial that they had looked forward to free lessons in science from Darrow's expert witnesses.

The first of the major protagonists to arrive in Dayton was William Jennings Bryan, who came into town on July 7 aboard the *Royal Palm* from Florida. The people caught an initial glimpse of their famous guest when he appeared on the rear platform of the train dressed in black coat and tie and white tropical helmet. Bryan was cheered by a crowd of three hundred spectators. After disembarking, he removed his coat and strolled among them under the hot sun to Robinson's drugstore, where he ordered an ice cream soda and chatted with his admirers.

Two days later Clarence Darrow arrived. No crowd like Bryan's greeted him, but he was not disappointed. He realized that his opponent, and not he, was the "ruler of the Bible Belt." A few supporters were there, however. One, a local banker, turned over his house to Darrow for his headquarters. Darrow settled in and went to work on his case. He noticed a collection of framed mottoes on the wall assuring him "Jesus loves you" and "The Lord will provide."

In the next few days Bryan and Darrow quickly impressed themselves upon the region. Bryan told the Dayton Progressive Club, "the contest between Christianity and evolution in Dayton is duel to the death." The next evening he delivered a lecture from the wood porch of a hotel in the hills; he stood in lantern light, speaking in his melodious voice to a crowd of country people who gazed at him with simple adoration. A storm of thunder and lightning in the hills blended well with his solemn and majestic presence.

The people in Rhea County had expected to like Bryan. They were surprised to find they also liked Darrow. Perhaps they had expected him to be overbearing and harsh. Instead, he impressed them with his homespun manners and modest demeanor. They liked his way of saying complicated things in a few simple words. If Bryan impressed Dayton as a spokesman of their own comfortable beliefs, Darrow excited them by his familiarity with science and the modern world.

The two attorneys were well chosen to represent the opposite sides in the trial. They were joined by other lawyers who would help present the case. In defending Scopes, Darrow had the assistance of Dudley Field Malone, a fashionable divorce lawyer; Arthur Garfield Hayes, perhaps the brightest attorney at the trial; and John Randolph Neal, a law school dean and proponent of academic freedom. Bryan would work with a battery of local attorneys including Sue Hicks, who had initially invited him to Dayton; and his son, William Jennings Bryan, Jr., a thirty-six-year-old Los Angeles attorney.

The basic strategy for each side was relatively simple. The prosecution would attempt to limit the trial to the simple question: Had John Thomas Scopes violated the law against teaching evolution in Tennessee schools? The defense would try to broaden the inquiry, claiming that the law violated the First and Fourteenth Amendments by writing a religious doctrine into law and that it was unreasonable because it forbade the teaching of a widely accepted scientific theory.

Such were the apparent legal boundaries of the trial, but it was inevitable that other issues would arise: evolution versus fundamentalism, modernity versus tradition, freedom of thought versus "established values." These were expected. The reporters in Dayton, the townspeople and visitors, the attorneys themselves recognized and welcomed the broad implications of the trial. Because the case touched such fundamental issues, the town was full of people of every sort: evangelistic preachers who held forth in the streets, showmen with pet monkeys, popcorn vendors. All had a stake in Dayton.

As Clarence Darrow walked through the crowded town to the courthouse on the hot first morning of the trial, he was aware that he was taking the case into the enemy's territory. Along his way he passed religious placards and banners attached to fences and buildings; they counseled him: "Read Your Bible Daily" and "Prepare to Meet Thy

Maker." Then he came to a two-acre park with more banners hanging in its oaks and maples. In the middle of the park stood a large brick building, the Rhea County Courthouse.

Darrow was surprised at the size of the courtroom. On the morning of Friday, July 10, it was packed with spectators. Reporters from a hundred domestic and foreign newspapers sat at makeshift desks at the front of the room. A telegraph wire connected the courtroom with the outside world. The benches, aisles, and walls were jammed with townspeople and farmers. Darrow noticed that "Read Your Bible Daily" banners hung by the bench, the jury box, and throughout the courtroom. "It looked as though there might have been a discount for ordering a wholesale lot," he quipped.

Through most of the day the two sides questioned prospective jurors. Several were excluded as too conservative in their faith, but even so eleven of the final twelve professed to read their Bibles. (The twelfth was illiterate.) Reporters were as intrigued by the attorney's attire as by the day's proceedings. In the close heat of the courtroom Darrow had stripped off his coat, revealing his bright suspenders. Bryan cooled himself with a large heart-shaped palm fan. When he wasn't questioning jurors, Darrow reflected on the temperature: "Tennessee must be very close to the equator," he thought, "or maybe the crust is thin under this little sin-fearing section."

After the long day the court adjourned for the weekend. While Darrow prepared his case, Bryan used the time to proselytize. On Sunday morning he delivered a lecture at the Methodist church, and in the afternoon he addressed a large audience on the courthouse lawn. In these talks he stressed the priority of religion over intellect and education. Christ's doctrines provide "so complete a moral code that no scholar has dared add a word to it." He denied that evolution laws restricted freedom of speech; they simply enabled parents "to guard the religious welfare of their children."

On Monday morning the trial began. Microphones had been installed to carry the arguments to loudspeakers outside the courtroom and to a nationwide radio audience. Thus technology would aid in publicizing the battle between tradition and evolution. The day was given over mainly to technicalities, but Darrow introduced a note of drama when he moved that the indictment be quashed. The evolution law was a "foolish, mischievous, and wicked act," he said; it was "as brazen and bold an attempt to destroy liberty as was ever seen in the Middle Ages." The motion was denied.

Darrow startled the court again next morning when he objected to the customary prayer that opened the day. In forty years of practice he had never seen such a ceremony. Because the case had strong religious overtones the practice seemed to favor the prosecution. He argued vehemently, but his motion was denied, and each morning a minister delivered a prayer before the court.

By now Darrow had impressed the spectators with his particular style. His bright suspenders and sense of humor gave him a casual air, but at the proper moment he could make sharp inquiries and rebuttals. In the early days of the trial Bryan's style contrasted sharply with Darrow's alert probing. He sat back, constantly fanning himself, and seemed to Darrow the portrait of indolence.

Darrow later amplified that portrait in his autobiography. "There sat Bryan," he wrote, "fanning himself, looking limp and martyr-like between assaults upon the flies that found a choice roosting-place on his bald, expansive dome and bare, hairy arms. He slapped away at them with the big fan, constantly and industriously. Somehow he did not look like a hero. Or even a Commoner. He looked like a common fly-catcher." The hostility and contempt that burns through this description would increase as the trial progressed. Although Bryan and Darrow had initially attempted to be civil to each other, the tension between them was bound to grow, for each believed that the other was not only wrong but morally wrong.

The prosecution had an easy time presenting its case. On Tuesday and Wednesday they showed that Scopes had taught evolution in his biology courses, a fact he never denied. In response, Darrow and Dudley Field Malone declared that they would prove there was no conflict between evolution and the Bible. On Thursday, July 16, the court considered whether the defense should be allowed to present the testimony of expert witnesses. Scopes's attorneys had gathered fifteen clergymen and scientists who could discuss evolution research and its relationship to the Bible. If the judge would allow the defense to explore the validity of the evolution law, this testimony would be crucial.

In opposition Bryan rose to present his first real address to the courtroom. He took a long drink of ice water and then began his argument. The experts were irrelevant, he argued. Their testimony might have been appropriate in the legislature when the law was being drafted, but now the law was a fact and the only issue was whether Scopes had broken it.

Bryan was perfectly correct in seeking to limit debate to Scopes's actual behavior and to skirt the issue of the evolution law's validity. But he incautiously abandoned this stable ground as he continued his oration. Palm fan in hand, gazing at the hundreds of Bible-reading Christians who regarded him as the protector of their faith, he felt compelled to engage the evolution question.

He held up a copy of George Hunter's *Civil Biology*, the text Scopes had used, and turned to a diagram of animal life. "We are told just how many animal species there are, 518,900," he began. Then he explained that the book divided the animals into groups, each represented by a circle. From the large circles representing protozoa, fish, and sponges, he came at last to a tiny circle containing man.

"Then we have mammals," he said, "3,500, and there is a little circle, and man is in the circle. Find him, find man."

Now Bryan's voice rose in indignation at the thought of this belittling of God's chosen creature.

"There is that book! There is the book they were teaching your children, teaching that man was a mammal and so indistinguishable among the mammals that they leave him there with 3,499 other mammals — including elephants!"

The audience was delighted. After five days the contest they had anticipated was finally taking shape. They laughed and applauded. Bryan continued.

"Talk about putting Daniel in the lions' den! How dare those scientists put man in a little ring like that with lions and tigers and everything that is bad?

"Tell me that the parents of this day have not any right to declare that children are not to be taught this doctrine. . . . Shall we be detached from the throne of God and be compelled to link our ancestors with the jungle?"

Here was an essential point in Bryan's critique of Darwin. By associating man with the beasts, evolutionary theory appeared to deny the divine origin of life and the existence of God. Bryan now held up a copy of Darwin's *Descent of Man*. To ease the tension in the room he complained facetiously that Darwin claimed man had descended, "Not even from American monkeys but from Old World monkeys."

Then he grew more serious. He complained that the evolutionists failed to consider the first cause of life.

"Did he tell you where life began? Did he tell you that back of all there was a God? Not a word about it. . . . They want to come in with their little padded-up evolution that commences with nothing and ends nowhere."

Bryan's gestures and intonations were so effective in the hot, stuffy courtroom that John Thomas Scopes was reminded of a symphony. Bryan now came to his final point. Without the divine creation, the essential link between God and man, there could be no moral standards. If man were merely a beast, he might as well act like a beast.

"The facts are simple," he said. "The case is plain, and if those gentlemen want to enter upon a larger field of educational work on the subject of evolution, let us get through with this case and then convene a mock court, for it will deserve the title of mock court if its purpose is to banish from the hearts of the people the word of God as revealed."

Bryan's speech was greeted with applause. Although he had begun and ended by claiming that the court should not go into larger questions of evolution, religion, and morality, he captivated the crowd by transgressing the boundaries he himself had established. The people wanted to hear about the broader issues.

The defense now followed with its own view of these larger issues, especially intellectual freedom. In a brief statement Darrow argued that risks are always involved in new ideas and inventions and that young people should be encouraged to "learn and choose." After this statement he turned the defense over to his co-counsel, Dudley Field Malone, who proved master of the occasion.

Malone, the New York attorney, had till now resisted the informality of the courtroom, but when he rose to speak he paused and removed his jacket, folding it carefully and placing it on the defense table. He then addressed the court with an air of deference.

"If the court please," he said in a low voice, "it does seem to me that we have gone far afield in this discussion. However, probably this is the time to discuss everything that bears on the issues that have been raised in this case; because, after all, whether Mr. Bryan knows it or not, he is a mammal, he is an animal, and he is a man. . . .

"I have been puzzled and interested at one and the same time at the psychology of the prosecution, and I find it difficult to distinguish between Mr. Bryan the lawyer in this case; Mr. Bryan, the propagandist outside this case; and the Mr. Bryan who made a speech against science and for religion just now....

"Mr. Bryan, Your Honor, is not the only one who believes in God; he is not the only who believes in the Bible."

Malone's voice rose, and each idea fell neatly into place as he continued with what most observers believed the oratorical masterpiece of the trial. The audience hung on his words as his voice filled the courtroom and boomed through the loudspeakers outside in the park.

Malone told of times in the past when authorities, believing they possessed absolute truth, had hindered science. The Muslims had burned the great library at Alexandria because it contained books contrary to the Koran. The Catholic church had tried Galileo because his astronomy appeared to contradict the Bible. In each case, history had repudiated the intolerant act. This should not happen again, Malone argued. Science and religion must be allowed to prosper side by side. He continued:

"These gentlemen say: 'The Bible contains the truth. If the world of science can produce any truth or facts not in the Bible as we understand it, then destroy science but keep the Bible.' And we say: 'Keep your Bible. Keep it as your consolation, keep it as your guide. But keep it where it belongs, in the world of your own conscience, in the world of your individual judgment.'"

Here Judge Raulston interrupted to ask Malone if he believed that the theory of evolution was compatible with the theory of "divine creation as taught in the Bible." Malone replied that he did so believe. God could have created the first single life cell and allowed man to evolve "serially." But whatever the actual process, men should be free to learn what they could through science.

Malone then turned to the question of morality. "What is this psychology of fear?" he asked. "I don't understand it." Science would not hurt the younger generation. "The children of this generation are pretty wise," he said. They did not produce the Great War that killed 20 million people. If they are allowed to think, he argued, "They will make a better world of this than we have been able to make of it."

By now Malone had the courtroom on his side. Fundamentalists as well as modernists hung on his words and interrupted him with applause. After twenty minutes Malone turned to the question at hand, admission of the expert testimony. Malone urged the court to admit it, to promote the free exchange of ideas.

"The truth always wins," he said, "and we are not afraid of it. The truth is no coward. The truth does not need the law. The truth does not need the forces of government. The truth does not need Mr. Bryan. The truth is imperishable, eternal, and immortal and needs no human agency to support it. We are ready to tell the truth as we understand it, and we do not fear all the truth that they can present as facts."

Malone now turned to Bryan. "We are ready," he said. "We feel we stand with progress. We feel we stand with science. We feel we stand with intelligence. We feel we stand with fundamental freedom in America. We are not afraid. Where is the fear? We meet it! Where is the fear? We defy it! We ask Your Honor to admit the evidence as a matter of correct law, as a matter of sound procedure, and as a matter of justice to the defense in this case."

Malone was finished, and now as he returned to the defense table, a remarkable thing happened. The courtroom exploded with cheering and applause. Even the policemen by the bench joined in the uproar, and people climbed over the rail to shake Malone's hand. Darrow exclaimed, "Tennessee needs only fifteen minutes of free speech to become civilized!" The cheering was reported to have been twice as long and twice as loud as that which greeted Bryan's earlier speech. Bryan, knowing he had been outdone, was gracious. "Dudley," he said, "that was the greatest speech I ever heard."

Malone's address was undoubtedly a masterful oratorical performance, and this was an age that admired good speeches. But even then
the response was puzzling. Why should fundamentalists, who were
surely in the majority that day, show such enthusiasm for a spokesman
of the opposition? Their behavior gives us a clue to one thread of the
conservative temperament in the 1920s. Curiously, Malone rather than
Bryan had articulated their deepest anxieties.

Were they worried about their children? So was he. But he had
confidence that they would grow up into wise and caring human beings.
Did they want to believe in God? So did he. But he assured them that
God could have chosen evolution as His method of creating human life.
Did they wish to face the future with confidence? So did he. But in place
of fearful rejection of the modern world, he offered them a vision of
triumphant progress. The unfettered search for truth, he assured them,
would bring mankind to a better future.

Here was a synthesis combining traditional values with confidence
in the future, a simple credo of optimism, morality, and progress. Its
appeal in the 1920s was enormous. The world was changing — that was
plain. And much of the progress — the telephone, the Ford car, the
radio — was exciting, even to the people of Dayton, Tennessee, and
thousands of towns like it. But where would it lead? What would it do
to the children's morals, to the faith in God? Didn't parents need to take
control, to put boundaries on freedom, even freedom of thought? Such
worries had led some Americans to favor Prohibition, the KKK, and
fundamentalism.

To all these anxieties, Malone had an answer. "Where is the fear?"
he had said. "We meet it! Where is the fear? We defy it!" His breastplate
in the struggle against fear was a simple belief in progress. Like Charles
Lindbergh, who to his contemporaries a few years later seemed to
combine frontier simplicity and mechanical wizardry, Malone believed
that America could have the best of its past in concert with the best of the
future.

If history were simply a fantasy written by a playwright, we might
let down the curtain over Dayton, Tennessee, with this account of
triumph — Scopes vindicated, Bryan and the fundamentalists converted, freedom of thought restored. But historical events seldom
resolve themselves into such tidy endings. Even Malone's great oratory
could not sweep away the Dayton of 1925, the America of 1925, or the
niceties of courtroom procedure.

After the wave of enthusiasm for Malone's address finally subsided,
Judge Raulston concluded the day's proceedings, and the people filed
out into the real world that ebbed and flowed around the courthouse.
Malone's speech had surely impressed many thinking people with the

idea that one could have evolution and the Bible, progress and tradition.

But there were also one's daily functions to perform. Farmers and laborers returned to their snug houses and to chores they had postponed to watch the trial. On the streets boys sold ice cream and popcorn. The men with monkeys moved aimlessly about. Evangelical preachers sought to attract audiences. The moist hot air muted the sounds and thoughts of men and women.

When the court convened again the next day, Friday, July 17, Judge Raulston ruled that the testimony of expert witnesses could "shed no light" on the questions before the jury and should therefore be excluded. But after further argument he modified the ruling to permit the witnesses to speak to the court with the jury absent. The defense therefore could put the expert testimony in the record for the purpose of appeal. The court then adjourned for the weekend.

By now both sides were becoming impatient. Bryan issued a statement on Saturday claiming he was fighting a "conspiracy against the Bible Christianity." Darrow replied that the scientist did not need "to call the aid of the law to enforce belief in his theories." Both men gave lectures that weekend to local groups, while Scopes, surprisingly relaxed, told reporters he hoped to return to college when the trial was over.

On Sunday evening the defense attorneys gathered at Darrow's lodgings — known as the "Monkey House" — and discussed strategy. They were particularly intrigued by a new idea: Why not call Bryan himself as an "expert witness"? They felt sure that Bryan would be unable to resist the temptation to express his views and that he would discredit himself and the evolutionists. To perfect the plan they practiced questions and answers, with one of the expert witnesses playing Bryan.

On Monday, July 20, the court convened for what many assumed would be the last day of the trial. The room was even more crowded than usual, and some worried that the floor might give way. After the midday break the judge reconvened on the lawn outside. He sat at a table on a platform built against the courthouse wall; hundreds of spectators assembled on benches in the park; boys climbed on tree branches above the crowd or circulated among the people selling soda pop.

The afternoon began with the reading of affidavits taken from the expert witnesses. Then the defense dropped its bombshell and called Bryan as a witness. Everyone was startled, including Bryan, who sat motionless as his fellow attorneys objected. He could easily have refused to testify; he was, after all, an attorney for the prosecution. But he was reluctant to appear timorous, and he was confident he could defend his position.

Bryan took a seat on a wood office chair on the narrow platform. Darrow, standing opposite him, began, "You have given considerable study to the Bible, haven't you, Mr. Bryan?"

"Yes, sir," Bryan replied, "I have tried to."

"Do you claim that everything in the Bible should be literally interpreted?"

"I believe everything in the Bible should be accepted as it is given there. Some of the Bible is given illustratively; for instance: 'Ye are the salt of the earth.' I would not insist that man was actually salt, but it is used in the sense of salt as saving God's people."

Darrow proceeded, pacing, leaning against a table, running a hand through his hair; occasionally he looked into a Bible for a reference. He mused, listened, and probed. What about Jonah and the whale? Did Bryan believe in that?

"It is hard to believe for you," said Bryan, "but easy for me. A miracle is a thing performed beyond what man can perform. When you get beyond what man can do, you get within the realms of miracles; and it is just as easy to believe the miracle of Jonah as any other miracle in the Bible."

Thus far, Bryan was doing well. The crowd applauded his answers. The other defense attorneys appeared pleased. Darrow continued:

"Do you believe Joshua made the sun stand still?"

"I believe what the Bible says," Bryan replied. "I suppose you mean that the earth stood still."

Darrow: "The Bible says Joshua commanded the sun to stand still for the purpose of lengthening the day, doesn't it? And you believe it?"

Bryan: "I do."

Darrow: "Do you believe at that time the entire sun went around the earth?"

Bryan: "No, I believe the earth goes around the sun."

Darrow was making progress. Bryan now had to admit that the authors of the Old Testament did not understand the world as well as modern man. Even Bryan would not claim that the sun moved around the earth.

Now Darrow asked about the Flood. Could Bryan give its date?

Bryan seemed muddled. He gave an answer but could not recall whether the information was in the Bible. The prosecution again objected, but Bryan wanted to continue, and Judge Raulston agreed. Agitated, Bryan turned to the audience. "These are the people whom you insult!" he said.

Darrow glared and shook his finger at Bryan: "You insult every man of science and learning in the world because he does not believe in your fool religion!"

The atmosphere grew more tense. Darrow continued his questions about the Flood. Bryan claimed that some four thousand years ago the only life on earth had been among the fish and on Noah's Ark. Then Darrow pointed out that some civilizations had existed for more than five thousand years.

Bryan was now forced to claim that all the world's civilizations must have sprung up after the Flood.

"Do you know a scientific man on the face of the earth that believes any such thing?"

"I cannot say," said Bryan, "but I know some scientific men who dispute entirely the antiquity of man as testified to by other scientific men."

"Oh," continued Darrow, "that does not answer the question. Do you know of a single scientific man on the face of the earth that believes any such thing as you stated, about the antiquity of man?"

Bryan faltered and replied, "I don't think I have ever asked one the direct question."

Bryan was obviously on the defensive now and tried to belittle the question. He said he had had more important things to do than "speculate on what our remote ancestors were." He seemed to forget that this was precisely the question that had brought them all to the crowded park in Dayton.

Darrow pressed on, exposing Bryan's ignorance of history, anthropology, and comparative religion.

"Did you ever read a book on primitive man? Like Tylor's *Primitive Culture,* or Boas, or any of the great authorities?" he asked.

"I don't think I have ever read the ones you have mentioned," answered Bryan.

"Have you read any?"

"Well I have read a little from time to time," he said weakly, "but I didn't know I was to be called as a witness."

"You never in your life made any attempt to find out about the other peoples of the earth — how old their civilizations are, how long they had existed on the earth, have you?"

"No, sir; I have been so well satisfied with the Christian religion that I have spent no time trying to find arguments against it."

"You were afraid you might find some?"

"No, sir; I am not afraid now that you will show me any — I have all the information I want to live by and to die by."

No phrase in Bryan's testimony more aptly summarized his view of science and religion. In affairs that mattered, the Bible provided enough information "to live by and to die by."

Darrow probed still further into Bryan's creed. Bryan believed that all the world's languages could be dated from the Tower of Babel, but had he read any scientific works on languages? Bryan admitted that he had not.

Once more a fellow attorney sought to rescue Bryan. "I want to interpose another objection," he said. "What is the purpose of this examination?"

Bryan was now feeling the strain of his ordeal. He shouted, "The purpose is to cast ridicule on everybody who believes in the Bible!"

Darrow snapped back, "We have the purpose of preventing bigots and ignoramuses from controlling the education of the United States!"

Now Bryan shook his fist at Darrow: "I am simply trying to protect the word of God against the greatest atheist or agnostic in the United States."

The audience burst into applause. Still the questioning continued. Darrow asked about Eve: Had she really come from Adam's rib? Bryan said yes. And what of Cain's wife: Where did she come from? Bryan had no answer.

Now Darrow returned to the creation of the world. He asked Bryan whether the six days of the biblical creation were twenty-four-hour periods. Bryan said probably not. They were "periods" of undetermined length. Here, as in the sun's standing still for Joshua, Bryan was admitting that the Bible could not always be understood literally.

Now Darrow came to his final line of questioning. He introduced Eve's temptation in the Garden of Eden. Did Bryan believe that women were compelled ever afterward to suffer childbirth pains because of Eve's sin?

"I will believe just what the Bible says," replied Bryan.

And did he believe that snakes were compelled to crawl on their bellies because the serpent tempted Eve?

"I believe that," said Bryan.

Darrow smiled. "Have you any idea how the snake went before that time?"

"No, sir."

"Do you know whether he walked on his tail or not?"

"No, sir, I have no way to know. . . ."

Before Bryan finished, the audience broke into a roar of laughter at the image of a snake walking on its tail. Bryan had finally had enough — he leaped to his feet and, in an angry, quivering voice, said, "Your Honor, I think I can shorten this testimony. The only purpose Mr. Darrow has is to slur the Bible . . ."

Darrow broke in, shaking his fist and shouting back, "I object to your statement. I am examining you on your fool ideas that no intelligent Christian on earth believes!"

As the two men glared at each other, the whole audience rose and joined in the noisy tumult. Realizing that things had gone too far, Judge Raulston immediately adjourned the court for the day. And so the interrogation of Bryan ended as abruptly as it had begun.

As the crowd dispersed, many spectators came forward to congratulate Darrow. He had proved that even Bryan could not defend a consistently literal interpretation of Genesis. Bryan had seemed a fumbling and ignorant defender of an embattled creed. He knew nothing about the scientific theories that he so glibly rejected, and even his support for the Bible was full of inconsistencies. At one moment he claimed it should be understood as literal truth; at another (the "days" taken to form the world), he showed it was susceptible to other interpretations.

When Darrow left the park, he looked back at the tired, deflated Bryan. "I was truly sorry for Mr. Bryan," he later wrote. "But I consoled myself by thinking of the years through which he had busied himself tormenting intelligent professors with impudent questions about their faith, and seeking to arouse the ignoramuses and bigots to drive them out of their positions."

That night both sides made plans for the final day of trial. Judge Raulston, fearing that violence might occur if it went on much longer, was eager to see the trial concluded. Bryan hoped to put Darrow on the stand in a reversal of the afternoon's roles in order to expose his agnosticism. But his associates saw no advantage in prolonging the trial. The defense attorneys also wanted to conclude. They had made a case for freedom of thought but realized that Scopes would be found guilty by the letter of the law. They hoped to overturn the conviction on appeal.

On Tuesday, July 21, Bryan and Darrow went to the courthouse under a rainy, leaden sky. The great drama of the trial was over. In the courtroom Darrow declared that to "save time" he would ask the jury to bring in a guilty verdict. Bryan was crushed: he would be unable to present a carefully prepared summation that he had been working on for days. But the prosecution gladly accepted the suggestion. A moment later the jury filed out, and in eight minutes they returned. Scopes was guilty.

No one was surprised; the jury could not change the law. The greater issues raised in the trial would have to be resolved in a higher court and by the American public. In the meantime, the hundreds of people who had been drawn to Dayton by the trial began to resume their ordinary lives.

John Thomas Scopes had lost his job and must pay a $100 fine for disobeying the law, but a committee was formed to raise money to send him to the University of Chicago. There he would study geology and embark on a new profession.

Bryan remained in Dayton to work on the address he had planned to deliver to the jury. This was typical of Bryan's career. He might suffer setbacks, but if he believed in a thing, he stuck to it with bulldog tenacity. He had arranged to have the speech printed in the *Chattanooga News,* where it appeared a few days later. And so it survives as testimony to his fundamentalist faith.

The undelivered address to the jury begins with a description of the simple virtues of Dayton. Bryan contrasted "the disturbing noises of a great city with the calm serenity of the country." In words that recalled his "Cross of Gold" speech, he drew together the land, the Lord, and the Bible in a web of righteousness: "I appreciate the sturdy honesty and independence of those who come into daily contact with the earth, who, living near to nature, worship nature's God, and who, dealing with the myriad mysteries of earth and air, seek to learn from revelation about the Bible's wonder-working God."

He did not oppose scientific progress. "Give science a fact and it is not only invincible, but it is of incalculable service to man." He praised science's contribution to humanity. Had it not produced the phonograph, the telephone, the sewing machine, the harvester, and "artificial ice"? Nor did he oppose freedom of thought. Atheists, agnostics, and evolutionists should be regarded as members of "sects," and like those in other religious groups they should be allowed to have their own schools.

But evolution must not be given the dignity of public support in the nation's classrooms. As in the trial, he complained that evolution associated man with the beasts and that it undermined morality. It replaced the wonderful, miraculous world of the Bible with a cold, sterile, godless universe. It depicted "a cold and heartless process." It left man to face a meaningless death. "Christ," he said, "had made of death a narrow, star-lit strip between the companionship of yesterday and the reunion of tomorrow; evolution strikes out the stars and deepens the gloom that enshrouds the tomb."

Bryan had not been able to deliver this address, but he spent the days after the trial working for the cause it celebrated. He visited the site of a proposed fundamentalist university on a hillside outside Dayton. He made a whirlwind tour through the region, speaking from the rear platform of a train to some fifty thousand people; the Scopes trial, he told them, had been a great victory for Christianity.

One day he drove through the Tennessee countryside with his wife, Mary. On a gravel road beside a cornfield he posed for a picture; standing in a dark suit beside the square black limousine with his face screwed up in a look that was half grin and half grimace, with his large farmer's hands at his side and his necktie slightly askew, he easily assumed the pose of the righteous, if aging warrior. His wife, whose confidence in Bryan was exceeded only by Bryan's confidence in himself, later wrote a description aptly describing the Great Commoner in these, his last days. "He met wave after wave of prejudice and animosity," she wrote, "as an old weathered rock will stand against angry seas."

On the Sunday morning after the trial Bryan delivered a sermon at Dayton's Southern Methodist church. After Sunday dinner he went upstairs to take a nap. In the late afternoon when Bryan had not reappeared, Mary began to worry. The room was checked, and Bryan was found dead. The heat and tension of these weeks had weakened him. But he was already an old man, aged beyond his years by diabetes.

Bryan's body lay in a house in Dayton overnight, while hundreds of tearful mourners gathered outside. On Monday morning the body was placed on a special train bound for Washington, D.C. As the train carried Bryan's body through the farmlands and hills of Tennessee and Virginia, crowds gathered in all the little towns along the way; people waved flags and sang hymns. In the Capital, Bryan's body lay in state, visited by thousands of mourners. On the afternoon of July 31, a day of fog and heavy rain, he was buried in Arlington Cemetery, hailed as a "great hero of the common people."

There was a dramatic fitness in Bryan's death. He had regarded Dayton as the scene of one of his greatest battles; its people were the plain, rural Americans he most loved. Some writers felt that the Dayton experience had crushed him, that he had died of a broken heart. But that was not Bryan's way. He had spent his life fighting for beleaguered causes. His undelivered speech to the Dayton jury concluded with the words of a hymn that conveyed this sense of pride in adversity: "Faith of our fathers, living still / in spite of dungeon, fire and sword." Others might have thought of the fundamentalist Bryan as bearer rather than victim of "dungeon, fire and sword." But Bryan was impervious to such doubts. His eyes had seen the glory of the Lord, and he held fast to the truth he found in the Bible.

Although Darrow was older than his opponent, he outlived Bryan by almost thirteen years. After the trial he gave a number of speeches on evolution, and in 1931 he narrated a full-length film on the subject entitled *The Mystery of Life*. He also handled several more important cases. Darrow, no less than Bryan, regarded himself as a protector of human dignity. A few months after leaving Dayton he was in Detroit, successfully defending a black family who had resisted with force when attacked by a white mob.

In 1928 Darrow returned to Dayton, where he was warmly received by friends he had made during the trial. His hosts drove him to the site of the new Bryan University. The fundamentalist backers had failed to provide the necessary money, and all that could be seen was a large hole in a Tennessee hillside. A few years later Darrow wrote: "My latest information is that the hole is still there on the lovely hillside, wide enough, long enough, and deep enough for a fitting grave for the monster project. Bigotry and opposition to learning are not a good foundation for any university in these modern times." Where Bryan had seen spiritual grandeur, Darrow could see only narrowmindedness.

The fundamentalist movement appeared to lose heart after the death of its best-known spokesman. But other evolution bills were debated in the next few years, and several were passed. The movement, however, never achieved the universal acceptance Bryan had anticipated. The spirited Scopes defense emboldened politicians and journalists elsewhere to denounce evolution laws. In Tennessee the law fell into neglect and was finally repealed in 1967.

In retrospect, it is remarkable how much Bryan and Darrow had in common. Each saw himself as a defender of the oppressed. Each represented a major cultural force in the 1920s. At Dayton each presented a program for American development. But where Bryan identified truth with tradition, the Bible, and rural America, Darrow embraced a creed of intellectual and social emancipation.

America observed the proceedings at Dayton with such avid interest because the trial brought out so many issues: parental authority, conventional morality, freedom of speech, science and the Bible. At times it seemed that the two forces would come to blows in the hot, muggy, hectic days of the trial. But somehow Dayton absorbed both sides. The crowd that applauded Bryan on the Bible also cheered Malone and Darrow on freedom of speech. The people seemed to want both sides to be right. They wanted the moral anchor and the spiritual certainty of the Bible, but they also wanted the personal freedom and scientific progress that were so alluring in the 1920s.

QUESTIONS

1. What features of modern American life did most Americans, fundamentalists as well as modernists, accept and enjoy? What did fundamentalists dislike about modern America?

2. Why did the teaching of evolutionary theory create such a stir? Why did fundamentalists object to it? How did modernists reconcile Darwinism and religion?

3. In what ways did Bryan's earlier career make him a natural choice for joining the prosecution in the Scopes case? In what ways did Darrow's career prepare him to defend Scopes?

4. Describe Dayton, Tennessee. In what ways did the town display fundamentalist conservatism? In what ways was it sympathetic to intellectual freedom? Why did the people in Dayton applaud Dudley Field Malone's speech on intellectual freedom?

5. What were the main issues in the Scopes trial? Why did Bryan condemn the theory of evolution? What was achieved in Darrow's examination of Bryan? Why was Scopes convicted?

6. Bryan is often regarded as the loser at Dayton. Why? Was there any validity in his critique of modern civilization, his rejection of materialism, and his emphasis on spirituality? Was he right to imply that other people were less moral or religious than he because they believed in Darwinian theory?

7. The author claims that despite the cultural schism revealed at Dayton, the opposing sides in the Scopes trial shared many values. What were their differences? On what issues were they in accord?

BIBLIOGRAPHY

ALLEN, FREDERICK LEWIS. *Only Yesterday* (1931). Lively social history of the 1920s.

BRYAN, WILLIAM JENNINGS. *The Memoirs of William Jennings Bryan* (1925). Bryan's autobiography.

DARROW, CLARENCE. *The Story of My Life* (1932). Darrow's autobiography.

FASS, PAULA S. *The Damned and the Beautiful* (1977). American youth in the 1920s.

FURNISS, NORMAN F. *The Fundamentalist Controversy* (1954). History of the fundamentalist movement.

GINGER, RAY. *Six Days or Forever?* (1958). Fine history of the Scopes trial.

LEVINE, LAWRENCE W. *Defender of the Faith* (1965). Biography of William Jennings Bryan covering 1915–25.

SINGAL, DANIEL J. *The War Within: From Victorian to Modernist Thought in the South, 1919–1945* (1982). The intellectual context for the Scopes Trial.

TIERNEY, KEVIN. *Darrow: A Biography* (1979). Probing explanation of Darrow's career and personality.

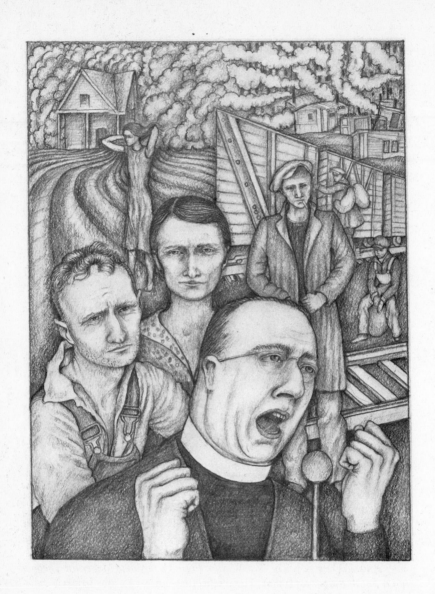

8

THE GREAT DEPRESSION

Father Coughlin and Social Justice

The Great Depression of the 1930s damaged the United States both physically and psychologically. It ruined thousands of businessmen and hurt millions of laborers. Breadlines and shanty towns appeared around the nation, making visible the plight of the unemployed. In a land whose resources had seemed boundless, where technology had promised unlimited progress, the depression destroyed dreams as well as jobs. Millions began to wonder if traditional American values could survive, and extremists advocated scores of fanciful programs for redistributing wealth. Charles Coughlin, one of the new prophets, denounced the supposed perpetrators of the depression and proposed far-reaching economic reforms. His popularity accentuates the decade's atmosphere of fear and privation; but his ultimate failure reveals American resistance to radical change.

On November 11, 1934, a Catholic priest, Father Charles E. Coughlin, made a radio broadcast announcing the formation of an ambitious political organization, the National Union for Social Justice. Under his direction the union would lobby for a broad reform program including a guaranteed annual income and the nationalization of oil, power, and light. These were revolutionary economic proposals, and in most periods of American history Coughlin would have commanded few followers. But in 1934, in the midst of the Great Depression, he was one of the most powerful men in America. His weekly radio broadcasts from a suburban Detroit parish commanded a larger audience than any other radio program in the 1930s. He claimed to have received as many as a million letters from supporters in a week.

Coughlin's popularity was made possible by the turmoil in American life during the 1930s. The depression brought with it not only unprecedented physical suffering but also unprecedented doubts about the American economic system. As a national challenge it overshadowed even World War I. In war a nation at least had a clear objective: to defeat the enemy in battle. But how did one defeat a depression when it was not even clear who or what the main enemy was? Its effects were pervasive, but its causes were elusive.

Only a few years before, America had enjoyed a decade of unprecedented prosperity, and the future seemed to promise continuing growth. Hard work, free enterprise, and inventiveness apparently opened the way to endless progress. Herbert Hoover summed up the people's optimism when he accepted the Republican presidential nomination in 1923. "We in America today," he said, "are nearer to the final triumph over poverty than ever before in the history of any land."

After the Great Crash in October 1929, however, American self-confidence suffered blow upon blow. Stock prices fell; businesses failed; farm income and manufacturing production declined by half; and new construction all but ceased. By 1932 millions of Americans were out of work. Many lived in squalid shacks on the edge of the cities and got their food from charity. Even those who were still employed frequently earned less from farm, job, or investments than in the previous decade. No one was beyond the reach of fear, for no one could anticipate what lay ahead.

Herbert Hoover, whose misfortune it was to be president at the onslaught of the depression, seemed helpless, and his opponents characterized him as an uncaring conservative. In truth, Hoover was neither heartless nor inactive; he purchased agricultural surpluses, inaugurated public works projects, and provided loans for homes and businesses. Even while making some changes, however, Hoover was determined to preserve the spirit of free enterprise. He believed that unemployment relief, currency inflation, and other popular reform ideas would undermine the American character.

In the presidential campaign of 1932 Democratic candidate Franklin Delano Roosevelt could easily suggest that Hoover's reticence about reform had worsened the depression. Roosevelt promised vigorous government action and was elected by a landslide. Significantly, he did not specify what action he would undertake. Nor did he need to: people voted for him in what amounted to an act of faith.

In the early days of his first administration Roosevelt was able to impress the country with his infectious optimism. On inauguration day, when the banks were closed and millions were still unemployed, he delivered a stirring address, claiming "The only thing we have to fear is fear itself." In the "First New Deal" of 1933 Roosevelt initiated measures to sustain the banks, support farm income, and provide jobs. His Civilian Conservation Corps employed young men in forest projects. The Agricultural Adjustment Act raised farm prices. The Tennessee Valley Authority provided flood control and electricity for a large region. Stimulated by these and other measures, production increased and the depression appeared conquerable.

But in 1934 more problems arose. The worst drought in American history created a great sterile dust bowl in Oklahoma and Texas, forcing tenants and sharecroppers by the thousands from their land. Laborers found Roosevelt's legislation inadequate to protect their unions; small farmers believed that Roosevelt's agricultural policies favored large farmers. Millions were still unemployed; and still there were breadlines; still there were shanty towns.

Again public confidence wavered. Roosevelt did well in the congressional elections of 1934, but new voices began to compete with his own, beckoning America to more extreme kinds of reform. The Socialist and Communist parties gained new adherents. And a host of radical reform programs enjoyed wide popularity. In this atmosphere of privation and frustration the melodious voice, colorful phrases, and radical ideas of Charles E. Coughlin won the attention of millions.

Coughlin was born in Hamilton, Ontario, on October 25, 1891. He loved to brag in later years about his background in the "laboring class" and his great-grandfather, who had "dulled many a pick with the pioneers who dug the Erie Canal." His father, Thomas Coughlin, had gone to work as a stoker on a Great Lakes steamer when he was sixteen. Forced by sickness to abandon his first job, the elder Coughlin became a sexton at Saint Mary's Church in Hamilton. He married one of the parishioners, a seamstress named Amelia Mahoney. Having secured a more lucrative position as foreman of a bakery, he located his family in a middle-class Irish neighborhood. Charles was their only child who survived infancy, and they lavished their parental affection on him.

At school Charles did well in both classics and athletics. When he was thirteen, he graduated from the local parish school and entered Saint Michael's College, forty miles away in Toronto. His doting parents were proud that their son was embarked on a course of studies that could lead to the priesthood, but they sorrowed at losing him. A week after she had left Charles at Saint Michael's, Amelia Coughlin wrote urging him to resign from the school and come home. The school authorities, however, intercepted the letter, and Charles did not learn about it until long after his mother had adjusted to his absence.

Charles compiled a good record in high school and college, graduating with honors in philosophy from the University of Toronto in 1911. He was an athletic young man with bright eyes and dark hair. With a keen mind and handsome features, he looked more like a charming escort and a rising businessman or politician than an incipient priest.

But his parents still hoped that he would enter the church. Partly to please them, partly from religious conviction, he entered Saint Basil's Seminary in Toronto, where he began an austere routine that included digging latrines, plowing fields, and washing floors as well as study and prayer. He hoped that he might combine religion with public service and was encouraged by Pope Leo XIII's 1891 encyclical, *Rerum Novarum* (Of New Things), which called upon Catholics to work toward a more just economic order.

In 1916 Charles Coughlin was ordained a priest in Saint Basil's Church, and a few days later he celebrated his first public mass at his parents' church in Hamilton. He was assigned by the church to teach at Assumption College outside Detroit, and he soon assisted at several neighborhood parishes.

Although his experience in debate and teaching had given him a good start as a pulpit orator, he entered upon his first preaching assignments with trepidation, composing draft after draft, then practicing his delivery, experimenting with different intonations, facial expressions, and arm movements. Father Coughlin soon established himself as an effective parish priest. His dynamic personality and effective preaching drew people to his services. After several assignments in other Michigan parishes, he was given the difficult task of establishing a new parish in Royal Oak, twelve miles north of Detroit. The town promised to attract many Catholic families in the future with the growth of the automobile industry, but in 1926 it had few Catholics and was a center of hostile Ku Klux Klan activity.

Detroit Bishop Michael Gallagher had ordered the construction in Royal Oak of a large wood barn of a church with a seating capacity of six hundred. When Father Coughlin took over the Shrine of the Little Flower — named for Saint Theresa, the "Little Flower of Jesus" — he entered upon his greatest challenge. The church sat at the intersection of two dirt roads in a mosquito-infested field. It had no rectory, so that Father Coughlin had to sleep in a small room at the back of his church and dine with his parishioners. And, as expected, the KKK soon paid a visit. In the night they arrived, hidden in white hoods, and burned a cross on the church lawn. Beneath this ominous, charred symbol of anti-Catholicism, Coughlin found the message "Move From Royal Oak." Instead of leaving, Father Coughlin vowed to build a monument on the spot where the cross had burned.

First, however, he had to solve the church's financial problems. He received unexpected help when a friendly baseball scout for the Detroit Tigers persuaded some local players plus a contingent of visiting New York Yankees, headed by Babe Ruth, to attend a widely publicized mass at the Shrine of the Little Flower. Thousands turned up, and under the Babe's direction baseball players passed hats and cardboard boxes while the great slugger shouted, "You can't get in without your money!" and "No change today!" At day's end the church was richer by $10,000, and Charles Coughlin had a new appreciation for the uses of publicity.

But in fall 1926 Coughlin was still sleeping in the cold room at the back of the church, worrying about heat bills, and struggling to provide $100 a week for the church mortgage. Because he could not expect a monthly visit from Babe Ruth, he hit upon the brash idea of a series of radio broadcasts. Many of his friends were skeptical; radio was a new medium, and religious programming was unusual. It might also be expensive.

But Coughlin, whose pulpit style was improving, wanted to try. He made an arrangement with station WJR in Detroit to broadcast one sermon from the Shrine of the Little Flower as an experiment. On October 17, 1926, at 2:00 P.M., Father Coughlin, soon to be known as the "Radio Priest," made his first broadcast. At the conclusion he was apprehensive. He was accustomed to winning an audience with his dramatic gestures and his infectious smile, and he had always been able to read his effectiveness in his congregation's faces; but this audience had been an abstraction hearing his disembodied voice over radio. How would they respond?

Within a few days Coughlin had his answer. He and the radio station received enthusiastic letters — enough to justify a weekly program. Coughlin's audience grew rapidly with each broadcast. His voice commanded attention: he spoke in a rolling Irish brogue, powerful and clear, that drew listeners to him. His words were plain and colorful, and he projected a sense of honest concern. As his reputation spread, new stations picked up the Sunday talks. Soon he could be heard all over Michigan, then across the Midwest, and in 1930 across the nation.

In Royal Oak his parish grew rapidly. His popularity actually encouraged a building boom in the area as Catholics sought to live near the now-famous Radio Priest. The church became wealthy, receiving donations from radio fans as well as from local parishioners. In 1928 Coughlin was able to begin planning for a new edifice, an octagonal church of stone topped by a great stone tower.

Coughlin's early broadcasts from the Shrine of the Little Flower were devoted primarily to religious themes. But during the depression his interest in social justice came to the fore. In Royal Oak he organized a relief society to distribute food and clothing. He sought in his broadcasts to identify the causes of the depression. Starvation and joblessness were bad enough, he argued, but they were merely symptoms of an elusive disease. Coughlin probed behind the symptoms and focused the anger of a distraught people on concrete, malevolent forces that, he claimed, had caused their suffering.

The most specific of his early targets were "international bankers." On January 4, 1931, he planned to announce on his weekly broadcast that the depression had been caused by an insidious band of financial magnates, whose hand had been strengthened by the Treaty of Versailles. When CBS, which carried his nationwide broadcast, learned of the proposed talk, the station's management asked him to change it. He promised to do so — but instead presented an attack on CBS itself for censorship. Buoyed up by a massive influx of supportive letters — he claimed he received more than a million after the speech — he next defied CBS and delivered the talk on bankers. Within a few months his relation with the network had become so strained that CBS dropped his program despite its enormous popularity. Undaunted, Father Coughlin created a new network by persuading scores of local stations to carry his Sunday broadcasts.

In this and other crises it was fortunate for Coughlin that he had the warm support of his superior, Michael J. Gallagher, a white-haired bishop, who believed, like Coughlin, that the church should be concerned with social justice. With his bishop's backing and radio's largest audience, Coughlin began to propose specific economic reforms. The bankers, he said, had caused the depression by restricting the money supply in order to increase their profits. Echoing the Populist rhetoric of William Jennings Bryan, Coughlin argued that the people had "been the pawns and chattels of the modern pagans who have crucified us upon a cross of gold." The solution was the abandonment of the "filthy gold standard." Coughlin also recommended that American industry be regulated in the public interest to curtail the "industrial rights and commercial rights greedily guarded by the few."

At first Coughlin refused to enter directly into the political arena, but as the depression worsened he became increasingly hostile to Herbert Hoover. In October 1931 he broadcast a direct attack on the president. Hoover, he said, was misleading the people with "airy platitudes." The president promised prosperity but refused to adopt what Coughlin regarded as adequate measures. In June 1932, when Hoover used the army against the Bonus Army, Coughlin castigated the president for giving "Billions to international bankers who never fought; but none to the soldiers who risked life and limb." Coughlin complained that the president tolerated "idle factories, long bread lines, millions of jobless" in a nation blessed with "abundance of foodstuffs, millions of virgin acres, banks loaded with money." By implication, the depression could easily be ended by an intelligent, creative leader.

Coughlin thought he had found that leader in Franklin Roosevelt, then governor of New York. Roosevelt, in turn, realized that Coughlin would be a useful ally. A cousin had written to him from Detroit that the priest had a "following just about equal to that of Mr. Gandhi's." During the election year an informal alliance developed between Coughlin and Roosevelt. When the priest had his troubles with CBS, Roosevelt wrote him an encouraging letter. One month before the election Coughlin wrote Roosevelt that his position prevented him from endorsing either candidate but that they should "work in harmony." Coughlin continued his attacks on Hoover throughout the campaign. It was clear that Roosevelt was his man.

In March 1933 Coughlin went to Washington to observe the inauguration of the new president. Millions were out of work. In January 272 banks had closed, and in February whole states — Michigan, Maryland, and Ohio — had closed their banks, threatening the savings of millions of Americans. On the eve of Roosevelt's swearing in, *The Nation* surveyed the wreckage of the American economy and lamented the passing of the American dream. "In all our previous history," the periodical declared, "it has been taken for granted that ours was a land of opportunity, and that rewards bore some relation to initiative, effort, and ability." This supposition was no longer true: "The promise of American life has been shattered — possibly beyond repair."

The people gathering for the inauguration needed to be reassured, not only that prosperity would return, but also that the country's traditional reliance on hard work and personal initiative would survive the ordeal. On March 4 the new president proved master of the occasion. He promised to reform the unpopular banking system and to create new jobs. The depression could be ended, he said, and America could be restored to her former greatness. But the people must first believe in themselves. His memorable words, "We have nothing to fear but fear itself," caught the imagination of Charles Coughlin along with millions of other Americans. Back in Michigan, Coughlin wrote the president that he had been "thrilled" with the address.

In the early days of his administration Roosevelt was able to impress the nation with his optimism and energy. His approach to reform was frankly experimental. The main thing was to do something. Congress shared this mood and quickly passed a series of reform measures. In the First New Deal, Roosevelt initiated programs to help banks, support farm income, and provide jobs. Of particular interest to Father Coughlin were the National Recovery Administration and the Agricultural Adjustment Act. The NRA encouraged businesses to work together for greater efficiency and profits and permitted unions to organize and bargain collectively. The AAA empowered the president to support farm prices and inflate the currency.

Coughlin carefully scrutinized each new measure. He appears to have considered himself an adviser — almost an informal member of the president's cabinet. In the early months of 1935 he frequently praised the New Deal. He described the NRA, for example, as the first legislation in many centuries to protect the worker; it was "an immortal step back to the principle of our being our brother's keeper." On November 27, 1933, he warmly praised Roosevelt before an overflow crowd of seven thousand at the Hippodrome in New York City. He had already decided that Roosevelt was a president to compare with Lincoln and Washington.

Coughlin would later claim that he could have been one of Roosevelt's inner circle, had he so chosen. Certainly the administration recognized his importance and encouraged his support. The White House always responded to his letters, and Coughlin's many admirers in Congress even encouraged Roosevelt to name the Radio Priest an adviser to an international economic conference in London.

But Roosevelt was wary of Coughlin. The priest sometimes presumed too much, as if he expected to dictate policy to the chief executive. At one time in 1933 Roosevelt, exasperated by Coughlin's constant communications, remarked, "He should run for the presidency himself. Who the hell does he think he is?"

The Radio Priest, in turn, began to cast a critical eye over Roosevelt's policies. He found fault with the wage provisions of the NRA — the minimum of 40 cents an hour was inadequate. Coughlin paid construction workers on his new church more generous wages: 55 cents an hour for laborers and $1.25 to $1.50 for carpenters and masons. He was particularly appalled by the administration's agricultural policy. To increase farm revenue the government decided to provide compensation for farmers who would reduce production. But this was not sufficient to end the current surplus, so that the administration encouraged farmers to destroy part of their cotton and wheat crops and purchased 6 million pigs for slaughter. The economic basis for these measures may have been sound, but to the millions of Americans who were ill clad and ill fed the fires that consumed the livestock and the plows that beat down the crops were symbols of an obscenely misguided policy.

Father Coughlin articulated this view, calling the farm program "foolish proposals aimed at starving us into prosperity." He denounced the policymakers "who have advocated the slaughter of six million pigs and have already defiled the countryside and the Mississippi River with their malodorous rottenness." He denied that there were surpluses. "There is no superfluity of either cotton or wheat," he said, "until every naked back has been clothed, until every empty stomach has been filled." This was the sort of issue that brought out Coughlin's best rhetoric. He thrived on issues where good and bad seemed clearly defined. And what could be worse than destroying food in a hungry nation?

Yet despite his concern, Coughlin was unwilling to exploit the issue. He still hoped to "work in harmony" with the president. His most caustic criticisms were addressed to the White House in private letters, proposing another course to the administration. If there was a farm surplus, let the market be expanded through Coughlin's favorite reform, currency inflation. If the country would just abandon the gold standard and create more currency, farmers could have their higher prices, and consumers could afford more goods. The only people who would suffer were the only people who should suffer — the bankers.

In January 1934 Coughlin presented his views on currency to a House committee considering a Roosevelt measure to reduce the gold content of the dollar. Coughlin heartily supported the measure. "President Roosevelt," he said, "is not going to make a mistake, for God Almighty is guiding him." If Congress failed to carry through the president's suggestions, he said, "I foresee a revolution far greater than the French Revolution. It is either Roosevelt or ruin." Two days later Coughlin visited the president at the White House and left an hour-long private conference praising Roosevelt as a man twenty years ahead of his time.

Despite the year's cordial beginning, however, events in the months ahead would soon strain relations between the priest and the president. In April, Father Coughlin could still declare, "The New Deal is Christ's deal." But his attitude toward Roosevelt had begun to sour as a result of both political conviction and personal ambition. With the powers granted him in the Gold Reserve Act of 1934, Roosevelt devalued the dollar by raising the price of gold from $20.67 to $35.00 an ounce. But Coughlin did not believe this inflationary measure was sufficient; the country needed to issue more paper, backed in part by silver.

Coughlin's belief that further reforms were needed was reinforced by economic developments. After a short growth period in 1933 the economy slowed down in 1934. Millions were still jobless. Businessmen and laborers alike were dissatisfied with the National Recovery Administration. The crippling drought in Oklahoma and Texas ruined many farmers. To make matters worse, the provisions for crop reduction in the Agricultural Adjustment Act forced many marginal tenant farmers off the land.

In the face of these developments, Coughlin began to ask himself whether he did not know better than Roosevelt what the country needed. His own vast audience and his personal surroundings encouraged his self-esteem. The Shrine of the Little Flower had grown into one of the most modern and impressive churches in America. Built of Vermont granite and Indiana limestone, it consisted of a basilica, a shrine, and a tower. In spring 1934 the basilica, a huge octagonal building that would hold 2,600 worshipers, was nearing completion. Its workmen, benefiting from Coughlin's belief in higher wages, had recently received a 10 percent pay boost. Next to the basilica was the shrine of Saint Theresa; above its altar was a relief of the saint carved from a single block of marble. Outside a massive stone tower reached 180 feet into the air. Shaped like a cross, the tower was decorated with carvings of Christ and the archangels; among these figures was a statue of Saint Michael that bore the features of Coughlin's white-haired bishop and patron, Michael Gallagher.

In 1934 the church was alive with activity. Parades of tourists, drawn to Royal Oak by the fame of the Radio Priest, came to the church from all parts of the United States. The visitors were greeted by guides who showed them the church and sold pamphlets by Father Coughlin. They arrived in such numbers that a collection of new motels and gas stations sprang up near the church to serve them. One establishment, the "Shrine Super Service Gas Station," was built directly across the street from Saint Theresa's.

Hidden from the tourists' view was a large soundproof room under the shrine where roughly a hundred clerks handled the Radio Priest's daily business. Well supplied with typewriters, mimeographs, and addressographs, the clerks sat on swivel chairs at long wood tables and sorted through mountainous piles of mailbags containing as many as two hundred thousand letters. They were mainly notes from supporters who praised Coughlin for articulating their hopes and fears. Many contained small donations; others requested copies of radio talks. Together, they made Coughlin's mail delivery the largest in the United States.

Coughlin's office was far removed from both clerks and tourists. It was inside the tower at the top of a dark, spiral staircase. Here, a few feet from the statue of Christ, Father Coughlin could withdraw completely from the world into a suite that had its own shower, kitchen, and sleeping room. A microphone on his desk fed Coughlin's Sunday addresses to millions of American households.

Father Coughlin, now in the prime of life, was an appealing figure. His bright eyes retained their luster, and his voice was warm and confiding. He spoke of himself with engaging candor. Was he a demagogue? one reporter asked. "Yes," he agreed, he was a "leader of the masses." He obviously enjoyed his fame. He took a puckish delight in walking around with a large dog, Pal, at his heels, and driving his car at high speeds. When he was not closeted in his tower, he cared for his church. He had designed the new basilica and raised the money to build it. Each Sunday he conducted two masses and delivered six or seven sermons.

But despite the efficiency of his clerical organization and the progress of his building program, he gave the impression of a man who was unsettled by his unique opportunities and responsibilities. His nervous temperament led him to eat constantly, and his weight rose steadily to more than two hundred pounds. One evening he collapsed in his tower room, thinking he was having a heart attack. He lay unconscious for half a day, only to awaken and learn that he had suffered from acute indigestion.

Surely the pressures on Coughlin were enormous. No man in America had ever spoken to so many people week after week. Although the pope and Coughlin's own bishop had urged Catholic priests to work for social justice, no priest in Catholic history had ever had such an opportunity to do so. He enjoyed telling people that he had addressed more people than Christ's apostles. All this was exciting, but producing dramatic new ideas week after week placed a terrible burden on Coughlin. He might reach more people than the apostles. But could he deliver as important a message?

Such doubts may have troubled Coughlin, but the challenge was exhilarating. By now he was a master of broadcast technique. His rich Irish brogue, his warm lyrical tone, and his engaging frankness made people feel that he was a man who understood and cared about their problems. He reduced complex economic issues to a few simple facts. He castigated villains by name and showed how they could be conquered. Herbert Hoover, J. P. Morgan, and the "international bankers" had already felt the sting of his rebuke.

Father Coughlin's voice and ideas had an astonishing magnetism. In New York City neighborhoods on a Sunday afternoon Coughlin's words seemed to come from radios in every building. In the mining town of Wernersville, Pennsylvania, unemployed miners and their families walked several miles to gather outside a Ford agency where they could hear Coughlin's strong voice over a loudspeaker. Throughout the United States were farmers who had paid their last doctor's bill in barter with a chicken or a sack of grain because they had no cash; families who sent their children to free camps for the summer because they could not afford to feed them; and salesmen who stood gaunt for months in automobile showrooms without selling a single car. In New York and Wernersville and across the nation such people nodded in approval when Coughlin told them that something was wrong with the country and that something must be done.

But what must be done? In his solitude in the tower office above the Shrine of the Little Flower, Coughlin pondered how to use his influence. Often it seemed that his best choice was to continue supporting Roosevelt. Coughlin had the gift of his oratory and the support of his audience, but Roosevelt had the power of his office. The president could actually make policy, and certainly his policies were better than Hoover's. Moreover, if Coughlin challenged the president, Roosevelt's popularity might well prove greater than his own.

Still the Radio Priest found himself increasingly at odds with the president. In April 1934 relations between Coughlin and Roosevelt reached a low point. Henry Morgenthau, Jr., secretary of the treasury, released a report showing that Coughlin's personal secretary had been speculating on the silver market, presumably with church funds. Her transactions were entirely legal, but in view of Coughlin's advocacy of a silver-based currency the investments were embarrassing.

Coughlin widened the breach with the administration in his final broadcast of the 1933–34 season. He reminded his audience that at Roosevelt's inauguration Americans had been "an optimistic people." Now, he said, "clouds of suspicion are darkening our hopes." Roosevelt, the "Moses" who had promised to lead his people out of their troubled circumstances, was "lost in his narrow confines of the desert."

During the next few months Roosevelt made conciliatory gestures toward the popular priest, sending Joseph Kennedy as an emissary to Coughlin, seeking a naval appointment for one of his friends, and inviting him to visit the White House. In response, Coughlin's first radio address was friendly. "More than ever," he said, "I am in favor of the New Deal."

But Coughlin still wanted to strengthen his political position and advance his program. His mail, showing "the pulse of the people," indicated that millions of Americans were dissatisfied with Roosevelt's reforms. In his second broadcast of the season he questioned whether either of the major parties could solve the country's economic woes. America needed something better than the "putrefying carcasses" of the old parties. Then, on November 11 in his regular Sunday broadcast, he announced the formation of the National Union for Social Justice and read its preamble and sixteen points.

Coughlin began by arguing that a "beneficent God" had bestowed "this world's wealth of field, of forest, of mine" on all mankind. The wealth taken from these resources belonged properly to all people. But the "harsh, cruel and grasping ways of wicked men" had "concentrated wealth into the hands of a few." Coughlin's introduction faintly echoes the preamble to the Declaration of Independence. Both documents portray a divinely ordained condition of equality; both see threats from ambitious usurpers. But Coughlin described a somewhat different kind of equality than Jefferson and a somewhat different breed of usurper. Jefferson cared less for economic equality than for equality before the law. Although Jefferson preferred agricultural to mercantile wealth, he did not find it unnatural that some Americans had amassed fortunes, nor did he object to the custom of rewarding such men with political power.

Coughlin, however, objected to inequality in the distribution of wealth. He favored something approaching equality of condition as well as equality of opportunity. His villains were those who misused the equality of opportunity to take more than their share of the world's wealth at the expense of others. Where Jefferson feared the tyranny of selfish politicians, Coughlin feared the tyranny of exploitive capitalists.

In some respects, he was an heir of William Jennings Bryan, Theodore Roosevelt, and other Populist and Progressive reformers who favored governmental restrictions on business. His program also reflected the emphasis on social justice set forth in the papal encyclicals of Pius XI and Leo XIII.

The sixteen points in Coughlin's reform program fall into four major categories. First, he called for personal freedom: liberty of conscience, worship, education, and vocation. Second, he made several proposals to improve the economic condition of the average person: a guaranteed annual income at a level meeting "the standard of American decency"; fair profits for the farmer; the right to unionize for the laborer; lower taxes for the average citizen; and maintenance of the cost of living on "an even keel." Third, he demanded that harmful concentrations of private economic power be ended. Certain resources, too important to be held in private hands, should be nationalized; the government should control banking and the coining and regulation of money; "non-productive" bonds should be recalled and tax-exempt bonds abolished; in wartime there should be "conscription" of wealth as well as men; and private property, though allowed to exist, should be regulated for the public good. Finally, the government should be simplified, its ever-expanding bureaucracy kept in check.

Clearly, the program raised many problems. It was full of contradictory and vague arguments. How could one establish a guaranteed annual income while reducing taxes and retiring bonds? What resources were too vital to be held in private hands? What was a "decent" income?

Such questions did not weaken the program's appeal. Coughlin's program may have been vague, but its attraction lay in its promise of things most Americans wanted: prosperity, security, and order coupled with personal freedom and economic independence. It did not anticipate the hard political decisions necessary to balance these blessings. But Coughlin did not have to involve himself in problems of implementation. His was the arena of dreams and emotions.

In the weeks following his November 11 broadcast, Coughlin urged his listeners to join the National Union for Social Justice. There were no dues, but, of course, contributions were welcome. By early 1935 Coughlin claimed 5 million adherents. (He later admitted that this figure was an exaggeration.) He argued that a new economic system must replace capitalism. The profit motive must give way to the needs of the community. All "honest needs within the nation" must be supplied. Coughlin called for construction of eighteen thousand miles of highways and nine hundred thousand homes. To pay for these improvements the government should issue "credit money" and so avoid bank loans and new taxes. The government should provide jobs for anyone unable to find employment.

During 1935 Coughlin was still reluctant to make a complete break with Roosevelt — his union could be a lobby rather than a political party — but he was well on his way to an independent course. On March 4 Gen. Hugh Johnson, the erratic former director of the NRA, went on national radio to denounce Coughlin as an opportunist and demagogue who should be excluded from public activity because of his clerical collar and foreign birth. Father Coughlin, who had long since become an American citizen, delivered an acrimonious reply defending the right of clerics to participate in politics and reviewing his American ancestry. He went on to describe Johnson as the victim of a bankrupt political program. He was a "political corpse" and a "chocolate soldier."

Another political figure, Secretary of the Interior Harold Ickes, joined Johnson's attack, but Roosevelt discouraged the exchange of barbs. He feared that such denunciations would drive Coughlin to form a third party that would sap Roosevelt's political strength. Roosevelt continued to flatter Coughlin through an emissary, Frank Murphy, a Roosevelt supporter and member of Coughlin's parish.

In the end it was not so much Roosevelt's actions as Coughlin's giddy success that drew the Radio Priest toward a third party movement. In 1935 he created a weekly newspaper called *Social Justice,* which enjoyed a wide audience, and gave speeches in Detroit, Cleveland, and New York that drew up to 25,000 people. His broadcast season grew by thirteen weeks, and he presided over the formation of NUSJ chapters across the nation. There appeared to be no limit to his power.

Coughlin must also have been encouraged in his militancy by the growth of other radical movements at this time. The failure of either major party to end the depression led others besides Coughlin to conclude that old parties and old ideas could not end the nation's problems. The best known of the extremists was Huey Long of Louisiana. Long was a heavy-set man with dark curly hair and rugged features. As governor of Louisiana he had become a hero of the common people, taxing the big corporations in Louisiana and building schools, highways, and hospitals. To his supporters it mattered little that he had established himself as virtual dictator of Louisiana and could remark unabashedly, "I'm the constitution around here now." He cared about the people, and he made things work. He was known affectionately as "The Kingfish."

In January 1932 Long took a seat in the U.S. Senate and brought his tough, outspoken politics to a national audience. With Louisiana safely governed by his associates, he began to press for an economic program known as "Share Our Wealth." He called for confiscation of all family fortunes of more than $5 million and a 100 percent tax on earnings larger than $1 million a year. These funds would, he claimed, help provide every family with an annual income of $2,000 to $3,000 and a "homestead" consisting of a car, a house, and other items. The idea was understandably popular. In 1935 Long claimed 4.6 million members for the Share Our Wealth movement and talked of a third-party presidential campaign in 1936.

Along with Coughlin's National Union for Social Justice and Long's Share Our Wealth program, a third radical panacea gained national prominence in 1935. This was Dr. Francis E. Townsend's Old-Age Revolving Pensions plan. Townsend was a retired physician who was worried about the plight of the elderly. He favored paying $200 a month to everyone above sixty. The recipients would be required to spend the whole sum within a month, and so the pensions would stimulate the economy as a whole as well as aid the elderly. Townsend was a colorless figure, totally lacking in the charisma of Long or

Coughlin, but his program appealed enormously to those who would benefit. In 1935 there were Townsend clubs throughout the United States and the *Townsend National Weekly* boasted a circulation of two hundred thousand.

While Roosevelt was courting Coughlin through Frank Murphy, Coughlin, Long, and Townsend were discussing a third-party movement. Their exchanges were awkward because each man was jealous of his own position, but Roosevelt was disturbed. A powerful independent party, drawing most of its strength from former Democrats, could ruin his chances for reelection.

In part to forestall such an alliance Roosevelt began the Second New Deal in summer 1935. Although he did not adopt the radicals' programs, his new measures, like theirs, did tend to redistribute American wealth and power. The National Labor Relations Board gave workers the right to bargain collectively. The Social Securities Act established an old age pension program. And the Wealth Tax Act increased taxes on large estates, incomes, and gifts.

As Coughlin picked his course, he had to evaluate a complex situation. His best hope lay in an alliance with Huey Long, for Coughlin was unwilling to leave the priesthood to run for office. If he launched a third-party movement, he would need a candidate like Long who was amenable to his program but capable of attracting votes on his own. Coughlin must have worried, however, that Long was too much his own man to carry out someone else's program.

His speculation ended abruptly on September 8, 1935, when a young Baton Rouge doctor approached Huey Long in the state capitol rotunda and fired a .32-caliber pistol into his stomach point-blank. Long's bodyguards immediately disarmed the assassin and riddled his body with submachine gunfire. He died immediately. Long struggled on for two days and died on September 10. By an odd chance Father Coughlin was having lunch with President Roosevelt at Hyde Park when they heard about Long's death. Both expressed their regrets, but each must have been secretly relieved: a formidable rival to priest and president had been removed.

Now Coughlin was without peer among American propagandists. Perhaps emboldened by his new prominence, he declared on November 17, 1935, that the New Deal and his Social Justice program were inexorably opposed. In January 1936 he announced that his NUSJ had organizations in 302 of the 435 congressional districts. Coughlin had not yet created a third party — his NUSJ was still a lobbying organization — but in April and May the union increased its political activities by endorsing local political candidates.

Coughlin finally embarked on an independent political campaign as the result of a bill in Congress sponsored by Senator Lynn Frazier and Congressman William Lemke of North Dakota. The bill called for refinancing of farm mortgages with the backing of $8 billion in paper currency. Coughlin strongly supported the measure, which combined inflation and agricultural reform, two important elements of his own program. The bill's defeat in the House on May 13 served as a catalyst for the formation of a new political party.

Coughlin soon held negotiations with Lemke that led to the announcement on June 19 that the congressman would run for president on a new ticket with the priest's backing. Although the Union party would have Lemke as its candidate, it was clear that Coughlin would be its leader. In his radio broadcast the week before Coughlin had hinted at what was ahead. "I shall lay down a plan of action," he said, "which will thrill you and inspire you beyond anything that I have ever said or accomplished in the past." Coughlin's growing egotism shines through this statement: his would be the inspiration, his the achievement.

The Union party platform, drawn up by Coughlin, was taken from the sixteen points of the NUSJ. As Lemke's running mate Coughlin favored Thomas C. O'Brien, a Boston labor attorney. In addition he courted Townsend and Gerald Smith, Huey Long's successor in the Share Our Wealth program, by including platform provisions for old age security and a limitation on personal income.

The next few weeks were spent in maneuvering by Coughlin, Smith, and Townsend. Smith had predicted that a coalition could poll 20 million votes; clearly, cooperation between the extremists was necessary for an effective third-party movement. But each was wary of the other.

In mid-July a Townsend convention met in Cleveland. Both Smith and Coughlin addressed the group. Speaking at the end of the convention in a hot, crowded auditorium, Coughlin labored to win the nine thousand elderly Townsendites to the Union party campaign. He pleaded and shouted; he removed his coat and clerical collar; he denounced Roosevelt as a "great betrayer and liar." The crowd cheered each new dose of rhetoric, and Coughlin returned to Detroit convinced that he had won the Townsendites for Lemke.

In the ensuing weeks he continued his attacks on Roosevelt. Now freed from the necessity of associating himself with the New Deal, he became increasingly vituperative, even blaming the great drought of that year on the president: God was punishing America for having elected Roosevelt. At the convention of the National Union for Social Justice in August he called the president "the dumbest man ever to occupy the White House."

But Coughlin's demagogy could not hold together the fragile

coalition of Lemke supporters, nor could it sway a great body of voters to the Union camp. Townsend was confused by the campaign and unable to deliver to Lemke his local Townsend clubs — many had been infiltrated by loyal Democrats. Gerald Smith was so taken by his popularity as orator and propagandist that he could hardly be harnessed to Lemke. Shortly before the election he began talking vaguely about leading a new movement to "seize" the government.

Moreover, Coughlin was in trouble with the Roman Catholic church. In the past some Catholics had found his reforms too radical. Now that he had broken with Roosevelt, many feared that he would discredit their church. In October, Monsignor John Ryan, prominent spokesman for liberal reform and onetime Coughlin supporter, accused Coughlin of fostering class hatred. In Rome in an official church publication, *L'Osservatore Romano,* he criticized the priest. Even Bishop Gallagher disliked his blunt attacks on Roosevelt.

And Coughlin's most loyal supporters were reluctant to vote for Lemke, fearing that by deserting Roosevelt they might help elect the Republican Alfred Landon. The Union candidate, with his genuine attachment to monetary and agrarian reform, was an attractive figure, but it was obvious that he could never win. Coughlin might say "Democracy is doomed," but many of his supporters still clung to words he had spoken earlier: to them, the choice appeared to be "Roosevelt or ruin."

When the votes were counted in November, Franklin Delano Roosevelt had scored one of the greatest triumphs in American political history, sweeping every state but Vermont and beating Landon by 9 million votes. Lemke polled less than 3 percent of the vote. The Radio Priest never fully recovered from the electoral debacle. It had once seemed that his influence on American politics was boundless, but his effort to translate his popularity into actual power had failed dismally.

For several years Coughlin charted a confused course in American public life. At first he retired from radio; then he let himself be "persuaded" to return. But his influence was clearly waning. The donations that had sustained the broadcasts declined. The president no longer courted his favor. His sympathetic bishop, Michael Gallagher, died and was replaced by a less supportive prelate.

Father Coughlin reacted strangely to his losses. At his best in the early years he had articulated many constructive ideas and served them up in engaging fashion. His barbs, aimed at bad policies and inept politicians, had often hit the mark. But in the years following the humiliation of 1936 his judgment was blinded by paranoia.

He had always succeeded best when he attacked specific villains, but he had been unable to induce his followers to regard Roosevelt as a villain. Now he identified a new enemy: the "international Jew," whom he associated with capitalistic and communistic oppression. Many of his erstwhile supporters refused to follow him into anti-Semitism, especially when the Radio Priest called for accommodation with Hitler, and radio stations dropped his broadcasts one by one.

He turned his attention to his journal, *Social Justice*. With America's entry into World War II, he became even more alienated from the American public, claiming that America had been drawn into the war by a Jewish-Communist plot aimed at "the liquidation of Americanism." As a result of his criticisms of the war, *Social Justice* was denied the use of the mails under the Espionage Act of 1917. In May 1942 Coughlin's new superior, Archbishop Edward Mooney, required him to cease all public pronouncements during the war. Forced to choose between his priesthood and his public career, Father Coughlin retired from politics.

Father Coughlin's career had been one of the most remarkable in American political history. For several years he "talked politics" with the largest weekly audience any American public figure had ever enjoyed. His success came in part from his own resources — from his fine oratory and his exciting ideas. But his rhetoric of denunciation depended ultimately on the existence of an unusual audience, consisting of millions of men and women who were already hurt, confused, and angry. Coughlin articulated their feelings. In Germany, Italy, or other countries he might have gone the next step and established a dictator-ship. In view of his appeal, it is remarkable that he failed so badly in his bid for political power.

Roosevelt had won because he commanded the respect of many of the same people who listened to Coughlin. Both Roosevelt and Coughlin wrestled with that perennial problem in American statecraft: how to nourish simultaneously the rights of the individual and the welfare of the nation. In his more freewheeling speeches Coughlin had frequently accused bankers and Jews of being both capitalistic and communistic. The association was illogical, but the accusation was revealing. Most Americans believed that the only solution to the depression lay in government-directed relief and regulation. But most believed that individual freedom had been the hallmark of America. By associating bad individualism and bad communalism and personifying them in the figure of the villainous "international banker," Coughlin had touched the vibrant chords of American frustration and hostility. His rhetorical onslaughts might not provide solutions, but they did articulate anxi-eties.

Significantly, his program itself was a great deal more practical than his oratory suggests. Many of the sixteen points in the NUSJ have been implemented as a whole or in part. The government has acquired more control over money, for example; labor unions are generally protected by law; unemployment insurance and poverty relief provide something approaching a guaranteed annual income. In such measures the anger that seethed through the nation's airwaves from the Shrine of the Little Flower and mingled with other voices of protest during the Great Depression was distilled into less dramatic but more enduring phrases in the nation's statute books.

QUESTIONS

1. Why was Charles Coughlin able to attract a national audience before the onset of the depression? What role did radio and his personality have in his rise to prominence?

2. Why was Coughlin critical of Herbert Hoover? What reforms did he propose during Hoover's presidency?

3. Why did *The Nation* declare in 1933: "The promise of American life has been shattered — possibly beyond repair"?

4. Why did Coughlin at first admire Franklin Roosevelt? What policies caused him to turn against Roosevelt?

5. What evidence do we have of Coughlin's popularity? Why was he so well liked during the depression?

6. Why did Charles Coughlin decide to run a third-party campaign against Franklin Roosevelt? Explain these factors: Roosevelt's policies, Coughlin's popularity, Coughlin's egotism, depression hardships, other extremists.

7. What was the program of the National Union for Social Justice? Which of its proposed reforms have been adopted? Which have not?

8. What were the similarities and differences between Coughlin's program and those of Huey Long and Francis Townsend?

9. Why was Coughlin unable to translate his enormous popularity into substantial political power? Evaluate the effect of these in his failure: William Lemke as a candidate, Charles Townsend and Gerald Smith, the Catholic church, "Roosevelt or Ruin."

10. Why did Coughlin embrace anti-Semitism after 1936? How did his audience react?

BIBLIOGRAPHY

ALLEN, FREDERICK LEWIS. *Since Yesterday* (1940). Social history of the 1930s.

BERNSTEIN, IRVING. *Turbulent Years* (1970). History of the labor movement during the 1930s.

BRINKLEY, ALAN. *Voices of Protest: Huey Long, Father Coughlin, and the Great Depression* (1982). Explores the conditions that gave birth to Long and Coughlin.

FRIEDEL, FRANK. *Franklin Roosevelt* (1990). Definitive one-volume Roosevelt biography.

LYND, ROBERT S., AND HELEN M. LYND. *Middletown in Transition* (1937). How the depression affected a small Indiana town.

SCHLESINGER, ARTHUR M., JR. *The Age of Roosevelt* (3 vols., 1957–60). Fine narrative history of Roosevelt and his times.

STEINBECK, JOHN. *The Grapes of Wrath* (1939). Moving fictional account of an Oklahoma family's trials as migrant laborers.

TERKEL, STUDS. *Hard Times* (1970). Evocative oral history of the Great Depression.

TULL, CHARLES J. *Father Coughlin and the New Deal* (1965). Biography of Charles Coughlin.

WARREN, ROBERT PENN. *All the King's Men* (1946). Compelling novel based on the life of Huey Long.

YOUNGS, J. WILLIAM T. *Eleanor Roosevelt: A personal and Public Life* (1985). Brief biography of America's foremost first lady.

9

TOTAL WAR

The Bombing of Hiroshima

Between 1941 and 1945 the United States took part in the most destructive war in history. During those years men who might otherwise have been factory workers, carpenters, lawyers, and businessmen became trained killers with one goal: to defeat Japan, Germany, and the other Axis powers. The United States went to war against these nations because they were ruled by totalitarian regimes; because they fought against our allies; and because, finally, one of them bombed Pearl Harbor. For four years mutual violence spread across the globe. The war came to a close after America exploded two atomic bombs, the most awesome weapons ever used in warfare. The story of Hiroshima, the first target, shows the horror of total war, and the experience of the bomber crews reveals how warfare can convert ordinary men into agents of ghastly terror.

In the predawn hours of August 6, 1945, three American B-29s droned through the darkness bound north from the Pacific island of Tinian toward the Japanese coastal town of Hiroshima. They flew at four thousand feet, where the air was close and humid, to avoid colliding with one of the hundreds of B-29s returning from bombing raids over Japan. Such massive raids were common. In the past year the balance of terror in the Pacific had swung irreversibly to the American side, and in summer 1945, B-29 Superfortresses could blast and burn Japanese cities almost at will. In comparison to such huge congregations of destruction, the three low-flying planes seemed unobtrusive, all but harmless. Not only were they few, but they did not bristle with guns like the other B-29s. Among them they carried only one bomb. Aboard the three planes there was little to suggest the historic character of the mission. The *Great Artiste*, so named for its commander's reputed prowess in love, carried a cargo of scientific instruments. A second ship, called simply *Number 91*, was full of photographic equipment. The third craft, named *Enola Gay* after its pilot's mother, carried the bomb. Until recently only the lead pilot, Lt. Col. Paul W. Tibbets, Jr., had known the character of this strange object they were soon to drop on Japan.

Tibbets was the commander of the 509th Composite Bomb Group, the first military unit ever trained in atomic warfare. He was a slender man with dark hair and heavy eyebrows. Despite his youthful, almost boyish appearance, he was a seasoned airman, the veteran of many B-17 bombing runs over Germany and Africa. He had trained his group with all the rigorous efficiency demanded of his unique mission. And he had guarded well the secret of the bomb. Through months of training with dummy prototypes, the crews had known their cargo simply as the "gimmick." The realization that they were to drop a weapon of enormous power had come slowly: it was implied first in the secrecy of their training and more fully revealed at a preflight briefing on Tinian. They now knew that the bomb had the potency of twenty thousand tons of TNT.

But even at takeoff several crewmembers had not been shown the last piece of the puzzle, the actual source of the bomb's power. In the first hour of the flight, Tibbets briefed the remaining men, scattered in various parts of the long, heavy aircraft. He sent William S. Parsons, his naval ordinance officer and a bomb expert, forward to explain the cargo to two men there, while he worked his way back through a narrow passage to the tail where the gunner, George Caron, sat in an isolated perch staring out at the darkness from under the visor of a Brooklyn Dodgers baseball cap. The gunner, who Tibbets described as a "pretty sharp type," was not surprised when he learned that the "gimmick" was an atomic bomb. He had heard people speculate about atomic-powered ships before the war, and he had guessed that the new bomb must have something to do with "splitting the atom." In the forward compartment the men who listened to Parsons were less communicative; they just raised their eyebrows in mute surprise.

After talking to Caron, Tibbets attempted to take a short nap. Expecting immediate orders to begin their mission, he and his men had been on edge for three or four days. He had not slept for twenty-four hours. Now he would try.

Parsons must have been tired, too, but he had a job to complete that banished all thought of sleep. The *Enola Gay* had taken off with an "unarmed" atomic bomb; the parts were all there, but some final adjustments had to be made before the bomb could be exploded. Ideally, the bomb would have been fully armed before the flight, but in the early days of August several B-29s had crashed during takeoff from Tinian. An accident with an atomic bomb would have destroyed half the island. Despite their fear that tools or parts might be left behind, the project commander, Gen. Thomas Farrell, had decided to let Parsons, an older man and much respected as a bomb expert, arm the bomb while in flight. Parsons had practiced for hours on the ground the day before and was ready to prepare the bomb for its final plunge over Japan.

He lowered himself slowly into the bomb bay and was followed by Lt. Morris Jeppson, another weapons expert. They stood in the narrow, pleasantly cool enclosure and began their work. The bomb had an unusual, almost makeshift form, as if it had been built as a high school shop project. Squat and diminutive, it gave no outward sign of the huge destructive power within. It measured ten feet from its blunt nose to its square tail and was twenty-eight inches in diameter. On its polished sides the ground crew had written messages cursing the Japanese and commemorating comrades lost at sea: "To Hell with the Emperor" and "This is for the boys on the Indianapolis."

Millions of hours of work had gone into devising the intricate mechanism of the bomb. The underlying physical principles had been anticipated almost a half century before, when Pierre and Marie Curie had argued that the atom, which had formerly been considered indivisible, could be broken. In 1905 Albert Einstein announced his famous formula, $E = mc^2$, which indicated that enormous energy lay in every particle of matter. Thereafter scientists throughout the world attempted to devise means to release and harness the energy of the atom. Some of the most famous of these men — including Niels Bohr, Enrico Fermi, and Einstein — were Europeans who fled to the United States to escape Hitler or Mussolini.

At the beginning of World War II many of the best nuclear physicists in the world lived in the United States. On August 2, 1939,

Einstein, the most famous of these exiles, wrote President Franklin D. Roosevelt that atomic research could lead to the creation of "extremely powerful bombs of a new type" and warned him that scientists in Germany were already seeking to develop an atomic bomb. The United States, then, was drawn into the nuclear race by the fear of atomic power in other hands as well as by the lure of possessing the "ultimate weapon" itself.

When America entered World War II in 1941, President Roosevelt established a scientific advisory committee, including Secretary of War Henry L. Stimson and Harvard President James B. Conant, to begin considering development of an atomic bomb. This group in turn established a committee of scientists, including Enrico Fermi and J. Robert Oppenheimer. In 1942 the "Manhattan Project" was organized, and work began on an atomic bomb. At its peak, the project employed 125,000 workers scattered among three top-secret plants: in Oak Ridge, Tennessee; Hanford, Washington; and Los Alamos, New Mexico. Most of the employees did not know what they were working on. The project's $2 billion budget was raised secretly without congressional authorization. Even Vice-President Harry S. Truman was kept in the dark.

On December 2, 1942, a controlled chain reaction was produced at the University of Chicago, establishing an early milestone for the project, but it was not until two and a half years later that the first atomic bomb was ready for testing. The site chosen was an airbase at Alamogordo, New Mexico, a remote place of desert and mountains 120 miles from Albuquerque. In mid-July 1945 scientists and military men from around the United States gathered at Alamogordo. Among them were James B. Conant; Gen. Leslie R. Groves, director of the Manhattan Project; J. Robert Oppenheimer, the scientist most responsible for the bomb's creation; and U.S. Army Air Corps Col. Paul Tibbets.

At Alamogordo they assembled at an old ranch house near a 120 foot-high steel tower at a remote corner of the base. The bomb was to be exploded atop the tower. In the early hours of July 16 they waited anxiously as torrents of rain and streaks of lightning delayed the firing. As the time for the blast drew near many lay face down with their feet toward the tower. Tibbets flew above in a B-29. No one knew what to expect. Even among the scientists who had developed the bomb, some harbored a fugitive hope that it would not work.

Then at 5:30 A.M., while darkness still hung over the stormy Southwest, the bomb was detonated. The steel tower disappeared, vaporized by the massive explosion. A tremendous flash appeared to Tibbets above the clouds. A brilliant light illuminated the desert and the mountains: "It was golden, purple, violet, gray, and blue. It lighted every peak, crevasse, and ridge of the nearby mountains with a clarity and beauty that cannot be described." Thus Gen. Thomas Farrell described the "searching light." Oppenheimer, stunned, recalled words from the Hindu epic *Bhagavad-Gita:* "If the radiance of a thousand suns were to burst into the sky, that would be the splendor of the Mighty One."

The light was followed by a shock wave, a tremendous sustained roar that knocked down men five miles from the bomb site and reverberated over the desert across thousands of square miles. In El Paso, Albuquerque, Socorro, and Gallup buildings shook and windows rattled. Above the bomb site a great, multicolored cloud rose eight miles into the air. Beneath, where the tower had stood, was a huge saucer-shaped hole in the hard earth.

Finally, after the light and the shock, after a few seconds that had seemed an eternity, the men jumped to their feet, shook hands, embraced, and shouted. It had worked. Their achievement was staggering: never before had men harnessed energy with such dramatic results. And yet, even in this time of scientific triumph, there were feelings also of shock and dismay. Farrell felt that "we puny things were blasphemous to dare tamper with the forces heretofore reserved to the Almighty." And Oppenheimer recalled a second line from the *Bhagavad-Gita*: "I am become death, the shatterer of worlds."

All this had happened only three weeks before. Now the "shatterer of worlds" would soon explode over people and houses instead of desert and cactus. The weapon sat snugly in the bomb bay while Parsons and Jeppson continued their work. They had plenty of time and moved carefully. First Jeppson removed the safety plugs and replaced them with arming plugs. (Even while doing this task, he thought of the importance of the mission and pocketed the safety plugs as souvenirs.) Then he and Parsons ran wires from the bomb to the electric monitoring equipment at the front of the plane. They finished the job within half an hour. Parsons later recalled that his hands were dirty, "as if I had changed the carburetor and distributor of my car." The two men then climbed to the forward compartment and settled down to watch the instruments. They were quiet, each thinking his own thoughts. Tibbets had been unable to sleep. He came forward to relieve his copilot, Maj. Robert A. Lewis, who was watching the plane's automatic pilot. The plane rumbled on toward the north through intermittent clouds and starlight. She rocked gently over patches of turbulent air and passed through light showers. Occasionally the sky was clear and the men could watch the moonlight on the sea.

It was fifteen hundred miles from Tinian to Hiroshima. The flight would take six and a half hours, and now there was nothing to do but wait. It should be a safe mission; the planes would be too high for enemy fighter planes or antiaircraft fire to reach them. But always on bombing runs there was fear. The three planes had only six 50-caliber guns among them, and they would go over Japan without a fighter escort. Then, too, there was the bomb itself, a curious device. Some of the men wondered uneasily whether the bumping of the aircraft would cause it to explode prematurely. Along with such thoughts for their own well-being, some of the men thought about the enemy. Aboard the *Great Artiste*, radio operator Abe Spitzer wondered vaguely what it would be like to be a Japanese pilot carrying an atomic bomb toward San Francisco.

In these ways the uniqueness of the mission impressed itself on the men. But for the most part they occupied themselves as hundreds of other crews had done on the long bombing runs over Japan. Maj. Theodore J. Van Kirk, the navigator, had flown with Tibbets in Europe, and attended to his job with routine efficiency. He did not appear to Tibbets to be particularly worried about the cargo: "He was a navigator: 'Where do you want to go, and when do you want to get there?'" The nineteen-year-old radio operator, Pfc. Richard Nelson, read a book about boxing. Lt. Jacob Beser, the radar countermeasures operator, was apprehensive about the mission but was reassured by Parsons, who seemed to "exude confidence." He lay on the floor and soon fell asleep, providing entertainment for some of the other men who rolled oranges and tried to hit him on the head. In the forward compartment the men watched in the dark as St. Elmo's fire, an eerie blue light common in the South Pacific, seemed to envelop the plane's four engines and clear plastic nose shield.

Despite the prosaic quality of these hours — Tibbets called it "the dullest trip anyone ever took" — the mission itself was the culmination of thousands of hours of preparation. In fact, the 509th Composite Bomb Group had been put together with the same care that had gone into fashioning its deadly cargo. In mid-1943 the Manhattan Project had reached the stage where it was necessary to contemplate the means of bomb delivery. The Allies had no sophisticated missiles comparable to the German V-1 and V-2 rockets, and at one time it was thought that the bomb would be so large that it would have to be taken into enemy harbors on shipboard. By 1943, however, it was apparent that the bomb could be carried by a plane.

After a period of preliminary planning, Col. Paul Tibbets was appointed in early fall 1944 to organize a new bomb group, the 509th, drawing men from other groups. He was assigned to an isolated base in a parched, treeless desert near the small town of Wendover, Utah. He assembled fifteen hundred men — mechanics and engineers as well as pilots and crews.

There were really two jobs to attend to at Wendover: creating a bomb capable of containing a nuclear armament and developing flight techniques to deliver the bomb. The metal shell, the nuclear cargo, the B-29, and the flight crews had to be adjusted to one another. The B-29s were modified to carry one large bomb, and test bombs were dropped so that they could be modified for accuracy. At first the stabilizing fins on the bombs were so weak they collapsed under the stress as the four- and five-ton bombs hurtled downward. The fins were rebuilt. Then there was the problem of adjusting the fuses. One of the lightly armed bombs exploded just after being dropped; had it been an atomic bomb, it would have demolished the plane. Finally, there was flight training. The crews practiced dropping bombs until they could come within nine hundred feet of a target from a height of six miles. After each drop they made a sharp, jarring turn, followed by an accelerated dive that took their craft far away from the falling missile.

During the months of training, emissaries traveled between Wendover, Oak Ridge, Los Alamos, and Hanford. Every activity was cloaked in unprecedented secrecy. The workers at Los Alamos did not know about Wendover, and those at Wendover did not know about Los Alamos. They called back and fourth over a coded phone system to mysterious colleagues working at Y and K. Most of the men in the 509th Bomb Group did not know they were being trained to drop atomic bombs. Moreover, they were warned to say nothing about their work, and they were watched by security agents. The phones out of the base were tapped. Sometimes government spies were sent aboard buses and trains to lure airmen on leave into talking. Those who failed these security tests were removed from the group.

This thick blanket of secrecy continued to shroud the 509th as the time came to transfer the operation to Tinian. The ground crew traveled in isolated cars on troop trains and ate only after all other soldiers were cleared out of the dining cars. They traveled across the Pacific in a special naval transport and were isolated in a dock warehouse during a stop in Hawaii. The movement of the planes was equally secret. Once the planes and crews reached Tinian, the bomb parts were transported covertly. After the Alamogordo explosion several transport planes flew nearly empty to Tinian carrying nothing but one or two couriers with parcels containing bomb mechanisms in their laps. The cruiser *Indianapolis* was called up to transport the bomb casings in closely guarded wood cartons on a fast voyage from San Francisco.

On Tinian all the pieces were put together. It was an unlikely place for such an enterprise. Recently captured from the Japanese, the island measured a bare five by twelve miles. But it was now home base for more than five hundred B-29s that daily rumbled three abreast down its long runways to climb over its coral shores toward Japan. Thirty-five thousand men and a thousand nurses were stationed on Tinian.

The 509th Bomb Group settled uneasily into an isolated special compound along with a group of scientists. Their separation annoyed the other airmen, who sarcastically called them the "Glory Boys" and pelted their barracks with rocks when they left on missions in the middle of the night. One of their rivals teased them with a poem:

> In the air the Secret rose,
> Where they're going nobody knows.

The men of the 509th had little time to worry about such teasing. They flew several practice missions over the Pacific and continued their training with dummy bombs. Meanwhile, the scientists and engineers worked on completing the real bombs. The commanding Air Corps officer, Gen. Curtis LeMay, had received orders to send out the first bomb as soon as the weather cleared over Japan. On August 5 LeMay learned that the weather over the target areas would be clear on the following day. The first bomb was moved from a shed into a concrete pit; the *Enola Gay* backed carefully over it; and hydraulic lifts raised the bomb into her metallic belly. Guards stood by the plane as Parsons worked inside, learning to arm the bomb in the crowded bay.

That night the crews had gathered under the curved roof of a metal quonset hut. They sat on wood benches while Tibbets, dressed in khaki shorts and an open-necked shirt, spoke quietly about the mission. For the men it was a familiar scene; they had met here several times on the previous days while Tibbets, pipe in hand, had discussed the mission — told them how important it was, how it would shorten the war by six months, how proud he was to be associated with them. In this room they had seen slides of the Alamogordo explosion and had been told that President Truman would release the news about their mission. Now there was little more to say. Tibbets simply told them that the mission would begin shortly and discussed the weather reports and provisions for rescue of downed aircraft. Chaplain William Downer closed the meeting with a prayer, a formality usually, now a solemn occasion. "We pray Thee that the end of the war may come soon," he said, "and that once more we may know peace on earth. May the men who fly this night be kept safe in Thy care, and may they be returned safely to us."

Following the days of anxious expectation, an atmosphere of calm deliberation had come over the group. In the last hours before the flight men ate sandwiches, drank coffee, and talked about how long the war would last and what they would do afterward. Radio operator Abe Spitzer noticed the serious tone of the conversations; there was no joking about women, the staple topic of the airmen's discourse, only these contemplative exchanges.

After midnight the men assembled by the planes. The *Enola Gay* was surrounded with floodlights and guards; the scene reminded some of the crewmen of a Hollywood set. They posed for photographs and waited for the order to depart. At 1:37 A.M. three weather planes lifted off to scout the targets. At 2:45 A.M. the *Enola Gay* was on the runway; her engines labored as the huge sixty-five-ton plane gained speed. Then came an anxious moment. She accelerated to 180 miles per hour, but was still on the ground with the sea rushing nearer. She was "gobbling up too much runway," Copilot Lewis shouted. At the end of the runway the plane finally left the ground. In the control tower the observers sighed heavily.

After the brief drama of the takeoff the flight assumed the routine character that allowed men to work, sleep, play, and think almost as they would on an ordinary mission. Caron might remind himself that this was "the one we had come over for," but the very fact of the months of training gave the early morning routine its almost commonplace quality. They were approaching the halfway point in their flight. Tiny streaks of light crept up beneath the clouds, then swiftly a curtain of light spread blue and purple across the sky, and it was day.

Ahead lay Iwo Jima, halfway to Japan, where the three planes would rendezvous and fly in close formation the rest of the way to the target. The *Enola Gay* began to circle above the tiny Pacific island. Iwo Jima looked peaceful in the early morning light, but just recently it had been a place of unspeakable horror and violence. It was already a legend in American military history and an essential link, strategically and psychologically, in the chain of events that brought the atomic bomb to Japan. In a sense, the dusty island lying below the planes symbolized the history of mutual violence that had led to the day's mission.

At the beginning of the war Iwo Jima had been of little strategic importance to Japan. In 1941 the perimeters of Japan's vast empire stretched well beyond this island through Korea, China, Indochina, Indonesia, Borneo, and the Solomon and Gilbert islands. Japan was on the offensive throughout the Pacific and could launch the surprise attack on Pearl Harbor that all but obliterated the American Pacific Fleet and killed 2,300 seamen. At first it had been an easy matter to overwhelm the Americans and to occupy the Philippines and the outer Aleutians.

Within two years, however, the Americans had beaten the Japanese navy and recaptured lost territory. In 1944 they captured the Mariana Islands, including Guam and Tinian. The fall of the Marianas placed American bombers within range of Japan and changed the status of Iwo Jima. Suddenly the island, at the middle of the bombing route, assumed enormous strategic importance. In Japanese hands it served as an observation point for warning the homeland of impending raids and as a base for fighters to harass the B-29s. In American hands it could serve as a fighter base and emergency landing field.

Twenty thousand of Japan's best troops were assigned to Iwo Jima. They honeycombed the island with bunkers protected by thick concrete walls and connected by miles of tunnels. From these positions machine guns and artillery could fire upon every part of the island. In an attempt to counteract these preparations the Americans dropped 6,800 tons of bombs and 22,000 shells on the dusty island. On February 19, 1945, following seventy-four consecutive days of bombardment, the Marines landed. Stumbling ankle deep through volcanic ash, they were hit by withering fire from hidden Japanese positions. In the first two days the Marines, clinging to the beaches, lost 3,650 men killed and wounded. Battle-hardened war reporters were appalled at the carnage: they saw arms and legs blown far from their bodies, men cut in half by flying steel, faces and bodies mangled by machine-gun fire.

On Iwo Jima the Marines suffered their worst casualties in the history of the corps. They fought their way across the island yard by yard, attacking the pillboxes with rifles, bazookas, flamethrowers, and bayonets. Although the Japanese were overwhelmed, they fought bravely for every inch of ground. In the end, more than 20,000 of them gave their lives, and only 218 were captured. The Marines suffered 20,000 casualties, including 6,821 killed. In less than a month 40,000 men had been incinerated by flamethrowers; blown apart by explosives; or cut by bullet, knife, and bayonet. Five men died for every acre of land on this desolate island.

In such places as Iwo Jima the Japanese showed themselves as tenacious in defeat as they had been forceful in victory. Each battle cost thousands of lives. On Okinawa, for example, where the two nations fought from April through June 1945, the Japanese lost 110,000 killed and 9,000 captured; the Americans lost more than 10,000 killed.

Such statistics testified to the Japanese resolve to die rather than surrender. The kamikazes gave further proof of Japanese persistence. In the final months of the war thousands of Japanese pilots agreed to become living bombs, flying heavily armed planes directly into American targets. During the fight for Iwo Jima the kamikazes fell upon the *Bismarck Sea* and the *Saratoga,* two light carriers, blasting huge holes in the first and sinking the second. In other battles the "Divine Wind" sank 29 ships, damaged 307, and killed almost 5,000 American seamen.

When Americans thought about ending the war with Japan, they thought about kamikazes and places like Iwo Jima. There were 2 million imperial troops in Japan, all of whom might fight as doggedly as their compatriots. Certainly the Japanese would lose, but at what cost to themselves and to their conquerors? Estimates of American losses in an invasion ranged up to half a million. Inevitably, any alternative to an invasion was attractive, and the long and bloody years of war had schooled the world in a brutal logic of violence, which encouraged the choice of harsh alternatives. In Hammurabi's Code it had been written that there must be "an eye for an eye." This code was rewritten many times during the war. The Russians had sworn that they would take "two eyes for an eye" in revenge for German depredations. In a less vengeful but equally stern spirit, Allied strategists, contemplating the bombing of German cities, had concluded that one eye now, even a civilian eye, could save two later. In 1939 such callous reasoning had been rare. But a new logic of violence had grown with experience. Across the globe hundreds of thousands of planes, ships, buildings, and houses had been destroyed. For six years men, women, and children had been killed by gun, bomb, knife, and gas. In all, some 20 million people had died. Gross violence had become the accepted path to victory — and ultimately, to peace and the cessation of violence.

In this atmosphere it had been easy to justify "saturation" bombing of German towns at the end of the war. The culmination was a massive raid on the refugee-swollen town of Dresden on the night of February 13–14, 1945. Eight hundred planes had leveled the town and inflicted between 250,000 and 400,000 casualties. Brutal? Yes, but the bombing had hastened the end of mutual brutality. So it was reasoned.

This cruel logic did as much as any scientist, engineer, pilot, or politician to hasten the *Enola Gay* toward Hiroshima on the morning of August 6. It had nourished the technology that built Japanese warships, German missiles, English planes, and American bombs. And it justified the use of each new instrument of destruction. Once the atomic bomb was available, it was a foregone conclusion that it would be dropped. Germany escaped because it surrendered before the bomb was ready, but Japan was less fortunate.

The final decision to use the nuclear weapon had been made in late July by President Truman. It was ironic that the responsibility was his, because he had learned about the new weapon only after his first cabinet meeting in April 1945 when Secretary of War Stimson called him aside to tell him about the Manhattan Project. Truman was at the Potsdam Conference when he learned about the Alamogordo explosion. Jubilant with the confidence that the new bomb would force Japan to surrender without an invasion, he issued a statement calling for immediate unconditional surrender, threatening Japan with "prompt and utter destruction" if resistance continued. The Japanese government sent no reply but announced to their people on July 28 that the Potsdam Declaration was "unworthy of public notice."

Hearing of Japan's reaction, Truman called for use of the bomb as soon as possible. Most of his staff were enthusiastic about the decision, but a few advisers had objected. A group of scientists, including Albert Einstein, warned Truman that use of the weapon against Japan would increase the possibility of future atomic warfare. A naval adviser suggested a blockade. A few men proposed demonstrating the bomb to the Japanese as an alternative to destroying a city. But after six years of total war, none of the alternatives was persuasive. The weapon that would kill and wound several hundred thousand Japanese could be seen as a blessing, a means to end the war and save lives. In this belief Truman had given the order to drop the bomb.

Now as the three B-29s made their rendezvous above Iwo Jima, all the threads of atomic policy — the research, the flight training, the history of mutual violence, the strategic planning — came together in a fabric of cold resolve. The *Enola Gay* carried the instrument of that resolve, rumbling toward its culmination in a moment of unimaginable horror.

After circling three times above Iwo Jima the *Enola Gay* joined the other planes and climbed to ten thousand feet. Navigator Van Kirk gave instructions to Tibbets for speed and altitude as the men ate a simple breakfast. Later they put on flak suits and checked the arc welder's goggles that would protect them from the atomic glare.

The men now showed signs of anxiety. In the tail section George Caron smoked cigarette after cigarette. He found that he was sweating from the waist up and freezing from the waist down. He fumbled nervously with a chain of rosary beads given him by his mother.

On the *Great Artiste* radio operator Abe Spitzer waited anxiously for the weather report from the targets. At 7:00 A.M. the three reconnaissance planes were supposed to send information on visibility over Hiroshima, Kokura, and Nagasaki. The planes were in range of all three targets, fast approaching the Japanese coast, but no message had arrived. Spitzer hunched over as chills ran through his body. At 7:10 A.M. there was still no word. Had he missed the signals? Was his radio broken?

Then at 7:20 A.M., when the planes were fifty miles from Japan, the first message arrived. Spitzer grabbed for a pencil but could not hold it in his shaking hand. It fell to the floor. He clutched another and wrote down the Hiroshima report: the target was clear. Soon similar reports followed from Kokura and Nagasaki. Weather conditions were good over all three cities. But Hiroshima was the primary target, and toward Hiroshima the *Enola Gay* now headed.

The planes climbed slowly to thirty thousand feet. Through the haze they could make out the coastline. They were flying over clouds at first, but fifty miles from the city they could see a large, clear space over Hiroshima. Tibbets conferred with Parsons. "Do you agree that's the target?" he asked. Parsons nodded yes. As they drew closer to Hiroshima, *Number 91* fell back to take pictures. *Great Artiste,* preparing to drop its cargo of instruments, stayed alongside the *Enola Gay.* Twenty miles from the target bombardier Thomas W. Ferebee fixed the doomed city in his bombsight.

Hiroshima stood out ahead in the sunlight: a triangle of buildings and houses, occupying six islets in the delta of the Ota River, nestled between green hills and the blue, island-studded waters of Inland Sea. At that moment in the city 245,000 men, women, and children were beginning their day.

Until recently Hiroshima had been an important point of embarkation for hundreds of thousands of imperial troops headed overseas. They had filled the town with a festive atmosphere and a sense of inevitable victory. Now, however, that atmosphere was changed. The town's war industries and the presence of the Second Army headquarters were reminders of war. But there were no more troop ships. The Americans had brought local shipping to a halt by mining the approaches to Hiroshima. All around were signs that Japan was losing the war. Bread was rationed. Coffee and good whiskey were unobtainable. Every day B-29s flew overhead.

With the remarkable buoyancy of youth the children of Hiroshima were proud of their ability to identify the hostile aircraft by sight and sound. They who had once thrilled at the parades of soldiers were now excited by the daily passage overhead of B-29s, calling them "B-san" or "Mr. B."

Thus far Hiroshima, alone of Japan's major cities, had been spared a major bombing. Five months before, on the night of March 9–10, hundreds of B-29s had swooped over Tokyo with incendiary bombs, burning sixteen square miles of the city, killing 97,000 people, and leaving more than 1 million homeless. Other raids had crippled most of Hiroshima's neighbors. But the city had been miraculously preserved. Fantastic rumors abounded to explain this good fortune: President Truman's mother lived nearby; the Americans liked the city and wanted to visit it after the war; and more accurately, the city had been spared for some special punishment. The Americans themselves had encouraged the latter view by dropping 720,000 leaflets on Hiroshima telling the people that their city and others would be destroyed if Japan did not surrender.

But despite such warnings, in Hiroshima it was difficult to maintain a sense of danger. Even the air-raid warnings had become routine. On August 7 when local radar stations picked up a single B-29 approaching the city the subsequent alert was lightly regarded by the citizens. They rightly assumed that the craft, the weather plane that preceded the *Enola Gay,* was an observation plane. When the all clear sounded at eight o'clock, most people were already at work or school.

Some busied themselves on the city's defenses. Soldiers dug hillside shelters and talked of resisting the invader "life for life." Others worked at dismantling wood-framed, tile-roofed houses to clear fire lanes in case of incendiary attack. But even in the midst of such war-related activities an atmosphere of civilian tranquility hung over the city in moments that years later would seem eternally present to the survivors of Hiroshima.

On the morning of August 7 Dr. Michihiko Hachiya is relaxing at home after a sleepless night on duty at the Communications Hospital. He lies exhausted on his living room floor, clad in drawers and undershorts. The morning is "still, warm, and beautiful" as he gazes contentedly through open doors at sunlight, "shimmering leaves," and shadows in his garden.

A few miles away Father John A. Siemes, S.J., is at work in his room at the Novitiate of the Society of Jesus. Throughout the war he and his colleagues have done missionary work first in Tokyo and then, with the bombing of that city, in Hiroshima. A sensitive man and a professor of modern philosophy, he enjoys the new location on a hillside above Hiroshima. From his window he can look down a broad valley to the edge of the city. He is pleased with the "bright, clear summer morning."

In the center of Hiroshima the eighth-grade students of the girls' school are preparing to help a demolition squad clear a fire lane. They meet in the school yard at 7:30 A.M., and happy in their mutual friendship, the novelty of their work, and the glorious weather, they walk to the worksite singing a cheerful song, "Blossoms and Buds of the Young Cherry Tree." Naoko Masuoka puts down her first-aid kit, which she always carries with her, and goes to work with her friend, Setsuko Sakamoto. The girls and their teacher begin to pass roof tiles from one to another, singing in unison as they work.

A few miles away from this activity the men on the *Enola Gay,* beginning their deadly approach, see a different Hiroshima. Six miles above the ground, traveling at better than three hundred miles an hour, they are unaware of Dr. Michihiko Hachiya and Father John Siemes and the students of the girls' school. Their delicate machinery allows them only to see a target, a large cluster of buildings and houses fixed at the center of a Norden bombsight.

Bombardier Ferebee is seated in front of Tibbets and Lewis,

looking intently at Hiroshima. As the target comes nearer, Tibbets orders the crewmen to fix their goggles on their foreheads, ready for use. With ninety seconds till the drop, Ferebee takes control of the aircraft, and radio operator Richard Nelson sends a signal to the *Great Artiste*, a thousand yards to the rear, to coordinate the instrument drop. Ferebee sees the aiming point, the Aioi Bridge, and sends a warning signal through the plane. An automatic device takes control, gauging the release. The bomb bay doors swing open. There is a pause, then the plane jerks suddenly upward as the nine-thousand-pound missile tumbles away. Seeing it fall, Ferebee shouts, "It's clear!"

Tibbets wrenches the *Enola Gay* into a sharp turn to the left, and the plane screams through the sky away from the bomb. "Make sure those goggles are on," he shouts. Ferebee can still make out the bomb as it hurtles downward. Higher up, the three instrument packages drift under their parachutes. The men wait anxiously, knowing the missile will fall free for exactly forty-three seconds.

The bomb rushes down with the sound of a freight train. Then, two thousand feet over Hiroshima, a gun fires inside its metallic shell forcing a small mass of fissionable material through a metal tube into a second mass. The two collide, and in less than a millionth of a second the atoms fly apart, vaporizing the four-ton bomb casing, issuing forth in a huge fireball, a blast of heat, and a thunderous concussion.

Aboard the *Enola Gay* several miles away a blinding purple light searches the interior of the plane and creeps up beneath the men's goggles. A shock wave shakes the plane, followed by another, then another. Caron can see the waves spreading through the air like ripples through water. At first Ferebee and Tibbets think enemy flak is exploding around them.

As the men look back, they see a gigantic multicolored cloud of smoke erupting upward. At the center is a huge ball of red flame; it looks as if the sun has been knocked out of the sky and is now rising again from the earth. Ferebee thinks he sees parts of buildings hurtling upward. A bubbling mass of flame spreads like lava over the city and into the hills. Overhead the cloud rushes upward mile after mile into the sky.

"My God!" says Lewis.

Hiroshima is hidden in a cloud of dust and flame. But on the ground the blast is registered clearly on buildings, trees, and flesh. A wave of radiant heat, traveling at the speed of light, burns granite blocks, melts hard roof tiles, and incinerates grass, trees, and houses. A shock wave follows, traveling at the speed of sound, knocking down everything in its way, collapsing buildings, tossing cars and trains through the air. Then dozens of fires started by the wave of heat or kindled by charcoal from overturned cooking stoves spread through the ruins.

More than two hundred thousand people are in the middle of this inferno. Near the center thousands are burned to cinders instantly. Some leave their shadows burned onto walls and roadways as their bodies vanish without a trace. Farther from the blast some are horribly burned by the wave of heat; others, indoors at the time of the explosion, are tossed about in their houses in a tangle of flying wood and glass. Some are pinned under beams; others are cut and bruised.

Even after the great heat and the deadening blast many are still alive. In the tortured quiet that follows the explosion, they look at themselves and one another with bewilderment. A man sees red strips of burned flesh hanging from his arm. A woman struggles to free herself from under a fallen roofbeam. A child stumbles through a ruined house looking for her parents. Everywhere people stare at one another with horror. They see burned, mangled faces; blood flowing from gaping wounds; naked bodies with odd burn patterns; people stumbling through the streets that are no longer streets, throwing themselves into the river seeking to quench the thirst that will not be quenched, to stop the pain that will not be stopped, moaning, vomiting, dying.

In such ways tens of thousands of people die quickly. But others struggle to live. In the Jesuit mission house, Father John Siemes seeks to escape from his room. He is conscious of having seen a "garish light" in the valley toward Hiroshima. The blast that followed shattered his window, cutting his face and hands. Now he pounds on his jammed door until it opens and he stumbles into the hall, finding it cluttered with broken glass and fallen books. Most of his colleagues have been cut, but none badly. They go outside and see that the explosion has blasted away all the doors and windows on the southeast side of the house and severely damaged the chapel.

Some minutes later they see people surging up the valley from Hiroshima, instinctively fleeing the horror behind them. Some come to the house seeking first aid. The priests apply fat on their burns but soon run out. They use bandages and drugs for the more seriously wounded and run out of these, too. By noon the chapel and library are filled with the wounded, but still they come.

A few miles away Dr. Michihiko Hachiya is closer to the blast and is more seriously injured than the Jesuit priests. As he gazes at the garden, he sees a flash of light. Then the garden disappears in a cloud of dust and he is vaguely aware of a wood support column "leaning crazily" at the corner of the house. Picking his way over fallen rubble into the garden, he feels weak, sees that he is naked, and finds slivers of wood and glass in his body.

Suddenly he remembers his wife. "Yaeko-san," he calls, "where are you?" She emerges from the ruined house, clothes torn and blood-stained.

"Let's get out of here as fast as we can!" he says.

As they walk away, their house sways and collapses. The wind grows vicious and fires begin to spread. Disturbed by his nakedness, Dr. Hachiya wraps his wife's apron around his loins. They move past a dead man, crushed by a falling wall; people with burned arms held out to their sides like scarecrows; a naked woman with her child. A wound in the doctor's thigh begins to spurt blood; he stops it with his hand, feeling faint and thirsty, but struggles on to his hospital. Friends greet him with alarm, place him on a stretcher, and begin to treat his wounds. He recognizes many of the other patients crowded into rooms and halls. It seems that the whole city is there.

At the clearance project the students from the girls' school have been badly burned by the blast. Some are already dead. The rest look with horror upon each other, faces scorched beyond recognition, clothes torn to rags. Their teacher, her hair turned white, holds her students close to her "like a mother hen protecting her chicks." The bewildered girls, "like baby chicks paralyzed with terror," thrust their heads under her arms.

Setsuko Sakamoto attempts to stay near her teacher. Her friend, Naoku Masuoka, searches for her family. Her hands are burned black; a yellow liquid drops "like sweat" from the broken skin. She feels lonely and afraid. "Why must I suffer?" she asks herself. "I don't want to die." As she wanders through the broken city, she sees someone pinned under a concrete wall, calling for help. Everyone hurries past. She sees a woman covered with burns writhing in agony and a bloody horse tied to a telephone pole, plunging wildly.

Fortunately, Naoku is picked up by a rescue squad and taken to a hospital. Lying on a blanket over a straw mat, she longs to see her family. Nearby another child dies after calling for her mother. Naoku is forlorn. Perhaps she will never see her parents again. In this moment of despair she hears her father calling her name. Tears come to her eyes, and when he appears, her "strong father" is crying, too. He can hardly speak as he cradles his badly wounded but still living daughter. Holding her to him, he repeats again and again, "I'm so glad, I'm so glad."

A few miles away, in another world, the men of the *Enola Gay* have little conception of what they have done. They saw smoke but not burned flesh, flames but not families, movement but not pain. They were separated from their victims by the mind-numbing toxins of war. Accordingly, their act was brave and useful. Like the millions of other men of every nationality who had killed in the past decade of war, the men of the *Enola Gay* lived in a world in which good men could cause horrible suffering in pursuit of patriotic goals.

After the explosion the men experienced three sensations. First there was elation. The bomb had gone off and destroyed the target; the mission was a success. Then there was relief; they could leave behind the dangers of flak, fighters, and atomic accident. Finally there was awe, an overwhelming recognition of the world-destroying power of the bomb.

The planes circled Hiroshima slowly, attempting to see the city through the clouds of smoke. The men had shouted their amazement at the size of the blast, but now they were silent, subdued by what they had seen. It was difficult to find appropriate words. Finally Tibbets announced to the crews of the three planes, "Well, boys, we've just dropped the first atomic bomb in history." He spoke slowly, seeming to labor over the words.

A few minutes after leaving Hiroshima, Tibbets and Parsons composed a concise report on the mission. It read: "Results clear-cut, successful in all respects. Visible effects greater than in any test. Conditions normal in airplane following delivery." With another six hours of flying ahead, the men ate C-ration sandwiches and drank coffee. Then, exhausted from the day and a half without sleep, they took turns napping. There was some small talk. Tibbets asked tail gunner Caron how he had felt during the sharp dive away from the bomb. Caron answered that it had been "better than the cyclone ride you pay a quarter for at Coney Island."

"Well, I'll collect a quarter from you when we land," said Tibbets.

But there was little of this banter. Aboard the *Great Artiste,* Abe Spitzer, his hands shaky and clammy as he watched the atomic explosion, heard one of his comrades say, "I wonder if maybe we're not monkeying around with things that are none of our business." Albert Denhart, a quiet, solitary Texan who was the *Great Artiste*'s tail gunner, was awestruck by the explosion. "I think I'd just as soon have missed it," he said. "Come to think of it, I won't be mentioning it to my grandchildren." Looking back, Denhart could see the smoke from Hiroshima for mile after mile. It was still visible when the planes had flown 250 miles.

At three o'clock in the afternoon of August 6 the three planes set down on the long runway at Tinian. They were greeted by a throng of high-ranking military personnel. Gen. Carl A. Spaatz, commander of the Strategic Air Forces, presented Tibbets with a Distinguished Service Cross. Tibbets apparently had not been expecting this ceremony; he put his pipe in a sleeve of his coveralls and received his award.

The men were then escorted to the officers' club, given lemonade well laced with bourbon, and questioned about the mission. It was not difficult to describe all that they had seen on the bomb run. Tibbets summarized it in four jaunty words: "Saw city, destroyed same." But the interrogators also asked a more complicated question: How had they felt? Even to the seasoned airmen and the men who had worked on the bomb, there was something disquieting about its power. One of the scientists remarked, "I'm not proud of myself right now." Abe Spitzer had difficulty with the question but replied, "It was hell, absolute hell." He answered the question more fully a few months later in a book. He wrote: "I felt that we were seeing a thing that man should never see, that was too big for the human mind really to understand and, moreover and more important, that even in a war, even in a war in which the enemy in the Pacific had been the most sadistic, most inhuman, most cruel, most hateful enemy in history, we had unleashed a force too great to be understood and properly feared. That we had, in short, learned how to kill too many thousands too quickly."

That night Abe Spitzer drank more heavily than he had ever done in his life. So too did many of his fellows. They had passed through a psychological ordeal the like of which few men ever had to face. Wearied by long hours without sleep, they had flown a strange mission that might easily have resulted in their own deaths, then dropped a bomb whose force was unearthly. There were many ways to see the event. It was a scientific triumph; it was a milestone in warfare; it was the death of thousands of people; it was an omen of future cataclysm; it was a way to shorten the war. In their minds feelings of triumph and tragedy, achievement and destruction, pleasure and regret mingled uneasily.

Abe Spitzer had difficulty sleeping. He kept seeing Hiroshima as he had imagined it a moment before the blast: "the green grass, the tiny trees, the bridges and the houses." Then he would see "that giant multi-colored mushroom and that black smoke that had covered the city."

What neither Spitzer nor any of the other men could see then was Hiroshima itself on the first night of its ordeal, an ordeal that made the discomfort of the bomber crews seem less than nothing. Four square miles in the center of the city were completely destroyed. Within a half mile of the blast 95 percent of the people had been killed. The survivors huddled in parks and ruined buildings. The night before they had slept safely in a thriving city. Now they struggled to survive amid ghastly horrors. In a city park hundreds lay in eerie silence under pines, laurels, and maples. Most were horribly injured, but none cried. In one hidden corner of the park a group of soldiers clustered together preserving a grotesque semblance of military order: their faces were burned; the fluid from their burned-out eye sockets lay encrusted on their cheeks.

In the Communications Hospital, Dr. Michihiko Hachiya was one of hundreds of patients. There were patients in every corner of the hospital, even in the toilets. Because most of Hiroshima's doctors and nurses had been killed or badly injured in the atomic blast, there were not enough trained personnel to care for the patients. Feces, urine, and vomit accumulated rapidly in beds and on floors.

In spite of all this human suffering, it was an animal that would impress many as the most grotesque symbol of their ordeal. For several days an injured horse — hairless, eyeless, and bloody — wandered through the rubble, bumping into walls and trees, apparently searching for a stable that was no more.

Surely no nation would continue to make war in the face of such a weapon. Such was the expectation of President Harry S. Truman when he heard the news from Hiroshima. He was eating dinner with the crew aboard the *Augusta* in mid-Atlantic on his way home from the Potsdam Conference. Jubilant, he told the sailors about the weapon that would end the war. They cheered as he made his way to the officers' mess with the news. "Keep your seats, gentlemen," he said, "I have an announcement to make to you. We have just dropped a bomb on Japan which has more power than 20,000 tons of T.N.T. It was an overwhelming success." He then issued a statement calling the atomic bomb "the greatest achievement of organized science in history."

On Long Island, Secretary of War Stimson released a longer, prepared statement describing the development of the bomb and calling on the Japanese to surrender. The communique reported that the atomic bomb derived its power from "a harnessing of the basic power of the universe. The force from which the sun draws its power." It claimed that Japan could have escaped if it had accepted the Potsdam Declaration. "Now," the statement continued, "if they do not accept our terms, they may expect a rain of ruin from the air, the like of which has never been seen on this earth." It was no idle threat.

Despite the awesome power of the bomb, Japan was not ready to surrender. The military chiefs were determined to fight to the end rather than capitulate, and so the official Japanese announcements on the bomb tended to minimize the danger from the weapon, even while characterizing the Americans as "inhuman" and "barbaric" for using it.

Two days after Hiroshima the men who had seen the cataclysm and thought the war was over had to prepare for another deadly flight to Japan. This time the crew of the *Great Artiste,* commanded by Maj. Charles W. Sweeney, would drop a new kind of bomb, made of an artificial element, plutonium, rather than uranium derivative U-235, as in the first bomb. Nicknamed "Fat Boy," it was almost eleven feet long and five feet in diameter, somewhat larger than the "Little Boy" that had shattered Hiroshima. The second bomb was said to be even more powerful than the first.

Sweeney's crew was to switch planes and fly another B-29, *Bock's*

Car, while *Great Artiste* followed as an observer. At 3:49 A.M. on August 9 they took off from Tinian and headed north on the familiar pathway of destruction. The mission was plagued with difficulties from the start. The gasoline in one of the tanks aboard *Bock's Car* could not be used, and so her range was reduced. A third plane failed to join the other two at Iwo Jima. The primary target, Kokura, was hidden in clouds when they arrived. The planes circled three times, the pilots hoping for a break in the clouds, but none appeared, and the men were not allowed to bomb through cloud cover; *Bock's Car* flew on to another target. In the incredible fortunes of atomic warfare, Kokura had been saved by bad weather.

The two planes turned toward Nagasaki, a city built on hills overlooking a bay in the East China Sea. As they approached, it was hidden in the clouds, but when they were overhead the city came into view. Bombardier Kermit K. Beahan fixed his sight on a stadium beside the banks of the Urakami River, and at 11:01 A.M. an atomic bomb fell away toward Nagasaki. The plane sped off in the dive away from the holocaust. Again there was a bright light, followed by searing heat, jolting shocks, and the billowing cloud. Again tens of thousands of men, women, and children were killed or mortally wounded and a city was destroyed.

On *Bock's Car* the men, who were seeing their second atomic blast in three days, were awestruck. This explosion seemed bigger than the last; it probed outward as if to swallow up everything in sight. "I've never seen anything like it," said Sweeney, with labored words, "and I hope I never do again." Ray Gallagher, the assistant flight engineer, was appalled as he looked at the huge fireball. Later he spoke the words that passed through his mind at that moment: "I thought maybe the world had come to an end, and we'd caused it." *Bock's Car* circled the remains of Nagasaki and then, perilously low on gasoline, headed for an emergency landing at Okinawa, where the crew ate and refueled. Flying to Tinian, they arrived home to a heroes' welcome. Most of the men were too exhausted to care.

In Tokyo it was evident to most that the end was near. Russia had declared war on Japan on the same day that the United States bombed Nagasaki. Reluctantly the emperor instructed his cabinet to sue for peace. On August 14 Japan accepted an arrangement that would retain the emperor but place him under Allied rule. In an unprecedented action the emperor went on radio and announced that Japan had surrendered.

Eight days after the bombing of Hiroshima the war ended. For many of the citizens of Hiroshima and Nagasaki the ordeal of atomic warfare had just begun. The initial impact of the bombs had been like that of conventional bombs, killing and maiming by heat and blast. But a few days later effects of a new sort appeared. Radiation from the bombs caused hair to fall out and wounds to resist treatment. People became acutely sensitive to infection and died quickly or lingered on in a strangely weakened condition. Children were born with birth defects. Such injuries would persist for years, even for decades.

A war characterized by terror had ended in horror of a new kind. Soon the questions would arise: Had it been necessary? Was there no effective alternative to the use of the atomic bomb? Although the logic of violence was widely accepted in 1945, it would seem less understandable later to a world at peace. But it is impossible to separate Hiroshima and Nagasaki from the worldwide fabric of violence that nourished the bomb's development and use. The ultimate tragedy of the atomic bomb was not that it was a careless aberration but that it was a "necessary" act according to the logic of that time. It was as necessary as Pearl Harbor or the German invasion of Russia or the D-day landing in France. Total war justified surprise attacks on merchant vessels, torture of prisoners, and the bombing of civilian targets. It provided a rationale for unspeakable suffering and enabled men to kill seventy thousand people in a day's work. But to those who suffered, pain was still pain. The destruction was no less grotesque for being "necessary."

If, however, war blinded one person to another's suffering, it also created curious and unanticipated sympathies. In the chaotic crucible of atomic warfare there was sometimes a peculiar mingling of sensibilities by which the victim comprehended the oppressor and the oppressor sympathized with the victim. Among the Japanese at Hiroshima and Nagasaki, many regarded the bombing as a predictable act of war; some citizens even reflected that they were being punished for Pearl Harbor.

And among the crews of the atomic bombers there were those who recognized that the logic of warfare makes everyone a potential victim. This perception entered a troublesome dream that haunted Abe Spitzer soon after the two atomic blasts. In the dream he found himself in a briefing room with his fellow officers. The commander was a man whose shoulders were covered with honorific silver laurels. But he was a disquieting figure. Where his face should have been there were no eyes, ears, nose, or mouth — just blank space. All the other men in the room were also faceless except his fellow crewmen. The briefing officer showed slides of the target, a modern port city with skyscrapers. He explained that the new bomb would be "much more destructive" than the previous two and would drop at 12:01 P.M. when people would be going out to lunch. All the faceless men laughed.

In the dream Spitzer's throat was dry and he was nearly paralyzed with apprehension. The city with its modern buildings and docks was disturbingly familiar. He waved his hand frantically and finally caught the commander's attention.

"Where's the target?" he asked.

The man with no face replied smugly, "The target is the Bronx, New York."

This was Spitzer's home. He protested wildly.

"That's an order, Sergeant," he was told. Then he awoke.

The radio operator had been dreaming. But there was a bizarre rationality in his vision. The commonplace and the monstrous were in reality intermingled in the logic of warfare. The men of the 509th Bomb Group were at one and the same time brave and resourceful airmen and fearsome agents of destruction. They would, of course, bomb only real enemies. But the destructive power they carried and the logic of warfare that justified their missions would soon be available to faceless commanders with other targets to bomb.

In later years a mythology would grow up around the men of the 509th Composite Bomb Group. In an age of peace it seemed incredible that men could kill tens of thousands of human beings without suffering remorse. Many people believed that the commander of the *Enola Gay* went crazy with guilt, even that all the atomic crewmen suffered emotional breakdowns. Other legends hold that there were several planes with "atomic" bombs on each mission, one with the real bomb and two with dummies, so that no one knew who really destroyed the cities. The implication of each myth is the same: men could not knowingly drop an atomic bomb without experiencing unbearable feelings of guilt.

There is a small degree of truth in these myths. Many of the crewmen did feel sorrow in later years when they saw pictures of bomb victims. Some sought to warn other people about the terrors of atomic warfare. And one officer, Maj. Claude Eatherly, commander of the weather plane, who gave the go-ahead report on Hiroshima, did have a mental breakdown that he attributed to guilt about the bomb. His experience fed the myths about other men's mental suffering.

But the story of atomic warfare during World War II is fundamentally a story of cold resolve rather than of reluctant acquiescence. That spirit was apparent on the 509th's last bombing run. After the two atomic missions the group made a final flight over Japan to drop conventional bombs on Koroma. As Abe Spitzer surveyed the results, the planes appeared to be pelting the city with "bean shooters." For a moment the men were disappointed. They had grown accustomed to atomic warfare.

QUESTIONS

1. Describe the role of the following in the preparation for the bombing of Hiroshima: nuclear scientists, the Manhattan Project, Alamogordo, Wendover.

2. What role did American experience at places like Iwo Jima have in the decision to use the atomic bomb? Would other nations have used atomic bombs in World War II if they had possessed them?

3. Why did the United States decide to use the atomic bomb against Japan? What other options were there? What was "the logic of violence"?

4. Would the United States have used the atomic bomb against Germany if it had been available before Germany surrendered?

5. What did the atomic bomb do to Hiroshima? How were people killed and injured? What did they think had happened?

6. How would you characterize the men who bombed Hiroshima and Nagasaki? Were they ordinary Americans? Did they care about the people they killed? How did they react to taking part in the bombing?

7 . Why did people believe that some of the atomic crewmen went mad?

8. Why didn't Japan surrender after the bombing of Hiroshima? Why did Japan surrender after the bombing of Nagasaki? Could it have been defeated by other means without great loss of American lives?

9. The author argues that in a state of total war acts of terrible violence become "reasonable." How does this transmutation happen?

BIBLIOGRAPHY

ALPEROVITZ, GAR. *Atomic Diplomacy* (1985). Argues that America's use of the bomb helped cause the Cold War.

BOYER, PAUL S. *By the Bomb's Early Light* (1985). American responses to the news of the bomb.

DOWER, JOHN. *War Without Mercy: Race and Power in the Pacific War* (1986). Documents the brutality practiced by all sides in the Pacific War.

FEIS, HERBERT. *The Atomic Bomb and the End of World War II* (1966). On the diplomatic significance of the bomb.

HACHIYA, MICHIHIKO. *Hiroshima Diary* (1955). A doctor's memories of the atomic bomb and its aftermath.

HERSEY, JOHN. *Hiroshima* (1949). Classic account of what it was like to be in Hiroshima in August 1945.

OSADA, ARATA, COMPILER. *Children of the A Bomb* (1963). Children's memories of the bomb.

RHODES, RICHARD. *The Making of the Atomic Bomb* (1988). How the bomb was built.

ROSS, BILL D. *Iwo Jima* (1985). Account of one island battle that helps explain American reluctance to invade Japan.

SCHELL, JONATHAN. *The Fate of the Earth* (1982). Discusses the dangers of modern nuclear warfare.

SIEMES, JOHN A., S.J. "Hiroshima: Eyewitness." *Saturday Review*, May 11, 1946. A Jesuit priest's memories of the bombing.

SPITZER, ABE. *We Dropped the A-Bomb* (1946). Radio operator's account.

THOMAS, GORDON, AND MAX MORGAN WITTS. *Enola Gay* (1977). Well-researched account of the bombing.

TIBBETS, PAUL W., JR., ET AL. "15 Years Later: The Men Who Bombed Hiroshima." *Coronet Magazine* (August 1960). Interview with the crewmen of the *Enola Gay*.

TOLAND, JOHN. *The Rising Sun* (1970). Good overview of the Japanese Empire from 1936 to 1945.

WYDEN, PETER. *Day One: Before Hiroshima and After* (1984). The story of those who made the atomic bomb — and were themselves surprised by its power.

10

Joseph McCarthy and Anti-Communism

The fundamental rules of American life were written into the Constitution and the Bill of Rights two centuries ago. But those rules have continually been reevaluated to govern new circumstances. After World War II the United States entered a historical era in which the superpowers, Russia and the United States, were engaged in a bitter rivalry that came to be known as the "cold war." The confrontation appeared so threatening that many Americans were willing to abandon the Bill of Rights in hunting Communist "subversives" in the United States. Joseph McCarthy's career reveals the urgency behind the anti-Communist crusade, but also suggests the enduring American commitment to free expression.

In 1954 the United States was at war. No troops were in the field and no ships were fighting at sea, but the country nonetheless was in a deadly struggle throughout the world against an "international Communist conspiracy." And in 1954 many Americans thought the Communists were winning. Communism had spread from Russia to China and Eastern Europe. It was winning in Vietnam. And worse still, Communist agents were active in the United States itself. In 1952 Senator William Jenner of Indiana charged that "this country today is in the hands of a secret inner coterie which is directed by agents of the Soviet Union." Senator Joseph McCarthy of Wisconsin declared that the United States had experienced "twenty years of treason" under Democratic Presidents Roosevelt and Truman.

McCarthy believed that Communists had infiltrated every corner of American life. Schools, libraries, newspapers, and movies all showed their influence. In 1954 he was on the trail of Communists who had infiltrated the last bulwark of American freedom, the United States Army. In April he pursued his army investigation before the largest public forum ever to watch an American political event. In that month the Senate began a public hearing on the army-McCarthy controversy and opened the council chamber to a new medium, television. Day after day for seven weeks millions of Americans would watch the nation's preeminent anti-Communist at work. The hearing, which McCarthy promoted as a lesson about the Communist conspiracy, became more than that: a lesson about American democracy in the modern world.

American anticommunism began in the nineteenth century, before the world had its first Communist nation. After Karl Marx published the *Communist Manifesto* in Germany in 1848, his ideas circulated rapidly in Europe and the United States. Marx's claim that the laborers of the world were cheated out of their fair share of industrial profits inspired a socialist movement in the United States during the latter part of the nineteenth century. The movement grew into several parties, diverse in program but alike in holding that the instruments of industrial production, distribution, and exchange should be owned by the people as a whole and managed cooperatively for the benefit of all rather than competitively for the benefit of a few. They looked at men like Andrew Carnegie as greedy oppressors: Why should Carnegie earn $25 million a year, when his workers earned less than a thousand?

The socialists advocated radical restructuring of American society. They ran several impressive presidential campaigns beginning in 1910, polling nearly a million votes for their candidate, Eugene V. Debs. But neither the socialists nor the Communist parties, which were formed later, could make much headway against a deep American antipathy to communism, which most Americans regarded as a foreign ideology. Naturally the "captains of industry" were unfriendly to any doctrine that would deprive them of their wealth; most believed that business success was a reward from God for hard work. By 1900 they were already using the term "communist" to condemn those who favored an income tax. And American workingmen, who might have supported socialism, were so imbued with the ideal of success through individual initiative that most regarded socialism and communism as exotic foreign doctrines, designed for men who were lazy and subversive, and not for American farmers and factory workers.

When the Russian Revolution in 1917 brought into being the first Communist state, most Americans were appalled. The United States actually stationed soldiers in Siberia between 1918 and 1920 to assist White Russians in an unsuccessful attempt to overthrow the Bolsheviks. During the same period the Communist party was founded in the United States under the direction of the "Russian International." Sporadic acts of violence by American radicals gave Attorney General A. Mitchell Palmer an excuse for attempting to root out Communists. The "Palmer Raids" resulted in more than 4,000 arrests and deportation of 556 supposed radicals.

American hostility toward communism softened somewhat during the Depression. Terrible economic conditions in the 1930s persuaded many Americans that unfettered capitalism could not provide for the economic well-being of all the people. Many American intellectuals and laborers joined the Communist party as an alternative to the individualistic ideals that seemed to have brought about industrial chaos. Roosevelt's own program, though far from communistic, involved many reforms that shifted power from individuals to the government. New Deal legislation enabled the government to provide jobs, housing, public works, and old age pensions. Most Americans regarded these measures as repairs to the political structure, not as a radical departure from traditional American values. But some feared "creeping socialism" and even accused Roosevelt himself of Communist leanings.

During Roosevelt's administration events in Europe encouraged a closer relationship with the Soviet Union. In 1933, when Hitler came to power, Roosevelt granted diplomatic recognition to Russia, and eight years later the United States and Russia were allies in World War II. The two nations fought in the same cause, plotted strategy together, met in Allied conferences, and cooperated in creating the United Nations. Joseph Stalin, dictatorial ruler of the Soviet Union, was known to American politicians and soldiers as "Uncle Joe."

Mutual enemies brought cooperation between Russia and the United States during the war, but with the defeat of Germany and Japan in 1945, suspicions soon resurfaced. Russia suffered far more casualties in the war than any other Allied nation: about 18,000,000 Russians lost their lives, compared to 300,000 American deaths — a 60 to 1 ratio. Russia's contribution to the war with Germany was apparent too in that three out of four German deaths in the war came in battles with Russians. For several years Stalin had tried in vain to persuade the Allies to open up a "second front" in Western Europe to take some of the burden off Russia, and he suspected that the D-Day landings in Normandy were delayed until 1944 because the Allies wanted Germany to weaken Russia.

Having fought two costly wars with Germany during the previous three decades, Russia decided to protect itself from further aggression by occupying not only the eastern sector of Germany, but also all the countries between Germany and the Soviet Union. Soviet occupation of East Germany was by joint agreement with France, England, and the United States, who occupied the western sector. Russia extended its influence into Poland, Hungary, Czechoslovakia, Rumania, and Bulgaria through force and guile. These acts, which Russia sought to justify as necessary defensive measures after a costly war, appeared in a different light in the west. In 1946 Winston Churchill composed a memorable description of Russian advances. Speaking at Westminster College in Fulton, Missouri, Britain's wartime prime minister declared: "From Stettin in the Baltic to Trieste in the Adriatic an iron curtain has descended across the continent."

The phrase "iron curtain" became a household word throughout the Western world. With Russia's expansion in Eastern Europe the image of Russians as friendly comrades-in-arms paled before the new Soviet spectre as brutal and aggressive. Other signs of Communist activity abounded. After Communist Mao Tse-tung consolidated his power in China with a victory over Nationalist forces at Nanking in 1949, there were two Chinas; the Communists controlled the whole mainland, and the Nationalists were left with the island of Taiwan. In Southeast Asia Communist Ho Chi Minh was waging war against colonial control by France. In Greece and Turkey Communist guerrillas were active.

Americans believed that communism was "monolithic," that each of these movements was sponsored by the Soviet Union. Moreover, the tentacles of Russian power seemed to extend to the United States itself and to its allies. In 1949, just four years after America had achieved a miracle in exploding the first atomic bomb, the Soviet Union exploded an atomic bomb. How had the Russians been able to develop a bomb so quickly? How, indeed, without help from the United States? In 1946 several Soviet spy rings were exposed in Canada. In 1950 Americans learned that a British scientist, Dr. Klaus Fuchs, had delivered atomic secrets to the Russians and that he had worked with an American, Harry Gold. During the same year a spy ring including Americans Julius and Ethel Rosenberg, David Greenglass, and Morton Sobell was exposed.

Shortly after the end of World War II Americans began to talk about a "cold war," a struggle with the Soviet Union that was waged by spying and subversion. The intense hostility toward communism that pervaded postwar America was stimulated by objective facts: real Russian expansion in Eastern Europe, real Communist gains in other nations, and real Russian spies in England, Canada, and the United States. The anti-Communist movement also grew out of partisan reactions to the alleged "creeping socialism" of the New Deal. Many conservatives believed that the social programs and economic regulations of the Roosevelt administration had undermined American values and traditions. The American traitors were not merely those who had access to atomic secrets and sold them to the Russians, but also those who worked within the system to promote un-American programs and ideas.

President Harry S. Truman did not embrace the conspiracy theory: he approved of the New Deal, and he doubted that America was as riddled with traitors as some anti-Communists contended. But he did adopt numerous policies designed to resist expansion of communism. He favored the Marshall Plan, under which the United States spent billions of dollars to strengthen economies in Western Europe. He announced the Truman Doctrine in 1947, which became the basic statement of America's position in the Cold War. There are "two ways of life," Truman declared, one free and one totalitarian. The United States should help "free people to maintain their free institutions and their national integrity against aggressive movements that seek to impose upon them totalitarian regimes." In particular Truman persuaded Congress to provide funds to support the governments of Greece and Turkey in their struggles against Communist insurrections. Moreover in 1949 the United States joined Canada and ten European nations in creating the North Atlantic Treaty Organization (NATO) as a bulwark against Russian expansion in Europe.

Truman also supported measures aimed at thwarting Communist activities in the United States. In 1947 he established a Loyalty Review Board to investigate government employees. During the next four years the government evaluated three million employees, dismissing 212 and forcing another 2,000 to resign under suspicion. In 1949 the government used the Smith Act, a 1940 law against advocating the violent overthrow of the government, as a basis for sending Communist leaders to jail. President Truman approved of these activities, but opposed more extreme measures, such as the McCarren Internal Security Act, which made it unlawful "to combine, conspire or agree with any other person to perform any act that would substantially contribute to the establishment . . . of a totalitarian dictatorship." Under the act, passed by Congress in 1950, "Communist-front organizations" were required to register with the attorney general. Members of such organizations could neither work in defense plants nor travel abroad.

Although Truman had been active in ferreting out Communists, he felt that the McCarran Act went too far. Truman vetoed the bill, declaring that it "put the government in the business of thought control." But by 1950 few congressmen shared the president's scruples; the bill gained a two-thirds majority, enough to override the president's veto.

In the following year the Supreme Court endorsed the anti-Communist movement in the case of *Dennis et al. v. United States* (1951). Three decades before, in *Schenck v. United States* (1919), the court had ruled that political expression could be limited only under rare wartime circumstances in which there was a "clear and present danger" of damage to the United States. In the Dennis case the court reviewed the convictions of the eleven Communists jailed under the Smith Act. Justice Hugo Black argued that the Smith Act violated the First Amendment, and Justice William O. Douglas said the Smith Act failed to distinguish between a "conspiracy to overthrow the government" and the simple teaching of "Marxist-Leninist doctrine." Black and Douglas were in the minority, however; the court endorsed the Smith Act and so the convictions held.

Every branch of the government was thus active in the anti-Communist movement, but some politicians questioned whether part of the problem might not be the government itself. These Red hunters favored a more rigorous effort to ferret out subversives within the government and charged that Truman himself was "soft on communism." He had opposed the McCarran Act, and he was clearly identified with the New Deal programs that had limited free enterprise in the name of communal welfare.

During the postwar years anticommunism was so powerful that the failure to be an ardent Red-baiter could, in itself, be regarded as evidence of pro-Communist sentiments. A young naval lieutenant, Richard Milhous Nixon, returned home to California after the war, and at thirty-three ran for Congress against H. Jerry Voorhis, a veteran politician. In platform debates Nixon charged that Voorhis was supported by Communists. The charges were unsubstantiated, but Nixon won the election. In Congress he helped write the anti-union Taft-Hartley Act, and he served on the House Un-American Activities Committee, which was created in 1938 as an anticommunism watchdog. Nixon prepared the House investigation of Alger Hiss, President of the Carnegie Endowment for International Peace and a former State Department official. In 1948 Hiss was accused by Whittaker Chambers, a former Communist, of having copied secret documents for the Russians. The evidence was flimsy, and President Truman called the case against him "a red herring." But Nixon insisted on pursuing the matter, and in 1950 Hiss was sentenced to five years in prison for lying about his involvement in the episode. In 1950 Nixon ran for the Senate against Helen Gahagan Douglas. As in his campaign against Jerry Voorhis, he launched an impassioned but unsupported attack on his opponent's loyalty, and again he won.

By 1950 many American politicians had learned the popularity of anticommunism. Fear of Communist expansion abroad and subversion at home led voters to admire any candidate who appeared to hate communism. In that year a young senator from Wisconsin, Joseph Raymond McCarthy, became the most outspoken anti-Communist in the Senate. In Wheeling, West Virginia, he delivered a shocking speech to the Women's Republican Club. "The reason we find ourselves in a position of impotency," he said, "is not because our only powerful potential enemy has sent men to invade our shores, but rather because of the traitorous actions of those who have been treated so well by this nation." Among the "traitors" known to McCarthy the most insidious were those who "infested" the State Department. Holding out his fist to the startled audience, he declared, "I have here in my hand a list of 205 — a list of names that were known to the Secretary of State as being members of the Communist Party and who nevertheless are *still working and shaping . . . policy.*" McCarthy was speaking from notes, and accounts vary as to his actual claim as to the number of Communists. At other times he spoke of 57 and 81 "card-carrying Communists" in the State Department. But whether 57 or 205, his claim and his pretense to authority — he had the list right in his hand — electrified not only the Women's Republican Club, but people all over the country. Within a few weeks Joseph McCarthy was hailed by many Americans as the bravest and best of the anti-Communist warriors.

Joseph Raymond McCarthy was in many characteristics a natural figure to champion traditional American values against treason. He was born in a simple clapboard farmhouse at Grand Chute, Wisconsin, in 1908. His grandfather, who pioneered in Wisconsin, had left Ireland in 1848 during the potato famine. Working as a farmhand in New York, he saved enough money to buy a half section of land — 320 acres in Wisconsin. He arrived at his farm in 1858 driving a wagon pulled by a team of oxen. Within a few years he had cleared the land, built a log cabin, and started a dairy farm. He and his wife had ten children, including Timothy McCarthy, who bought a nearby farm and married a tall, heavy-set woman, Bridget Tierney.

The Timothy McCarthys, Joseph's parents, lived on a 142-acre farm in the "Irish settlement" near grandfather McCarthy's farm. They raised corn, hay, barley, oats, and cabbage along with some cows, pigs, and horses. They had seven children, of whom Joseph, or "Joe," was the fourth. They were apparently a close, hardworking, and religious family. They rode to nearby Appleton for mass every week, whatever the weather. The McCarthy children generally finished eighth grade in the local one-room schoolhouse and then left and went to work.

Joe McCarthy was fourteen when he quit school. He was good looking, with black hair, blue eyes, and a light skin, and he spoke with a slight Irish brogue. Joe was different from his six brothers and sisters in his enormous energy. He could get by on a few hours of sleep a night; he loved boxing, wrestling, and baseball; when an older brother brought home a motorcycle, Joe, age thirteen, had to ride it. A neighboring farmer remembered him as "always driving, always driving."

After quitting school Joe did farm chores for a time, but soon got bored and used $65 he had saved to build a chicken shed and stock it with chickens. He tended his poultry carefully, and by the time he was seventeen he owned 2,000 laying hens and 10,000 broilers. But three years later his profitable business was ruined when a disease killed most of the chickens. Joe moved to nearby Appleton, Wisconsin, and became manager of a grocery store. His was the smallest store in a chain of twenty-four, but it was soon the most profitable. Joe won customers by walking the country roads and introducing himself to farmers, inviting them to the store. At work he flattered old ladies, joked with teenagers, and made his shop into a kind of community center. He was gifted with an extraordinary memory and could recall hundreds — and later thousands — of names. Anyone who came more than once to the store was an old friend.

Joe McCarthy next turned to completing high school. At Appleton's Little Wolf High School, which he entered as a freshman, he was allowed to work on his own in the school study hall, taking examinations whenever he completed a subject. He completed first-year algebra in six weeks, was a sophomore by Thanksgiving, a junior at midterm, and a senior by Easter. He graduated that spring, with honors. While doing schoolwork for twelve hours a day, McCarthy also played basketball, taught boxing, and completed an extension course for the University of Wisconsin.

That fall he entered Marquette University. He intended at first to be an engineer, but decided law was more interesting. He supported himself by working as a janitor, salesman, and short-order cook. At the end of his second year ar Marquette he was managing two service stations. He spent much of his time working and enjoying life in a fraternity house, where he was an outstanding poker player. In just five years McCarthy earned a B.A. and a law degree. McCarthy's work was impressive, but in many areas his knowledge was superficial. He tended to get by with hasty memorization and other shortcuts that left him with only a hazy perspective on history and philosophy.

After a brief spell on his own, McCarthy took a job in a law office in Shawano, Wisconsin. He was so poor when he arrived that he had to sell his typewriter to set himself up in a boarding house. At Shawano he joined the Young Democratic Club and was soon president for his district. Although his boss was a Republican, Joe McCarthy supported Roosevelt's reelection in 1936 and distributed Roosevelt-for-President buttons. McCarthy proved himself an adequate attorney, and in 1937 he became a partner in his firm, but his real talent seemed to lie in his personal relationships. In 1938 he decided to run for the position of judge in Wisconsin's Tenth Circuit against an able incumbent, Edgar V. Werner.

Circuit judges were usually senior attorneys, but McCarthy believed that through hard work and personal contacts he could win the election. The district encompassed three rural counties, and McCarthy set out to meet every farmer in the region. During his visits he would swap stories, discuss farm problems, and even, occasionally, milk a cow. After each stop he would record notes on a dictating machine in his car while driving to the next farm. Using this information he sent each family a personal postcard before the election. Because he needed to send out thousands of cards, he left the writing to friends — he had many — so that each card was handwritten and appeared to come from the candidate himself. When the vote was tallied on April 5, 1939, Werner's total exceeded McCarthy's in Appleton, but McCarthy swept the rural areas, winning overall with 15,160 votes to Werner's 11,154. Only ten years after beginning high school McCarthy was the youngest Circuit Court judge in Wisconsin's history.

Judge McCarthy showed the same frenetic energy on the bench that had won him the election. He took office with a backlog of 250 cases. Holding that "justice delayed is justice denied," he held open his court twelve hours a day to work through the cases. He was a popular judge, liked for his even-handed running of the court and his good sense of humor. McCarthy might have spent his life on the bench, but he soon grew restless for other challenges. By 1941 he had decided that he wanted to be senator. He began exchanging circuits with other judges, in part for variety, in part to make political contacts throughout the state.

After Pearl Harbor, McCarthy considered joining the armed forces. His judicial position gave him an automatic deferment, but patriotism, a sense of adventure, and the obvious political advantages of a good service record all drove him to enlist. After finding that he could take a leave from his judgeship, he joined the marines. He took his political instincts with him. Reporters asked Judge McCarthy whether he expected to be made an officer, and he told them he was "more interested in a gun than a commission." Just before leaving for active duty he presided over a Milwaukee courtroom in his marine uniform.

McCarthy spent sixteen months in the South Pacific, most of it as an intelligence officer for a dive-bomber squadron. His work kept him at a desk most of the time, but he was able to go on a dozen missions as a photographer and tail gunner. The muscular Irish-American was popular with his fellow marines. He got around a liquor ban by filling three trunks with bottles and labeling them "office supplies." And he was an outrageous poker player. "He'd sit in a game," one friend recalled, "and suddenly, for no reason at all, bet $101.50, or $97.90. Not only would the bet knock other players off balance, but they'd have the problem of counting out the exact sum. Most times, they'd let him have the pot just to get on to the next game."

McCarthy's military career was honorable, but like his inflated poker bets, his hand in the war was subject to exaggeration. He slipped off a ladder and fractured his leg. The leg was further injured when an orderly mistook a caustic acid for a fluid used to soften the cast for cutting and, pouring the fluid on McCarthy's leg, gave him a severe burn. In different tellings this injury became a war injury and a battle injury. Similarly the story of McCarthy's missions grew with the telling. He parlayed his twelve flights into thirty-two, and on that basis he received a Distinguished Flying Cross. That was in 1952, when few people were willing to challenge anything McCarthy said.

At the war's end "Tail Gunner Joe" was again "Judge McCarthy." But he was already planning his run for the Senate. His political views, however, had not yet crystallized. He would soon be considered a conservative Republican, but in recent years he had been a New Deal Democrat, and an advocate for the United Nations. "There ought to be machinery to back such an international tribunal with force," he said, "As a circuit judge, my judgments would not have been worth the paper

they consumed without the authoritative presence of the sheriff's department on another floor of the courthouse." A liberal Democrat could
hardly have spoken more clearly in favor of a strong United Nations.

McCarthy's conservatism was a product of the postwar years, and
he decided to become a Republican when he had assessed the political
leanings of the voters in Wisconsin. He had won election to the bench
in a nonpartisan race. To switch parties all he needed to do was register
as a Republican. That much was easy. Winning recognition in a
statewide election was much more difficult. While continuing his work
as a judge, McCarthy stumped the state speaking tirelessly wherever he
could find an audience. Voters were worried about Russian advances in
Eastern Europe and about a rash of strikes in American factories; so
McCarthy bemoaned the "loss" of Eastern Europe and warned about the
corrosive influence of Communists in the labor unions. He was on the
conservative side on issues that troubled many Americans, but his
greatest asset was his personal appeal. If any political figure in the decade
following World War II filled the role of "all-American boy," it was Joe
McCarthy. He was a strong, handsome war veteran. And he was the
incarnation of hard work and imagination: in one year he fought his way
through high school and when he was only thirty he won a position on
the bench. His mother had taught her children, "Man was born to do
something." In his campaign speech he echoed her words. "I don't claim
to be more brilliant than the next man," he announced, "but I have
always claimed that I worked harder. I am going to work harder. That's
a promise."

McCarthy had to face two opponents in the Senate race. First he
must beat Robert M. La Follette, Jr., the popular incumbent senator, in
the Republican primary; then he would face the Democratic nominee.
During the campaign season McCarthy drove 80,000 miles, visiting as
many as twenty-eight towns in four days — all while continuing his
work on the bench. He engineered another postcard blitz, paying people
half a cent per card to send a "personal" message to each of the hundreds
of thousands of voters in Wisconsin. The other side of the card was a
smiling picture of Judge "Tail Gunner Joe" McCarthy. La Follette ran
a lackluster campaign; assuming that he would easily defeat the upstart
McCarthy, he appeared in Wisconsin for only ten days. The vote was
close — 207,935 to 202,557 — but McCarthy managed one of the
biggest upsets in Senate history.

Ironically, La Follette was on many issues a more ardent conservative than McCarthy in 1946. He opposed the United Nations and was
critical of Stalin; after the election he claimed that Communists in the
labor unions had contributed to his defeat. In the postwar era
anticommunism was virtually a national credo. The question was not so

much whether a politician was anti-Communist as how far that politician would go to demonstrate loyalty.

McCarthy still had to face the Democratic nominee, Howard McMurray, but by now the momentum was behind his campaign. He knew how to make the most out of his agrarian roots: "I'm just a farmboy, not a professor," he told a pleased audience. Upon hearing that Henry Wallace, the liberal former vice president, was going to speak in Wisconsin on behalf of his opponent, McCarthy declared. "The people of Wisconsin completely understand only one language — the American language, and Mr. Wallace does not speak that language." McCarthy claimed that Communists, who surely did not understand the "American language," had moved into positions of power in business, labor, and the government. Pro-McCarthy newspapers joined the crusade. McMurray, said one, is "in favor of the enemies of our country." When the votes were tallied in November McCarthy had won by 250,000 votes.

A few weeks later Senator Joe McCarthy went to Washington. At thirty-eight he was the youngest member of the Senate, but he was neither awed by his success nor humbled by the company of his seniors on Capitol Hill. He held a press conference shortly after his arrival, ducked a prickly question about why a junior senator would do such a thing, and declared that coal miners, then on strike, should be drafted into the army. McCarthy insisted on being called "Joe" by everyone, not only fellow Senators, but office workers and laborers, too. He invited eight Senate newswomen to dinner and cooked fried chicken. Friends remembered him chatting with black workers at a construction site and befriending the woman who made sandwiches in the Senate cafeteria. He was a popular figure in his neighborhood, too, where he shared an apartment with friends and played on the street with the local children. Joe McCarthy's personal tastes in Washington kept alive his man-of-the-people image. He wore inexpensive suits until they were shiny with age; at bedtime he read western pulp novels.

In an age of anticommunism McCarthy soon established himself as one of the leading opponents of communism in the Senate. He opposed the appointment of David E. Lilienthal as chairman of the Atomic Energy Commission because Lilienthal, while director of the Tennessee Valley Authority, had appointed men of dubious loyalty to positions of power. The stain of disloyalty was thin: one appointee was married to a woman with allegedly left-wing connections and another had a brother who was possibly a member of the Communist party. But this hint was enough for McCarthy. "I'd much rather run the risk of discarding a competent man than run the risk of being stuck with a dangerous man," he said. Lilienthal's appointment received a Senate vote of 51 to 30, enough to win confirmation, but far from a unanimous endorsement. A few weeks later the Taft-Hartley Bill, limiting the power of labor unions, came before the Senate. McCarthy approved of the bill wholeheartedly, but wanted to add an amendment encouraging labor unions and employers to get rid of workers who were Communists. The proposal was poorly written and was probably unconstitutional. Senator Robert Taft, a conservative and an anti-Communist, felt that it would add nothing to his bill. Senator Millard Tydings of Maryland warned that it would encourage a "witch hunt." The proposal was rejected.

Although McCarthy met defeat on both the Lilienthal and the Taft-Hartley issues, he had added to his credentials as an anti-Communist. In July 1947 he was interviewed on "Meet the Press." "We are at war," he said, "We've been at war with Russia for some time now. . . . Everyone is painfully aware of the fact that we are at war — and that we're losing it."

Despite these early signs of anticommunism, however, McCarthy's Senate career had not yet taken a clear direction. One of his biggest projects as a freshman senator was to conduct hearings on public housing. Although he felt that building should be left mainly to private enterprise, he wanted the government to help disabled veterans find suitable housing, and he fought corrupt business practices that inflated building costs. After the war "gray marketeers" hoarded scarce materials and sold them to contractors for inflated prices. McCarthy grilled a New York attorney, Isidore Ginsburg, one of the most active hoarders. Ginsburg responded, "We deal in nothing but free enterprise and take a reasonable profit, and nothing more." McCarthy snapped back, "Your enterprise is just too damn free, Ginsburg." The attorney claimed that "only in Russia" could his business be curtailed, and a newspaper claimed that McCarthy's attack on the gray marketeers could put America "in the straightjacket of Russia." Charges of Communist leanings came easily in the 1940s; anyone with a sympathetic word for government regulation or a harsh criticism of private enterprise could be labeled a Red, anyone including "Tail Gunner Joe."

McCarthy's most dramatic cause in his early years in the Senate was the investigation of alleged army brutality in the treatment of Nazi soldiers accused of massacring American troops at Malmédy, Belgium, in 1944. McCarthy read a report that American guards had placed hoods over prisoners' faces and beaten them with brass knuckles to extract confessions detailing their involvement in the massacre. Friends warned him that it would be political suicide to investigate the army for its activities at Malmédy. But McCarthy insisted that every suspect has a right to a fair trial. "We have been accused by the Russians," he said, "of using force, physical violence, and have accused them of using mock trials in cells in the dark of night, and now we have an army report that comes out and says we have done all the things that the Russians were ever accused of doing, but they are all right because it created the right psychological effect to get the necessary confessions."

In the Malmédy hearings McCarthy showed his willingness to adopt an unpopular cause when a matter of principle was involved, and he showed an attorney's regard for the importance of fair judicial proceedings. But his conduct in the hearings revealed a less attractive aspect of his character. The investigation was conducted by a Senate committee of which McCarthy was not a member, but an observer. Soon, however, he established himself as the most outspoken senator in the room, badgering the witnesses and the committee members with incessant questions, making wild charges, and accusing the committee chairman of a whitewash. He also claimed that he had seen damaging evidence that he could not produce and had, in fact, never seen. The Malmédy charges against the army proved mostly groundless, but McCarthy was so obsessed with his own view of the situation that he lost the ability to react intelligently to the evidence. The more the facts refuted his preconceptions, the more he insisted that he saw a coverup.

In the Malmédy proceedings McCarthy showed a tendency to combine genuine personal conviction (that all people, even ex-Nazi soldiers, deserve a fair trial) with a pathological compulsion to be right (blustering, intimidating, and lying to make his points). His fellow senators had difficulty evaluating their colleague from Wisconsin. Off the Senate floor he was friendly, thoughtful, and buoyant. But at work he was rude and obsessive. His behavior alienated many of the senior senators, who controlled committee appointments, and McCarthy soon found himself relegated to obscure committees on which he could have little influence on important public policy.

In 1949 Senator McCarthy finally tied himself to the cause that would win him lasting fame — and infamy. He had flirted with anticommunism in the past, but so too had many other congressmen. McCarthy's involvement became more intense in 1949 when he began a campaign to discredit the *Capital Times*, a Wisconsin newspaper that accused him of poor conduct in running for office while a judge and in failing to file proper tax returns. McCarthy claimed that the *Capital Times* was "the Red mouthpiece for the Communist party in Wisconsin." To substantiate his charge he claimed that the best way to evaluate whether someone was a Communist was to see whether they followed the "Communist party-line." "If a fowl looks like a duck, walks like a duck, swims like a duck, and quacks like a duck, then we can safely assume it is a duck."

As evidence that the *Capital Times* did indeed swim like a Communist duck, McCarthy found instances in which articles in the Times were printed shortly after similar articles in the Communist *Daily Worker*. He also pointed out that the paper complained about a double standard of justice in the United States, one for the rich and one for the poor — another sign of Communist leanings. The charges were totally unfounded. In fact, the *Capital Times* had a long history of *anti*-Communist articles and editorials. But McCarthy's charges were given favorable publicity throughout Wisconsin.

In McCarthy's account of his evolution as a crusader against communism he stresses a trip he made to rural Arizona, where he met "real Americans without any synthetic sheen." Among them, he says, he laid plans for "the one great fight" he would make as a senator. In 1950 McCarthy agreed with Republican party leaders to deliver five Lincoln Day speeches to Republican gatherings across the country. This type of tour was standard fare in senatorial politics, but the consequences of McCarthy's efforts were explosive. Some time before leaving he decided that he would claim to have a list of known Communists in the State Department. No such list existed, but McCarthy assumed he could persuade willing listeners that he had the information. As in a good poker bluff he would bid high on an empty hand. In Wheeling, West Virginia, on February 9, he first claimed to have the names of Communists in the State Department. He repeated his claim at stops in Colorado and Nevada; by the time he reached Huron, South Dakota, his charges were headline news across the country.

McCarthy was evasive, of course, when reporters asked to see the list. He told one reporter he had left the list in a suit that had gone astray on an airplane. After drinking late at night with two other journalists, he claimed they had stolen the list. One of the newsmen reported cynically, "He lost his list between his eighth and ninth bourbons." The *Washington Post* accused McCarthy of "sewer politics" and Communist tactics. "Rarely has a man in public life crawled and squirmed so abjectly," they declared. Such papers demanded facts, and McCarthy had no facts to give them. But scores of papers reported McCarthy's accusations uncritically, and millions of Americans needed little convincing. Like McCarthy they knew something was wrong with the country, and the more he was criticized the more they believed his charges were true. He was a brave patriot, they reasoned, and so naturally the Communists would attack him. After he spoke in Huron, South Dakota, the local paper ran a characteristically sympathetic letter by someone who had heard the senator speak. "He left us feeling proud we were Republicans. . . . McCarthy is a thinking, acting leader, not just a politician. There is a tremendous difference."

Soon afterward the senator from Wisconsin delivered a five-hour

speech in Congress repeating his charges about the State Department
and giving vague details about some of the alleged Communists. The
public outcry following McCarthy's allegations was so great that the
Senate decided to hold hearings to evaluate his evidence. McCarthy still
had no evidence of Communists, but his assertions forced other anti-
Communists to come to his assistance. J. Edgar Hoover, a friend of
McCarthy's, was angered by his premature allegations, though he
worried that if the senator was discredited the FBI's own investigations
would be discredited. Hoover therefore tried to help McCarthy find
evidence to support his claims. Richard Nixon urged McCarthy to be
more cautious in his accusations, but he favored McCarthy's cause and
helped the senator gain access to documents accumulated by the House
Un-American Activities Committee. Dozens of conservative politicians
came to McCarthy's assistance because they realized that if he were
discredited, their own anti-Communist efforts would be hampered.
Veterans of the conservative movement were often surprised at how
little McCarthy actually knew about the history and theory of the
Communist movement. He had placed himself at the center of
anticommunism through a monumental bluff.

McCarthy's initial test came a few months later. A Senate committee headed by Senator Millard Tydings of Maryland met to explore
McCarthy's allegations. In highly publicized hearings the Tydings
Committee heard a patchwork of charges put together by McCarthy and
his supporters. Lacking the name of *even one* Communist in the State
Department, McCarthy defined communism so broadly that any American who had supported a liberal cause during the previous twenty years
was suspect.

McCarthy's first name was typical of his list as a whole. Dorothy
Kenyon was a sixty-two-year-old New York attorney who had served on
the United Nations Commission on the Status of Women from 1947 to
1949. The case for her Communist leanings was based on her association
with various organizations that McCarthy and others described as
"subversive." One was the "Abraham Lincoln Brigade" — Americans
who had fought as volunteers against the fascist dictator, Francisco
Franco, during the Spanish Civil War. Another was the League of
Women Shoppers, a consumer rights organization. Others whom
McCarthy mentioned include Philip C. Jessup, the State Department's
ambassador-at-large, and Owen Lattimore, an adviser on China policy.
In none of these cases did McCarthy prove membership in the Communist party, to say nothing of treasonous conduct. Eleanor Roosevelt, the
president's widow, might have said of all the accused what she said of the
first: "If all the honorable senator's 'subversives' are as subversive as Miss
Kenyon, I think the State Department is entirely safe and the nation will

continue on an even keel." Margaret Chase Smith, a Republican senator from Maine and a strong supporter of the House Un-American Activities Committee, accused McCarthy of trying "to ride the Republican party to victory through the selfish political exploitation of fear, bigotry, ignorance, and intolerance." Senator Tydings summed up his view of the hearings by calling McCarthy's charges "a hoax."

The charges were flimsy, but the press often printed them without comment, and millions of Americans were ready to believe whatever McCarthy said. Despite the unfavorable response of the Tydings committee, the senator's popularity continued to grow. His influence now spread to the film community, where he numbered John Wayne among his good friends. In the fall elections of 1950 McCarthy spoke on behalf of sympathetic candidates across the country, reserving his best efforts for John Marshall Butler, a Maryland attorney who ran for the Senate against McCarthy's foe Millard Tydings. The senator from Wisconsin assigned his whole staff to take part in a campaign to slander the incumbent, and helped Butler upset Tydings. The political lesson was clear: those who opposed McCarthy risked their own political futures.

In 1951 McCarthy's self-assurance was so strong that he could launch an attack on one of the most popular men in America, George C. Marshall, the secretary of defense. The address, delivered on June 14, 1951, lasted almost three hours and is the classic expression of McCarthy's anti-Communist rhetoric. Marshall had been Army Chief of Staff during World War II and proposed the postwar European Recovery Program that bears his name. But his position as foreign policy adviser to President Truman tainted him, in McCarthy's estimation. Having alerted reporters in advance, McCarthy delivered his attack to packed galleries. Men like Marshall, he said, were responsible for every recent failure in American foreign policy, especially the "loss" of China. Marshall was engaged in "a conspiracy on a scale so immense as to dwarf any previous such venture in the history of man. A conspiracy of infamy so black that, when it is finally exposed, its principals shall be forever deserving of the maledictions of all honest men."

Collier's magazine declared that McCarthy's speech "set a new high for irresponsibility." But McCarthy's supporters were uncritically appreciative. Senator Henry Jackson of Washington would later declare, "Throughout this whole period the major thread was fear." The rapid spread of communism through Eastern Europe and China nourished the fear that the "Red menace" was close to worldwide domination. The Russian development of the atomic bomb raised the specter of a nuclear holocaust — a danger so believable that thousands of Americans built concrete bomb shelters in their backyards and stocked them with food and water. Fear also dominated many Americans' thinking about their

"Tail Gunner Joe." McCarthy served with the Marines during World War II. His service was honorable; later, in his own telling, it became heroic.

fellow citizens. A Wisconsin farmer summed up the way millions of Americans felt: "Yes," he said, "I guess almost everybody in this part of the country is for McCarthy. He's against communism — and we're against communism. Besides, if he wasn't telling the truth they'd 'a hung him long ago. He's one of the greatest Americans we've ever had."

And what of Joe McCarthy, himself? How did his meteoric rise to power affect his own life? Somehow he had to forget who he had been just a few years before — a Democrat supporting Roosevelt and the New Deal. And he had forgotten also the principles underlying his declaration in the Malmédy hearings that one of "the basic principles of American justice" was "the rights of the innocent." There were no innocent men or women in McCarthy's hunt for Communists, only insidious conspirators in a massive plot that he alone understood. In the early stages of McCarthy's political career his commitment to causes was balanced by an engaging ability to laugh at himself. Even when he began to number the State Department Communists, he confided to reporters that his figures were a bluff — he just wanted to see what he could find out. But as his career unfolded he became more and more of a true believer in his own anti-Communist crusade. Ambition and paranoia led him to believe that he represented the forces of light, and his enemies the forces of darkness — period.

At the same time he was discovering, however, that there was very little to discover about Communists in high places. Despite all the help he received from J. Edgar Hoover, Richard Nixon, and other public figures he could not identify a single Communist in government. The men and women he singled out for his attacks were, in fact, persons whose ideas differed from his, but who were as fundamentally loyal as McCarthy himself. In his true believer's mind, however, the lack of evidence was itself evidence of the insidiousness of the plot — the traitors were so clever that you could not pin them down. Some writers have accused McCarthy of cynically manipulating events to his political advantage, while realizing fully the hollowness of his own accusations. But it is more likely that he was swept by events and by his own personality into deeper and more obsessive commitment to his crusade. He had staked his political future on the existence of a massive Communist conspiracy in government. His friends agreed with him.

International events fed the American fear of communism and encouraged McCarthy's rise to power. On June 25, 1950, Communist North Korea invaded South Korea. The United Nations Security Council adopted a resolution urging member states to assist South Korea, and during the summer a UN force consisting mainly of American soldiers landed in Korea. After being forced south to a tiny foothold of land near Pusan on the tip of the peninsula, they pushed the North Koreans back to the Chinese border. Then on November 25, 1950, China entered the war and forced the South Koreans and their allies back to the 38th parallel, roughly at the center of Korea. During the next three years the two sides traded deadly assaults, gaining and losing ground in the neighborhood of the 38th parallel. McCarthy and his followers were discouraged by the indecisiveness of the war. The enemy was, of course, a formidable opponent, and bombing raids into China — favored by some Americans — might have resulted in a wider war with both China and Russia. But McCarthyites blamed the stalemate on American treason. The failure to whip the Chinese and North Koreans was looked on as yet another sign of the corrosive power of the Communist conspiracy.

McCarthy believed the conduct of the Democrats at their presidential convention in 1952 was a good example of their disregard for Korea. He remarked that on a day when they all sang "Happy Days Are Here Again," the Democratic theme song, 208 Americans had died in Korea. McCarthy was a leading figure at his own party's presidential convention, where he delivered a well-received speech about the Communist conspiracy.

His power was evident. Even General Dwight David Eisenhower, the American commander in Europe during World War II and now the Republican candidate for president, was reluctant to offend him. Eisenhower would never forgive McCarthy for his attack on General Marshall, Eisenhower's comrade-in-arms during the war. He knew Marshall's loyalty was unassailable, and he despised the senator from Wisconsin for his unwarranted attack. But politics makes strange, and sometimes reluctant, bedfellows. The general could not avoid a campaign swing by train through Wisconsin. Eisenhower was barely civil to the senator, who accompanied him. He would not mention him by name in his speeches, and he planned to deliver a rousing defense of Marshall at a political rally in Milwaukee. His advisers, however, urged him to remove the remarks, arguing that he needed the McCarthyite vote to win the election. Eisenhower was "purple with rage," according to one observer, but he agreed to expunge the offending remarks.

Although Eisenhower realized that the Red scare was a hoax as it touched on his friend Marshall, he tended otherwise to accept uncritically the views of the anti-Communists. In Milwaukee he claimed that Communists had penetrated American schools, newspapers, labor unions, and the government itself, and thus they had "poisoned two whole decades of our national life." The enemy, he said, had infiltrated "our most secret councils."

Learning that Eisenhower had abandoned his friend Marshall, Adlai Stevenson, the Democratic presidential nominee, charged that his Republican opponent was "grasping" for votes and had mortgaged "every principle he once held." Stevenson refused to join the Red-scare bandwagon. He shared the antipathy of most Americans to Communist expansion, and he was as opposed as any to domestic subversion, but he distinguished between actual and imaginary threats of subversion. In the atmosphere of the Red scare many men and women were unwilling or unable to make that distinction.

Eisenhower easily defeated Stevenson in 1952. The election was not simply a referendum on anticommunism. Many voters turned to Eisenhower because of his war record or because they felt that it was "time for a change" after five terms of Democratic presidents. But millions of voters were impressed by McCarthy's charge that the Democrats were responsible for "twenty years of treason." McCarthy, himself, was reelected in 1952 along with many other outspoken anti-Communists, all of whom redoubled their efforts to find subversives.

The Senate Internal Security Subcommittee under William Jenner of Indiana investigated allegations of communism in education. The House Un-American Activities Subcommittee, chaired by Harold R. Velde of Illinois, explored charges of communism in Hollywood. And

Joe McCarthy continued to probe for Communists in government. As chair of the Senate Permanent Investigating Subcommittee of the Government Operations Committee he investigated between 1953 and 1954 the Voice of America, which produced pro-American radio programs for broadcast around the world, the State Department, and other organizations and individuals. One observer remarked that the Senate caucus room where the McCarthy Subcommittee met "stank with the odor of fear and monstrous silliness."

By now an increasing number of Americans were beginning to ask whether the crackdown on supposed Communists was going too far. In 1953 President Eisenhower denounced "the book burners" and insisted that everyone has a right to meet his or her accuser "face to face." McCarthy's campaign, however, knew no limits, and a year after Eisenhower took office the senator claimed that the United States had now experienced "twenty-*one* years of treason." He would try to prove his point by demonstrating that the army, itself, was full of Communists.

He focused his attack on alleged subversion in the Signal Corps Engineering Laboratories at Fort Monmouth, New Jersey, where he discovered that an army reserve dentist, Irving Peress, had been promoted and given an honorable discharge despite his refusal to sign a loyalty oath. Peress was never proven a Communist, but he had attended Communist meetings some ten years before. Refusal to sign the loyalty oath would normally have been grounds for a less-than-honorable discharge from the army, but here the system processing information about soldiers had broken down. Sensing a plot, McCarthy had demanded to know "Who Promoted Peress?" The question became a rallying cry, a kind of anti-Communist slogan. The Peress promotion was a clue McCarthy thought he could follow to the heart of the foul conspiracy he imagined to be at work in the army.

In the meantime the army had its own grievance against McCarthy. One of his assistants, G. David Schine, had recently entered the military. McCarthy and his staff bombarded the army with requests for special treatment for the young private. Congressmen often sent polite letters to the army on behalf of favored constituents, but McCarthy's badgering was unprecedented. The conflict between the army and McCarthy was so heated that the Senate finally decided in spring 1954 to hold special hearings to evaluate both sides of the quarrel.

The Army-McCarthy Hearings began on the morning of April 22, 1954. Eager to watch one of the most heralded debates in congressional history, hundreds of spectators and reporters crowded into an ornate caucus room on the third floor of the Senate Office Building. At the front of the room glaring television lights illuminated a twenty-six-foot mahogany table where McCarthy's Permanent Investigating Subcommittee sat without McCarthy. The Wisconsin senator had stepped down temporarily to preserve the neutrality of the body and had appointed another senator to take his place. The committee consisted of four Republicans and three Democrats, with Senator Karl Mundt as chairman. At one side of the room sat representatives of the army, led by Robert T. Stevens. Opposite him sat McCarthy and his staff.

As the trial developed, the two figures who captured the public imagination were McCarthy and army counsel Joseph Nye Welch, a short, balding Boston lawyer with the twinkling eyes of a leprechaun. Like McCarthy he was born on a farm. His parents were Iowa pioneers who raised seven children near the little town of Primghar. Joe Welch, born in 1890, was the youngest of the seven. Like McCarthy, Welch worked hard as a young man, traveling by foot, buggy, and bicycle from door to door throughout the Midwest and in Pennsylvania and New York, selling state maps for $1.95 apiece. He later remarked that it was "hateful, hard work," but it helped him understand people. "It ranks above, or with, my law school training in value," he said.

Welch worked his way through Grinnell College in Iowa and then won a scholarship to Harvard Law School. The mental distance he would travel from his parents' home was apparent in a conversation he had with his father on the night before his departure.

"Josie," the elder Welch said, "You're going off to Harvard?"
"That's right."
"That's a long way, ain't it?"
"Yes, it's a long way."
"Somewhere's in Michigan?"
"No it's near Boston — or maybe in Boston...."
"It'll take a heap of money, won't it?"
"Yes."
"You know that little gray box up on the shelf? Well, you go and get it."

Welch did, and his father dumped the contents into his hands. "There was $19," Welch recalled, "all he had, his savings of 14 years, and he gave it all to me."

Welch went on to become a successful attorney with a respected Boston law firm. He put some of his wealth into a wardrobe that included eighteen suits and more than 150 bow ties. But he retained a simplicity and charm that suggested his Iowa farm background. Joe Welch, like Joe McCarthy, believed in hard work and scorned communism. But unlike McCarthy he was aware that anticommunism can itself become a threat to American values. During the eight weeks of the

Army-McCarthy hearings the interchanges between these two midwestern farmboys-become-lawyers furnished revealing moments of high drama, and helped the American public evaluate the various forms of anticommunism.

The army began by charging McCarthy with improper behavior in seeking privileges for his former assistant, Private Schine. Before the hearing was half an hour old McCarthy interrupted, shouting "Point of order, Mr. Chairman!" and complaining about the way the army was presenting its case. This procedure, which McCarthy repeated again and again, allowed him to dominate the hearings, even though he was a party in the dispute. During the next two months he would raise more "points of order" than all the other participants combined.

McCarthy's behavior in the hearings was like his conduct in previous Senate committee meetings. He was loud, rude, deceitful, and at times, vicious. On the first day he cross-examined Major General Miles Reber, a thirty-five-year veteran and winner of a Distinguished Service Medal. Reber testified about the times that McCarthy's assistant, Roy Cohn, had pressured him on behalf of Private Schine. Unable to refute the facts in Reber's testimony, McCarthy announced that Reber's brother had resigned from the State Department because he was "a bad security risk." The charge was irrelevant to the case, but it was typical of McCarthy's tendency to "smear" everyone who crossed his path. Committee member Henry Jackson, senator from Washington, complained that "we may be trying members of everybody's family involved before we get through." But by now McCarthy was so accustomed to assigning guilt by association that Jackson's warning had no effect.

As the hearing dragged on day after day Senator McCarthy worked feverishly to establish his case that the army and not he had acted improperly in their exchanges. He spent the evening working with staff members and then stayed the night in his office, where he would work over papers, fortifying himself with glasses of bourbon and five-minute naps. An assistant would often stay until six in the morning and leave the senator still at work. Then would come the hearing and McCarthy would enter the fray like a boxer, issuing "points of order," and ripping at his opponents with volleys of words. At the two-hour lunch break he would confer with his staff, his jacket on a chair, his shirt soaked with sweat. Then he would go back to the hearing and more charges and countercharges.

In the past only a few spectators at a time had witnessed the frenzy of a McCarthy hearing. But now two television networks carried live broadcasts of the hearings nationwide. Television was still a new medium and relatively few families had sets, but friends gathered around them across the nation to watch the famous senator from Wisconsin at work. In all, ten million Americans saw the hearings on television. Millions more saw newsreels, heard radio broadcasts, or read newspaper accounts. In hundreds of schools, saloons, and theaters one could hear amateur and professional comics intoning the words, "Mr. Chairman, point of order. . . ."

Among the millions who watched the army hearings was a young French student named Madeleine Biskey. Newly arrived in America, she was attending Columbia University, where she learned about the McCarthy hearings from fellow students. On a trip to Washington she talked to a soldier from Wisconsin who told her that McCarthy was the greatest man alive and that there were Communists everywhere. Curious about American ways, she attended the senate hearings. "It was McCarthy's show," she later recalled. And a strange show it was, led by a curiously bloated McCarthy and his strangely intense assistants, David Schine and Roy Cohn. From the vantage point of her own culture, the frenzy of anticommunism seemed strange to Mlle. Biskey. At home the French Communists had been active in the resistance to Hitler, and the great war hero, Charles de Gaulle, accepted them into his post-war government. Why were Americans so frightened of people who in France were simply members of another political faction? As the trial progressed and McCarthy's personality was revealed to millions of Americans, others came to ask the same question: What was the country afraid of?

The actual issues of the trial were less important than the exposure given to the character and tactics of Joe McCarthy as the nation's foremost Red hunter. McCarthy presented a photograph suggesting that Private Schine and army Secretary Stevens had met privately: the picture proved to have been doctored to leave out other men standing nearby. McCarthy presented a carbon copy of an alleged FBI document: the document proved to be a forgery. It was, said army Counsel Welch, a carbon copy of nothing at all. With each new performance by the senator, Welch's face showed bemusement and indignation. That face appeared on millions of television screens, and many viewers saw in it the echo of their own astonishment at McCarthy's behavior.

The hostility between the two men erupted on June 9 when Welch was examining McCarthy's assistant, Roy Cohn. The testimony was going badly for Cohn, and so McCarthy began to attack Fred Fisher, a young law associate in Welch's firm. Fisher had once belonged to the Lawyers' Guild, a legal organization that was associated with the Communist party. He was never a Communist and had quit the Guild some time before, but McCarthy had found a weakness in Welch's law family and went to the attack.

Roy Cohn was horrified at his boss's tactic. They had agreed in advance that McCarthy would not mention Fisher, and that Welch, in turn, would not mention that Cohn had flunked the physical test for admission to West Point. He scribbled a hasty note to McCarthy: "This is the subject which I have committed to Welch we would not go into. Please respect our agreement as an agreement, because this is not going to do any good."

McCarthy, however, had lost all sense of discretion and attacked Fisher before the committee and millions of television viewers who had no way of evaluating the charges, or even knowing why they mattered. Before those millions of witnesses the quiet lawyer from Iowa, trembling with emotion, addressed McCarthy. "Until this moment, Senator," he said, "I think I never really gauged your cruelty and your recklessness."

Welch explained that Fred Fisher was a young man starting "what looks to be a brilliant career" with Welch's law firm. He had accompanied Welch and his chief assistant, Jim St. Clair, to Washington for the hearings. Welch asked both men if there was anything in their backgrounds that might cause embarrassment at the hearings, and Fisher volunteered that while in law school he had belonged to the Lawyers' Guild, as McCarthy alleged. Welch thought that the former connection was harmless, but decided not to use Fisher on his staff in Washington, explaining to him, "If I do, one of these days that will come out and go over national television, and it will just hurt like the dickens."

"So, Senator," continued Welch, "I asked him to go back to Boston. Little did I dream you could be so reckless and cruel as to do an injury to that lad. It is true he is still with Hale & Dorr. It is true that he will continue to be with Hale & Dorr. It is, I regret to say, equally true that I fear he shall always bear a scar needlessly inflicted by you. If it [is] in my power to forgive you for your reckless cruelty, I will do so. I like to think I am a gentleman, but your forgiveness will have to come from someone other than me."

McCarthy tried to resume his attack, but Welch interrupted:

"Senator, may we not drop this? We know he belonged to the Lawyers Guild, and Mr. Cohn nods his head at me. . . .

"Let us not assassinate this lad further, Senator. You have done enough. Have you no sense of decency, sir, at long last? Have you no sense of decency?"

McCarthy tried one last time to attack Fisher. Welch cut him off: "Mr. McCarthy, I will not discuss this with you further. You have sat within six feet of me and could have asked me about Fred Fisher. You have brought it out. If there is a God in heaven, it will do neither you nor your cause any good. I will not discuss it further. I will not ask Mr. Cohn any more questions. You, Mr. Chairman, may, if you will, call the next witness."

The audience in the Senate caucus room had listened in stunned silence. When Welch finished, their applause thundered through the room, engulfing a tearful Welch and a stunned McCarthy. The hearings went on for a few more days, but for most observers the encounter over Fred Fisher was the climax of the proceedings. Never had McCarthy's anticommunism seemed more petty, malicious, and stupid, and never had an opponent of the senator's called more effectively for understanding, charity, and wisdom in the difficult task of distinguishing between patriots and traitors.

A few months later the committee issued a report criticizing both the army and McCarthy for misconduct. More important, during fall 1954 the Senate as a whole considered a motion to censure McCarthy. He had made many enemies by riding roughshod over fellow senators as well as by attacking hundreds of other loyal Americans. Additionally, questions about his campaign funds had arisen that McCarthy failed to answer satisfactorily. On December 2, 1954 all of the Senate Democrats and half the Republicans joined in adopting a resolution "condemning" McCarthy's actions.

Neither his humiliation at the Army hearings nor the Senate condemnation removed McCarthy from the political scene. In November 1954, 1,500 supporters attended a birthday dinner at Milwaukee's Pfister Hotel. Huge banners with the slogan "WHO PROMOTED PERESS" decorated the banquet hall, and the band played a song declaring "Nobody's for McCarthy but the people." Most of the people, however, no longer admired the senator. His popularity rating in Gallup Polls dropped from a solid majority to a distinct minority. He was excluded from the White House invitations that went to other congressmen; journalists and politicians failed to take him seriously. Humbled and isolated, the senator became increasingly alcoholic, gulping down whole glasses of liquor before breakfast. His liver began to fail him, and in spring 1957, at age forty-seven, Joe McCarthy died.

The fear of communism did not disappear with McCarthy's death. Real spies would still be discovered from time to time in the United States. Moreover, international events laid the seeds for more anti-Communist activities abroad. During the Army-McCarthy hearings, Dien Bien Phu, a French stronghold in Vietnam, fell to the Communist insurgents under the leadership of Ho Chi Minh. A reporter asked Richard Nixon, now vice president of the United States, what the country would do if France were forced to withdraw from Vietnam. Nixon replied that if there were no other recourse, the administration would have to send troops. Even Joseph Welch, who so ably exposed McCarthy's vicious tactics, was an ardent anti-Communist.

But the events of 1954 discouraged the more repressive expressions of anticommunism. Soon it was apparent that thousands of innocent

Americans had been slandered — and often lost their jobs — in the atmosphere of hysteria surrounding the anti-Communist crusade. Ironically, McCarthy, who had been the champion of anticommunism, became the symbol of its abuse. "McCarthyism" entered the dictionary as a word to describe harmful and irresponsible charges of disloyalty. The senator's tumultuous career thus encouraged Americans to distinguish between treason, the conscious effort to betray the country to an enemy, and freedom of expression, one of the strengths of American public life.

QUESTIONS

1. Apart from McCarthy's efforts, in what ways did the American government attack communism at home and abroad? Mention specifically the activities of the president, Congress, and the Supreme Court.

2. What were the objective reasons for American anticommunism in the postwar era?

3. During the decade following World War II nearly everyone in American public life, including Presidents Truman and Eisenhower, and McCarthy himself, was accused of Communist leanings. Cite instances of these accusations and explain why they occurred.

4. In what ways did some anti-Communists confuse the ideas and actions of loyal Americans with treason?

5. What elements in Joe McCarthy's character and background made him an appealing national figure? What flaws in his character were apparent early in his life?

6. Assess McCarthy's anti-Communist crusade. Why did many Americans admire his efforts? In what ways were his investigations fair or unfair?

7. How did the army hearings discredit McCarthy? Examine especially the role of Joseph Welch.

8. What was the political legacy of McCarthy's career?

BIBLIOGRAPHY

CAUTE, DAVID. *The Great Fear* (1978). Surveys anti-Communist activities during the presidencies of Truman and Eisenhower.

COHN, ROY. *McCarthy* (1968). Written by one of McCarthy's chief assistants.

GOODMAN, WALTER. *The Committee* (1968). History of the House Un-American Activities Committee.

HOFSTADTER, RICHARD. *The Paranoid Style in American Politics* (1952,

1963). Classic examination of the tendency of some Americans to see conspiracies where none exist.

LATTIMORE, OWEN. *Ordeal by Slander* (1950). Personal account by a man accused by McCarthy of Communist leanings.

MCCARTHY, JOSEPH R. *America's Fall from Grace: The Story of George Catlett Marshall* (1951). Based on McCarthy's vituperative attack on Marshall in the Senate.

MACDONALD, CALLUM A. *Korea: The War Before Vietnam* (1986). Lucid account of the Korean conflict.

PHILBRICK, HERBERT A. *I Led Three Lives* (1952). Autobiographical account by an American counterespionage agent.

REEVES, THOMAS C. *The Life and Times of Joe McCarthy* (1982). Superbly researched and carefully balanced account of McCarthy's life.

ROVERE, RICHARD H. *Senator Joe McCarthy* (1959). A journalist's damning account of McCarthy's career.

11

THE CIVIL RIGHTS MOVEMENT

Martin Luther King, Jr., and the Road to Birmingham

The civil rights movement of the 1950s and 1960s is often called the "Second Reconstruction." It changed the lives of black Americans more significantly than any other event since emancipation. Although freed from slavery, blacks had been imprisoned in a circle of discrimination that restricted most to menial jobs and inferior public facilities. During the civil rights movement many formal barriers to black equality were removed by tactics of nonviolent confrontation that exposed racial injustice and won public support for remedial legislation. The movement's success would encourage women, native Americans, Mexican Americans, and other "minorities" to claim for themselves the birthright of equality.

In the last years of his life Martin Luther King, Jr., liked to tell the story of Birmingham. He regarded the great struggle of 1963 in that city as a turning point in the civil rights movement. Not only did it result in reforms in Birmingham, but it also helped persuade Congress and the president to give their full support to civil rights legislation. When King described the episode in lectures and sermons, he depicted a cosmic struggle between justice and injustice, the forces of light and the forces of darkness. The leader of the opposition to integration in Birmingham, Eugene ("Bull") Connor, who directed the police attacks on civil rights demonstrators, was in King's view not merely a bigot but the very embodiment of injustice. The civil rights demonstrators, on the other hand, by resisting injustice without being tainted by violence, symbolized the moral superiority of an oppressed people and thereby won worldwide support for their cause.

As King told an audience at the Mount Zion Baptist Church in Cincinnati, "Bull Connor was always happy when some of the spectators on the sidelines would begin to throw rocks and throw bottles. He was very happy when he saw Negroes doing that. Now he was happy because he's an expert in violence and in dealing with violence." But when demonstrators protested peacefully Connor was confused. He "didn't understand this. He didn't know how to handle this. Because of this, that community, which said that it would never integrate its lunch counters and many of its facilities, has to face integration at its lunch counters today and in many other facilities. There's power in this method."

King's "method" consisted of nonviolent resistance to oppression. He regarded the civil rights movement as a great moral struggle between the oppressor and the oppressed; the villain was the person who lived by injustice, and the hero was the person who resisted tyranny without being degraded by it. Cowards ran from injustice; knaves became corrupted in fighting it. But the virtuous man won the struggle by forcing the oppressor to reveal his villainy to the world; for when the cruelty of segregation was fully exposed, no right-thinking person would accept its continuation. At Birmingham, King believed, the mindless villainy of segregation had been revealed in all its tawdry colors, and the heroic persistence of integration had won a great moral and political victory.

King's efforts to end segregation through nonviolent confrontation made him at once the most loved and most hated man in America. But Birmingham was more than simply the test of one man or one idea. It was the culmination, rather, of two forces that had been active in the country for almost a century: the effort to segregate blacks from the mainstream of American society and the movement to resist segregation.

The issue in Birmingham was whether whites could exclude blacks from a wide range of segregated facilities, including jobs, the ballot box, schools, parks, public transportation, housing, restaurants, hotels, rest rooms, and drinking fountains. Such restrictions were so familiar in many areas that they seemed inevitable — the natural course of human affairs. Segregation had begun long before emancipation, as Frederick Douglass learned after he escaped from slavery in Maryland. Even in the North he was a second-class citizen and had to ride on segregated jim crow railroad cars. In the antebellum period most northern states denied blacks the ballot, and some of the territories passed laws declaring that nonwhites could not live within their borders.

The freeing of the slaves did nothing to end the racial prejudice that had contributed, in the first place, to black enslavement. The freedmen soon faced limitations on their social, economic, and political freedom that reminded them of their inferior status. This system of racial separation was widely accepted throughout the first half of the twentieth century. In the 1940s black athletes played on segregated clubs. Baseball players who were as skilled as any contemporary white athletes were restricted to the Negro leagues. One player recollected traveling from game to game in an old bus; denied the use of segregated service station rest room facilities, he and his teammates frequently had to urinate at the side of the road. During World War II thousands of blacks gave their lives without achieving equality for themselves. In the army blacks were barred from white social facilities. At a typical training camp in Arizona there was only a white swimming pool; when a group of blacks sneaked in during the night to use it, the base commander punished them, then drained and refilled the pool, thus isolating his white troops — who were about to fight the race supremacist Hitler — from contamination by their nonwhite fellow soldiers.

During the war black soldiers who conducted German prisoners by railroad between camps in the United States had to go unfed while the Nazi captives ate in white-only restaurants. As late as 1949 blacks were not admitted to theaters in downtown Washington, D.C., even to hear such celebrated black performers as Marian Anderson. The examples of segregation in the land of the free were unending. The policy of separation was not as restrictive as slavery, but like slavery it put strict limits on black enterprise. It meant that blacks were, as a matter of course, denied jobs, schooling, political power, and cultural and recreational opportunities.

From the earliest years of segregation some blacks had resisted these restrictions. When they began to realize in the late nineteenth and early twentieth centuries that segregation was a fact of life, they offered many responses to the situation. The most famous was Booker T.

Washington's proposal in 1895 that his people work their way to equality by developing their own skills so highly that all whites would recognize the mutual dependence of the races. Although not endorsing segregation, Washington argued that even without social equality blacks had "a man's chance" to succeed if they worked hard. Washington was considered the foremost black leader of his time by blacks and whites alike. His belief that the path to black progress lay through hard work, rather than in tearing down the barriers to white society, was reflected in the Supreme Court's 1896 *Plessy v. Ferguson* decision, which endorsed the segregationist concept of "separate but equal."

There were, however, those who criticized the ever-tightening hold of segregation on the nation's political and economic institutions. W. E. B. Du Bois, a Harvard graduate and black intellectual, approved of Washington's emphasis on hard work but felt that he overlooked "the emasculating effects of caste distinctions." In 1905 Du Bois met with a small group of black intellectuals and professional men at Niagara Falls to discuss the race question. This was the beginning of the Niagara Movement. In the following year the participants met at Harpers Ferry and demanded an end to discrimination in public accommodations, education, and politics. "We are men!" they said, "we will be treated as men. And we shall win!"

After several more annual meetings most of the supporters of the Niagara Movement joined forces with a new organization, the National Association for the Advancement of Colored People. The NAACP was formed by discontented blacks and by antisegregation whites, such as the socialist journalist William English Walling, who opposed racial injustice and wanted to revive "the spirit of the abolitionists." The NAACP charter of 1910 declared that the organization would seek "to advance the interests of colored citizens; to secure for them impartial suffrage; and to increase their opportunities for securing justice in the courts, education for their children, employment according to their ability, and complete equality before the law."

The NAACP soon embarked on an ambitious program of fighting segregation and racial injustice through publicity, politics, and the courts. When rioters in East Saint Louis killed thirty-two blacks in 1917, the NAACP organized a protest parade in New York City. After more than a thousand blacks had been lynched throughout the nation between 1900 and 1920, the NAACP campaigned for a federal anti-lynching bill. When blacks were convicted of crimes on flimsy evidence, the organization appealed their convictions to higher courts.

Although the NAACP enjoyed considerable support from both whites and blacks, it could only chip away at the great national edifice of racial injustice. Segregation continued; disfranchisement continued;

lynchings continued. In response, some blacks concluded that white America was hopelessly bigoted and that the only refuge for the oppressed was in Africa.

The foremost exponent of the black to Africa movement was Marcus Garvey, a Jamaican black who immigrated to the United States and in 1917 founded the Universal Negro Improvement Association in Harlem. Garvey publicized the idea of the fraternity of blacks throughout the world and advocated the creation of an independent black nation in Africa. In 1921 a Garvey convention in New York attracted 25,000 participants, who immediately formed a provisional government for the proposed state and elected Garvey as president general. Although the movement declined after 1925 when Garvey was imprisoned for mail fraud, it had revealed the profound discontent that many blacks felt. Black nationalism found another prophet in the 1930s in the person of Wallace Fard, a young Detroit black who declared that the true Afro-American religion was Islam. Christianity currently ruled the world, but soon, he said, members of his Black Muslim faith could overthrow white supremacy. Fard built up a strong following in the Detroit ghetto but relinquished leadership to Elijah Poole, soon to be known as Elijah Muhammad, who recruited more than one hundred thousand members of the new faith and established fifty temples across the United States. Although the Muslims did not advocate integration, they did share with other reformers a belief that the race problem was, in part, an economic problem. Thus, they encouraged blacks to establish independent department stores, restaurants, grocery stores, and other businesses. While other leaders saw such enterprises as a route to equality and integration, however, Elijah Muhammad favored business activity as a means of increasing the independent power of his people.

One of the most important civil rights initiatives in the 1930s was the Jobs for Negroes movement, which began in Detroit in 1933. The program organized boycotts to force white employers to hire blacks. Among its leaders was the Reverend Mr. Adam Clayton Powell, who later became a U.S. congressman. Through his influence blacks began to get jobs in stores, public utilities, and transportation in New York City.

Reform continued in a piecemeal fashion in the 1940s. Blacks were particularly successful in winning concessions from the nation's defense industries, in part because of their need for employees, and in part through federal action. When blacks found that most war contractors refused to hire them, they threatened to organize a massive march on Washington in summer 1941. President Roosevelt wanted to avoid the embarrassment of this demonstration at a time when war with Germany seemed imminent, and so he met with the parade leaders and agreed to issue an executive order prohibiting discrimination in war industries.

His Executive Order 8802 — perhaps the most beneficial document for blacks since the Emancipation Proclamation — established the Fair Employment Practices Commission. Although the new agency did not completely end discrimination in defense production, it did persuade many employers to hire blacks.

At the war's end discrimination still prevailed in schooling, politics, employment, and public services. But whereas in 1890 all the signs pointed to the elimination of black rights, in 1945 the system of segregation seemed to be weakening. In sports Joe Louis was in the eighth year of his reign as heavyweight champion of the world. In the ring, at least, a black man could stand up to a white man without fear of being lynched. When Louis had won the crown from James J. Braddock in 1937, a black boy named Malcolm Little remembered that in Lansing, Michigan, his people "went wildly happy with the greatest celebration of race pride our generation had ever known."

Throughout the United States young blacks took up boxing as a means of moving up in the world. But there could be only one champion at a time, and most ended up like Malcolm Little — whose second and last fight lasted only ten seconds — seeking other forms of self-expression. For the great mass of Black Americans the less dramatic court victories of the postwar decade were more important than boxing victories.

The NAACP now focused most of its energies on legal challenges to segregation and disfranchisement. In 1944 the Supreme Court declared in *Smith v. Albright* that states could not prevent blacks from voting in political primaries, thereby eliminating — by law, at least — one of the most popular southern tactics for destroying the electoral influence of blacks. Equally important, the Court made a series of decisions that upheld the idea of equal access to public institutions of higher education.

But the most significant change of all came in 1954 with the Supreme Court's decision in *Brown v. Board of Education.* The case involved a young girl in Topeka, Kansas, who had been denied admittance to an all-white school. The NAACP, representing the plaintiff, argued that the old separate-but-equal doctrine was specious: the mere fact of separation put the black in a demeaning and discouraging position. The NAACP counsel, Thurgood Marshall, cited sociological and psychological evidence to show that segregation damaged black children. "The policy of separating the races," he said, "is usually interpreted as denoting the inferiority of the Negro group. A sense of inferiority affects the motivation of the child to learn." The court decided unanimously in favor of the plaintiff. Separate educational facilities were inherently unequal and contrary to the equal protection clause of the Fourteenth Amendment.

The *Brown* decision was greeted as the death knell of segregation. But like the earlier decisions against segregation in higher education and discrimination in political primaries, the decision reflected a de jure, not a de facto condition. In 1954 segregation was still the reality in the South.

That reality was represented in a state of near perfection in the bus system of Montgomery, Alabama. Throughout the South blacks were required to ride at the back of the bus. But in Montgomery blacks were not merely prevented from riding in the preferred white section. Local law required the blacks to board the bus at the front, pay their fares, then disembark, walk along the street to the rear, and reboard the bus. Thus, blacks were forbidden even to pass in the midst of the superior race. A further regulation set aside a middle section of the bus as a neutral area. If no whites needed its seats, blacks could occupy them. But if one white wanted to sit in the middle area, all the blacks seated there must get up and stand at the back of the bus.

These laws were demeaning inherently. But there were other indignities. Although the majority of the city's transit passengers were black, all the drivers were white. Some were polite enough to the blacks; but others lorded it over them, calling them "niggers," "black cows," and "black apes." They sometimes allowed black passengers to pay at the front and then drove off while they were walking outside to the back. There were stories, too, of passengers injured when the doors caught them halfway in — a blind man hurt when he was dragged along the ground, another man killed.

For the most part, the Montgomery blacks accepted the situation, for they had never known anything better. When the buses rolled past the state capitol the passengers could look up and see a Confederate flag flying in all its glory — above the American flag. Blacks did not elect the state government or run the transportation system or go to school with whites. The back of the bus was the only place they had known.

Occasionally a black would become disgusted with the system and refuse to occupy the designated seats. The driver could then summon the police, and punishment would be inevitable. Until 1955 any such resistance was isolated and futile. But on December 1 a black seamstress named Rosa Parks refused to give up her seat and inadvertently inaugurated a new era in the civil rights movement.

Mrs. Parks had spent the day working downtown at the Montgomery Fair Department Store. When she left, her shoulders and neck ached from leaning over the fabric press. Wanting a comfortable ride home, she did not board the first bus that passed her on Cleveland Street because it had passengers standing in the aisles. The next bus was less crowded; she paid the driver, walked along the street to the rear entrance, and found a seat with three other blacks in the middle section.

The bus began to move, and Rosa Parks relaxed.

But after three stops whites had filled all their designated seats, and one white man was left standing. The driver turned and said that he would need "those seats." The four blacks would have to stand so that the one white man could sit.

For a moment no one moved. Then the driver said, "You all better make it light on yourselves and let me have those seats."

Three blacks left their seats, but Rosa Parks refused to move. She was a proud, handsome woman with strong features and an expression that revealed both intelligence and toil.

"Are you going to get up?" the driver asked her.

"No," she said.

"If you don't stand up, I'm going to have you arrested," said the driver.

Rosa Parks didn't move. The driver left the bus to find a policeman. The other passengers remained calm, but some of them began to leave the bus. The driver came back with a police officer and pointed out the troublemaker.

"Why didn't you stand up?" asked the officer.

"Why do you push us around?" she answered.

"I don't know, but the law is the law, and you are under arrest," he said.

With that, Rosa Parks picked up her purse and shopping bag and went to the waiting police car. Within a few minutes she was booked at city hall and put in jail. "I felt very much annoyed and inconvenienced," she recalled, "because I had hoped to go home and get my dinner, and do whatever else I had to do for the evening. But now here I was sitting in jail and couldn't get home."

It is hard to imagine a more prosaic beginning to a revolution than Rosa Parks's refusal to give up her seat on the Cleveland Street bus. Vehicles in Montgomery and hundreds of other cities had carried millions of blacks from place to place in segregated seats. The affront to Rosa Parks was no worse than she and others had borne for many decades. She might not even have thought twice about relinquishing her seat if she had not been especially tired. But she had said no, and soon the whole system of segregation would be affected.

It weakened, however, not only because of the quiet stand of one woman, but also because of blows already delivered by the Supreme Court and because of the activities of Montgomery's black community. The word of Rosa Parks's arrest soon spread through the city. Her refusal to leave her seat had been a spontaneous act of defiance, but the news reached many black leaders in Montgomery who were prepared to turn her random act into a well-organized protest. There was Jo Ann

Rosa Parks. Tired after a hard day's work, she refused to give up her seat on a bus to a white passenger. With her arrest the modern civil rights movement began.

Robinson, president of the local Women's Political Council, a black equivalent of the segregated League of Women Voters; E. D. Nixon, a member of the Brotherhood of Sleeping Car Porters and leader of Montgomery's black community; and Ralph Abernathy, pastor of the First Baptist Church. They all had deep roots in Montgomery, but the man who was destined to lead the protest had been in the city for only one year. He was the pastor of the Dexter Avenue Baptist Church, Martin Luther King, Jr.

King was twenty-six years old at the time. His background linked him both to the strong Christian traditions of the black South and the intellectual formulations of modern theology. He had grown up in Atlanta, Georgia, where his father was pastor of the Ebenezer Baptist Church. He graduated from Morehouse College when he was nineteen, then went to Crozer Theological Seminary in Chester, Pennsylvania, and to Boston University, where he received a Ph.D. in systematic theology in 1955. In the meantime, he had begun work as a pastor in Montgomery.

King saw the problems of the South through the perspective of his training in philosophy and religion. He believed with many modern theologians that "sin is separation" and applied this concept to the separation of the races. He was impressed with Henry David Thoreau's argument in the "Essay on Civil Disobedience" that man could not accept injustice without being corrupted by it, and he was impressed with Gandhi's belief that people can change history by nonviolent protest.

During his career as a civil rights leader, King often reminded blacks that they could never attain full equality without working to improve themselves. "We must set out to do a good job," he liked to say, "and do that job so well that the living, the dead, and unborn couldn't do it any better. So if it falls your lot to be a street sweeper, go on out and sweep streets like Michelangelo painted pictures, sweep streets like Beethoven composed music, sweep streets like Shakespeare wrote poetry, sweep streets so well that all the hosts of heaven and earth will have to pause and say, 'Here lived a great street sweeper, who swept his job well.'"

These words show that the legacy of Booker T. Washington, with its emphasis on honest toil, affected even Martin Luther King, Jr. But unlike the sage of Tuskegee, King did not believe that black Americans could greatly improve their condition without the elimination of racial injustice. Blacks, he said, "live within two concentric circles of segregation. One imprisons them on the basis of color, while the other confines them within a separate culture of poverty. His struggle to escape his circumstances is hindered by color discrimination. He is deprived of normal education and normal social and economic opportunities. When he seeks opportunity, he is told, in effect, to lift himself by his own bootstraps, advice which does not take into account the fact that he is barefoot." True progress could come only with the removal of barriers to racial equality.

King had thought to spend his life as a minister. His wife, Coretta, believed that her husband could have been perfectly happy as a country pastor, living close to his congregation. But Rosa Parks's refusal to leave her seat changed King's life. He had already established himself as an effective preacher and an opponent of segregation. When Montgomery's black community wanted a leader for their protest against segregation, King was a natural choice.

The protest began with a one-day boycott of the city's buses. Sermons and leaflets proclaimed that segregation in busing must end and that the bus company must hire black drivers. On the first day almost the whole black community abandoned the buses. Some walked to work; others rode in black taxis at a reduced fare. The black leaders decided to continue the boycott until their demands were met and created the Montgomery Improvement Association to coordinate boycott activities.

They were highly conscious of their public image. They chose Rosa Parks as the focal point for their protest because she was well respected by her community. With the same regard to the dignity of their movement, they were attracted to King in part because he had received a prestigious degree from a northern university.

King became president of the Montgomery Improvement Association and spoke at its first public meeting held on the night after the opening day of the boycott. He addressed an enthusiastic audience of five thousand in a manner that would become familiar in the future years of the civil rights movement.

"You know, my friends," he said, "there comes a time when people get tired of being trampled over by the iron feet of oppression. There comes a time, my friends, when people get tired of being flung across the abyss of humiliation where they experience the bleakness of nagging despair. There comes a time when people get tired of being pushed out of the glittering sunlight of life's July, and left standing amidst the piercing chill of an Alpine November. We are here this evening because we are tired now."

It was oratory such as this that projected Martin Luther King, Jr., into national prominence as a statesman for his race. He knew how to find the right words to express the sorrow and longings of his people. He could take a phrase like "people get tired" and weave it into melodic cadences that beat upon the heart. He could take images like "the abyss of humiliation" and "the piercing chill of an Alpine November" and form them into sounds that pulled at the emotions.

It was a rhetoric that grew out of his own southern black Christian heritage, from religious meetings at which people sang old spirituals, clapped their hands, and punctuated the minister's sermon with shouts of "Yes, Lord!" and "Tell it, Brother!" King was short and stocky; his hair and mustache were close clipped; his face was heavy and muscular; in the pulpit or behind the lectern his eyes seemed riveted on some eternal truth. When he spoke, he usually began slowly, a preacher "opening" a biblical text. As he got into his subject, his voice became powerful and melodious, building to a thundering evocation of righteousness.

The circumstances might change, but King's fundamental ideas and his mode of expression remained the same. That night in Montgomery he made two points that he would repeat again and again throughout the civil rights movement. First, men and women must not accept injustice. Second, they must resist nonviolently in order to win the contest with a display of loving forbearance.

King's address was well received. The Montgomery bus boycott went on from day to day, week to week. The black people of Montgomery walked through the winter of 1955–56, when the cold winds blew;

through the spring, when the rains fell over the city; through the summer, with its sweltering heat; and into the autumn, when the leaves began to fall alongside the road. They negotiated with city officials; they spoke encouragement to one another. They refused to be provoked into violence. One night an angry segregationist threw a bomb onto Dr. King's front porch; it exploded, destroying the front of the house but luckily injuring no one; a crowd of three hundred angry blacks gathered, eager to retaliate; King spoke to them about nonviolence.

The Supreme Court finally decided the segregation issue at Montgomery. On December 13, 1956, it declared that Alabama's state law requiring racial segregation on public buses was unconstitutional. The bus company agreed to integrate and hire black drivers. For several months recalcitrant whites periodically attacked the buses, but the change took hold. Blacks had shown that they could break down the walls of segregation by refusing to accept an inferior status.

The victory at Montgomery enlivened the civil rights movement throughout the United States. It was not actually the first American victory for nonviolent protest. The Congress of Racial Equality, founded in 1942, had been engaged in "non-violent direct action" in the North for many years. In 1943 they had forced a Chicago restaurant to serve black customers, and they had engaged in many other local protests after that date.

But never before had a protest been organized on the scale of the Montgomery bus boycott. The boycott demonstrated the value of effective organization and strong leadership. It raised King to national prominence as a civil rights leader. And it showed how an effective demonstration could win sympathetic press coverage: the lines of determined black citizens walking to work furnished good photographs for the news journals and film for the newly available television news shows.

Even without systematic organization the idea of nonviolent protest would have proved infectious. The civil rights movement was like a great body of water pressing at cracks in a weakening dam. In 1956 a twenty-six-year-old black woman, Autherine Lucy, decided she wanted to attend the University of Alabama to study library science. She was unsuccessful, but in the next year nine black students integrated all-white Little Rock High School. When they were initially barred by Governor Orval Faubus and the National Guard, President Eisenhower sent a thousand paratroopers into Little Rock to keep order and protect the students. Five years later an air force veteran, James Meredith, became the first black to enter the University of Mississippi. Governor Ross Barnett tried to bar him from the school, and campus riots after his arrival resulted in two deaths. But he gained admission with the help of federal marshals, a detachment of army troops, and the federalized Mississippi National Guard.

In such episodes three forces were joined: blacks who demanded their legal rights; federal courts that overturned segregation laws; and presidents who enforced integration edicts. The effectiveness of all three was ensured by the national public response to each issue. When Americans outside the South saw pictures of young schoolchildren in Little Rock marching between lines of angry whites or James Meredith seeking a college education on a riot-torn campus, their support went to the blacks. In each case the white segregationists seemed violent, irrational, and cruel while the black students seemed calm, deliberate, and patient.

Efforts to desegregate public accommodations followed the same pattern. In 1960 four black college students in Greensboro, North Carolina, tried to buy food at a local Woolworth's lunch counter. They were denied service but refused to leave their seats. For three months they and their fellow students conducted a sit-in, finally forcing Woolworth's to integrate its lunch counter. The technique caught on throughout the South in the early 1960s. Groups of blacks, joined by sympathetic whites, would take seats at lunch counters and demand to be served. Hostile whites abused the demonstrators — pouring sugar or catsup over them, cursing them as "niggers" and "nigger lovers," and sometimes attacking them with fists or clubs. The demonstrators, trained in nonviolence, usually endured the taunts silently. Again they won national sympathy. Within two years, hundreds of restaurants, theaters, hotels, and other facilities had been integrated.

Martin Luther King, Jr., was often at the center of such protests. After the Montgomery bus boycott he and other black leaders created the Southern Christian Leadership Congress, whose aim was desegregation of all public facilities in the United States. Under King's direction the SCLC became the most powerful organization in the civil rights movement, raising funds, planning demonstrations, publicizing black grievances. Through private contributions and benefit concerts featuring such entertainers as Dick Gregory, Harry Belafonte, Jack Benny, and Sammy Davis, Jr., the SCLC was able to create an organization and a treasury capable of supporting large demonstrations in target cities.

In the years immediately following the Montgomery bus boycott, King devoted himself to many local activities, joining lunch counter sit-ins and preaching about civil rights. In 1957 alone he gave more than two hundred lectures throughout the country. In the half decade following Montgomery, he was arrested more than a dozen times. In 1961 he became a spokesman for the Congress of Racial Equality's Freedom Rides. These were busloads of black and white volunteers who set out from Washington, D.C., to drive through the South on interstate highways in order to challenge segregation of public facilities. In several cities the volunteers were badly beaten and their buses were burned or pelted with rocks. But they won their point. On September 22, 1961, through Attorney General Robert Kennedy's intervention, the Interstate Commerce Commission ruled that passengers in interstate commerce must be seated without regard to color and that terminals must be desegregated.

Such victories were numerous in the five years after Montgomery. But King did not personally organize a single major protest movement during this time. His contribution had been primarily supportive. During the Freedom Rides, however, several hundred blacks were arrested in Albany, Georgia, for civil rights activities. King decided then to use Albany as the focal point for a new kind of demonstration aimed at abolishing discrimination in all public facilities. Hitherto, reform had been incremental — a school or a lunch counter in one place, a bus company or a theater in another.

The SCLC joined with the NAACP and CORE in Albany to mobilize the black community. During 1962, 6 percent of the blacks in the city were arrested for protest activities. Despite the willingness of many local residents to go to jail, however, little was achieved in that year. The black leaders had made few plans and could not agree on strategy; and the Albany police were discreet, avoiding dramatic incidents that would win sympathy for the demonstrators. At the end of the year there was little public interest in the confrontation; people were beginning to suggest that the era of King's leadership was at an end.

It was even possible that the public might have grown apathetic about civil rights. Television shows and newspapers had publicized many black victories in the past few years. It was easy to forget that most southern blacks still attended segregated schools, could not vote, had inferior jobs, and had access only to second-class public facilities. Within the past few years blacks who had attempted to register to vote in Fayette County, Tennessee, had been evicted from their homes. A man who photographed a "WHITE ONLY" sign on a Coke machine in Jackson, Tennessee, was arrested and fined for disorderly conduct. In Montgomery, Alabama, the average black earned only half as much as the average white, and fewer than 50 percent of the black families had indoor toilets. In many respects, the condition of black Americans had changed little in the previous decade.

Birmingham, Alabama, typified the persistence of the old racial barriers. King once called it "the most segregated city in America." A steel town with a population of three hundred thousand, it was proud of its ability to keep blacks "in their place." Of the ninety thousand registered voters in Birmingham only ten thousand were black. The NAACP had not gained a foothold in the city because it was outlawed by Alabama law as a "foreign corporation." Efforts to change the racial situation in the city were often met with violence. Between 1957 and 1963 alone there were seventeen unsolved bombings of black churches and homes in Birmingham. In 1961 a mob had beaten a group of freedom riders in the local bus station. The city government was as diligent as its citizens in enforcing segregation. When it became evident that the city's sixty-eight parks, thirty-eight playgrounds, six pools, and four golf courses would have to desegregate to comply with federal law, the city fathers closed them. The city's tough attitude toward black unrest was ably represented by Eugene ("Bull") Connor, one of Birmingham's three commissioners of public safety. Connor was a popular ex-baseball announcer who ran one of the toughest police forces in the South.

Many of Birmingham's black leaders were reluctant to attack segregation in the city head-on, but in 1962 the Reverend Mr. Fred L. Shuttlesworth, leader of the Alabama Christian Movement for Human Rights, organized a boycott of Birmingham businesses that discriminated against blacks. After studying the situation, the Southern Christian Leadership Council under King's direction decided to join Shuttlesworth in attacking segregation in Birmingham. If they could win in Birmingham, they concluded, they could win anywhere.

The SCLC began planning for demonstrations in Birmingham in winter 1962–63. They wanted to avoid the error they had made in Albany of beginning without extensive preparation. King and other leaders became acquainted with the local black community and began to teach them the philosophy and method of nonviolent resistance to segregation. Andrew Young, then vice-president of the SCLC, remembered that in Birmingham this was a hard lesson to convey. Many of the city's tough young blacks believed that in a confrontation they would have to "kill or be killed."

The civil rights leaders established three major goals: removal of racial restrictions in stores, including segregated lunch counters, dressing rooms, drinking fountains, and rest rooms; adoption of nondiscriminatory hiring practices; and creation of a biracial city commission to negotiate further desegregation. They made prospective demonstration participants sign a pledge of nonviolence. The signers agreed to "Remember always that the non-violent movement in Birmingham seeks justice and reconciliation, not victory"; to "Observe with both friend and foe the ordinary rules of courtesy"; and to "Refrain from the violence of fist, tongue, or heart." These rules and others like them were not mere window dressing. They were at the heart of the civil rights movement as King and others understood it. King carefully explained this Gandhian creed of peaceful protest at dozens of meetings of Birmingham blacks.

At the scores of organizational meetings that were held before and during the demonstrations King, Ralph Abernathy, Fred Shuttleworth, and other leaders also taught their people the "freedom songs." These were adaptions of old slave songs to modern times. King believed that both the words and the music of the songs reinforced the patient resolve that was essential to the movement. "Woke Up This Morning with My Mind Stayed on Freedom," he said, "is a sentence that needs no music to make its point." Another song, "Ain't Gonna Let Nobody Turn Me 'Round," taught persistence. "It is not just a song," wrote King. "It's a resolve."

The civil rights organizers set April 3 as C day in Birmingham — C for confrontation, for the great demonstration against segregation. The predominantly white electorate of Birmingham had just voted in favor of a new type of city government and had chosen a moderate segregationist for mayor over Bull Connor. But the election did not appear to signal an end of racial discrimination, and Connor was still in office at the time anyway. And so the demonstrations began.

On the first few days the organizers sent small groups of blacks downtown to sit in at department store lunch counters. They wanted to build up to the full force of confrontation slowly. On April 6 a crowd of demonstrators marched on city hall. The police ordered them to disperse but approached them cautiously. Connor had been persuaded that he should not allow himself to appear brutal, because the demonstrations were receiving national press coverage.

On April 12, Good Friday, King led a march toward city hall. The authorities had obtained a court injunction against the march, but King decided that he would disobey it. As he later wrote: "Any law that uplifts human personality is just. Any law that degrades human personality is unjust." As the marchers moved along the street singing "We Shall Overcome," the police moved in and arrested King along with fifty other demonstrators.

In prison King found himself in solitary confinement. He was not allowed to make calls or receive visitors. On Saturday morning shafts of sunlight coming through a high window barely illuminated his dismal cell. Then the beams of sunlight were gone. The day had ended, and he still had not been allowed to communicate with anyone outside the prison. He later wrote: "Those were the longest, most frustrating and bewildering hours I have lived." On Sunday his attorneys were finally allowed to visit him. The next day King learned that singer Harry Belafonte had raised $50,000 in bail for the prisoners. King was deeply relieved. After he was alone again, he contemplated his feelings of the last two days. He was stunned by "a profound sense of awe. I was aware," he wrote, "of a feeling that had been present all along below the surface of consciousness, pressed down under the weight of concern for the movement: I had never been truly in solitary confinement; God's companionship does not stop at the door of a jail cell."

King is so well known as a political figure that we easily forget the deep current of piety that influenced his life. But his sense of the reality of God infused his oratory and leadership with its prophetic tone. It was the minister in him that told his followers to "Refrain from the violence of fist, tongue, or heart."

While he was in prison, Martin Luther King, Jr., read in the newspaper that eight white ministers in Birmingham had criticized the demonstrations as "untimely." King decided to reply. Not being allowed any writing paper, he began his composition on the margins of the newspaper, then continued on a legal pad obtained from his attorneys. The result was the "Letter from Birmingham Jail," the most important document of the civil rights movement.

The eight clergymen asked why King had come to Birmingham. King answered that his Southern Christian Leadership Conference had branches throughout the South and that he had been invited by a local affiliate to come to the city. "But more basically," he said, "I am in Birmingham because injustice is here." Segregation in Birmingham was not merely a local matter, he argued. "Injustice anywhere is a threat to justice everywhere. We are caught in a inescapable network of mutuality, tied in a single garment of destiny."

King's critics chided him for leading demonstrations. He replied that they should be equally concerned about "the conditions that brought about the demonstrations." They said that the demonstrators should seek change through negotiation. King replied that the city had never acted in good faith through negotiations. "We know through painful experience," he said, "that freedom is never voluntarily given by the oppressor; it must be demanded by the oppressed."

The eight ministers questioned whether the demonstrations were "well timed." King replied that blacks had waited 340 years "for our constitutional and God-given rights" and that was long enough. In the most eloquent passage in the long letter he described just what it meant to "wait" in a condition of inferiority: "When you have seen vicious mobs lynch your mothers and fathers at will and drown your sisters and brothers at whim; when you have seen hate-filled policemen curse, kick, and even kill your black brothers and sisters; when you see the vast majority of your twenty million Negro brothers smothering in an airtight cage of poverty in the midst of an affluent society; when you suddenly find your tongue twisted and your speech stammering as you seek to explain to your six-year-old daughter why she can't go to the public amusement park that has just been advertised on television, and see tears welling up in her eyes when she is told that Funtown is closed to colored children, and see ominous clouds of inferiority beginning to form in her little mental sky, and see her beginning to distort her personality by developing an unconscious bitterness toward white people; when you have to concoct an answer for a five-year-old son who is asking: 'Daddy, why do white people treat colored people so mean?'; when you take a cross-country drive and find it necessary to sleep night after night in the uncomfortable corners of your automobile because no motel will accept you; when you are humiliated day in and day out by nagging signs reading 'white' and 'colored'; when your first name becomes 'nigger,' your middle name becomes 'boy' (however old you are) and your last name become 'John,' and your wife and mother are never given the respected title 'Mrs.'; when you are harried by day and haunted by night by the fact that you are a Negro, living constantly at tiptoe stance, never quite knowing what to expect next, and are plagued with inner fears and outer resentments; when you are forever fighting a degenerating sense of 'nobodiness' — then you will understand why we find it difficult to wait. There comes a time when the cup of endurance runs over, and men are no longer willing to be plunged into the abyss of despair. I hope, sirs, you can understand our legitimate and unavoidable impatience."

This was what segregation was really like. This was what it did to its victims. The rest of King's letter explained the philosophy of nonviolent resistance to injustice. One could break an unjust law, he said, if one did so "openly, lovingly, and with a willingness to accept the penalty." He cited early Christian and American Revolutionary precedents for civil disobedience and argued that such acts were often the path to human progress.

He had been called an extremist. But he was really a moderate, King asserted, standing between those blacks who were afraid to act at all and those who tended toward violence in the face of oppression. Or if he was an extremist, he acted in the tradition of Jesus, Paul, and Luther, who were extremists for love. "Perhaps," he said, "the South, the nation and the world are in dire need of creative extremists."

In contrast, too many southern ministers were cautious men who could go to church without ever troubling themselves about racial injustice. He had once hoped that southern white churchmen would rally around the civil rights movement. But he had been disappointed by their indifference or hostility. He now called upon the church as a whole to "meet the challenge of this decisive hour."

Lastly, King's critics had praised the Birmingham police department for doing its job well. King conceded that they had not engaged in any acts of overt violence. But the very system they were supporting was wrong; they were using "the moral means of nonviolence to maintain the immoral end of racial injustice." They were not the heroes of the South.

Yet the South did have its heroes, men and women who stood up for justice. "One day," King said, "the South will recognize its real heroes." Those were people like James Meredith, who went alone to integrate the University of Mississippi. They were people like the seventy-two-year-old black woman in Montgomery, Alabama, who joined her neighbors in refusing to ride the segregated buses. Asked whether she was tired, she replied, "My feets is tired, but my soul is at rest."

The "Letter from Birmingham Jail" was a celebration of such people and of the aspirations and achievements of the civil rights movement. King concluded on a note of optimism for the future: "Let us all hope that the dark clouds of racial prejudice will soon pass away and the deep fog of misunderstanding will be lifted from our fear-drenched communities, and in some not too distant tomorrow the radiant stars of love and brotherhood will shine over our great nation with all their scintillating beauty."

Such were the thoughts that Martin Luther King, Jr., committed to paper in his narrow cell. Eight days after his arrest he was released on bail and rejoined the civil rights workers in Birmingham. He revised the letter and released it to a sympathetic world. The rhetoric of King's letter was made all the more compelling by the events of the next four weeks.

Day after day large groups of well-organized demonstrators walked to downtown Birmingham. On May 2 a thousand young people marched. The civil rights leaders were criticized for exploiting children. In reply, King asked where these critics had been when the children had been forced to enter segregated schools and were barred from downtown lunch counters. With the passage of time the tensions in Birmingham mounted, and Bull Connor became frustrated with the failure of his restrained police work to end the demonstrations. So he began using police dogs and firehoses.

There were now more than a hundred newsmen in Birmingham who sent out pictures of Connor's men at work: five policemen pinning a middle-aged black woman to the ground; demonstrators thrown against a wall by streams of water powerful enough to strip the bark off trees; police dogs sinking their teeth into unresisting blacks. Bull Connor did nothing to dispel the image of brutality. When the local demonstration leader, Fred Shuttleworth, was injured by a hard blast of water and carried away in an ambulance, Connor told reporters that he wished "they'd carried him away in a hearse."

After several weeks of pictures and comments like these, there was strong nationwide support for the Birmingham demonstrators. President Kennedy, who had been following the confrontation closely and sensed the surge of public sympathy for the demonstrators, remarked, "The civil rights movement owes Bull Connor as much as it owes Abraham Lincoln."

The leaders attempted to keep their "moral edge" over the opposition by demanding that their followers keep to the tactics of nonviolence. On May 10 their followers broke ranks briefly after bombs exploded at the A. G. Gaston Motel, the demonstration headquarters, and in front of the home of King's younger brother. For three hours blacks rioted, burning stores and vehicles. King and Ralph Abernathy responded by conducting a "pool hall pilgrimage" urging tough young blacks to practice nonviolence.

By late spring 1963 the Birmingham demonstrations were beginning to achieve results. The city government and downtown merchants in Birmingham finally agreed to desegregate public facilities and to hire blacks. President Kennedy began to advocate strong civil rights legislation. He had initially been reluctant to offer King more than token support, telling him that his narrow electoral margin of barely one hundred thousand votes in the 1960 presidential contest against Richard Nixon did not justify an aggressive integration policy. But during the Birmingham crisis both he and his brother, Attorney General Robert Kennedy, had been in frequent contact with the demonstration leaders in Birmingham. On June 19, 1963, John F. Kennedy delivered a speech endorsing strong civil rights legislation. No one had ever barred black Americans from fighting and dying for their country, he said. It was time that they be fully accepted in other areas of American life.

In the next two years the favorable current of public opinion created by the Birmingham demonstrations carried the civil rights movement to its greatest triumphs. In fall 1963 King and other leaders spoke to a crowd of 250,000 supporters in Washington, D.C. King delivered there his famous "I Have a Dream" speech, calling for Congress and the people to "let freedom ring" for blacks throughout the United States.

Although the movement lost one of its great supporters with the assassination of President Kennedy on November 22, 1963, his successor, President Lyndon Johnson, continued to support new legislation. With his urging, Congress passed the Civil Rights Act in 1964 and the

Voting Rights Act in 1965, the most significant legislation for blacks since Reconstruction.

King, too, went from victory to victory. He won a Nobel Peace Prize in 1964 — becoming the youngest person to win the award — largely on the strength of his leadership in Birmingham and his letter from the city's jail. In the next year he led demonstrations at Selma, Alabama, to dramatize the continuing disfranchisement of blacks.

Despite these triumphs, however, King's position would become increasingly different in the last five years of his life. Between 1963 and 1968, when he was assassinated in Memphis, Tennessee, it became more and more difficult to rally blacks and whites around the clear-cut distinctions between segregation and integration. New black leaders began to assert that blacks could achieve more with fists and guns than with nonviolence. They and other new leaders were often less interested in integration than in black nationalism. Some of their young proteges in American colleges and universities even demanded separate dormitories and dining tables to preserve black identity. At the same time, the problem of providing equal access to jobs resulted in "affirmative action," which sometimes replaced favoritism for whites with favoritism for blacks. Then, too, the nation discovered that de facto segregation in the North was almost as extensive as de jure segregation in the South.

All these new cross-currents of opinion, fact, and policy would complicate issues that King had so ably expressed in words like justice and injustice, light and darkness. The civil rights movement of the 1950s and early 1960s had exposed the most glaring examples of racial injustice in America. It had succeeded, quite simply, because the racial bars — disfranchisement and segregated public facilities — were so blatantly inconsistent with American ideals of human dignity and equality. Civil rights leaders revealed those inconsistencies and moved American blacks a stride toward the just society that glittered so brightly in Martin Luther King's moral armament.

QUESTIONS

1. In what ways were blacks discriminated against in the 1940s and 1950s? Why was segregation harmful to blacks? How was it harmful to American society as a whole?

2. In what ways did these individuals, organizations, and events anticipate the civil rights movement: W. E. B. Du Bois, the NAACP, Marcus Garvey, Jobs

for Negroes, Executive Order 8802, Joe Louis, *Smith v. Albright,* and *Brown v. Board of Education?*

3. Why did blacks decide to boycott buses in Montgomery? What tactics were used in Montgomery that were significant for the later civil rights movement? What role did Rosa Parks play?

4. Martin Luther King, Jr., was the most articulate spokesman for the civil rights movement. Explain the significance of these King statements: (a) "Sweep streets like Beethoven composed music"; (b) blacks "live within two concentric circles of segregation"; (c) "God's companionship does not stop at the door of a jail cell"; (d) "Freedom is never given voluntarily by the oppressor"; (e) "We find it difficult to wait"; (f) "One day the South will recognize its real heroes."

5. What role did these play in the civil rights movement: nonviolence, civil disobedience, sit-ins, Freedom Rides, the media, the Southern Christian Leadership Conference, the Congress of Racial Equality, civil rights songs, Bull Connor?

6. Why was Birmingham chosen as a target for civil rights action, and why was victory there so important to Martin Luther King, Jr.?

7. In what ways did segregationists try to resist the civil rights movement? How did their resistance affect the movement?

8. Why did John F. Kennedy decide to take a strong stand for civil rights legislation?

9. In what ways did new currents in racial relations in the late 1960s complicate the struggle for racial equality?

10. In what ways did the civil rights movement of the 1950s and 1960s improve conditions for blacks? In what respects were blacks still disadvantaged in relationship to other Americans?

11. What role did the media play in the civil rights movement?

BIBLIOGRAPHY

ANSBRO, JOHN J. *Martin Luther King, Jr.: The Making of a Mind* (1982). Explores the philosophical basis of King's nonviolence.

BASS, JACK. *Unlikely Heroes* (1991). Account of the role of federal judges in implementing desegregation in the South.

BRANCH, TAYLOR. *Parting the Waters* (1988). A history of America during "the King years," 1954–63.

BRAUER, CARL M. *John F. Kennedy and the Second Reconstruction* (1977). Kennedy's role in the civil rights movement.

CARSON, CLAYBORNE. *In Struggle: SNCC and the Black Awakening of the 1980s* (1981). History of the Student Nonviolent Coordinating Committee.

GARROW, DAVID J. *The F.B.I. and Martin Luther King, Jr.* (1981). Describes surveillance of King, whom the F.B.I. considered a threat to the social order.

KING, MARTIN Luther, JR. *Stride Toward Freedom* (1958). King's account of the Montgomery bus boycott.

_____. *Why We Can't Wait* (1963). King's account of Birmingham with his "Letter from Birmingham Jail."

LAWSON, STEVEN F. *Black Ballots: Voting Rights in the South. 1944–1969* (1976). Expansion of voting rights in the South.

Lewis, David Levering. *Martin Luther King* (1978). Definitive King biography.

MALCOLM X. *Autobiography* (1966). Life story of the foremost black nationalist of his time.

MEIER, AUGUST, AND ELLIOTT RUDWICK. *CORE: A Study in the Civil Rights Movement* (1973). Close examination of one of the most influential civil rights organizations.

MORGAN, CHARLES, JR. *A Time to Speak* (1964). Account of Birmingham by a white citizen who spoke out against segregation and violence — and was forced to leave.

NUNNELLEY, WILLIAM A. *Bull Connor* (1991). Biography of the police commissioner who opposed King at Birmingham.

12

AMERICA DIVIDED

The Vietnam War and the 1968 Democratic Convention

For better or worse, war usually fosters national unity. Critics might argue that wartime patriotism cloaks domestic injustice and stifles free speech, but in an international crisis people rally around the flag. The Vietnam War, however, was an exception. Divisive in itself, it reinforced rather than obscured other divisions in American society: minorities against the dominant culture, young people against the "establishment," liberals against conservatives. The war protesters who shouted, "Hell, no, we won't go!" and the war supporters who jeered, "America, love it or leave it!" might have lived in separate nations. In 1968 the Democratic party, torn between supporters and opponents of the war, attempted to unite behind a presidential candidate. Their convention in Chicago dramatized but did not heal their divisions.

Democratic party conventions have always been renowned for their no-holds-barred politics. But none was more tumultuous than the 1968 convention in Chicago. Its major participants could have been the cast of characters in a melodrama. First there was Lyndon B. Johnson, the president of the United States, a powerful and complex man. He was by turns imaginative, manipulative, warm, cynical, humane, and tough. He had won a landslide victory over his Republican opponent, Barry Goldwater, in the 1964 election, but now, four years later, he was a lame duck, a political victim of the war in Southeast Asia.

At his right hand stood Vice-President Hubert Humphrey, ready to succeed Johnson. No man in the United States had a better civil rights record than Humphrey. In the Senate and as vice-president he befriended labor, minorities, and the poor. But he had followed his chief in supporting the Vietnam War, and now he often heard himself vilified as a warmonger and oppressor. He sought to maintain his accustomed posture of benevolent rectitude, but he was troubled by these criticisms.

Humphrey's supporters assumed that he had already won the prize to be awarded at Chicago, the Democratic nomination for the presidency. But a third figure, Senator Eugene McCarthy of Minnesota, planned to fight them and their policies. He had audaciously challenged President Johnson in the New Hampshire primary six months before and had nearly won. Known for his reserve and intelligence, McCarthy had expected only to frighten the president and to publicize his antiwar views. But having nearly bagged the chief executive, he had suddenly taken his own campaign more seriously. He built up an organization and won impressive primary victories in Wisconsin and Oregon.

In the meantime, McCarthy's near success in New Hampshire had persuaded Lyndon Johnson to withdraw from the campaign and encouraged New York's Senator Robert Kennedy to throw his hat into the ring. Kennedy was the most glamorous political figure of his time. Handsome, vigorous, and articulate, he inherited the political image and following of his brother, John F. Kennedy. The New York senator had overtaken McCarthy in the Illinois, Nebraska, and California primaries, only to fall victim to an assassin's bullet on the night of the California primary. Kennedy's specter loomed over the gathering at Chicago, contributing to the moral outrage that beat upon the convention.

That outrage was dramatized by another character, or rather by a chorus of characters, gathered under a loose affiliation to the Youth International Party, or "Yippies." This coalition of antiwar demonstrators, student activists, and civil rights militants not only challenged President Johnson's war policies but also denounced the social ills they associated with that policy: materialism, imperialism, racism, and moral absolutism.

Standing between the political professionals and the new dissidents there was, finally, Richard J. Daley, the mayor of Chicago. A short, corpulent man with a hard, plump face, Daley was the foremost representative of a dying breed in American public life, the political boss. Daley's machine was so effective that in his periodic reelection bids he could sweep precincts in Chicago by 95 percent. Daley had little sympathy with idealistic politicians like McCarthy, and none whatsoever with the Yippies. He placed police barricades around the convention hall and declared that he would keep order in his city.

These men differed on many issues, but the most abrasive was the problem of the Vietnam War. Every American war has had its opponents; some, like the Mexican and Spanish-American wars, have proved quite divisive. But these were short conflicts, easy victories for American arms. The Vietnam War, on the other hand, was in its fourth year, with no end in sight, and opposition to it had become as important as the war itself.

Americans in 1968 divided into hawks and doves. The hawks were those who approved of the war, or even wished for the use of more force against the enemy. The doves believed that the United States had no vital interest in Vietnam and should withdraw its troops. If you were to ask a hawk and a dove to explain what the United States was doing in Vietnam, he or she would give you two entirely different answers, based on completely opposed views of history.

A hawk would explain that the United States had a vital interest in South Vietnam. The little nation was a democratic country and depended upon American aid for its survival; it had been attacked by North Vietnam, a Communist nation that was armed and encouraged by Russia and China. If the United States failed to support South Vietnam, democracy everywhere would be affected. President Dwight David Eisenhower had articulated this view many years before. Remarking that the world's failure to halt Adolf Hitler's initial acts of aggression had facilitated his rise to power, Eisenhower and other Americans concluded that tyranny should be nipped in the bud. The fall of South Vietnam would lead to the fall of Cambodia, Laos, Thailand, and the rest of Southeast Asia. The fall of Southeast Asia would lead to the fall of Indonesia, the Philippines, and Australia; eventually we would be fighting "them" in Hawaii and California. "You have a row of dominos set up," Eisenhower said, "you knock over the first one, and what will happen to the last one is that it will go over very quickly."

This "domino theory" furnished the ideological basis for American involvement in Vietnam even before Eisenhower's presidency. In the late 1940s France was nominal sovereign of Vietnam, having established a colonial empire in Southeast Asia in the nineteenth century. France was fighting a war against an independence movement led by Ho Chi Minh, and the Truman administration concluded that because Ho was a Communist, the French effort deserved American support. Truman sent supplies rather than men, but by 1954 the United States was paying almost 80 percent of the French war costs.

In that year France was on the verge of a major defeat. The Viet Minh, Ho's revolutionary army, cut off an important French base at Dien Bien Phu. France sought American aid, and President Eisenhower was tempted to intervene. He wrote British Prime Minister Winston Churchill that if Vietnam fell into Communist hands the effect on Britain and America would be "disastrous." "We failed to halt Hirohito, Mussolini and Hitler by not acting in unity and in time," he said. "That marked the beginning of many years of stark tragedy and desperate peril. May it not be that our nations have learned something from that lesson?"

Churchill was unconvinced, however, feeling that intervention would do little to change the situation in Vietnam and might lead to a major war. Eisenhower's chief of staff, Gen. Matthew B. Ridgway, believed that the massive use of planes and men in Vietnam would not change the situation. And John Kennedy, then a young senator from Massachusetts, declared that the Vietnamese countryside was "the most difficult terrain in the world." The United States could not possibly win a war there without the Vietnamese people's support. And the people regarded France as a foreign oppressor.

In view of opposition from Congress, the military, and his allies, Eisenhower decided against intervention in 1954. Dien Bien Phu fell to the Communists, and France agreed to withdraw from Southeast Asia. An international conference at Geneva established the independence of Vietnam, Cambodia, and Laos, and partitioned Vietnam at the seventeenth parallel. Emperor Bao Dai, the former ruler of Vietnam under the French, was left in control of South Vietnam, and Ho Chi Minh became ruler of the North.

The United States soon established close ties with South Vietnam. But the emperor's position was immediately threatened by Communist revolutionary activity in South Vietnam. In 1955 Ngo Dinh Diem overthrew the emperor and established a more popular pro-Western government. He continued the emperor's struggle against the Communists and persuaded the United States to send military assistance in the form of equipment and advisers. By the end of Eisenhower's presidency in 1961, 3,200 American military advisers were in Vietnam. John F. Kennedy, now president of the United States, continued the Eisenhower policy of helping South Vietnam attempt to suppress the persistent Communist insurrection and increased the number of advisers. In 1963

16,000 Americans were in Vietnam. They were all "non-combat" troops, but in the guerrilla warfare waged by the Communists, or Vietcong, the lines of battle were seldom clear, and American soldiers occasionally found themselves in combat zones. In this fashion 120 American soldiers were killed between 1956 and 1963.

Although this was war, of a sort, few Americans knew anything about Vietnam. If they read occasional illustrated articles about the country in *Life* or *National Geographic,* they were left with the impression of a pretty little country, full of lush jungles and muddy brown rice paddies. The war in this quaint and remote land seemed like an adventure in a storybook — the periodic rebel attacks on military outposts created a sense of adventure but hardly seemed to pose a serious threat to the South Vietnamese government.

In 1964, however, Americans became more aware of the Vietnam War. In Saigon, Ngo Dinh Diem was killed in a coup and a succession of military rulers attempted to run the country. Meanwhile, the Vietcong gained control over scores of isolated hamlets. In August 1964 President Johnson announced that North Vietnamese patrol boats in the Gulf of Tonkin had attacked American destroyers off the Vietnamese coast. He easily persuaded Congress to pass legislation authorizing him to "repel any armed attack against the forces of the United States and to repel further aggression." With the backing of the Gulf of Tonkin resolution, he stepped up the American involvement in Vietnam with air strikes against North Vietnamese oil supplies in Haiphong and by sending thousands of soldiers to South Vietnam. At the same time, in his electoral campaign against Barry Goldwater, Johnson advocated restraint in Vietnam. Whereas his Republican challenger called for heavy bombing in North Vietnam to bring the war to a hasty conclusion, Johnson insisted that the South Vietnamese must fight their own war. "We are not going north and we are not going south," he said on September 28, a few weeks before the election; "we are going to continue to try to get them to save their own freedom with their own men."

Johnson won the election with an overwhelming 61 percent of the popular vote, but he found it difficult to fight the limited war he had advocated in his campaign. The more advisers he sent to Vietnam, the greater the chance of casualties. In February 1965 thirty-one American soldiers were killed in Vietcong attacks on Pleiku and Qui Nhon in South Vietnam. In retaliation, the United States bombed North Vietnam and began using B-52s against Vietcong strongholds in the South. At the urging of Gen. William C. Westmoreland, Johnson sent more troops to protect American positions in Vietnam. It was now apparent that the Communists were so strong that without substantial military aid South Vietnam would fall. Accordingly, the United States continued to increase the American forces in Vietnam. Congress did not, however, declare war. It was difficult in fact to pinpoint a date on which American fighting actually began in Vietnam. A new word, "escalation," was coined to describe the gradual but inexorable American involvement.

By the end of 1965, 184,000 American soldiers were in Vietnam; in mid-1968 there were 538,000. With this military buildup the Americans abandoned their noncombat posture. They fought a complicated, frustrating, and often brutal war. Because there were no "front lines," battles could erupt in the far North near the seventeenth parallel, to the south of Saigon in the Mekong Delta, or anywhere between. A town might be "loyal" to Saigon one day and be a Vietcong stronghold the next.

Americans fought from helicopters, gunboats, and B-52s. They marched through rice paddies, thick forests, and rugged hillsides. But even the physical challenge of fighting the war was only half the problem in Vietnam. It soon became clear that the United States would have to help create the nation it was attempting to save. America had to choose between the rival political factions in Saigon, and men had to visit hundreds of Vietnamese villages to encourage war-weary civilians to resist the Communists.

The Vietnam War dragged on year after year, but the administration hoped that each year would end the fighting — surely if the United States sent over a few more planes and a few more men the enemy would collapse. This was, one must admit, a very old hope in Vietnam. In 1952, when the French were still fighting the war, Secretary of State Dean Acheson had remarked, "The military situation appears to be developing favorably." Two years later Secretary of Defense Charles Wilson declared that a French victory was "both possible and probable." After a trip to Vietnam in 1962 Secretary of Defense Robert S. McNamara stated confidently, "We're winning this war." In 1967 the columnist Joseph Alsop said that within a few months, "the chances are good that the Vietnamese war will look successful."

Such hopes had been dashed in the past, and in 1968 optimism about the war suffered its worst setback since the 1954 French debacle at Dien Bien Phu. On January 30–31, during the lunar new year holidays (Tet), roughly one hundred thousand Communist troops attacked seventy-four cities and towns, including thirty-nine of South Vietnam's forty-four provincial capitals and every major American base. The Communists captured Hue, the old imperial capital of Vietnam, and occupied parts of Saigon. American jets had to bomb enemy positions within the national capital. Eventually the Vietcong and North Vietnamese were driven back from most of their new positions, and within a month they lost tens of thousands of men. But American and South

Vietnamese losses were heavy, too, and the Communists had proved that the frequent rumors of their demise were, indeed, greatly exaggerated.

What did one make of the Vietnam War? What was the United States trying to achieve? Was American policy likely to benefit the South Vietnamese, the rest of Southeast Asia, or the United States? Hawks had one set of answers to these questions, doves another.

In opposing communism in Vietnam, Presidents Truman, Eisenhower, Kennedy, and Johnson had operated on the assumption that Ho Chi Minh and his allies were in the wrong for two reasons. First, they were unjust in imposing a "foreign" ideology on the Vietnamese people. With the partition of Vietnam in 1954 the South should have been allowed to develop as a democratic nation without outside interference. The Communists were also in the wrong because, according to the domino theory, their threat to South Vietnam was a threat to other nations as well. As Lyndon Johnson remarked at a Democratic fund-raising dinner in Chicago in 1966, "We have learned over the past half century that failure to meet aggression means war, not peace." Johnson argued that the whole world would be affected by what happened in Vietnam. "Not just that one little country of 14 million people," he said, "but more than a hundred other little countries stand tonight and watch and wait." Characterizing the opponents of the war as "Nervous Nellies," he promised to fight on until "peace is secure — not only for the people of America, but peace is secure for peace-loving people everywhere in this world." Johnson made many statements like this during his administration. In the early years of the war, most of Congress and the press shared his sentiments. The Tonkin Gulf resolution and subsequent war appropriations passed both houses of Congress by lopsided majorities.

Many Americans, however, did not see the situation in Southeast Asia as Johnson and his supporters did. The United States was supposed to be supporting a democratic regime in South Vietnam. But Diem had been a dictator who deposed an emperor, and he in turn had been assassinated by other military chiefs. Even when the government held national elections at the insistence of the United States, Saigon did not encourage free speech, a free press, and the other personal liberties Americans identified with freedom. Thus, the various Saigon regimes failed to live up to the image of beleaguered democracy.

It could be argued too that Ho Chi Minh was a fitting ruler for Vietnam. Although he was a Communist leader, Ho was also a nationalist. Some doves claimed that America should have supported him in the first place when he waged his war of national liberation against the French. After all, they argued, we ourselves had achieved nationhood in a Revolution against an imperial power. Moreover, Ho's 1945 Declaration of Independence of the Democratic Republic of Vietnam showed his admiration for the American political system. It began with words familiar to all Americans: "All men are created equal. They are endowed by their Creator with certain unalienable rights, among these are Life, Liberty and the pursuit of Happiness."

Johnson's critics also pointed out that the Vietcong consisted almost entirely of South Vietnamese opponents of the Saigon government. Even when North Vietnam began to send troops to the South in large numbers after 1964, many of these soldiers were natives of the South who had gone north after the partition in 1954 anticipating that the country would eventually be reunited. The conflict in Vietnam was a civil war, said the doves. It was an issue that the Vietnamese must work out for themselves, just as the United States had solved its political problems in the Civil War.

The domestic situation in Vietnam was further complicated, critics argued, by the presence of rival factions that owed allegiance neither to the Communists nor to Saigon. In 1966 a Buddhist uprising throughout the country nearly toppled the Saigon regime. The Buddhists were not Communists but were opposed to the military leaders in Saigon and to American intervention. The complexities of Vietnamese politics did not fit the comfortable distinction between communism and freedom, right and wrong.

Doves viewed the Vietnam War as brutal and senseless. They were appalled by the sheer magnitude of the American involvement. Between 1964 and 1968 the United States dropped more explosives on North and South Vietnam than the Allies had unloaded over Germany and Japan during the whole of World War II. The United States used weapons that seemed calculated to destroy the entire country: high-flying B-52s that accidentally bombed friendly villages; napalm that stuck to the flesh and burned horrible wounds, chemical defoliants that destroyed forests.

The United States was allegedly "saving" Vietnam from the Communists. But, the doves argued, America was actually doing more damage to Vietnam than the Vietcong. Every evening before dinner Americans sat in front of their television sets and observed the war at first hand. In their living rooms they watched as U.S. Marines set fire to Vietnamese huts, soldiers told about cutting off Vietcong ears as "trophies," or officers admitted that their men used water torture or dropped captives from helicopters in order to obtain information. One particularly gruesome report showed a helicopter flying over the countryside with a huge net dangling at the end of a long rope from its belly. The net held the bodies of several dozen dead Vietcong.

Worse were the stories of American brutality to Vietnamese civilians. The war against the Vietcong guerrillas tested the patience of even the best American soldiers. A village that appeared friendly would harbor Vietcong soldiers; an apparently harmless peasant woman would suddenly throw a grenade. Under these circumstances, Americans sometimes "shot first and asked questions later" and even massacred civilians, including women, children, and babies. The worst such incident occurred at the village of My Lai in March 1968, when American soldiers rounded up and killed several hundred noncombatants. At the time of the Democratic Convention the Defense Department knew about the My Lai massacre but was attempting to cover up the story. But already in 1968 the Vietnamese people appeared to be paying a tremendous price for American assistance — a price that was aptly described by an American officer after his men had demolished a village suspected of harboring Vietcong soldiers. "It became necessary," he said, "to destroy the town to save it."

The hawks could point to innumerable Vietcong atrocities to place American policy in perspective. When American and South Vietnamese forces recaptured Hue, for example, after the Tet offensive, they discovered three thousand civilian bodies in mass graves. The Vietcong had massacred these enemies of their revolution, sometimes torturing them first. Both sides were proving that "War is hell." From the dove's point of view, however, there was no point in engaging in brutal war where civilians as well as soldiers were killed by both sides as a matter of course, when the issue in South Vietnam was a matter of local politics, and neither the Communists nor the Saigon government could claim the full allegiance of the people.

The divisions in America between hawks and doves were made all the more bitter because of other divisions in American society in the 1960s. The civil rights movement had exposed the glaring injustice of racial discrimination. Although Martin Luther King, Jr., espoused a nonviolent approach to the problems of race, many young black leaders were impatient with moderation. In 1966 Bobby Seale and Huey P. Newton organized the Black Panthers in Oakland, California, along paramilitary lines. H. Rap Brown declared in the following year that violence is "as American as apple pie." Between 1964 and 1968 more than a hundred people, mainly black, were killed in race riots in Watts, Detroit, Newark, and elsewhere. Violence and injustice seemed to haunt American society.

During this same period traditional restraints on personal and social action seemed to fall away like worn-out creeds. Young people began to experiment with drugs, to engage more freely in sexual relations, to question the ideal of material success. Nothing was sacred except, perhaps, honesty to oneself and a genuine feeling for one's fellow human beings. Bob Dylan summed up the sentiment of the young in the title of his most famous song, "The Times They Are A changin'." On college campuses it became fashionable to challenge the grading system, course requirements, and admissions policies. At Berkeley, Columbia, and a thousand other colleges and universities students adapted civil rights tactics to campus politics by staging sit-ins at administration buildings, and speakers exposed the evils of a decadent world, punctuating their comments with the phrase, "you know."

Inevitably attitudes toward the war, the youth movement, and other issues tended to come together. Campus radicals spoke about the "establishment." *The establishment, you know, was that cozy relationship between big business, big government, and the military. The war was good for business because it meant bucks for war contractors. It was good for politicians because it made them seem patriotic. And it was good for the university, too, because academe was part of the "military industrial complex"; it owned stocks in defense companies, you know, and did research on military contracts. The establishment was screwing the Vietnamese and it was screwing the blacks and other minorities. But you didn't have to go along with it.*

Above all, the dissidents said, you didn't have to go along with the war. The antiwar movement made its beginnings on America's campuses. Shortly after the Tonkin Gulf incident, faculty and students across the United States engaged in teach-ins, long meetings devoted to an exchange of views on the situation in Vietnam. From these meetings came a substantial number of students and adults who believed that the United States should not be in Vietnam. Realizing that they were a small minority, they organized peace marches and rallies to publicize their opposition to the war and gain converts. Initially these were parades of a few thousand people in places like Berkeley, where antiwar feeling was already strong. But with each year of escalation, the movement grew stronger.

The nightly news of events in Vietnam was accompanied by stories of war resistance in the United States. Usually the acts of resistance were symbolic: peace marches, ceremonial burning of draft cards, slogans and chants — "Hell, no, we won't go!" and "Make love, not war" — sit-ins at military depots and induction centers. For draft-age men the war problem could require a more difficult course than simple protest. The law allowed a person to gain a draft deferment on the basis of religious objection to war. But this exception did not help the hundreds of thousands of young men who opposed the Vietnam War but did not oppose all wars or who had no formal religious affiliation. Some feared disapproval by parents or friends and went into the military despite their feelings about the war. Others refused induction and went to jail as draft resisters. (Muhammad Ali, the heavyweight boxing champion, refused to be drafted on the basis of his Muslim religion. "I ain't got nothing against them Vietcong," he said.) Thousands more went to Canada, Sweden, or other foreign countries as draft dodgers or deserters.

The burden of war resistance fell most heavily upon young men, but the movement to end the war soon involved men and women of all ages. Dr. Benjamin Spock, author of the most respected child-care book in America, dismayed some admirers and thrilled others when he announced his strong opposition to the war. Martin Luther King, Jr., holder of the Nobel Peace Prize, announced in 1967 that he opposed the war as a matter of conscience even though he realized his opposition might damage his position in the civil rights movement.

The peace movement gained strength in Congress, too. Senator Wayne Morse of Oregon was the first and most outspoken Senate critic of the war. He was suspicious of Johnson's policies from the start. On August 5, 1964, he challenged the Johnson administration's account of the Tonkin Gulf incident. Morse suggested that the American ship in question had been inside the North Vietnamese twelve-mile limit and may have been covering a South Vietnamese naval raid. He and Ernest Gruening of Alaska voted against the Tonkin Gulf resolution. Morse denounced the February 1965 air strikes against North Vietnam as a "black page in American history."

The administration was able, initially, to isolate Morse and Gruening. Most of their colleagues either supported the war or were afraid to speak out against the president. But in 1966 dissent became more respectable when Senator J. William Fulbright, chairman of the Senate Foreign Relations Committee, held nationally televised hearings on the situation in Vietnam. In this respectable forum some senators and witnesses expressed their doubts about the sagacity of American war policy. Within a year Senators Frank Church of Idaho, Eugene McCarthy of Minnesota, George McGovern of South Dakota, Gaylord Nelson of Wisconsin, and Stephen Young of Ohio began to criticize the war.

In early 1967 Eugene McCarthy considered taking the war to the people with a campaign to win the Democratic presidential nomination. Before entering politics McCarthy had been a philosopher, poet, and college professor, and in some respects he retained the aloof intellectualism so often associated — though often mistakenly — with academic life. With his gray hair, intelligent face, and quiet manner of speech, he was a man of ideas more than a man of organizations. He did not especially concern himself with "practical" politics. The main thing was to change people's ideas.

When word began to circulate that McCarthy was considering running against Lyndon Johnson, antiwar activists around the country warmly encouraged him. McCarthy was especially well received on college campuses where he quietly but firmly denounced the war. On November 30, 1967, he announced that he would run. He briefly summarized the costs of the war — 100,000 to 150,000 civilian casualties in South Vietnam, the loss of nearly 110,000 Americans killed or wounded, a monthly American expenditure of $2 billion to $3 billion, the loss of funds available for internal improvements in the United States, the growth of inflation. He was worried too about the psychological costs of the war. "There is growing evidence," he said, "of a deepening moral crisis in America: discontent, frustration, and a disposition to extralegal — if not illegal — manifestations of protest." While stating that he was not for "peace at any price," he called for a "political solution" to the war.

McCarthy's announcement gave heart to the antiwar movement. Doves, who had been frustrated by their lack of political power, felt now that they could do something to change American foreign policy. Few politicians in American history have had less trouble than Eugene McCarthy in finding volunteers to do the busywork of a political campaign: to stuff envelopes, make phone calls, ring doorbells. In winter 1968 some five thousand students converged on New Hampshire, the first primary state, to take part in the McCarthy campaign. Most were from local colleges, but many came from Michigan, California, and other distant states. Many would stay with him until Chicago.

McCarthy was characteristically reticent about the rough-and-tumble of politics. He refused to make the usual courtesy calls on local politicians; he frequently dined alone; and he was once late for a speech because he was enjoying a private conversation with poet Robert Lowell. But when necessary, he could prove himself a man of the people by bowling, riding a snowmobile, and engaging in an old-timer's hockey game.

His opponents claimed that a vote for McCarthy would encourage Communists and draft dodgers. His supporters argued simply that he would end a disastrous war. New Hampshire went to the polls on March 12. Earlier opinion samples had indicated that he would receive 10 to 20 percent of the vote. But McCarthy surprised the pollsters and the Johnson administration by receiving 42.4 percent to the president's 49.5. McCarthy and his followers were ecstatic. They had proved Johnson's vulnerability in a traditionally conservative state. McCarthy began to talk about actually winning the presidential nomination.

The New Hampshire primary forced both Lyndon Johnson and Robert Kennedy to reevaluate their political futures. Kennedy had long since concluded that the war must be ended, and he had been considering a presidential bid for months. He had proved himself an accomplished administrator during his tenure as attorney general under his brother, and he had inherited many of his brother's political supporters. He was also known for his genuine feeling for the underprivileged in America. Whereas other statesmen might philosophically regret the condition of the poor and oppressed, Kennedy's feelings went deeper. He was a natural leader in a movement that associated the Vietnam War with injustice at home. On March 16, four days after McCarthy's fine showing in New Hampshire, Robert Kennedy announced that he was running for president.

Eugene McCarthy was dismayed at Kennedy's apparent opportunism. He had fought the tough fight in the first primary, he reasoned, and now that he had proved Johnson vulnerable, here was Kennedy trying to snatch his prize. When people asked him about Kennedy's candidacy, he frowned and talked about how cold it had been in New Hampshire.

Faced with two strong competitors from his own party, Lyndon Johnson began to reevaluate his candidacy. In three years he had suffered a painful fall from grace. In 1964 and 1965, with most of the country behind him, he had passed his Great Society legislation; improving schools, health care, and minority rights. But the Vietnam War had ruined his popularity. On college campuses students shouted, "Hey, hey, LBJ, how many kids did you kill today?" In Congress, the press, and his administration there were many criticisms of the war. The news from New Hampshire had been bad, but the news from Wisconsin, the next primary state, was even worse. Some ten thousand volunteers for McCarthy were canvasing Wisconsin voters while Johnson's campaign barely stumbled along. The president's headquarters in Madison was an empty shell, whereas McCarthy's office was a flurry of activity.

Johnson was also deeply tired. People who could remember how he had looked in the heyday of his presidency noticed the lines that creased his face and the sickly pallor of his flesh. The strain had been terrible, and the election campaign would be worse. Johnson decided finally that for his own sake, and for the sake of his country, he should withdraw from the race. On March 31, on the eve of the Wisconsin primary, he went on national television to announce, "I shall not seek and I will not accept the nomination of my party for another term as your president." The McCarthyites in Wisconsin were delighted. They had forced the president to withdraw from the contest. But they still had to face Robert Kennedy.

Kennedy won in Indiana and Nebraska but lost in Oregon. Then came California. Kennedy swept through the state carrying his concern for the disadvantaged and his opposition to the war to college campuses, the black ghettos, and the great Central Valley. Everywhere he attracted huge, enthusiastic crowds. People pressed in upon him seeking a handshake, a glance, a word. McCarthy, too, traveled widely in the state, offering his image of calm rectitude as an alternative to the charismatic, almost messianic appeal of Kennedy.

On June 6, the day of the primary, Kennedy relaxed with his family at a friend's beach home by the Pacific. He walked along the beach, swam with his children, and talked with friends. In the evening he went to a boisterous party at his campaign suite at the Ambassador Hotel in Los Angeles. Early predictions showed him leading McCarthy by 10 percent. Satisfied that he had won, Kennedy went downstairs to the hotel ballroom to make a brief victory speech to his followers. "What I think is quite clear," he said, "is that we can work together in the last analysis." The divisions in American society could be healed, he said, "whether it's between blacks and whites, between the poor and the more affluent, or between age groups or on the war in Vietnam."

Nearby in the hotel kitchen a young Arab nationalist, Sirhan Sirhan, did not join in the cheering for Kennedy. Angered at Kennedy's views on Israel, he waited for his chance. The door to the kitchen opened, and Kennedy walked in with a group of friends, taking a deadly shortcut out of the hotel ballroom. A second later Robert Kennedy was lying on the kitchen floor in a pool of blood. He died a few hours later.

The year 1968 had already been a turbulent one. The Vietnam War had taken a turn for the worse. President Johnson had been forced to abandon his reelection campaign. On April 4 Martin Luther King, Jr., had been assassinated after telling supporters in Memphis the night before that he had "been to the mountain top . . . and seen the promised land." After these shocks, Kennedy's death seemed to confirm the bleak visions of America's gloomy critics. Among the young and the disadvantaged there was a feeling that the forces of darkness were destroying their people and their dreams.

After June 6 the Kennedy forces scattered. Some joined McCarthy; others supported George McGovern, who announced his candidacy only two weeks before the convention; the rest gave their support to Hubert Humphrey. The vice president had announced his own candidacy in April but declined to enter any primaries, preferring to rely on the political professionals in nonprimary states, who would tend to support him as the president's chosen successor.

Humphrey's record of support for civil rights and social welfare measures was unmatched by any other living politician. A veteran of many years in the Senate, he was popular with labor. But his association with Lyndon Johnson spoiled his reputation with the antiwar Democrats, and McCarthy ran ahead of Humphrey in many state popularity polls.

Nonetheless, as the convention drew near, it was Humphrey who had the largest slate of delegates, perhaps as many as fifteen hundred, more than enough to win the nomination. Among the idealistic followers of McCarthy and Kennedy, the process seemed unfair. They had gone to the people with their cause and had won a great popular following. Then an assassin had destroyed one of the antiwar candidates, and the political professionals had ruined the chances of another. What could they do?

In late August, delegates and demonstrators began to arrive in Chicago for the Democratic Convention. The delegates had been chosen in local elections and caucuses. The demonstrators were self-selecting. Eugene McCarthy had urged his youthful campaign workers to stay home. But other voices were urging dissidents from across the country to meet in Chicago. David Dellinger, chairman of the National Mobilization Committee to End the War in Vietnam, called for five hundred thousand war protesters, and hoped for at least one hundred thousand.

In the week before the convention some twenty to thirty thousand dissidents began arriving in Chicago, fewer than Dellinger had hoped for but more than enough to disrupt the convention. They were not, strictly speaking, under anyone's command. Dellinger, a fifty-three-year-old veteran of antiwar protests, organized some protest activities. But the protesters themselves — a diverse group consisting of McCarthy campaigners, concerned doves and civil rights workers, pseudorevolutionary activists, and culturally alienated hippies — acknowledged no leader. They were often lumped together by the press as Yippies for lack of another name. Many of them slept in Grant Park near the Hilton, the major convention hotel. They symbolized, in their persons, the nation's troubled disaffection with the Vietnam War. Walking among them in Grant Park, one reporter would detect a bunch of bearded and doped-up social misfits; another would see the passionate idealism of American youth. Like the war itself, the protesters aroused different feelings in different observers.

Two of the most influential youth leaders in Grant Park were Tom Hayden and Rennie Davis, founders of the militant Students for a Democratic Society. Hayden, a veteran of confrontation politics, carried several disguises so that he could elude the police. He expressed the more radical aims of the dissidents in a speech to eight thousand followers when he declared that the whole city had to be "so disrupted it begins to charge around like a mad dog."

The Yippies first captured national attention on Friday, August 23, several days before the beginning of the convention, when they staged their own mini-convention in Grant Park and attempted to nominate a swine — whom they called Pigasus — as president. The Chicago police were not amused by this satire on American politics and "arrested" the unfortunate pig. Thereupon the demonstrators christened a handy sow Mrs. Pigasus and offered her as their candidate.

While such activities on the Chicago streets were making news, final preparations were under way for the Democratic Convention. Mayor Richard Daley was determined to maintain order in his city. The son of a workingman and a Chicago native, he was fiercely proud of his town. He had worked his way up through the local Democratic machine and first won his mayoral office in 1955. Having been reelected three times, he was probably the best-known mayor in the United States. A proud man, he had fought hard to have his party's convention in Chicago, and now he would prove that he could maintain order. In cooperation with President Johnson he prepared for the event as a general might plan for battle. His 11,900 police officers were to be on twelve-hour shifts during the convention. Housing was ready for 7,500 additional National Guardsmen, and army bases in Colorado, Oklahoma, and Texas were on the alert to send more troops if needed. A high chain-link fence surrounded the convention site; manholes inside the fence were sealed to thwart saboteurs; and security men prowled catwalks ninety-five feet above the convention floor to prevent mischief.

While Daley and the Yippies were preparing for confrontation, the Democratic platform committee argued about the party's position on the war. The majority, loyal to Lyndon Johnson, favored a war plank calling, in essence, for continuation of current policy. It renounced unilateral withdrawal, supported the current Paris peace talks, and called for a halt in the bombing of North Vietnam only if the safety of American soldiers could be ensured. This was Hubert Humphrey's position. The platform committee doves drafted an alternative plank calling for an immediate end to the bombing, withdrawal of American and North Vietnamese forces from the South, and a coalition government of South Vietnamese Communists and non-Communists. McCarthy, McGovern, and their supporters favored this minority plank. The convention as a whole would make the final choice.

When the convention convened on Monday, August 26, Hubert Humphrey seemed assured of winning the nomination. But despite his apparent command of delegate strength, he was insecure. Lyndon Johnson was behaving strangely. During the summer the president had frequently belittled Humphrey, calling him old-fashioned and weak. "He cries too much," Johnson told one reporter. The president was in command of the convention machinery and seemed eager to make Humphrey aware that he was not his own man. The vice-president even had to send someone to get in line each morning with other ticket hunters to get convention seats for his family. There were rumors that the president, who stayed in Texas during the convention, planned to snatch back the nomination when Humphrey faltered.

Edward Kennedy presented another problem. The last and youngest Kennedy brother, he was favored by many of Robert's former supporters. And Eugene McCarthy, realizing his chances were, as he put it, "zero," would support Kennedy in order to block Humphrey, although the young Massachusetts senator, still grieving deeply over the loss of his brother, was unwilling to encourage a draft Kennedy campaign. The threat of Kennedy's entry into the race, however, actually helped Humphrey win the nomination. The southern delegates, who might have spearheaded a draft Lyndon Johnson movement, were frightened by the prospect of Kennedy, whose views on the war and civil rights differed so greatly from their own. They fell in behind Humphrey, and by Tuesday, the day before the voting for the candidates, it was clear that the vice-president would win.

On Wednesday, August 27, the Democrats debated the Vietnam War planks. Speakers for the majority position spoke about national honor and the safety of American "boys" in Vietnam. They presented a taped statement by Gen. Creighton Abrams, American commander in Vietnam, arguing that if the United States stopped bombing North Vietnam, the Communists would find it much easier to supply their forces. Speakers for the minority position argued that the war hurt America without helping Vietnam. Paul O'Dwyer, a New York senatorial candidate and one of the war's most outspoken critics, claimed that the Kennedy-McCarthy primary victories showed that millions of Americans believed "that the war is unconscionably cruel, that it is highly immoral, that it is disastrously wasteful, that it is unbelievably savage."

The issue required almost three hours of often acrimonious debate. In the end it was put to a vote, and as expected, the war plank carried by a 3 to 2 majority. The antiwar delegates, especially large groups from California and New York, stood on their chairs and sang "We Shall Overcome." While other delegates filed out of the convention hall for the dinner break, several hundred doves wrapped black crepe around their flags and chanted "Stop the War" and "We Want Peace." The official band in the gallery tried to drown them out with cheery music. "We Got a Lot of Living," played the band. "We Shall Overcome," sang the peace delegates.

Band: "I'm Looking Over a Four-Leaf Clover."

Doves: "We Shall Overcome."

Band: "If You Knew Suzy, Like I Know Suzy."

Doves: "The Battle Hymn of the Republic."

Finally the band left the hall. The peace delegates marched around the auditorium, among them civil rights leader Charles Evers, economist John Kenneth Galbraith, and playwright Arthur Miller. They prayed, sang, and chanted slogans. But beneath this show of bravado they knew they had lost.

In the streets the Yippies soon learned that the peace plank had been voted down. During the past few days they had held marches and demonstrations. Now they moved through the streets with new determination. In the early evening a crowd of some two to three thousand demonstrators gathered outside the Hilton Hotel. Nearby stood hundreds of helmeted policemen, armed with clubs. From hotel rooms above the streets, other dissidents leaned out of the windows, jeered at the officers, and threw bottles. Then the policemen began to move into the crowd, clubs swinging, and the street was a chaos of blows, cries, and shouts. Some of the injured demonstrators escaped to the McCarthy headquarters in the hotel, and his workers bandaged them with torn sheets and pillow cases. In a few minutes two hundred demonstrators were arrested and a hundred Yippies and policemen were injured.

In a hotel room twenty-five floors above the street Hubert Humphrey was above the noise of violence. But he could not escape its influence. In his crowded suite he and his supporters watched television as the convention, now reconvened, began to choose its candidate. The process that should have been a simple triumph for Humphrey was shattered by reports of the violence outside the hotel. The televised reports cut back and forth from the convention to the violence in the streets. On the convention floor, delegates learned what had happened through their portable television sets. Senator Abraham Ribicoff of Connecticut, having a chance to address the crowd, denounced the "Gestapo tactics in the streets of Chicago." The police actions, following upon the bitter defeat of the war plank, confirmed the belief that America had been corrupted and brutalized by the Vietnam War. In his suite Hubert Humphrey maintained his composure for the benefit of photographers, reporters, and friends. But he felt sick at the realization that his nomination would appear to have come about through violence. Finally the convention settled down, and the nomination procedure continued. The vice-president's supporters prevailed on the first ballot. The next day Hubert Humphrey appeared before the bitterly divided convention to accept his tarnished prize.

Humphrey did not win the presidency in 1968. Alabama Governor George Wallace, running as a prowar third party candidate, swept the Deep South, and Richard Nixon, the Republican nominee, picked up enough of the remaining states to have a commanding lead in the electoral college. It is tempting to conclude that the Chicago Democratic Convention had ruined Humphrey's chances. But the election turned on many factors. Both Humphrey and Nixon spoke vaguely about peace and honor in Vietnam. Many people voted for Nixon because they wanted a change. Even then, he won by a narrow margin, less than 1 percent.

Events at Chicago did less to change American politics than to symbolize the turbulence and agony of the Vietnam era. In 1968 the American conscience was badly divided. Some Americans honestly believed that their country's involvement in Southeast Asia would benefit Vietnam, the United States, and democracy. Others believed genuinely that the issues in Vietnam could best be settled by the Vietnamese themselves. The hawks won in 1968, and Americans fought in Vietnam for almost five more years. Finally, the United States negotiated a settlement that allowed disengagement of United States troops in 1973. The independent South Vietnamese government survived for two more years. Then in 1975 the Communists overran the country in a brief struggle and completed the unification anticipated by Ho Chi Minh thirty years before.

By then Vietnam was a remote land again, and America's attention had turned to other issues. It was difficult to remember that a few years before the war had cut through the fabric of American life like a sword plunged into the breast.

QUESTIONS

1. Summarize the main events in America's relationship with Vietnam between 1945 and 1963. Why did the United States support first French colonialism and then the Bao Dai and Diem regimes?

2. Why did the United States begin to escalate its intervention in Vietnam after 1964? Why did so few congressmen oppose escalation?

3. Why did doves oppose the Vietnam War? In what ways did they disagree with hawks about Vietnamese history, the domino theory, and the value to Vietnam of American assistance?

4. Describe the protest movement against the war.

5. How did the opposition to the Vietnam War relate to other kinds of current discontent in American society and culture?

6. What were the strengths and weaknesses of each of these 1968 presidential candidates: Lyndon Johnson, Hubert Humphrey, Eugene McCarthy, and Robert Kennedy?

7. Who were the Yippies and what was their influence on the Democratic Convention?

8. Why was Hubert Humphrey's triumph in Chicago a "tarnished prize"?

BIBLIOGRAPHY

DICKSTEIN, MORRIS. *Gates of Eden* (1977). History of the cultural rebellion in the 1960s.

FITZGERALD, FRANCES. *Fire in the Lake: The Vietnamese and the Americans in Vietnam* (1972). Sensitive account of the effect of the war on American and Vietnamese peoples.

HALBERSTAM, DAVID. *The Best and the Brightest* (1972). Explores how State Department personnel developed Vietnam policy.

HERRING, GEORGE C. *America's Longest War* (1968). Surveys American involvement in Vietnam, 1950–1975.

JOHNSON, LYNDON BAINES. *The Vantage Point* (1971). Johnson's autobiographical account of his presidency.

KEARNS, DORIS. *Lyndon Johnson and the American Dream* (1976). Perceptive biography based on close observation of the president.

KOVIC, RON. *Born on the Fourth of July* (1976). A soldier's forthright account of his youthful longing for martial glory, the brutality of war, and his injury by enemy fire.

MCCARTHY, EUGENE. *The Year of the People* (1969). Autobiographical account of the McCarthy campaign,

POWERS, THOMAS. *The War at Home* (1973). History of the American antiwar movement.

SCHLESINGER, ARTHUR M., JR. *Robert Kennedy and His Times* (1978). Intimate and exhaustive portrait of Robert Kennedy.

SHEEHAN, NEIL. *A Bright Shining Lie* (1988). Vivid account of John Paul Vann, critic and hero of the Vietnam War.

SUMMERS, HARRY G., JR. *On Strategy: A Critical Analysis of the Vietnam War* (1985). Influential critique of the political and military facets of American involvement in Vietnam.

VIORST, MILTON. *Fire in the Streets: America in the 1960s* (1980). Fourteen biographical sketches illustrating the civil rights and antiwar movements.

WHITE, THEODORE H. *The Making of the President: 1968* (1969). Fine narrative history of the 1968 campaign.

13

THE NEW COMPUTER AGE

Bill Gates and Microsoft

The computer industry is the fastest growing business in the world. In 1960 there were roughly 10,000 data-processing computers in operation. The number reached 100 million by 1990. Experts predict that by the year 2000 worldwide, the computer industry will be second only to agriculture in revenue. While falling behind in other areas, such as automobile manufacture, the United States has led the world at almost every stage in the development of the modern computer and computer software. In 1990 the American computer industry was the largest in the world, employing one million people and producing $100 billion in revenues. U.S. citizens owned about half of the world's computers, 50 million in all. The success of Bill Gates in establishing Microsoft as the world's preeminent software manufacturer illustrates the charac-teristics of inventiveness and entrepreneurship that made possible the creation of a new industry.

O n a December morning in 1974 a young man named Paul Allen
was browsing through magazines in Harvard Square, when he
caught sight of the current issue of *Popular Mechanics*. On the cover was
a story about a computer kit, called the Altair 8080, marketed by a small
company in Albuquerque, New Mexico. Allen ran across campus to find
his friend Bill Gates. In one version of a conversation that has become a
legend in the computer industry, Allen shouted to Gates, "Look, it's
going to happen! I told you this was going to happen, and we're going
to miss it!" Gates was 19 at the time; Allen was 21.

Bill Gates and Paul Allen, who had been friends since childhood in
Seattle, Washington, were members of a fledgling American community of computer enthusiasts. Until the Altair, which actually went on
the market in 1975, the only computers in the world had been large,
expensive machines owned by governments and businesses. Throughout the United States, however, a few thousand young Americans like
Gates and Allen acquired a degree of computer literacy by experimenting with computers at school or at work. Many dreamed of a time when
they could have their own machines.

With the introduction of the Altair, people drove through the
night to buy a computer. One man arrived in Albuquerque with his
trailer, and camped for several weeks, waiting for his machine. The
hobbyists, as they were called, soon formed clubs and held national
meetings. For the computer enthusiasts of the mid-1970s, the Altair was
a godsend. Years later Bill Gates recalled, "What excited us more than
the kit itself was the realization that the personal computer miracle was
going to happen." Eager to be involved, Gates and Allen adopted a
strategy that made their fortunes and accelerated the computer revolution. They decided to make "software" for the Altair.

Fifteen years later in 1990 Bill Gates, then in his mid-30s, was the
youngest billionaire in the United States. Two years and several billion
dollars later, he was the wealthiest man in America. When the Seattle
Mariners baseball team was up for sale for roughly $100 million, and
Northwesterners feared they would lose their team, a local journalist
noted that Gates could afford to buy the team *sixty* times over. Nonetheless, Gates demurred, explaining that his business was computer software, not baseball.

Although his life and Andrew Carnegie's are separated by more
than a century, Gates's career begs comparison with that of the great
nineteenth-century steel magnate. In real dollars, Gates's fortune is
roughly equal to Carnegie's when Carnegie turned from steel manufacture to philanthropy. Certainly, there are differences. Carnegie was a
poor immigrant; Gates is the son of a prominent Seattle attorney.
Carnegie dealt in heavy iron bars; Gates sells feather-light computer

programs. But the similarities are striking. Each supplied a product vital to American growth. Each man, though a genius in his own right, depended on the inventions of other brilliant entrepreneurs — who in turn depended on him. Each had the vision to map out for himself a crucial role in an emerging world of business and technology. Seeing a new era of railroads, skyscrapers, and bridges, Andrew Carnegie recognized the need for good inexpensive steel. Envisioning a new age of computer electronics, Bill Gates recognized the need for software to help the machines run.

One of the remarkable features of Bill Gates's career — shared with other pioneers of the computer revolution — is that he grew up in an age when American entrepreneurship was thought to be dead. During the 1950s and 1960s, the idea of "the organization man" became a cliché. The typical American businessman was said to be the servant of convention, from his "grey flannel suit" to his unimaginative and slavish devotion to the company. Americans looked back with nostalgia to the robust age of Thomas Edison and Andrew Carnegie, when it had been possible for a young person with "luck and pluck" to invent wonderful devices and create new industries. Conventional wisdom held that an Edison or a Carnegie would not stand a chance in modern America. No one could create a new company to manufacture automobiles or steel. The business world was controlled by the giant corporations.

During the 1970s and 1980s, however, something happened that virtually no one had anticipated: the computer revolution. Bill Gates was one of a group of inventors and entrepreneurs who upset the notion that there could be nothing new under the sun in the world of American business. Like the industrial pioneers of the nineteenth century, the new computer wizards looked at the world, imagined new possibilities, and brought them into being.

The origins of the computer can be traced back hundreds, even thousands, of years. The early history of mechanical computing begins with the Greeks, who used pebbles to make calculations. In about 500 B.C. Babylonians strung counters on wires, mounted on a frame. This invention, the abacus, was popular in Egypt, India, and China. In 1642 Blaise Pascal, a 19-year-old French scientist, devised a calculator consisting of wheels and cogs. The machine was intended to help his father, a French official, and worked like a modern odometer. It was not popular in seventeenth-century France, however, because the elder Pascal's fellow clerks feared that it would put them out of work.

The nineteenth-century British inventor Charles Babbage first envisioned the modern computer. He called his device an "analytical engine." Babbage envisioned a machine with 50,000 moving parts —

thousands of wheels, levers, and belts, working together in perfect unison. Babbage worked on the idea for 40 years, and built a simple model, but the craftsmen of that age were unable to machine the parts required for the analytical engine. Moreover, the device would have been the size of a football field and would have required six steam engines for power. Babbage's machine was forgotten until 1937, when his writings were rediscovered.

The first person to build a working computer was an American, Herman Hollerith, who developed a calculating machine during the 1880s. The U.S. government, fearing that it would take a decade to tabulate the 1890 census, sponsored a competition to develop a machine to help with the census. Hollerith won. His machines used cards with holes punched to indicate data on topics such as age, sex, marital status, race, and occupation. The machines substantially reduced the time required to analyze the census.

Hollerith founded the Tabulating Machine Company in 1896. During the next few years, it went through several mergers and was finally absorbed into a company that in 1924 adopted the name International Business Machines Corporation (IBM). IBM's punch-card machines, the successors to Hollerith's computers, were the dominant business information system until the 1960s. In comparison to modern computers, however, they were slow and unreliable.

A much more promising technology had its inception during the 1930s, with the application of the binary numbering system to computing. The binary system, which uses only the digits 0 and 1, seems cumbersome. To represent a 2, you move a column to the left, as in the decimal system to create the number ten. So in the binary system, two is represented by 10. Three is 11, four is 100, five is 101, six is 110, seven is 111, and eight is 1000. A nineteenth-century British mathematician, George Boole, devised a system of mathematics — "Boolean Algebra" — using only 0 and 1.

Boolean Algebra was simply an arcane branch of mathematics, until two American physicists, John V. Atanasoff and Clifford Berry, noted that the binary system could easily be represented in electrical circuits, which were switched either on or off, representing 0 or 1. The modern computer term "bit," for one on-off switch, is derived from the binary system. A bit is a *b*inary dig*it*. In early computers, bits were shuttled around within the computer eight at a time. Clusters of eight bits came to be known as "bytes."

Bits and bytes are the building materials of the modern computer programs. Each byte is a cluster of eight switches that can be either on or off. All together there are 256 possible permutations, or arrangements, of eight switches. In word processing, these 256 possibilities are used to represent characters, including lower- and uppercase letters from A to Z, accented letters, spaces, and tabs. The standard binary code for the letter "A," for example, is 01000001.

Such possibilities grow out of combinations of switches that are either on or off. In sufficient quantity, switches can also be used to represent other information, such as computerized drawings. In such a case the switches are used to tell dots on a screen whether they should be black or white, or even what color they should represent. The first computers lacked the capacity, however, to undertake such complex activities. They were huge in size, but minuscule in capacity compared to modern computers.

With World War II, scientists in Germany, England, and the United States devised computers using the binary system. Howard Aiken, a Harvard mathematician, worked with IBM engineers to develop the Harvard-IBM Automatic Sequence Controlled Calculator, later called the Mark I. Using 3,304 on-off switches, it created ballistic tables used by naval artillery. The British developed a computer using vacuum tubes instead of switches that they used to decode German messages.

After the war, two Americans, John W. Mauchly and J. Presper Eckert, Jr., created the first general-purpose computer, known as the Electronic Numerical Integrator and Calculator (ENIAC). Weighing 30 tons, it contained 17,468 vacuum tubes, connected by 500 miles of wire. The ENIAC occupied 1,500 square feet, and was housed at the University of Pennsylvania. Its vacuum tubes were an improvement over earlier computers that used electromechanical relays as switches, but ENIAC was temperamental, functioning only in short bursts. When it worked, it could perform 5,000 simple calculations per second. This was 1,000 times faster than the Mark I, but much slower than the modern personal computer.

To perform new operations ENIAC had to be rewired by hand, like the wire and plug connections made on an old telephone switchboard, a process that took several days. According to a computer legend, one day ENIAC would not function, and could not be fixed until someone found a moth caught in the machine — the origin of the computer term "bug."

A new stage in computer sophistication came with the UNIVAC I, which beat out an IBM competitor for a Census Bureau contract in 1951. It became the world's first commercially distributed computer. In 1952 a UNIVAC I was used to tabulate the results of the American presidential election. The machine astonished the country by accurately predicting the overwhelming victory of Dwight David Eisenhower only 45 minutes after the polls closed. In fact the UNIVAC worked so fast, and its prediction of an Eisenhower landslide was so unanticipated that the TV network using it suspected a flaw and fudged the figures, announcing a lesser margin of victory than the computer had indicated. Later it turned out that the computer had been right.

Vacuum-tube computers were notoriously unreliable — the tubes often overheated and failed. So the next step in computer evolution came with the introduction of the transistor in 1947, developed by three scientists at Bell Labs. Fortunately for the growth of the computer industry, transistors came to be made from silicon, an inexpensive substance taken from sand. Smaller than a vacuum tube, transistors were also faster, cheaper, and more reliable. They revolutionized many branches of electronics besides computing, including radio and television.

During the late 1950s the invention of the integrated circuit allowed many transistors to be connected on a silicon chip. Developed simultaneously by Jack Kilby of Texas Instruments and Robert Noyce of Fairchild Semiconductor, the microchip was the fundamental ingredient of the modern computer. Over time, engineers were able to increase the number of electronic components on a chip. By 1990 they could manufacture chips with one million transistors on a surface area of one square inch. It may eventually be possible to place as many as ten million electronic components on a microchip the size of a fingernail.

Another essential element of the modern computer arrived in 1971 when the central processing unit (CPU) of the computer was put on a silicon chip. This device, the microprocessor, was invented by American engineer Ted Hoff. The first such chip was known as the Intel 4004. It and subsequent variations are the essential component in the computer. They can be programmed for a variety of tasks from running a watch to steering a spacecraft.

By the 1970s microchips and microprocessors had reduced the cost of computing, but no one had yet built a computer for general consumption. In 1974 Micro Instrumentation Telemetry Systems of Albuquerque, New Mexico, brought computers one step closer to the general public by introducing the first personal computer. This was the Altair 8800, the machine that propelled Bill Gates into the computer revolution.

In 1974 Bill Gates was not yet old enough to buy a six-pack of beer, but he was already a veteran computer programmer and entrepreneur. Born on October 28, 1955, in Seattle, he showed signs of his genius before he was out of grade school. Even his more critical biographers seem mesmerized by a certain energy that Bill Gates showed early in life. Just as medieval hagiographers traced the piety of saints to their infancy,

Gates's biographers have found unusual qualities even in his early life. In his fourth-grade class, Bill Gates submitted a 30-page report when only five pages were required. As an 11-year old he memorized the Sermon on the Mount. In high school he scored 800 on the college boards in math.

In the 1960s, as he was growing up, Gates did not have the easy access to computers common to students a generation later. The technological assets of the typical American household usually included a television set and a record player, but there were no VCRs, CD players, pocket calculators, Nintendo games, or personal computers. The idea that computers would one day appear in American households was inconceivable only a few years ago.

Bill Gates's first contact with a computer came at Lakeside School in Seattle in 1968. At that time, computers were far too expensive for a high school to own, but Lakeside bought time on a PDP-10 computer, located in downtown Seattle. Manufactured by Digital Equipment Corporation, the PDP-10 was a "minicomputer," about the size of a refrigerator. It was linked to Lakeside by Teletype. One spring afternoon Gates's math teacher, Paul Stocklin, took his class to the "computer room." Gates typed a few words into the Teletype, and watched enthusiastically as it printed a reply from the computer. His teacher later recalled, "I knew more than he did for the first day, but only for the first day."

At Lakeside, Gates made friends with Paul Allen, his future partner in founding Microsoft. The two students shared an insatiable appetite for computers. While other students were absorbed in dating and sports, Gates and Allen were obsessed with computers. "We were off in our own world," Gates remembered. "Nobody quite understood the thing but us. I wanted to figure out exactly what it could do." Among their discoveries was the fact that the PDP-10 included a program for playing chess. Gates and Allen soon exhausted the Lakeside computer budget.

Ironically, a software malfunction paved the way for the two students to acquire more computer time for free. The PDP-10 was frequently "down" because of its many bugs. Gates himself crashed it once simply because he typed in a program name that was too long. The company that owned the PDP-10 offered to let Gates and Allen use the computer in the evenings and on weekends for free if they would simply keep track of what they had done each time it crashed. The two students suddenly had the chance to become "hard-core" computer users. Bill Gates was then a 13-year-old eighth-grader.

As a high school student Gates showed an unusual aptitude for computers, but possibly even more important for his later career, he also showed promise as an entrepreneur. In 1971, when Gates was a junior, he and Paul Allen created a company called Traf-O-Data. At any moment across the United States hundreds of metal boxes were busily recording traffic on counting devices stretched across the roadway. Gates and Allen figured out a way to analyze the data by computer. They made about $20,000 from Traf-O-Data. They might have made much more, but the U.S. government entered the business, offering traffic data analysis for free.

During Bill Gates's senior year, he took a leave from Lakeside so that he could work on a project to help computerize the Bonneville Power Administration, which controlled much of the electrical power from dams along the Columbia River. The company hired teenagers Gates and Allen for the project because they knew about their work in tracking down bugs in the PDP-10. That summer Gates and Allen talked about founding their own software company.

In 1973 Bill Gates entered Harvard University. At college his work habits were legendary. He would stay awake for 36 hours, sleep for 10, then eat a pizza and go back to work. Under pressure, he was reputed to work for as many as three days at a stretch without sleep. He put some of that time into classwork, but many more hours into computers. During his freshman year, he worked on a computer baseball game. Gates taught the computer to portray baseball players on the screen, hitting, throwing and catching. One night he was overheard talking about the program in his sleep, "One comma, one comma, one comma. . . ."

Like most of the leaders of the computer revolution, Bill Gates learned a lot about computers by writing and playing computer games. At Harvard's Aiken Computer Center (named for the genius of the Mark I), Gates played games such as "space wars" on a PDP-10 computer. He also read books and magazines about corporate law and business management. Despite his achievements at Harvard, Bill Gates felt a sense of ennui while at school, uncertain about his future career. He considered mathematics and law, but his real gift was computers. So on that December day when Paul Allen saw the *Popular Mechanics* article on the Altair 8080, Gates was ready for a new challenge.

Ed Roberts, the father of the Altair, was typical of the hobbyists who fueled the computer revolution. He was an electronics buff who joined the Air Force to learn more about the field. In Albuquerque he founded a company called Model Instrumentations and Telemetry Systems (MITS), which he operated out of his garage. At first Roberts sold mail-order model rocket equipment and radio transmitters for model planes. In 1969 he moved MITS into a building previously occupied by a restaurant. MITS became the first company in the United States to sell calculator kits. Roberts's profits soared, but then Texas

Instruments and other companies began manufacturing calculators, and MITS was in trouble.

At that point, when his fortunes looked bleak, Ed Roberts made an audacious decision. He would build a personal computer and sell it for $397. In retrospect a few years later, after millions of personal computers had been sold across the United States, Roberts's decision seemed like a safe bet. But in 1974 computer manufacturers were building machines designed for big business and government. Companies like IBM could no more imagine selling to a mass market than the Boeing Corporation today would envision building airplanes to fit in the family garage.

The brain of Roberts's machine was an Intel microprocessor, the 8080 chip, which came on the market in early 1974. Normally the chip would sell for $350, but Roberts persuaded Intel to sell them for $75 apiece. His 12-year-old daughter suggested the name "Altair" from a star visited by the *Enterprise* on "Star Trek." Roberts himself coined the term that soon became a household word, "personal computing." He later recalled, "I was trying to convey a small machine you could afford to buy that didn't sound like a toy."

By the standards of a few years later, the Altair was a primitive machine. Buyers paid $397 for their computer, unassembled. After they put it together, they had to work the machine with switches rather than a keyboard. It had no permanent memory — no floppy disks or hard drive; so if the power went out, the user had to begin all over. The typical Altair had a random access memory of about 2000 bytes, or 2K. In contrast, the 1991 Hewlett-Packard palmtop computer, smaller than a paperback book, had more than 250 times the memory of the Altair, cost less in real dollars, featured a keyboard, and came fully assembled.

One of the Altair's limitations was that it came without software. Most fundamentally, it needed language software. A computer language provides an easy way for a user to instruct a machine to operate in a particular way, that is, to program it. Over the years, many languages had been developed for computers. One of the most popular was Beginner's All-purpose Symbolic Instruction Code, or BASIC, developed by two Dartmouth College professors, John Kemeny and Thomas Kurtz, in the mid-1960s. It had proven useful to people working with large computers such as the PDP-10, but it was unclear whether BASIC could be adapted to a machine with such a small capacity as the Altair 8080.

In Cambridge, Massachusetts, Bill Gates and Paul Allen thought they could solve the puzzle, and called Ed Roberts at MITS to tell him so. It turned out that dozens of other callers had made the same claim. Roberts said he was willing to work with whoever could actually deliver the product. Gates and Allen went to work at Harvard's computer center, laboring day and night for eight weeks refining BASIC for the Altair. Gates would fall asleep at the keyboard, wake up, and continue working. Or he would take a catnap behind the PDP-10.

In February 1975 Gates and Allen decided their program was ready. Allen flew to Albuquerque to meet Ed Roberts. He may have pictured MITS as a company with an impressive corporate headquarters. So he was disappointed to find that MITS was located in a shopping mall with a massage parlor on one side and a laundromat on the other. He was pleased, however, to find that the Altair at MITS headquarters had a paper tape reader. Otherwise he would have had to enter BASIC into the computer by flipping the toggle switches on the front of the machine roughly 30,000 times, all in the right sequence.

Paul Allen had never seen an Altair before. He had no way of knowing for certain whether the program would work until the morning after he arrived, when he tested it in front of Ed Roberts, his prospective customer. Allen fed the program into the computer, then anxiously entered the command, "print 2 + 2." The Altair answered, "4." "I was pretty stunned myself that it worked the first time," Allen later admitted. With that humble beginning, Paul Allen and Bill Gates were on their way to creating a billion-dollar software company.

Ed Roberts was impressed: "I was dazzled. It was certainly impressive. The Altair was a complex system, and they had never seen it before." Using BASIC, Allen then ran a computer game, a lunar landing program. This was the first software ever run on what came to be known as Microsoft BASIC. When Allen returned to Boston, he and Gates, not yet old enough to drink, celebrated over ice cream and 7 Up.

That spring Paul Allen went to work in Albuquerque as MITS software director. Bill Gates completed his academic year at Harvard, then joined his friend for the summer. They created a company called MicroSoft, for *Micro*computer *Soft*ware — the capital "S" in soft was later dropped. Based on their respective contributions to developing BASIC, they agreed to a 64/36 split, with Gates having the major share. In a separate agreement MITS agreed to pay Microsoft $30 for each copy of BASIC sold with the Altair.

For a few months the Altair was at the center of the personal computer revolution. It was a catalyst for meetings of computer fans across the country, and in many cities, clubs were formed where enthusiasts could trade ideas. One of these was the Homebrew Club, founded in March 1975 in Menlo Park, California. Two of its members, Steve Wozniak and Steve Jobs, dissatisfied with the Altair, would soon found their own company, which they would call Apple.

Bill Gates first came to the attention of many of these computer buffs as a cranky young man complaining about their "piracy" of his software. Microsoft had developed a good version of BASIC, but more copies were being copied for free than sold. This is a problem that plagues the software industry to this day. In some countries, copies of Microsoft products, complete with the standard packaging and literature, are manufactured and sold as the real product, with no payment going to Microsoft. In 1975, seeing the potential profits for Microsoft vanishing, Gates published an article entitled, "An Open Letter to Hobbyists."

In the letter Gates was alternately whining and persuasive. "Is this fair?" he complained. But the letter was more than a lament for profits lost. It was a farsighted analysis of the danger of piracy to the infant software industry and to computer users themselves. "One thing you can do is prevent good software from being written," he argued. "Who can afford to do professional work for nothing. . . . Nothing would please me more than being able to hire ten programmers, and deluge the hobby market with good software." The point may seem obvious in retrospect, but at the time it ran contrary to the dominant philosophy of the thousands of computer hobbyists, who like Gates and Allen were pioneers in the personal computer revolution. In his book *Hackers,* Steven Levy summarizes their philosophy: "At the heart of the problem was one of the central tenets of the Hacker Ethic: the free flow of information, particularly information that helped fellow hackers understand, explore, and build systems."

Bill Gates repeated his attack on the hacker ethic in a speech at a computer convention sponsored by Altair in 1976. When he stepped to the microphone, he was barely 20 years old, known better for his shrill denunciation of computer pirates than for his role in developing the new BASIC. His disheveled hair, his too-large glasses, and his high-pitched voice accentuated his youth. Yet his speech impressed many in the audience. One computer magazine editor recalled agreeing with young Gates, "How do you get your money back?"

Ironically BASIC piracy actually helped Gates and Allen in the long run. At the infancy of personal computing, a Microsoft product found its way — partly by sale and partly by theft — to thousands of users. Computer enthusiasts became accustomed to using Microsoft BASIC. In a later version, the product became the industry standard, complete with royalties duly paid.

In 1976 Microsoft acquired two important customers for BASIC, National Cash Register and General Electric. Microsoft's revenues in 1976 were $100,000, enough to persuade Gates to drop out of Harvard after the fall semester. The next challenge facing the inventors of BASIC was in the arena of business negotiation rather than computer programming. Although Microsoft was an independent company, its fortunes were closely tied to those of Altair. Their contract limited them to selling BASIC to companies that were not business rivals to MITS. For a short time the Altair dominated the personal computer industry, but the machine was badly flawed, and big companies like Tandy and Commodore were entering the market with their own computers. Gates and Allen would have liked to sell BASIC to these and other companies, but MITS blocked their efforts. A potential giant of a software company was held in check by a small and declining hardware manufacturer. Microsoft revenues declined to a trickle.

Fortunately for Microsoft, Ed Roberts then sold MITS to another company, Pertec, which apparently underestimated the scruffy youngsters of Microsoft. Pertec sent a letter to Gates and Allen saying that it would no longer allow BASIC to be sold to any other companies because it considered all others as business rivals. This was contrary to an original contract by which MITS had agreed to make its "best efforts" to find suitable markets for BASIC. After three intense weeks of hearings before an arbitrator, a decision was rendered freeing Microsoft from the MITS agreement. Orders poured into the now independent software company.

In 1977 Microsoft licensed BASIC to Tandy, for its new computer, the TRS-80, and to Apple, for the Apple II. Bill Gates was on the way to realizing a dream, marketing a product that eventually could accompany any personal computer in the world. "We set the standard" became Microsoft's motto.

As time passed, Bill Gates's proficiency as entrepreneur was more in demand at Microsoft than his skill as computer programmer. Other bright young programmers came to Albuquerque to develop new versions of BASIC and other computer languages. Gates practiced his programming skills by taking part in informal competitions with these employees to write programs in the fewest lines. He also reviewed every line of code for their new programs. Much of his energy, however, went into finding new markets for Microsoft products. Sensing that Japan would play an important role in the computer industry, Gates began negotiations with Japanese firms.

Life at Microsoft in Albuquerque was characterized by a youthful exuberance. The handful of employees wore jeans and open shirts to work. Some went barefooted. They worked hard and played hard. Bill Gates turned his early Microsoft profits into a new Porsche, which he loved to drive fast on the roads around Albuquerque. He discovered a construction site out in the country, figured out how to start the bulldozer engines, and late at night he and other programmers raced the bulldozers.

In 1978 the company moved to the Northwest, partly because Paul Allen missed the "trees and water" after his years in Albuquerque, partly so that both he and Gates could be near their families. A location in Bellevue near Seattle also gave them better access to domestic and international flights at a time when contacts with other companies were increasingly important.

During the 1980s the personal computer industry was similar to the American automobile industry in the early 1900s, when dozens of companies marketed automobiles for a few years, then fell to the competition. Today we look back at the Pierce Arrow and the Stanley Steamer as elegant failures of the early automotive age. Similarly, many computer companies were begun and ended in the 1980s. In 1983, for example, a historian purchased a sleek machine called an Otrona. Weighing about 20 pounds, the Otrona was one of the first of a new breed of portable computers. The owner took it to the Roosevelt Library at Hyde Park on a research trip, and the librarians there were so impressed — it was the first PC ever used at Hyde Park — that they convened a special staff meeting to see how it worked. To their amazement the machine performed such marvels as cutting and pasting text. The exotic machine thus had its moment of glory. Then followed a pitiful decline. During the next two years the Otrona went into the shop four times for major repairs, while the historian learned new terms like "mother board" — usually in the context of sentences like this: "Your mother board has failed." In the meantime the Otrona company also had failed. So the last time the computer went into the shop, no new parts were available. Calling for a report on his machine, the owner encountered a light-hearted repair man:

"Do you own a boat?"

"Why do you ask?"

"Because you've got a new anchor."

The failure of Otrona, one of many companies that did not survive the 1980s, was a result of the survival of other companies, a process familiar to the nineteenth century, known then as the "survival of the fittest." The hardware and software companies that did survive carried forth one of the most important revolutions in the history of technology, manufacturing products that were hardly imaginable a few years before. The industry was driven from success to success by a remarkable relationship between hardware and software. The early versions of BASIC pushed the capabilities of the original CPU, the 8080 chip, to its limits. For that reason among others, there was a need for a more powerful central processing unit, and along came the 8086 chip, later followed by the 286, 386, and 486 chips. At the same time, hardware manufacturers improved the random access memory and disk storage on their computers. These innovations created the need for new versions of BASIC, which, along with other programs such as spreadsheets and word processing programs, became more complex and thus pushed the limits of each new hardware configuration.

It was as if a symbiotic relationship existed between bread and toasters, where each new toaster design would enable bakers to manufacture more sophisticated bread, which in turn would create the demand for more complex toasters, which in turn would encourage the development of more intricate bread. No such culinary relationship exists, of course, which is why a 30-year-old toaster does the same job as this year's model. But in the computer industry more powerful machines have enabled software manufacturers to design programs unimaginable a few years ago, thus creating a demand for more sophisticated computers. Microsoft was able to be in the right place at each phase in the industry's growth, marketing key software products to facilitate the sale of not only its own products but computer hardware and other software as well.

After the move to the Seattle area, Allen devoted most of his time to hiring and supervising programmers, while Gates was active in pursuing new contracts for the company. Its staff of programmers developed several versions of such computer languages as FORTRAN, COBOL, and Pascal, along with BASIC. Gates met computer manufacturers and sold them on Microsoft products. Still in his mid-20s and often dressed informally in jeans, he impressed older, well-dressed business executives from large corporations with his drive and vision. Among Microsoft's new clients were AT&T and Xerox.

The transformation of Microsoft from a small company to a software giant was possible in part because of the drive and vision of its founders. It was also possible because of the remarkable growth of the computer industry as a whole during the 1980s. As in the nineteenth century, success came from a combination of luck and pluck. In 1979 Microsoft logged $4 million in annual sales. So far the company had been involved in computer language products, but there were other promising areas in computer software it had not yet tested. At the most basic software level, a computer needs an operating system, which enables it to save, copy, and delete files, and perform other basic functions. Thanks to some help from a multibillion-dollar industry, IBM, the fledgling Microsoft came to own the most important operating system in the world.

During the mid-1970s IBM had made a halfhearted effort to enter the personal computer market, which it soon abandoned. But after seeing the success of Apple and other companies, IBM decided to try again. Eager to produce a computer quickly, IBM asked Microsoft to develop a disk operating system for its new machine. At the time a system called CP/M was the industry standard, but IBM wanted new software.

Fortunately a local company, Seattle Computer Products, had developed a product called QDOS, which stood for "quick and dirty operating system." (The modern name DOS stands for the more prosaic phrase, "disk operating system.") Tim Paterson, the father of QDOS, agreed to let Microsoft develop refinements in the software for an undisclosed customer. Microsoft bought all rights to QDOS for $50,000.

By some measures it was one of the best bargains in the history of American business. In 1991 Microsoft made $200 million just selling copies of DOS. But it would be inaccurate to say that Microsoft bought a billion-dollar product for just $50,000. Before DOS was worth anything at all, it had to be refined to work with particular computers, and other software, such as word processing programs, had to be developed to work with DOS. The first step was refining QDOS to work with the new IBM personal computer.

In November 1980, Microsoft agreed to supply a disk operating system to IBM within a year. IBM insisted on top secrecy. No one must know about their PC, code named "Acorn," until its release in 1981. The prototypes with which Microsoft would work were to be kept in a special room in Bellevue, with the door locked even when employees were inside working with the machine. Manuals were to be left in a safe or locked file drawers. Further to discourage spying, IBM wanted Microsoft to install a shield of chicken wire above the ceiling tiles. On that demand Microsoft refused, but the other conditions were met, and programmers worked in secrecy in a hot, stuffy room.

Microsoft produced the new version of DOS on schedule, but at the time no one seems to have realized how important the new software would be. There were then many different software operating systems for computers, just as trains in the early days of railroading ran on many different-gauge rails. In 1981 Microsoft, whose current revenues had reached $16 million annually, anticipated that its principal revenues in the future would come from producing language and other software for many different operating systems.

The situation was radically altered, however, with the success of the IBM personal computer and the movement of all other PC manufacturers except APPLE toward producing IBM "clones." Within a decade most of the world's personal computers would be IBMs or clones, and most of them — 80 million in all — would run Microsoft DOS. In a sense, Microsoft "got a ride" with IBM. Microsoft profited as IBM became the industry standard. But the reverse was also true. DOS became the standard operating system for most software applications in part because Bill Gates was able to persuade other software manufacturers to develop good applications to run on DOS. In 1982 the software industry was a chaotic world where manufacturers had to choose among many different operating systems. With the success of Microsoft DOS, the industry was able to focus on producing the best possible programs for one of two platforms, Apple or DOS. Because Gates was able to persuade many software manufacturers to develop programs run on Microsoft DOS, the IBM personal computer could offer customers an attractive assortment of activities from games to word processing to spreadsheets. In that sense Big Blue caught a ride with Microsoft.

In 1982 the leading software applications were a spreadsheet called VisiCalc, made by VisiCorp, and WordStar, a word processing program from MicroPro. Bill Gates was eager to enter the applications market, and the company went to work on a spreadsheet called Multiplan, which it released in 1982. It enjoyed a few months of glory, having been named "product of the year" by the computer journal *InfoWorld.* Then, however, Lotus introduced a spreadsheet called 1-2-3 that outperformed Multiplan.

At this point Bill Gates may have adopted a strategy reminiscent of Andrew Carnegie at his most crafty. DOS was due for an upgrade to DOS 2.0. Lotus 1-2-3 ran on DOS. According to one Microsoft programmer who is cited by James Wallace and Jim Erickson in their Gates biography, *Hard Drive,* the key programmers working on DOS 2.0 wrote a few bugs into the new DOS that caused Lotus to fail when it was loaded. Allegedly their motto was, "DOS isn't done until Lotus won't run."

If the story is true, the tactic was shortsighted and uncharacteristic of Microsoft's sense of its relationship to the software industry as a whole. Admittedly, Microsoft wanted its spreadsheet to be more popular than 1-2-3. Competition is an important part of the computer industry, but the most resourceful hardware and software companies have often profited from each others' successes. During the early 1980s Lotus 1-2-3 helped IBM and its clones gain popularity. People bought IBM PCs in part because they could run Lotus on them, and that in turn helped with the success of Microsoft DOS, just as the efficiency of DOS contributed to the popularity of Lotus and IBM. So Microsoft had as much to gain as to lose from the success of Lotus.

In recent years Microsoft has developed a competitive spreadsheet, Excell, as well as one of the top word processing programs, Word. But Microsoft has also continued to improve DOS, and encouraged hundreds of smaller firms to write their own DOS based programs. During the late 1980s, Microsoft gained a still more powerful position in computer software by developing a program using icons and a mouse to facilitate computer use.

Programs that use what is called a graphical interface — images as well as words — trace their origins to an experimental program undertaken by Xerox during the 1970s in Palo Alto, California. Eager to find a way to make computers more "user friendly," the researchers at Xerox PARC experimented with children in developing computer drawing programs. One of their achievements was creating the illusion of an office on the screen with folders for storing and manipulating documents.

For a short time Xerox marketed a computer for $45,000, but then the company withdrew from an area where it had made such a promising beginning. Learning from Xerox, Steve Jobs and Steve Wozniac developed the Apple Macintosh, which featured a mouse and an icon-based "desktop." To delete a document, for example, you simply "clicked" on it with the mouse, and "dragged" it to the trash basket icon.

In another example of the symbiotic relationship between the various companies in the computer industry, Microsoft developed word processing, spreadsheet, and other programs for the Macintosh. Both companies prospered from the arrangement: Microsoft sold more copies of Word and Excell because they worked well on the Macintosh, and Apple sold more "Macs" because of the good software provided by Microsoft and other software manufacturers.

For millions of computer users who ran Word and Excell on their Macs, the names Apple and Microsoft were virtually synonymous. But the relationship between the two companies was strained when Microsoft developed its own graphic program called Windows. The new program helped push Microsoft's annual revenues above the $1 billion mark. Alarmed at this competition in a domain they had controlled, Apple cried "foul," and sued Microsoft, claiming that the "look and feel" of windows was stolen from Apple. In response, Microsoft pointed out that both companies could trace the inspiration for their graphics to a common source, Xerox PARC. Both Microsoft and Apple employed several Xerox stars. In 1992 a judge rejected Apple's claim that the "look and feel" of an icon interface was its exclusive property. That decision alone added a quick $1 billion to the value of Microsoft stock, and increased the value of Bill Gates's fortune by several $100 million.

The Apple suit is one example of the complexity of the business world in which Microsoft operates in the 1990s. Bill Gates's success is based on a delicate balance between cooperation and competition with the other players in the computer revolution. Because of Microsoft's success in both arenas, a company that began with a handful of employees came to employ hundreds, then thousands of workers. During the 1980s Paul Allen resigned from Microsoft and formed another software company. Microsoft bought a large tract of land in

Redmond, Washington, and built its new corporate headquarters, a facility on the scale of a university campus, complete with soccer and baseball fields.

Increasingly Bill Gates's personality dominated Microsoft. Gates was noted for the "seven hour turn around." That is, whenever he left Microsoft, he would be back at work seven hours later. If he worked until 2:00 A.M. he would return to work by 9:00 A.M. It became a status symbol at Microsoft to enter messages on electronic mail late in the night, evidence of diligence. Bill Gates is still noted for his frankness in discussing the work of his employees. More than one has been told in public, "That's a dumb idea."

In such ways, Gates's career recalls steel-plant manager William R. Jones's parody of his boss, Andrew Carnegie: "Puppy dog number three, you have been beaten by puppy dog number two on fuel. Puppy dog number two, you are higher on labor than puppy dog number one." Was Bill Gates, like Andrew Carnegie (in another of Jones's observations), "born with two sets of teeth and holes bored for more"? Certainly, the two men are comparable in their relentless drive. They both managed to embitter some of their own employees as well as their business rivals.

The sort of entrepreneurial drive of a Carnegie or a Gates, however, is as inspiring to some as it may be daunting to others. Despite his frank appraisal of his boss's style, plant manager Jones basically liked and admired Andrew Carnegie. The people who work closely with a Gates or a Carnegie tend to enjoy the sense of excitement that comes with hard work and innovation. At Microsoft a good example is Charles Simonyi, who came to Seattle from Xerox PARC. Born in Hungary, he was like Gates as a youngster, craving computer time. He agreed to work as night watchman in a room containing the most powerful computer in the country, a Russian machine called the Ural II. Unlike modern computers whose switches are invisible to the naked eye, the Ural II was laid out before him. Simonyi later recalled, "Hundreds of orange lights flickered behind glass doors and cabinets. The whole life of the machine pulsed right in front of your eyes." From humble origins Simonyi came to Microsoft, helped develop the company's application programs, became one of Gates's most trusted lieutenants, and came to own his own Lear Jet.

Many other workers at Microsoft became millionaires — a much rarer phenomenon at Carnegie Steel. Reports in 1992 indicated that some 2,000 Microsoft employees had received stock options worth $1 million by that time. While the financial rewards of work at Microsoft were clearly an advantage to joining the company, Gates's greatest success as a boss was arguably his ability to create an atmosphere where, in Robert Frost's phrase, "work is play for mortal stakes." With his background as a computer programmer, Gates understands the social psychology of programming: "I think most great programmers like to be around other great programmers. When they think up an incredible algorithm [computer instruction], they like having peers who can appreciate the cleverness that went into it, because when you're creating something like that and you have that model in your mind, it's a lonely thing." Gates's remark points to an underlying feature in Microsoft's success, and the success of the computer industry as a whole: It has involved a *community* of effort by innovators who were inspired and empowered by one another's achievements. Sometimes they have been business rivals, but the total effect of their efforts has been to push computer technology to new levels of excellence.

Microsoft's latest challenge is to establish a position in the new world of computer multimedia. With new technologies, computers can now produce documents that include not only words and spreadsheets, but also music, pictures, and even video. Commercial CD-ROM products can be stored on single "CD-ROM" disks that can hold roughly 1,000 books or thousands of images.

Software companies like Microsoft, which formerly produced the tools that others would use to write books and articles, are now beginning to market end products in the form of CD-ROM disks. The *Microsoft Bookshelf*, for example, is a collection of reference works on a single disk, including Bartlett's *Familiar Quotations* and *The Concise Columbia Encyclopedia.* With a computer and CD-ROM drive, the *Bookshelf* user can easily find facts and quotations and even hear historical speeches delivered by John Kennedy and others. Even more suggestive of the marvels at hand in CD-ROM technology is *Multimedia Beethoven,* a CD-ROM product developed by another company and now released by Microsoft. It combines images, text, and the music of Beethoven's Ninth Symphony. The CD-ROM user looks at *Microsoft Bookshelf* and is impressed by its usefulness. Looking at *Multimedia Beethoven,* the user is carried to a higher plane of appreciation: Here is something new and astonishing in the realm of communication.

The multimedia market today is as volatile as computers themselves were a few years ago. Companies like Microsoft, Apple and IBM are struggling to shape the new industry at several levels, defining not only the end products of CD-ROM technology, but also determining which software "platform" will become the industry standard for running CD-ROM. To complicate matters further, new products are emerging, such as hand-held computers capable of plucking information from satellites, and the gigabyte memory card, the size of a credit card and capable of storing thousands of books. Such innovations could unsettle multimedia at the very inception of the infant industry.

Tom Corddry of Microsoft. With multimedia, he says, "You have a little world, and you can create all sorts of objects in that world."

   Among the pioneers in multimedia is an enthusiasm comparable to the spirit found among the computer hobbyists of the mid-1970s, who were suddenly presented with the opportunity to own and develop their own computers and software. At Microsoft, multimedia specialist Tom Corddry is a good example. He is a graduate of Brown University, where he majored in English — a far cry from the computer training background of most of Microsoft's original employees. He studied documentary filmmaking in graduate school, worked in radio, produced slide shows and videos, consulted for Microsoft, and became interested in interactive videos.

   In an interview in 1992, Corddry discussed the challenge of multimedia. "The first question that comes up," he said, "is how can we presume to be that business? There are already people doing it. . . . There are publishing companies, and television networks, and painters. . . . Essentially what it comes down to is, what value can we add?" Corddry noted that in many ways the computer is less attractive than a book. Grasping a volume from his desk, he asked whimsically, "How do we address this as a technology? What does the book do well in computer language? It has a good user interface, you know. It has high resolution; it has full color; it's portable; it requires no batteries; it comes without a manual. . . . In an instant you know what you're dealing with there. People don't have any of that going for them on a computer."

So what value can a computer add to communication? Corddry continued, "The one thing that a computer can allow information to do differently than print is *behave.* . . . It has the opportunity to react and interact, and the microprocessor allows you to perform functions with the information. It's really a thought support system. . . . And so there are ways in which it can add this capability for behavior to what you generally think of in information as just the capability to appear."

Corddry wrestled with the question of just how the multimedia "behavior" of CD-ROM products can add value to traditional ways of communicating ideas. "The most general basic principle is that we're multisensory, and life is multimedia. Hence our normal experience is to integrate input all the time from all directions. . . . . One theory says that there are most appropriate media for different kinds of information, and they should be in that medium instead of being forced into another one, and computers can handle all those different media equally well and integrate them and let you choose the priorities. . . . [With multimedia] you have a little world, and you can create all sorts of objects in that world and give them behavior and have that behavior dependent and conditioned on what the user is doing and has done. It is virtual reality. . . ."

With multimedia, Microsoft and other companies find themselves on a new frontier in the 1990s, as pregnant with possibility as the personal computer revolution of the 1970s. CD-ROM technology has already proven its ability to retrieve bibliographic data and reference information more quickly than traditional methods. It may also revolutionize the way historians *re-create* the past, allowing them to bring sound and images into their work as never before. In Tom Corddry's phrase, historians will be able to design "little worlds" with multimedia.

Bill Gates, whose success owes much to his ability to foresee the future of the computer industry, is betting that the availability of attractive multimedia products will carry computers to a new level of success. "Our goals are simple," he says, "We are going to create the software that puts a computer on every desk and in every home. . . . CD-ROM is the technology we're going to use to get personal computers into the home."

Gates's multimedia goal — to set the industry standard — is reminiscent of his earlier goals for BASIC, DOS, and Windows. At the computer programming level, developing multimedia will involve many of the same challenges. And yet multimedia also involves a new kind of challenge because the art of designing computer tools is different from the art of creating, say, a historical presentation. Similarly, Johannes Gutenberg, who brought movable type to Europe, was different from

William Shakespeare, whose plays were printed on movable type. Each person was a product of the Renaissance, and each was a creative spirit, but Gutenberg could no more have written *Romeo and Juliet* than Shakespeare could have designed a printing press.

Tom Corddry's rhetorical question — "how can we presume to be that business?" — is one measure of the challenge ahead for hardware and software companies. Multimedia is a new frontier that will draw on the combined talents of humanists and scientists. Like the computer itself, it has the power to suggest new and exciting possibilities for human creativity. In multimedia, as in the computer revolution as a whole, the innovative spirit of the nineteenth-century "Age of Invention" is apparent in late twentieth-century America.

Now the richest man in America, Bill Gates is eager to retain the freshness of spirit he brought to the first years of Microsoft. While enjoying the fruits of his riches — fancy cars and fine champagne, for example — he seems to regard wealth as a potential distraction, to be enjoyed with caution. He dresses casually, and he still uses youthful slang: "scary," "cool," "hardcore," "superneat." Asked recently why he doesn't fly first class or in a private plane rather than coach, he remarked, "It sets a bad example. I think eventually you get used to those things, then you're just abnormal. I'm afraid I'd get used to it."

QUESTIONS

1. In what ways did the computer revolution contradict the assumption that only an "organization man" could succeed in America? In what ways did it revive the business characteristics of the age of Thomas Edison and Andrew Carnegie?

2. What are the major similarities between Andrew Carnegie and Bill Gates? What are the main differences between them?

3. Explain the contribution of each of the following to the computer revolution: Herman Hollerith, John V. Atanasoff and Clifford Berry, ENIAC, UNIVAC I, transistors, integrated circuits, Ted Hoff, the Altair 8080, Steve Wozniak and Steve Jobs, Xerox PARC.

4. Explain the role of the following events in the growth of Microsoft: BASIC for the Altair, "An Open Letter to Hobbyists," arbitration with Pertec, the "seven hour turn around," DOS, selling software manufacturers on DOS, Word and Excell, Windows.

5. The author argues that there was a "symbiotic relationship" between several of the big players in the computer revolution, particularly Microsoft,

Apple, IBM, and Lotus. Describe ways that the success of each of these companies helped the others.

6. During the nineteenth century people commonly spoke of "luck and pluck" as the fundamental ingredients in business success. How did these factors influence the growth of Microsoft?

7. In what ways do multimedia and CD-ROM technology take the computer industry to a new frontier?

BIBLIOGRAPHY

CRINGELEY, ROBERT X. *Accidental Empires: How the Boys of Silicon Valley Make their Millions* (1992). Makes the interesting, but flawed, argument that the founders of Microsoft, Apple, and other companies achieved their success largely by accident.

ICHBIAH, DANIEL, AND SUSAN L. KNEPPER. *The Making of Microsoft* (1991). Concise overview of Microsoft history.

KIDDER, TRACY. *The Soul of a New Machine* (1981). The prize-winning account of the efforts of computer "whiz kids" at Data General to build a new computer.

LAMMERS, SUSAN. *Programmers at Work: Interviews with 19 programmers Who Shaped the Computer Industry* (1989). Personal recollections of Charles Simonyi, Bill Gates, and other software writers.

LEVY, STEVEN. *Hackers: Heroes of the Computer Revolution* (1984). Colorful account of the informal origins of the personal computer revolution.

SLATER, ROBERT. *Portraits in Silicon* (1987). Biographical sketches of computer pioneers including Howard Aiken, H. Ross Perot, Ted Hoff, Steven Jobs, and Bill Gates.

WALLACE, JAMES, AND JIM ERICKSON. *Hard Drive: Bill Gates and the Making of the Microsoft Empire* (1992). A well-written and extensively researched account of the rise of Microsoft.

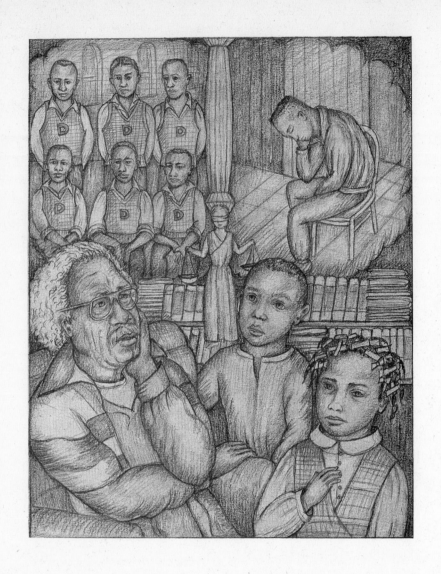

14

CONTEMPORARY AMERICA

The Worlds of Osborne Jones

In the present, we are all participants in history. Historical forces are active in our individual lives, drawing us into politics, popular culture, economic issues, and other movements. One of the best ways of exploring modern history is to go straight to the sources — to the men and women around us who can remember, say, the Great Depression, the birth of Rock and Roll, or the rise of environmentalism. This kind of scholarship, known as oral history, is as accessible as our friends, neighbors, and relatives.

The story of Osborne Jones illustrates the value of oral history for exploring a fundamental topic, the history of American race relations. Jones is an African-American, in his 70s, whose life began in the segregated South, and whose mentors included his grandparents, who were former slaves. His story covers the transition from segregation to civil rights, and his current life highlights enduring problems in American society. Jones's experience reveals, too, a deep stratum of human decency in American life, an influence that may yet prove stronger than the forces of ignorance and greed.

My phone rang: "Dr. Youngs, this is Osborne."
The raspy voice on the other end of the line was Osborne Jones —resurrected. Osborne was an M.A. student during the 1970s at Eastern Washington University. We renewed our acquaintance in 1990 when, in retirement, he visited me on campus at Cheney, Washington, and we discussed the idea of his writing an autobiography. I liked the idea. For me, Osborne Jones was already a part of history. He makes a brief appearance in Chapter 11 of *American Realities*. Osborne was my source for the story of the African-American soldiers who were disciplined during World War II for swimming in the white officers' pool. Osborne was a good authority: He was one of the black officers who got caught in the "crime" of swimming.

In 1990 almost a half century later, we began work on his autobiography. Whenever Osborne came to see me on campus, he dressed in a jaunty three-piece suit with a triangle of pink handkerchief showing in his breast pocket. He is a short man with long gray hair and twinkling eyes. He was enjoying the project. Newly retired, he wanted something to do, and he had plenty of good stories to tell. But the autobiography also caused him pain. Parts of his life were easier to forget.

Through his ancestors, Osborne's story goes back to slavery itself. At one point in his youth he went to live with his grandmother and grandfather, who had both been slaves. Osborne recounted a family tradition: "My grandfather had met my grandmother, and they were not married. She was sold from South Carolina into Arkansas. After the Emancipation Proclamation, he walked from South Carolina to Arkansas and found her."

That spring, Osborne gave a guest lecture at Eastern Washington. In an accent flavored by his Arkansas boyhood, he spoke eloquently about his experiences in black and white America. Although he was 70 years old in 1990, he became youthful as he described his distant past:

"My mother knew I was going to be small," he said, "so she used a parable of the elephant and the mouse to motivate me. She said that the elephant is one of the largest animals in the jungle, but he is no match for the tiny mouse who used his brain and small size to outwit the elephant."

Osborne told the story with a particular relish; its moral had helped to shape the man he became.

"One of my earliest recollections," he said, "was of reciting Paul Lawrence Dunbar's 'A Negro Love Song.' This has remained my favorite over the years, and I can clearly see in my mind a little boy saying:

'Seen my lady home las' night,
Jump back, honey, jump back.

Hel' huh han' an' sque'z it tight,
    Jump back, honey, jump back.
Hyeahd huh sigh a little sigh,
Seen a light gleam f'om huh eye,
An' a smile go flittin' by —
    Jump back, honey, jump back.

Hyeahd de win' blow thoo de pine,
    Jump back, honey, jump back.
Mockin'-bird was singin' fine,
    Jump back, honey, jump back.
An' my hea't was beatin' so,
When I reached my lady's do',
Dat I couldn't ba' to go
    Jump back, honey, jump back.

Put my ahm aroun' huh wais',
    Jump back, honey, jump back.
Raised huh lips an' took a tase,
    Jump back, honey, jump back.
Love me, honey, love me true?
Love me well ez I love you?
An' she answe'd, ' 'Cose I do!'
    Jump back, honey, jump back."

We were in a small classroom, about two dozen of us with chairs arranged in a semicircle around Osborne. He had been sitting, but he stood up to recite the "love song."

"I still remember a little boy in knickers," he said, "as he said the poem taking a backward step."

And with that, the 70-year-old man took a perky step backwards.

Osborne went on to discuss other experiences, including life in the segregated army. He also described his work, more recently, with the employment and penal systems of Washington State. The session was charmed, and we could have gone on all afternoon. But Osborne had a social engagement. The day, June 19 (sometimes called "Juneteenth," he told us), was the anniversary of the day the slaves were freed in Texas, now noted as emancipation day among many African-Americans through-out the United States. "A great day in black culture," said Osborne. He and some friends were celebrating with a picnic.

That was in June 1990. With the end of the school year, Osborne and I did not see each during the summer. We started the autobiography project again in the fall, but then Osborne hurt himself by dropping an iron pipe on his foot. The accident aggravated his gout and arthritis, leaving him lame. Osborne had to put off one meeting, then another. I began to worry about ever seeing him again. He was a young man in spirit, but in addition to the persistent gout and arthritis — reminders of his age — he had suffered a massive heart attack some years before. I also feared that writing his memoirs might be painful. Being a soldier in a segregated army was not an experience to remember fondly. Then, too, I wondered whether he really wanted me, a white, to help him tell a story in which white America had sometimes played a cruel role. After Osborne's health caused him to cancel several meetings, we lost contact.

I continued, however, to think about Osborne Jones. I wondered how he was, and I fretted that he might have passed away.

When he called me in the winter of 1992, my first thought was, "Osborne is *alive!*"

For me, and I think for both of us, it was one of those wonderful moments when a friendship, postponed or delayed, suddenly rekindles. He was in Seattle and was interested in starting up the autobiography again. Osborne had written about 30 pages of the autobiography, but wanted some ideas on how to continue. We decided to combine memoirs and oral history. I would meet with him regularly and record our discussions about his past, providing material to expand the autobiography. We agreed to get together at his house in Seattle. So one afternoon in the winter of 1992, I got in my car and left my Bellevue, Washington, home to drive the ten miles to Osborne's home.

FROM BELLEVUE TO SEATTLE

The trip would take only 20 minutes, but my thoughts along the way were one measure of the distance between black and white America today, almost four decades after the Montgomery bus boycott. I live in Bellevue, Washington, an affluent city of 80,000. Bellevue has little poverty or crime.

Certainly there are African-Americans in Bellevue, but relatively few. In Seattle, a much larger city, most blacks live in the Central District. Most whites live anywhere else. Go to a play in Seattle and you will see an audience that is almost entirely white. Go to church on Sundays and you will likely worship in a congregation that is mostly white or mostly black.

This kind of separation can be found, of course, almost anywhere in the United States. I spent some time recently at the National Archives. In the lunch room at that cosmopolitan institution, I never once saw blacks and whites sharing a table, although equal numbers of each race were eating there. In a performance hall at the Smithsonian a few years ago, I attended a musical tribute to Rodgers and Hammerstein. There were no blacks in an audience of roughly 400. A year or two later I was in the same auditorium at the Smithsonian, watching an African drum band with my wife, who served with the Peace Corps in Nigeria, and another Peace Corps couple. Again the audience was roughly 400, but this time the crowd was almost entirely black.

During the 1960s, at the height of the civil rights movement, many Americans anticipated that we would become a "café au lait" society, completely homogenized. In one of his most concise and significant phrases, Martin Luther King, Jr., said, "Sin is separation." Many Americans agreed, yet members of both races seemed to embrace separatism, even in the midst of integration. During the 1960s black college students demanded separate dining tables, fraternities, and even dorms. In the South and other parts of the country whites withdrew their children from integrated schools and started a parallel system of private education. Today blacks in New York are warned to stay away from Bensonhurst, and whites are warned away from Harlem.

The final years of the twentieth century have brought with them a troubling combination of progress and decline in American race relations. In some areas the progress is remarkable. Only a few decades ago African-Americans were barred from participation in major league football, basketball, or baseball — now they dominate all three sports. Until after World War II the army was segregated. In 1992 the Chairman of the Joint Chiefs of Staff, Colin Powell, is an African-American. In 1961 Sammy Davis, Jr., was invited to John Kennedy's inaugural ball, then at the last minute was told that the invitation had been withdrawn — the country was not "ready" for a black to attend a presidential ball. Subsequently Davis became a frequent guest at the White House, along with many other blacks. Today, Americans hear the news from black reporters, buy products endorsed by black superstars, and elect black mayors in our major cities. Our only national holiday honoring an individual American is Martin Luther King Day. Such things were inconceivable just 40 years ago.

In these ways and many others the civil rights movement of the 1950s and 1960s has transformed the United States. And yet in the 1990s, America remains a disunited nation. It is all too easy for Americans to go through their entire lives without forming a close friendship with men and women of other racial and ethnic backgrounds. We can see a change in our culture in the fact that the most popular television program during the 1980s was the "Cosby Show." A few years before, blacks had appeared on family programs mainly as servants. Now an African-American family became a kind of model to tens of millions of households throughout the United States. But the "Cosby Show" also embraced a kind of segregation; it showed a world in which only one race existed. Whites were as rare on the "Cosby Show" as blacks were on the family shows of 30 years ago.

In addition, the problems of poverty, crime, and illiteracy continue to haunt large sectors black America. In 1992 the inner city was a harsher environment than it was 50 years before, made more dangerous by guns and drugs. Almost 25 percent of young black males were in jail or on probation. Two thirds of black babies were born out of wedlock. Rap music offers a blunt explanation for black hardships: whites do not *want* blacks to succeed. In the music video "Can't Truss It," for example, rap group Public Enemy chronicles a history of white injustice to blacks. In one compelling scene a white plantation owner rapes a black servant girl; when she becomes pregnant her black lover thinks the child is his and is overjoyed; but then a light-skinned child is born, and the vicious planter gloats over his triumph.

To some viewers such rap images seem a valid historical explanation for the ills of the black ghetto. Others see the effort to blame whites for drugs, illegitimacy, and other ills as a cop out. Instead of complaining about the activities of slaveowners a hundred fifty years ago, they say, more black men should take advantage of the opportunity they now have to marry and raise their children. Instead of complaining about the weakness of inner city schools, inner city residents should make certain that talented black and white teachers are not driven from their schools by abuse and violence. "Can't Truss It" has become a kind of motto for all sides of the inner city debate. Blaming someone else is apparently easier than solving the problems.

On the winter afternoon of 1992 when I drove to Seattle to visit Osborne Jones, I was carrying a burden of suspense inherited from contemporary American culture. Crossing the Interstate 90 floating bridge on Lake Washington, with Seattle looming in the distance, I was not sure what to expect. Would my white face in his black neighborhood arouse curiosity or even hostility? I took the freeway off ramp to Rainier Avenue, turned east into the Central District, and continued across Martin Luther King Way. The faces changed from predominantly white to predominantly black. I drove on, looking for Osborne's address, came to the crest of a hill, and caught a beautiful view of Lake Washington, with the Cascade Mountains in the distance. Unexpectedly, I had driven right through the Central District. Osborne, it turned out, lived in Leshi, a more prosperous and racially mixed neighborhood on the eastern slope of Seattle.

AT HOME WITH OSBORNE

Osborne was waiting for me on a porch swing. Instead of the three-piece suit I had always seen him in, he was wearing a bright jogging suit. His smile was infectious. We went inside his house, and within a few minutes I was seeing facets of Osborne Jones that I had never envisioned. The walls of the living-dining room were crowded with family portraits, his parents, a brother in military uniform, his wife, Jean, with a child, grandchild, and great-grandchild — along with her mother. I was particularly struck with a poster-sized portrait of Osborne and his wife at a party — the governor's inauguration ball. He was wearing a tuxedo, and she an evening gown. She was a striking woman of about 55 and stood almost a head taller than her husband. They looked as happy as if they had just won the lottery.

Between the living-dining room were two little plastic tables and plastic chairs. Osborne explained to me that when his and Jean's two adoptive children came back from day care each day, he gave them a snack at the table. Osborne had mentioned the children before, but until now they had been an abstraction. During the next few weeks, they would become very real indeed.

After a few minutes, Osborne settled into an armchair, I arranged myself with tape recorder on a neighboring couch, and we went to work. He began by telling me about his new children. A few years ago, Osborne and Jean agreed to provide a home for a young girl. In her early teens, she had been in foster homes most of her life. "She wasn't really bad," said Osborne, "I considered her more mischievous. And then again, she had learned how to work the system." When she was 14, she became pregnant. "I had sort of sensed," said Osborne, "that a lot of her male friends were older men. . . . I was very angry, and I told her, 'If I find out who it is, he's going to prison.'"

The baby was given up for adoption, and a year later the mother was pregnant again. "We questioned her about who was the father, but we never got any information." She gave birth to a girl, and had complications. "My wife went and brought the little girl home, while she stayed in the hospital. So we had the baby before she came home. I was very angry at that time. I wouldn't even go to the store to get the baby milk. I said, 'I won't have nothing to do with this baby.' And one day I was sitting in here, and the little baby come crawling up and pullin' on my pants leg. And I guess that was the end of me. [laughs]

"Well, it was more than that. . . . I had become smitten with the little girl. Now, because of my age, I wasn't considered as a good possibility for adoption." Now Osborne chuckled, and his eyes twinkled. "I guess in order to put things in my favor, I said, 'As many black kids as there are out there, and here's a black parent who would adopt a kid, and we're having problems?!'" In telling me the story, Osborne's voice was charged with playful outrage. But the tension of uncertainty had been real enough at the time. While waiting for a decision, Osborne attended a course at a local community college on early childhood development. "I was trying to learn more about children, you see. We were getting a lot of resistance because of my age. But I was just determined that we would get the child. We had kept her so long that we both had fallen in love with her. As far as she's concerned right now, I'm her 'Papa' and my wife is her 'Mommy.'"

Eventually the state did approve the adoption. Today Osborne and Jean are raising Kiki and another child, her little brother Tavon. I asked Osborne, "Do you ever read to them?"

"Oh, yes, I read to them *every* night. Last night we did *Jack and the Bean Stalk*. You talking about books, now. [laughs] Oh, we got all kind of children's books." Osborne walked to a pile of children's books by the dining-room table and proudly opened a workbook where Kiki had drawn circles and triangles. "They wanted to know about the *Town Mouse and the Country Mouse*. I said it's like the Seattle mouse and the Pasco mouse. [Pasco is a small city 150 miles from Seattle.] To me it's something that keeps me busy. It keeps me busier than I would like to be, but. . . ." Osborne's voice trailed off. Going through the pile of books, he found a dinosaur book. "Most little boys love dinosaurs," he said.

He returned to the living room. "So that is how the children arrived here," he said. Osborne settled back in his armchair and began to talk about his career with the criminal justice system in Washington State.

"I was and still am interested in the correctional system," he said, "because I see the racism that's involved. . . . You've got to have money to get a good defense. The defense attorneys are backlogged; they have hundreds of cases; they go try to defend people they've never talked to. That's really not good, it's not good. It's making a lot of bitter people.

"I guess I was naive early in my career. When I was a young officer, I had been appointed to a court martial board. One day we were sitting in a room playing poker, you know, three or four of us, and a senior officer came in and said,

'Well, you've got this court martial coming up. I don't want the guy to go to jail. Just take his stripes, you know.'

"And I said to myself, 'This is not the *way* things are supposed to be done.' I didn't talk too much, you know, but I became kind of interested in the justice system then." Afterward Osborne had worked for a judge advocate in the army, and years later that experience helped him land a job with the Washington State criminal justice system during the 1970s and 1980s.

"I got into it, and I really liked it. If you like what you're doing, you gonna really do it well. I used to do things like come home at night, and I'd look in the mirror, and I'd laugh. I'd say, 'You did it.' You know. You feel good within yourself when you accomplish things, when they said, 'You can't do this.' or 'We don't have no money to do this.'"

Osborne learned to lobby the legislature and to write grants for the programs he supported. "One of the things that really makes me feel good now," he said, "is when I'm in the store, shopping, and some guy will come up to me, and he has a wife and two or three kids. He says, 'Don't you remember me. . . . I wouldn't be here today if it wasn't for you.' And then he'll go on and tell me. 'You helped me get out of jail,' or 'You helped me get a job,' and so forth. 'I'm off of parole now, and this is my wife and children.' And that to me is a good feeling. Just to know that you have made an impact on others' lives. People who work with people, they don't look for a lot of monetary rewards. Their reward is to see others take what you had to give them, and they give it to someone else. It's like what I tell the kids about the broken line and the solid line. It's an unbroken line. You give to someone — it's like passing the baton. That's the way I feel about it.

"I've reached this age. I sit on the front porch out there. I say, 'I've *had* a good life.' But I'm still not satisfied. You look at the youth today. To me, I don't see anything. . . . I see disaster. Our young people are putting a lot of values on money, and obtaining money."

We spent the rest of the afternoon outlining Osborne's autobiography: his youth in Arkansas and California, his army career, an interlude of teaching in North Carolina, then graduate school and civil service in Washington. Osborne talked about various episodes in his life, picking events at random from his seven decades.

Toward the end of the afternoon, Osborne wanted to introduce me to his wife, who was at work a couple of miles away at her store, "Jean's Boutique." Any remaining idea I had of a frail elderly Mrs. Jones was dispelled the moment I stepped through the door into the small shop. It was like walking into a rainbow. The room was alive with colorful dresses, blouses, and hats. Jean was in the middle of a small crowd of models, who it turned out were preparing for a fashion show that evening. She greeted us warmly, all smiles for the two of us. It was Valentine's Day, and I was soon in the middle of a conversation about a present for my wife. Jean and her models were full of advice. The topic of a present, however, made one of them a little sad. "I wish I had someone to buy me something for Valentine's Day," she remarked. Her daughter, sitting nearby, came over, kissed her, and said, "*I* love you, Momma."

I suddenly noticed that Osborne had disappeared. I looked around, and he was by the door, almost in hiding. I sensed then — and he later admitted to me — that he felt quite awkward around so many women. At the same time, he was proud of Jean for starting her own business. He told me that people came from as far away as Olympia, 70 miles to the south, to do business with Jean. A lot of the money she earns goes to buying clothes for the children.

I drove Osborne back home. We discussed when we would meet again. "We can make it a schedule," said Osborne. "We can make it a once a week schedule. Then I can say, 'Well, once a week, I'm on schedule.'" That sounded fine to me.

DUNBAR HIGH SCHOOL, 1936

A week later Osborne greeted me with a collection of documents from Dunbar, his high school in Little Rock, Arkansas. Named after poet Paul Lawrence Dunbar, the author of his favorite childhood poem, it was the only black high school in the city at the time. We spent the next hour discussing his schooling. "This is my yearbook," Osborne said, handing me a pamphlet called the *Bearcat*. It was 24 pages long, stapled. The date was 1936. Framed between two Grecian columns on the yellow front cover was a poem, "Farewell to Dunbar."

> Dunbar we're leaving your portals renoun,
> Thy teachings still in our ears resound. . . .
> So farewell to you Dunbar you've done your best
> Believe in us Dunbar We'll do the rest.

Leafing through the *Bearcat*, Osborne showed me his picture. He was wearing a suit, with a flower on the lapel. With bright eyes and a crew cut, he had a look of innocence and vulnerability — possibly because he was only 16 at the time, the youngest student in his class. Osborne's nickname was listed as "Tapper," and his favorite quotation read, "In spite of all [that] learned men have said, I still my opinion keep." He said that the quotation "followed me through life."

Most of the 95 students in his class had nicknames: "Butch," "Lacie," "Lambchops," "Mug," "Pip," and "Little Burton," among others. And each had a favorite quotation, invariably brimming with optimism:
"It is only the ignorant who despise education."

"No one can make, break, or decide your destiny, but you yourself."

"The mill will never grind with the water that is past."

"The best angle to choose in life is the try-angle."

"Pessimism leads to weakness. Optimism leads to power."

One student admitted some apprehensions as she faced the world, and wrote as her motto, "To do my best under any circumstances — hopefully." The only student to strike a less exalted — though still optimistic — note was a senior named C. R. English, who wrote, "C. R. English likes to make a big show, if your car stops, call him and he will make it go."

In addition to student sketches, the Dunbar High School *Bearcat* had all the other ordinary features of a modern "annual." The "Class Will" bestowed on various members of the class other students' assets, such as "talkativeness," a "million dollar smile," "cooking ability," "money wasting habit," "friskiness," "winning ways," "punctuality," "long hair," and "fishing tackle." The "Class Prophecy" predicted recognition for many graduates in the 1946 *Who's Who in Colored America*. Among their destinies were "missionary to South Africa," "concert pianist," "popular band leader," "efficient architect," "jockey," and "economics teacher."

Because Osborne was a year or two younger than most of his classmates, he was left out of some of the activities. Even his crush on a fellow student went amiss. "I remember in my high school, one time, I got in trouble because I liked a young lady. She was in the glee club, and I joined the glee club, but I can't sing. One day in glee club practice — this song has always remained in my mind because of this incident that happened — they were practicing, 'The hounds are dancing, horses prancing, tally ho.'" (At this point Osborne shook his head to the rhythm and repeated, "The hounds are dancing, horses prancing, tally ho.")

"I got carried away. Now I can't sing, and I noticed the instructor kept walking up and down the aisle. Undoubtedly, she was trying to find the discord, you know. And she came up and stood beside me, and she said, 'Osborne I'd like to see you when class is over.' So when class was over I went to see her. 'How long have you been in the glee club?' she said, 'Have you been singing all the time?'

"I really hadn't been doing too much singing," Osborne continued, "I was 'lip synching' or whatever they call it. She said, 'Well, I don't think we can use you any longer.' See I had really gotten in the glee club so I could get a chance to see the 'little girl' in the afternoon. But I always remember getting kicked out of the glee club," he said, laughing.

Growing more serious, Osborne said, "Somehow I seem to feel that the high school had a lot to do with me all through the years." At Dunbar, it was "important" to be a member of the National Honor Society — even more important than to be a member of the football team. "If you were a member of the National Honor Society, you were more recognized in the school." One of Osborne's classmates became president of Tuskegee. Another taught the Ninety-Ninety Pursuit Squadron at Tuskegee, the crack World War II fighter pilots. "I can say we had some dedicated teachers, and these teachers instilled a lot of things. But we came along in a different era. I can always remember my parents saying to me, 'I want you to achieve things that I haven't had an opportunity to. I don't want you to have to go through things I had to.'"

Osborne began to explain his job in the criminal justice system when we were interrupted by a noise on the porch. The dog barked, the door opened, and 4-year-old Kiki exploded into the room, just home from nursery school. Oral history gave way to living history, as Kiki began showing us her favorite photographs. I asked whether I could take a picture.

"Oh, yes," said Osborne. "Kiki, do you want to put on your little uniform sweater?"

"Noooo," said Kiki.

"Noooo," said Osborne, playfully imitating her, as I took the picture.

Kiki was lovely. Her hair was gathered into 40 or 50 braids, each held with a bright plastic clip. Her eyes were bright and inquisitive. Apparently she and Osborne had discussed my visit, and agreed that she would tell me some of the things she had learned in school. Osborne asked her, "What did you say you were going to tell Bill when he came? What did you learn in your school? You are intelligent. . . ."

"I am intelligent," said Kiki.

"And you are what?"

"Smart!"

"She's intelligent and she's smart!" said Osborne.

"I want to say my prayers," said Kiki, who was fully into the spirit of showing off her knowledge by now. Then she sat on Osborne's lap and looked at him as she said the "Lord's Prayer." Osborne whispered each phrase after her, confidingly. Kiki stumbled over "temptation" and began to repeat herself toward the end. "Papa" helped her finish.

While Kiki went to change out of her school uniform, Osborne described Zion Preparatory School. It covers preschool and day care, with classes through grade eight. Kiki's brother Tavon, who was sick that day, had already learned his ABC's at Zion, even though he was only two. "Since it is a private church school," said Osborne, "they are able to teach religion."

Once the children are ready for first grade, they will go to public school. "We're just trying to give her a foundation, you know, to take her as far as we can — because we've seen so much, the generations on welfare, and young girls who have become pregnant at early ages, and don't even finish high school, or don't even finish sixth or seventh grade. All they know in life is having babies and staying on welfare. I'm determined to give her as much as I can. . . ."

"Oh, there he is!" said Osborne, seeing Kiki's little brother coming shyly into the room. "Tell him what's your name."

"Tavon," said Tavon.

He was a little boy with a big cold, clothed in pajamas. Tavon demonstrated his ABCs, and then both children discovered the interesting things we could do with a tape recorder besides recording "Papa's" memoirs.

SEGREGATION

Arriving one afternoon for our weekly oral history session, I found Osborne amused and perplexed. At 72 he was reflecting on the inquisitiveness of a 4-year-old child. He had recently been trying to impress on Kiki the importance of not lying. So he told her about the little boy who cried wolf. "She wanted to know his *name*." He didn't have an answer for that.

Since neither of us could come up with the name of the little boy who cried wolf, we went on to other subjects. Since talking to Osborne about Dunbar High School, I had been pondering another problem. What had it been like to leave Dunbar for a segregated world? There had been all those idealistic students, looking forward to interesting careers, and they were graduating into the segregated world of the 1930s. They could not go to the University of Arkansas, or become mayor of Atlanta, or even ride in the front of the bus in Montgomery or other Southern cities.

Osborne's answer surprised me. It had not been bad at all, he said, because they lived in their own world. "Blacks lived then in what I call now a self-contained little community. We had everything we needed, doctors, lawyers, our movie theaters. I knew of no racial prejudice." He said that the people looked out for each other. "I don't know whether there was more pride, but there was more togetherness." He described his neighborhood in Little Rock, drawing a map to illustrate his points. Near the center of the African-American community was a restaurant, owned by his uncle, with a wonderful name, the "Chat and Chew." Here was the liquor store and next to it the pool hall. "My mother didn't care for me to go into any of those places, but she allowed me to go into the pool hall to clean up to make extra money. So one day I was in the pool hall, and I was really cutting up, you know, and I was saying, 'Who wants to shoot the devil one.' I was calling myself the devil because I really thought I could play. I had my back turned to the door, and suddenly I felt something had a hold of my ear, and I looked around, and there was my mother. So she took me out by the ear in front of all my friends."

A safer form of entertainment came at the local movie theaters. On Osborne's map, here was the Realto theater and there was the Gem. The Gem was the black theater, the Realto was for whites, but blacks were allowed to sit in the balcony. Segregation worked both ways. The big bands would come to town, Duke Ellington and Count Basie, and they would play in the black Masonic Hall. Whites could sit and watch, but they had to stay behind a rope and could not dance.

Osborne's first experience with segregation came in the army, even though when he enlisted he was assigned to a special new program for black officers. In a draft of his autobiography, he has written about the shock of being treated as an inferior. He reported to a post in Fort Knox, Kentucky, in July 1942. The commanding officer told him there was no discrimination on the base, but all the other candidates, who were white, slept in a barracks, while Osborne slept alone in the squad room.

"My day to day relations with whites were more or less that of being tolerated. It seems as if the attitude was, 'Why bother, we will always be in command.' I was once told by a classmate of mine that he had only had contact with one black before in his life, a 'boy' who had worked for his family for about 50 years. I asked him how old did boys grow where he came from, and he answered that they usually called 'them' boys until they started calling them 'uncle.'

"As we marched to class one day a young black girl pushing a white child in a baby carriage drew the following comment from one of my fellow candidates, 'That is why I want to be an officer so I can have a nigger maid.'"

When Osborne needed a haircut, a staff car took him to the "Colored Troop Area." "It was a separate camp within a camp. There was almost everything, but of lesser quality."

A few months later he was presented the gold bars of a second lieutenant in a ceremony he recalled as "one of my proudest moments." But he adds, "My bubble was soon to burst."

He was sent to Louisiana. "As I arrived at the train station I had my first encounter. Being a new second lieutenant, I was anxious that I should be recognized. So when two white enlisted men passed me without saluting, I stopped them, saying, 'Soldiers, what do you do when you see an officer?' They looked at me with blank stares. I finally said, 'Have you not been taught to salute an officer when you see one?' One of them replied, 'I don't salute niggers,' and they walked away."

Osborne rose to major in the army, but might have gone much further in today's integrated military. A senior officer once told him that if he were white, he might have become a general. Despite the many hard times in the army, one moment at home was particularly rewarding. He was visiting home with his brother, another officer.

"My mother wanted to go down to Main Street. She didn't believe that the Caucasian soldiers would salute black officers. My brother and I took my mother, and we stood on the main street. Some soldiers came by, and they saluted us. That's all she wanted to see." She was proud of her two soldier sons. "She talked about it for a long time."

With the end of our session, Osborne and I decided that our next meeting should take place at the children's school. In a sense, I would thus accompany Osborne to two schools in two time periods, Dunbar in 1936 and Zion more than a half century later.

ZION PREPARATORY ACADEMY, 1992

Zion Preparatory Academy, though a private school, is inexpensive, and provides day care and education to children from diverse backgrounds. Of about 500 children, most are black; about ten are white. The school is on a pleasant street overlooking downtown Seattle and Puget Sound. When I arrived the children were presenting a convocation, the various grades each giving a presentation. "Dr. King, Dr. King, Dr. King was a civil rights leader," sang one class. "Oh, Freedom," sang another. Another group of children put on sunglasses and danced to rap music. When one class appeared on stage carrying signs indicating their professional goals, I was reminded of Osborne's Dunbar High School. Each shyly named a profession into a microphone: "judge," "flight engineer," "model," "architect," "interpreter," "scientist," "teacher," and "civil rights leader," among others.

One of the mothers watching the show was a Seattle police officer, complete with uniform and gun. She came over in a break between performances and gave Osborne an embrace. A beautiful woman, she had been a model in Chicago before moving west. Osborne explained that she was one of his and Jean's "kids." They try to assist young people, he said, and they had helped this model make the transition to the police force.

Later Osborne took me to meet Doug Wheeler, the president of

Zion Prep. He is a handsome, athletic African-American in his middle years. In an office decorated with children's pictures, he sat behind a simple wooden desk. Osborne and I described our oral history project, and my interest in learning more about the school. Wheeler explained that lots of the children at Zion have older parents. "It's incredible the number of grandparents that are raising children, mainly because — for some reason I still haven't put my finger on yet — there is a generation of parents who don't seem to take the responsibility, whether it's a boyfriend or girlfriend situation, whether it's lack of responsibility, maturity, whatever it is, there is a tremendous increase of grandparents playing a custodial role of children — a tremendous increase." In many cases the grandparents are in their thirties. They may think, "Now I can do for my grandchildren what I wasn't able to do, or mature enough to do, or stable enough to do, when I was growing up."

Zion Prep takes children as young as 2 1/2. Whatever their ages, all the children have homework assignments. "It's to get you trained that you have to take something home that you're responsible for, and you have to bring it back. As you go through this system, you don't have to worry about homework because it's already *been* in their minds." Wheeler explained that the school also develops the most basic study habits: "You sit at your desk, there's work to do, there's a responsibility, and it's hard work."

I asked Wheeler about the argument that the biggest problem with American education is parents who fail to encourage their children. He rejected that idea. "I always cause a lot of problems," he said. "People don't like to hear me talk. [laughs] I don't accept that at all, because if that was acceptable, and we accepted it, then the students are going to accept it, and no one's responsible from that point on. I won't get into whether that's right or wrong, but the consequences of that, I will. And the consequences of that are that you have a child who is saying it's not my fault because it's the home; the parents are saying it's not our responsibility, it's the school; and the school is saying there's not enough money. So we can do that *all* day, OK?

"So I decided the bottom line is, the consequences are, if these children don't take the responsibility for *themselves,* they're going to be lost. I may *never* see a parent; a parent may *never* help a child with homework; a parent may *never* spend time with a child. I can't do anything about that. But what I can do, is when I have that child here six and seven hours a day, I can say, 'Regardless, *you* have a responsibility to do this and this and this. And I'm going to teach you, and make sure you meet that responsibility. No matter what goes on around you, you know what your responsibility is.'"

Osborne had been listening intently. He told us how the system

Doug Wheeler, president of Zion Preparatory Academy. He tries to teach by example: "Self-esteem is something that's alive, that moves, and how you move, and how you present yourself."

works on Kiki: "Sometimes in the morning she's ready to come back to school, I'll sometimes forget it, and she'll say, 'Oh, no, no, Papa. I've got to have my homework.'"

I wondered how the homework system worked. There are many high schools in America today that have given up homework. "But how many levels of *consequences* do they have?" asked Wheeler. "You have to have a consequence. If you don't turn in your homework the first time, you automatically go to detention after school. If that doesn't work, then you have Saturday school, and the school costs you *five* bucks to help pay for the teacher, and then you do labor. If you have to come a third time, then a parent has to come with you. . . . Believe me, parents do not want to be here — it costs twenty bucks. So momma's on your case about the twenty dollars, and her takin' her time!"

To help children — and parents — avoid Saturday school, Zion provides a phone number for a recording of the day's assignments. "A little thing like that empowers you," said Wheeler. Out of curiosity, I called the number one weekend. Doug Wheeler's friendly voice read the assignments: "Second grade, Brother Mark, they have to write misspelled spelling words five times, and they have to convert their problems on their math test; third grade, Brother Jordan, they have a reading and a writing project to do — they have to write in their journals; sixth grade, social studies, you have to write two paragraphs comparing and contrasting the Philippines and Indonesia. . . . This is the homework line for the weekend, and God *bless* you, and be sure to go to church."

What about problem children? The challenge, said Wheeler, is "taking each child, and building your curriculum around the needs of that child. For example, we have a beautiful child, who is nothing short of a genius. But he has real problems, violence: swinging bats, sticks, kicking, and biting. We kept working, kept working, saw some improvement. But the one thing that changed his whole life is that we had a promotion ceremony for him from first grade to second grade, a year ahead, because he's a genius, and he got a certificate. And he'll run down all the time with his papers with the stars and stuff on them because his whole mind-set about himself has been changed over a little piece of paper, like the Wizard of Oz, you know," he laughed.

Crack children — born to mothers who were addicts — have begun to arrive at Zion. With his characteristic optimism, Doug Wheeler anticipates that the school will be able to handle the problem with special care. "It is an opportunity to find a solution," he said, "and there is one for it. You just have to change the environment for that."

I asked Wheeler how he had become an educator. "It was really weird," he said. "I went into education back in 1968. I taught high school, 1968–69, and I *hated* it with a passion. So I went into a safer profession — I went into law enforcement. And I stayed in law enforcement for about 18 years." His wife and father-in-law in the meantime had started the school, and Wheeler would help out in his spare time. The school was understaffed, and his wife urged him to leave his police job. Eventually, he agreed.

"I had been a probation officer," Wheeler said, "and I always felt as a probation officer that I was never accomplishing anything. In the police department I always would see these kids in a setting that I didn't think was right. I met some wonderful young men who were in real trouble. And I always thought, what could I do if that was my son? I always thought, I could really make a difference, and that's why I was so interested in the building of this school."

So the change to teaching had been welcome, but Wheeler still works as a consultant for police and communities as an expert on victimology and the traumatic impact of crime and accidents. His work has taken him to such scenes as a plane crash in Detroit or a murder in Oklahoma. "I just got back from the Dahmer murder case," he said. Jeffrey Dahmer was the man who killed and cannibalized a dozen people in Milwaukee, Wisconsin, before he was apprehended in 1991. In Milwaukee, Wheeler counseled police officers and victims' families, held a community meeting, and met with school officials. "That brings a balance to what I'm doing," said Wheeler, "because what it allows me to do — with the insight I have for people — is to work with my kids to prevent them from things I already see. So it's an easy transition."

Doug Wheeler went on to talk about values he tries to inculcate. He emphasized self-esteem. "Self-esteem is not something that people can say, 'OK, I'm going to teach you self-esteem.' Self-esteem is something that's *alive,* that *moves,* and how *you* move, and how you present yourself — how you walk, how you teach children, how you cater to them, how you love them, how you listen to them, how you spend time and make sure they're successful — that puts self-esteem in children, that's what self-esteem is, it's an *action,* a movement."

Toward the end of our conversation, we turned again to the topic of victim counseling. Wheeler told us that after the Dahmer case, he put out a notice that he would not be able to travel anymore on a regular basis for counseling. "It was hard, Bill. It's getting harder and harder to deal with as far as — for my own mind. So I was kind of losing it a little bit, crying when I didn't know why I was crying, and not wanting to watch TV, not wanting to talk to people. I was beginning to find an isolation and numbness in my life. So I had to back off some."

He paused. We could hear sounds of children playing in the courtyard outside the window. Then Wheeler seemed to shake off the gloom of the Dahmer memories. "I'm just having a ball up here," he said. "God, this is incredible, it really is. I look forward to it every day."

"I can see that," I said. "I get a charge out of just seeing Osborne here with Kiki."

"He's very good," said Wheeler. "We see him every day, almost every day. It is fun, isn't it?"

Osborne answered thoughtfully: "It gives you the *will* to do things that you ordinarily wouldn't do. It's tiring. [laughs] 'Cause they're never without energy — no, no. But if you really want your children to excel, you've got to show them that you're *interested* in what they're do-ing. . . ."

Doug Wheeler looked at Osborne with affection. "We'll make a difference, won't we?" he said.

THE RODNEY KING RIOTS

Osborne Jones and I were able to work out the main contours of his autobiography during the winter of 1992. Then other work kept me away from our project for a while. I had not seen Osborne for a month when a California jury rendered a verdict in the Rodney King case. A black man arrested after a high-speed chase, King had been badly beaten by the police. A videotape of the beatwing, shown often on TV in America and throughout the world, appeared to offer irrefutable evidence of police brutality. And yet the jury failed to convict any of the four officers involved. Immediately following the acquittal, riots erupted in Los Angeles and spread to San Francisco and Seattle. The riots, in turn, revealed another level of bigotry: many of the targets of looting and burning in Los Angeles had been Korean-American businesses. Apparently not even black Americans, the traditional victims of prejudice, were free of the taint of racism.

I called Osborne during the riots. I told him that I was checking to make sure he was all right; although I did not say so, I also wanted to assure him — and myself — that we were still friends. That day a white truck driver had been badly beaten in Los Angeles, just because he was a white man in a black neighborhood. For the moment black and white America appeared to be at war. I was not even sure I would be safe driving across Seattle to visit Osborne, or whether he would want to see me.

"I'm not a nice person to talk to," Osborne said in opening our conversation. "I'm just so concerned about what's happening. . . . I think it's making the split greater between the races."

Eager to reestablish the friendly rapport of the past few months, I asked a serious question in a playful manner. "What do you think?" I asked, "If you were God, what would you do."

Osborne cut to the heart of the question. "I would try to make everybody feel that they had an equal chance at what we call the good life. Now, I don't know what the good life is — the good life is one thing to this person and another thing to another person. But there are people born in America today who feel from the day of birth that they're fighting a losing battle."

We talked for half an hour, trading ideas on what the riots meant. Osborne was clearly struggling to understand all facets of the conflict. He blamed President Bush for fostering racism with the Willie Horton campaign ads of 1988, which focused on a black murderer paroled by his opponent, Michael Dukakis. And he argued that Bush's lack of support for affirmative action had undercut black progress. But he also found fault with the rioters. He noted that among the Seattle rioters shown on TV, there did not seem to be a single "working person." A lot of them appeared to be "opportunists," taking advantage of the situation. They were clearly irresponsible, Osborne said, but he did not leave it at that. In most cases their upbringing was at fault, he said; they had never been taught responsibility.

"What are we saying?" I asked. "Are we saying that the problem is society and it's racism, or are we saying the problem is low life 'scumbags' who aren't taking responsibility for their own lives?"

"Well, I think it's all of them!" said Osborne.

The answer was typical of the Osborne Jones I had come to know. He could not be pigeon-holed as either a "liberal" or a "conservative." He could be equally passionate in advocating personal initiative and political reform — the system hurt people, and people hurt themselves. We talked for a half hour about the many facets of the riots and racial relations in America today. Then, after agreeing to continue our autobiography project during the summer, we said goodbye.

Born in an America where racism was vastly more powerful than it is today — where blacks could not vote in the South, or mingle with white crowds at a movie, or even serve in an integrated army —Osborne Jones has managed to live a productive, even a triumphant life. A man whose upbringing included living with ex-slaves, he will project his life forward through his adoptive children deep into the twenty-first century. The gray-haired man who is sharing his retirement with Kiki and Tavon is communicating to them a sense of life's wondrous possibilities. Doug Wheeler is teaching the same lesson at Zion Preparatory Academy, inculcating personal pride in his 500 students.

At one level their story is a uniquely African-American story of courage in the face of adversity. In a larger sense, it is a more universal story of personal initiative, and the "pursuit of happiness." At the same time, Osborne Jones's story shows the role of social environment in personal success. Osborne was raised by a mother who inculcated a sense of personal responsibility; he attended one of the finest black high schools in the country; he entered an army which, although segregated, was beginning to experiment with integration; and he became a public servant in Washington State after the civil rights movement had expanded opportunities for African-Americans.

Arguably, the most fundamental problem facing Americans in the 1990s is the challenge of defining areas where individuals must be responsible for their own fate, and areas where society must provide opportunities. In such diverse matters as poverty, illiteracy, and illegitimacy the nation is faced with the task of knowing when to say, "You are responsible," and when to say, "We are responsible." Osborne Jones has achieved so much in the face of such hardships that it might be tempting to make him into a model of rugged individualism, to conclude from his experience that any American ought to be able to achieve success on their own initiative. But in Osborne's own awareness of who he is, there is no facile sense of superiority. In our conversation after the Rodney King riots the deepest impression was left by these haunting words:

"there are people born in America today who feel from the day of birth that they're fighting a losing battle."

QUESTIONS

1. While growing up in Little Rock during the 1930s, Osborne Jones did not experience segregation. Why?

2. In what ways did Jones become aware of racial discrimination while he was in the army?

3. What are the similarities between Dunbar High School in Little Rock in 1936 and Zion Preparatory Academy in Seattle today?

4. Osborne Jones and Doug Wheeler suggest that success in life is a matter of personal effort *and* supporting environmental conditions. How does each describe these vital personal traits? How does each describe ways that a healthy social environment contributes to a healthy person?

5. This article is based mainly on interviews with living persons rather than books and documents. In what ways does this sort of oral history differ from other kinds of history?

BIBLIOGRAPHY

HACKER, ANDREW. *Two Nations — Black and White, Separate, Hostile, Unequal* (1992). A polemical book with a point to make about racial divisions in modern America.

SCHLESINGER, ARTHUR M., JR. *The Disuniting of America* (1992). A historian's reflections on the modern emphasis on ethnicity.

Songs of My People (1992). Contemporary African-American life documented by black photographers.

TERKEL, STUDS. *Race: How Blacks and Whites Think and Feel about the American Obsession* (1992). America's preeminent oral historian explores contemporary racial attitudes.

Index